Volume 1

DAILY STRENGTH

DEVOTIONS FOR BIBLE BELIEVING STUDY

Douglas D. Stauffer
Andrew B. Ray

Bonus: Includes weekly Bible study tips

For more information, contact:

McCowen Mills Publishers
Dr. Douglas D. Stauffer, President
6612 Hickory Way Lane
Knoxville, TN 37918
1-866-344-1611 (toll free)
Website: *www.BibleDoug.com*
Email: *Doug@BibleDoug.com*

LTB Publications
Pastor Andrew Ray
5709 North Broadway Street
Knoxville, TN 37918
(865) 688-0780
Website: *www.LearntheBible.org*
Email: *pastorray@LearntheBible.org*

Acknowledgments

The authors would like to express their deepest appreciation to the following:

Most preeminently, the precious Lord Jesus Christ for His saving and sustaining grace.

Those who invested the time and effort into our spiritual development, along with the men and women who have been persecuted and sometimes put to death for the faith and their trust in the Saviour and His word.

Our devoted wives for their constant support, encouragement, and understanding through our years of marriage and ministry together. They are truly God's *second* greatest gift to each of us *(Romans 6:23)*.

Mrs. Candace Jones for her assistance in the initial formatting of the chapters.

Mrs. Lois Barnes for her many hours of proofreading and grammatical suggestions.

Mr. Rick Quatro for his invaluable assistance in formatting the book text.

Mr. Tom Rood for his creativity reflected in an impressive cover design.

Lastly, the members of Antioch Baptist Church, Knoxville, TN for their faithful support and encouragement during this long process of writing a book.

Author Biographies

Dr. Douglas D. Stauffer is an internationally recognized authority in the field of Bible history and defense. He is a prolific author, having written ten books along with many writings published in Christian periodicals. Because of his biblical expertise, *Oxford University Press* commissioned Dr. Stauffer to work as a consulting editor.

Immediately, following high school, Doug served a four year tour of duty in the USAF. Upon discharge, he returned to Pennsylvania to attend *The Pennsylvania State University,* graduating with a BS degree in accounting. A few months later he began attending Bible college.

While attending Bible college, Dr. Stauffer passed the CPA exam. He then worked as controller of several organizations. In 1994, he gave up his work as CFO of a multimillion dollar company along with managing his own firm when God began dealing with him about dedicating his time more fully to the ministry. Since that time, he has earned his ThM and PhD in Religion from *International Baptist Seminary.*

Along with being a frequent guest speaker on radio and television, he has served ten years in pastoral ministries and logged thousands of hours teaching in churches and at the college level. Dr. Stauffer currently serves as an evangelist and president of *Partners for Truth Ministries.*

Doug and his wife Judy are blessed with two children, Justin and Heather.

• • • • • • •

Dr. Andrew B. Ray is the pastor of Antioch Baptist Church in Knoxville, Tennessee. He has a heart for the Lord, His word, the church, families, as well as the next generation. He spends countless hours counseling and obediently declaring "all the counsel of God." As a diligent student of the scriptures, he earned his Doctor of Theology degree and faithfully preaches and teaches at the church and the Bible institute.

Before becoming pastor in May 2007, Dr. Ray served as assistant pastor for four years at Antioch Baptist Church under Dr. David F. Reagan. Upon Dr. Reagan's death, Andrew was unanimously voted as pastor of Antioch Baptist Church.

Bro. Ray is the author of *The Fingerprint of God* along with a four year series of devotional books called *Daily Strength: Devotions for Bible-Believing Study*. He has also written several gospel tracts and is currently serving as an editor for a songbook that incorporates scriptural songs, bringing back original lyrics altered or removed by modern hymnals.

God has blessed Bro. Ray and his wife Lula with four children: Noah, Hannah, Sara, Charity, and Lord willing, soon to be little Isaac.

How to Use This Book and an Admonition to the Reader

Two vital admonitions for personal use of the scriptures entail reading *(1 Timothy 4:13)* and studying *(2 Timothy 2:15)* the Bible. Yet, far too many Christians allow books and other materials to supersede their personal interactions with God's word. This devotional series should never usurp either of these crucial admonitions. Rather, the role of this volume serves to assist, expand, and help focus personal or group Bible study. This book is intended to be more like a springboard to launch the student deeper into the most precious book ever written. It is not intended to be an end-all to Bible study. Each devotion consists of five component parts.

I. Scripture Passage

The first section before the *Introductory Thoughts* presents the relevant scripture. Be sure never to skip over the reading in its entirety of each *Scripture Passage*. If you are using the book to lead others in Bible study, make sure to read and meditate on the passage and its context ahead of time though you may want to break the passage into shorter segments while teaching. The devotion will be completely ineffective when the *Scripture Passage* has been overlooked or discounted.

II. Introductory Thoughts

The *Introductory Thoughts* immediately follow the *Scripture Passage*. Apart from the scripture, this section communicates the heart of the devotion. Read it carefully and completely, taking time to examine each referenced scripture. If you are leading a study for others, it is not necessary to read this section verbatim to them. Instead, study the contents ahead of time and use it as a guide for your words and thoughts. Doing so will increase the study's effectiveness and add a personal element to the study.

III. Devotional Thoughts

The *Devotional Thoughts* section serves to make the study more personal by offering some questions to stimulate self-examination. The first section in the series of questions or thoughts is geared toward younger children. However, older children, teens, and adults may also find these thoughts helpful. Feel free to skip this first portion if there are no young children in the study group. If you are studying alone, be sure to take the time to consider each thought or question to see how it might improve your walk with the

Lord. If you are leading or studying with a group, this section should help provoke discussion and prayerful consideration.

IV. Prayer Thoughts

Prayer Thoughts serve to guide the reader to thoughtfully going to the Lord with specific prayer requests. Be sure to pray as God leads. Prayer should always be a matter of the heart so you should never merely repeat the written words. If you are studying as a group or as a family, you could take time for prayer requests followed by one person leading the group in prayer. You could also dedicate some time for each member to pray. Remember that this prayer time can offer a great opportunity for teaching children the importance of prayer.

V. Song

The final section, *Song*, is self-explanatory. Some of the songs will be unfamiliar but each has been prayerfully chosen. Each of these songs will eventually be included in a single songbook. Though some individuals and families might shy away from the thought of singing out loud in a group or alone, it was historically common for people to sing together during times of study. Follow the "song" link at *www.DailyStrengthDevotions.com* for many of the lyrics and tunes of the recommended songs.

Table of Contents

1

Compassion

Occurrences: found forty-three times in forty-one verses

Variations: compassion, compassions

First usage: *Exodus 2:6* (compassion)

Last usage: *Jude 22* (compassion)

Defined: *Compassion* means to suffer with someone; painful sympathy excited by the distress or misfortunes of another.

Interesting fact: *Compassion* is found five times in Psalms and six times in Matthew. Jude mentions those who have compassion, *"making a difference."*

Bible study tip: When a verse contains a compound word, a helpful study tool involves considering the biblical usage of the root word.

Sunday, Day 1—Church Day (no devotional)
Monday, Day 2—*What Is Compassion?*
Tuesday, Day 3—*A Compassionate Saviour*
Wednesday, Day 4—Church Night (no devotional)
Thursday, Day 5—*God: Full of Compassion*
Friday, Day 6—*The Sighing Saviour*
Saturday, Day 7—*The Only Son of a Widow*

Day 1: Church Day

*Psalm 86:15 But thou, O Lord, art **a God full of compassion**, and gracious, longsuffering, and plenteous in mercy and truth.*

Day 2: (Monday)
What Is Compassion?

*Lamentations 3:22 It is of the LORD'S mercies that we are not consumed, because **his compassions fail not.***

23 They are new every morning: great is thy faithfulness.

INTRODUCTORY THOUGHTS

The word *compassion* consists of two components: "com" plus "passion." ***Acts 1:3*** defines the root word "passion" as suffering. The prefix "com" means with. Therefore, the compound word, com-passion means to suffer with someone. God expects every true child of God to demonstrate compassion, but even more impressive is the thought that the Lord Jesus Christ manifested compassion during His earthly ministry. What an amazing truth—the Lord of glory willingly humbles Himself to suffer with others. One might assume this only became possible because Christ took upon Himself the likeness of sinful flesh *(Romans 8:3)*. Yet, the Bible attributes compassion to God prior to the first coming of Christ.

DEVOTIONAL THOUGHTS

- **(For children):** How do you feel when someone gets sick or hurt? What can you do to help them? You want to do these things because you *hurt* for them. That is how you express compassion.
- **(For everyone):** Upon what is the Lord's compassion based? How does this help us understand God's ability to have compassion before His Son came in the likeness of sinful flesh?
- What are some ways in which the Lord has had compassion on you? Were you completely deserving of His compassion? Were you grateful to Him for having this compassion upon you?

PRAYER THOUGHTS

- Take time to thank the Lord for His compassion toward you.
- Ask God to give you opportunities to be more compassionate toward others.

SONG: *GREAT IS THY FAITHFULNESS!*

Day 3: (Tuesday)
A Compassionate Saviour

Hebrews 4:14 *Seeing then that we have a great high priest, that is passed into the heavens, Jesus the Son of God, let us hold fast our profession.*

*15 For we have not an high priest which cannot be **touched with the feeling of our infirmities**; but was in all points tempted like as we are, yet without sin.*

16 Let us therefore come boldly unto the throne of grace, that we may obtain mercy, and find grace to help in time of need.

INTRODUCTORY THOUGHTS

The scripture plainly declares that God was compassionate prior to the coming of Christ. His coming to earth in a body of flesh simply confirmed that He is a compassionate Saviour. The coming of Christ, in the likeness of sinful flesh, enabled God the Son to experience the temptations and struggles of mankind *(Romans 8:3, Hebrews 5:8)*. His compassion on earth reveals that He suffered *with* man, but more importantly, He suffered *for* man. He took the sins of the world upon Himself *(2 Corinthians 5:21; 1 Peter 2:24)*, and gave man His own righteousness *(2 Corinthians 5:21)*. One of the greatest demonstrations of His compassion is the fact that God Himself loved us enough to be housed in a body of flesh *(Hebrews 10:5)*.

DEVOTIONAL THOUGHTS

- **(For children):** How would you feel if someone took you out of your home and put you in a home where you were not loved by everyone and even got mistreated? Jesus willingly did this for you.
- **(For everyone):** Did Jesus learn anything by coming in a body of flesh? If so, what did He learn? What are some of His experiences while on earth that you might also have to endure?
- God's compassion stems from His mercies *(Lamentations 3:32)*. Since each of us is undeserving of His mercies, isn't it also likely that we are undeserving of His compassion?

PRAYER THOUGHTS

- Ask God to help you sacrifice for Him like He sacrificed for you.
- Ask God to help you understand the benefits of His compassion.

6-18-2021 ☑ Completion Date

SONG: *AND CAN IT BE, THAT I SHOULD GAIN?*

Day 4: Church Night

Lamentations 3:31 *For the Lord will not cast off for ever:*

32 *But though he cause grief,* **yet will he have compassion** *according to the multitude of his mercies.*

Day 5: (Thursday)
God: Full of Compassion

Psalm 145:8 *The LORD is gracious, and* **full of compassion***; slow to anger, and of great mercy.*

9 *The LORD is good to all: and his tender mercies are over all his works.*

Introductory Thoughts

God's compassion originates from His mercy and grace and the way He deals with man displays this compassion. For example, He is *"slow to anger"* and *"good to all,"* etc. It is important to note that compassion is not something God simply does but rather a manifestation of His character. The Bible emphasizes the importance of this truth by stating that God is *"full of compassion"* on five separate occasions in the book of Psalms **(Psalm 78:38; Psalm 86:15; Psalm 111:4; Psalm 112:4; Psalm 145:8)**. God's actions (past, present, or future) can all be traced back to His compassion. This even includes His acts of judgment. When the Bible refers to God's longsuffering it means that He will suffer for a long time before bringing judgment against a person, nation, or the whole world.

Devotional Thoughts

- **(For children):** When you do something wrong, your mom or dad does not just simply snatch you up and discipline you. Rather, they generally first warn you to change your behaviour. Yet, if you keep doing the same thing after you've been warned, correction usually follows. God is like that with us—He is slow to anger.
- **(For everyone):** Can you think of a time when God was slow to anger with you? What kind of judgment did you deserve? What kind of judgment did you receive?

- When you think of the compassion of God, what comes to mind? How has God's compassion helped you through some difficult times?

PRAYER THOUGHTS

- Thank the Lord for the benefit of compassion.
- Ask the Lord for help in not abusing His compassion.

SONG: *COME, YE DISCONSOLATE*

Day 6: (Friday)
The Sighing Saviour

Mark 7:31 And again, departing from the coasts of Tyre and Sidon, he came unto the sea of Galilee, through the midst of the coasts of Decapolis.

32 And they bring unto him one that was deaf, and had an impediment in his speech; and they beseech him to put his hand upon him.

33 And he took him aside from the multitude, and put his fingers into his ears, and he spit, and touched his tongue;

*34 **And looking up to heaven, he sighed,** and saith unto him, Ephphatha, that is, Be opened.*

35 And straightway his ears were opened, and the string of his tongue was loosed, and he spake plain.

36 And he charged them that they should tell no man: but the more he charged them, so much the more a great deal they published it;

37 And were beyond measure astonished, saying, He hath done all things well: he maketh both the deaf to hear, and the dumb to speak.

INTRODUCTORY THOUGHTS

The journey of the Lord from Phoenicia (Tyre and Sidon) to Decapolis covered between 50 and 75 miles. No doubt much of the traveling might have taken place on foot. When He arrived at the Sea of Galilee, the Lord must have been drained physically. Yet, there was no time for rest because a man in need of healing was brought to Him. The man was deaf and had a speech impediment. The Lord separated from the multitude and healed the deaf and dumb man. He first put His fingers in the man's ears, then spit and touched the man's tongue. The Lord looked toward heaven and sighed, then commanded the man's ears to be opened. Immediately, his eyes were opened and his tongue was loosed and he could both see and speak.

DEVOTIONAL THOUGHTS

- **(For children):** Discuss how mom and dad show their love by still caring for their family even when they are tired or sick. God helps them to do this. Jesus cared for people even when He was tired. He even took care of people even while suffering on the cross.
- **(For everyone):** How would you feel after a journey of 50-75 miles? (Remember travel was not the same as it is today.) Would you easily be able to focus on helping others?
- What problems did the man in need have? How did Christ heal him? If *compassion* means "suffer with someone," why is it significant that the Lord touched the man's ear and tongue?

PRAYER THOUGHTS

- Thank the Lord for being touched with the feeling of our infirmities.
- Ask God to help you become more aware of His compassion.

SONG: *COME UNTO ME, AND REST (WHITTLE)*

Day 7: (Saturday)
The Only Son of a Widow

Luke 7:11 And it came to pass the day after, that he went into a city called Nain; and many of his disciples went with him, and much people.

12 Now when he came nigh to the gate of the city, behold, there was a dead man carried out, the only son of his mother, and she was a widow: and much people of the city was with her.

*13 And when the Lord saw her, **he had compassion on her**, and said unto her, Weep not.*

14 And he came and touched the bier: and they that bare him stood still. And he said, Young man, I say unto thee, Arise.

15 And he that was dead sat up, and began to speak. And he delivered him to his mother.

16 And there came a fear on all: and they glorified God, saying, That a great prophet is risen up among us; and, That God hath visited his people.

17 And this rumour of him went forth throughout all Judaea, and throughout all the region round about.

18 And the disciples of John shewed him of all these things.

INTRODUCTORY THOUGHTS

God is a compassionate being. The earthly ministry of Christ repeatedly demonstrated this truth. In Luke chapter 7, the Lord entered into a city only to find that a widow (a woman whose husband died) had just lost her only son to death also. It was a very sad time for this dear lady. The loss of her husband had been hard to bear, but her son was a daily reminder of the husband whose love she treasured so greatly. Yet, now the son too was gone. Perhaps the young man worked to help support his mother, but now she was alone without her husband and without their son. Fortunately for this woman, God is rich in mercy *(Ephesians 2:4)*. He intervened on behalf of the woman bringing her son back to life. Her tears of mourning *(Luke 7:13)* turned into tears of joy.

DEVOTIONAL THOUGHTS

- **(For children):** God cares for everyone. He is interested in listening to your prayers. He cares for you when you are sick or hurting. You are important to Him.
- **(For everyone):** How do you think Jesus understood the pain the widow would experience in losing her son? (Think about the separation of God the Father and God the Son.)
- Out of all the things the Lord needed to do, He took time to raise this young man from the dead. Out of all the people who needed the Lord, He took time for a lonely widow. What does that teach us about our great Saviour?

PRAYER THOUGHTS

- Take the burden of your heart to the Lord and seek His help.
- Ask God to help you understand that He cares for you.

SONG: *DOES JESUS CARE?*

Notes: _____

_____

_____

_____

_____

_____

_____

_____

_____

_____

_____

_____

_____

_____

_____

_____

_____

_____

Quotes from the next volume

(VOLUME 2, WEEK 1)

Subject: Church Attendance

The incarnate Son of God had no need of the fellowship and spiritual blessings derived from attending places of worship; yet, His faithfulness to do so clearly testifies to the importance of faithful church attendance for those who know the Lord.

2

Compassion (con't)

Occurrences: found in twenty-one verses in the Old Testament and twenty in the New Testament

First usage in the New Testament: *Matthew 9:36* (compassion)

Last usage in the Old Testament: *Zechariah 7:9* (compassions)

Interesting fact: Compassion occurs twice as often in the gospels (fourteen times) than in any other section of the Bible. God displayed the epitome of compassion when He took on a body in the likeness of sinful flesh to suffer for the sins of mankind.

Bible study tip: Consider not only the number of times a word occurs in scripture, but also where it occurs. If a word appears repeatedly in one section of the Bible, this usually signals an emphasis of teaching a specific Bible truth.

Sunday, Day 8—Church Day (no devotional)
Monday, Day 9—*Moved with Compassion*
Tuesday, Day 10— *The Compassionate Samaritan*
Wednesday, Day 11—Church Night (no devotional)
Thursday, Day 12— *A Compassionate Father*
Friday, Day 13— *Love with Action*
Saturday, Day 14— *Compassion One of Another*

Day 8: Church Day

*Psalm 78:38 But he, being **full of compassion**, forgave their iniquity, and destroyed them not: yea, many a time turned he his anger away, and did not stir up all his wrath.*

Day 9 (Monday)
Moved with Compassion

*Mark 6:34 And Jesus, when he came out, saw much people, and was **moved with compassion** toward them, because they were as sheep not having a shepherd: and he began to teach them many things.*

35 And when the day was now far spent, his disciples came unto him, and said, This is a desert place, and now the time is far passed:

36 Send them away, that they may go into the country round about, and into the villages, and buy themselves bread: for they have nothing to eat.

37 He answered and said unto them, Give ye them to eat. And they say unto him, Shall we go and buy two hundred pennyworth of bread, and give them to eat?

38 He saith unto them, How many loaves have ye? go and see. And when they knew, they say, Five, and two fishes.

39 And he commanded them to make all sit down by companies upon the green grass.

40 And they sat down in ranks, by hundreds, and by fifties.

41 And when he had taken the five loaves and the two fishes, he looked up to heaven, and blessed, and brake the loaves, and gave them to his disciples to set before them; and the two fishes divided he among them all.

42 And they did all eat, and were filled.

43 And they took up twelve baskets full of the fragments, and of the fishes.

44 And they that did eat of the loaves were about five thousand men.

INTRODUCTORY THOUGHTS

One's actions demonstrate true compassion. Five times the Bible uses the phrase *moved with compassion (**Matthew 9:36; Matthew 14:14;***

Matthew 18:27; Mark 1:41; Mark 6:34). Four of the five references refer to Christ's compassion toward others. True compassion always moves people to do something for others. In *Mark 6:34-44*, the disciples wanted to send the crowd away hungry, but Christ refused to send them away empty. He would not allow the multitudes to leave His presence still in need. In this one example, Christ's compassion fed thousands when others would have sent them away faint and hungry. The Lord not only fed thousands with two small fishes and five loaves of bread, but also produced a miraculous amount of leftovers.

DEVOTIONAL THOUGHTS

- **(For children):** Jesus loved the people and did not want them to go away hungry. Amazingly, He fed a hungry crowd of more than 5,000 men with one boy's lunch. Dad and mom love you and ensure that you always have food enough to keep you healthy.
- **(For everyone):** It is obvious, from the context, that the Lord and His disciples were very tired. Yet, we find the disciples learning an important lesson about serving others. What does this teach us about serving others rather than making excuses?
- The Lord performed a miracle of compassion using what the disciples already had. What does this teach us about what the Lord wants us to use in serving Him?

PRAYER THOUGHTS

- How do you feel about your level of compassion for others? Is this something with which you need God's help?
- Ask God to open doors of opportunity for you to demonstrate your compassion toward others.

SONG: *THE GREAT PHYSICIAN*

Day 10 (Tuesday)
The Compassionate Samaritan

Luke 10:30 And Jesus answering said, A certain man went down from Jerusalem to Jericho, and fell among thieves, which stripped him of his raiment, and wounded him, and departed, leaving him half dead.

31 And by chance there came down a certain priest that way: and when he saw him, he passed by on the other side.

32 And likewise a Levite, when he was at the place, came and looked on him, and passed by on the other side.

*33 But a certain Samaritan, as he journeyed, came where he was: and when he saw him, **he had compassion on him**,*

34 And went to him, and bound up his wounds, pouring in oil and wine, and set him on his own beast, and brought him to an inn, and took care of him.

35 And on the morrow when he departed, he took out two pence, and gave them to the host, and said unto him, Take care of him; and whatsoever thou spendest more, when I come again, I will repay thee.

36 Which now of these three, thinkest thou, was neighbour unto him that fell among the thieves?

37 And he said, He that shewed mercy on him. Then said Jesus unto him, Go, and do thou likewise.

INTRODUCTORY THOUGHTS

The Lord expects His followers to demonstrate the same compassion that He has for His creation. Perhaps, the best biblical example is the Samaritan mentioned in Luke chapter 10. The story begins with a man who took a journey to Jericho. On his way, evil men robbed and wounded him. As he struggled for his life, lying on the ground, a priest passed by him. The priest saw the man but passed on the other side. A Levite came and did likewise. Then a Samaritan (a person who was partly Jewish yet bitterly despised by the Jewish people) approached the man in need. Unlike the others, this man stopped and helped the injured man. He bound up the wounds, placed the man on his beast and took him to an inn. He paid for the inn and offered to pay any additional expenses.

DEVOTIONAL THOUGHTS

- **(For children):** Jesus cares for others and wants us to do the same. If you saw someone get hurt, what should you do? How could you help if a friend was sick or lost his toy? How would he feel if you did not help?

- **(For everyone):** What are some reasons the men might offer for deciding to pass by the man in need? Would you offer similar reasons? Are these reasons good reasons for failing to help or just excuses?
- Since we understand that compassion is suffering *with* someone, in what ways did the Samaritan show compassion? What did he provide that he might otherwise have used for himself?

PRAYER THOUGHTS

- Ask God to help you give of yourself when you see others in need of help.
- Ask the Lord to help you care more for others by putting them first.

SONG: *WHERE HE LEADS I'LL FOLLOW*

Day 11: Church Night

Psalm 111:4 *He hath made his wonderful works to be remembered: the LORD is gracious and **full of compassion**.*

Day 12 (Thursday)
A Compassionate Father

Luke 15:11 *And he said, A certain man had two sons:*

12 And the younger of them said to his father, Father, give me the portion of goods that falleth to me. And he divided unto them his living.

13 And not many days after the younger son gathered all together, and took his journey into a far country, and there wasted his substance with riotous living.

14 And when he had spent all, there arose a mighty famine in that land; and he began to be in want.

15 And he went and joined himself to a citizen of that country; and he sent him into his fields to feed swine.

16 And he would fain have filled his belly with the husks that the swine did eat: and no man gave unto him.

17 And when he came to himself, he said, How many hired servants of my father's have bread enough and to spare, and I perish with hunger!

18 *I will arise and go to my father, and will say unto him, Father, I have sinned against heaven, and before thee,*

19 *And am no more worthy to be called thy son: make me as one of thy hired servants.*

20 *And he arose, and came to his father. But when he was yet a great way off, his father saw him, and had compassion, and ran, and fell on his neck, and kissed him.*

21 *And the son said unto him, Father, I have sinned against heaven, and in thy sight, and am no more worthy to be called thy son.*

22 *But the father said to his servants, Bring forth the best robe, and put it on him; and put a ring on his hand, and shoes on his feet:*

23 *And bring hither the fatted calf, and kill it; and let us eat, and be merry:*

24 *For this my son was dead, and is alive again; he was lost, and is found. And they began to be merry.*

25 *Now his elder son was in the field: and as he came and drew nigh to the house, he heard musick and dancing.*

26 *And he called one of the servants, and asked what these things meant.*

27 *And he said unto him, Thy brother is come; and thy father hath killed the fatted calf, because he hath received him safe and sound.*

28 *And he was angry, and would not go in: therefore came his father out, and intreated him.*

29 *And he answering said to his father, Lo, these many years do I serve thee, neither transgressed I at any time thy commandment: and yet thou never gavest me a kid, that I might make merry with my friends:*

30 *But as soon as this thy son was come, which hath devoured thy living with harlots, thou hast killed for him the fatted calf.*

31 *And he said unto him, Son, thou art ever with me, and all that I have is thine.*

32 *It was meet that we should make merry, and be glad: for this thy brother was dead, and is alive again; and was lost, and is found.*

INTRODUCTORY THOUGHTS

Compassion forgives. A familiar parable of the Lord displays this truth. A father had two sons. One stayed home with his family and worked the land, while the other son decided to leave and travel the world. Before leaving, he asked for his inheritance (what he would have received upon his father's death). Instead of being a wise steward with this inheritance, he foolishly wasted it. Afterward, he found himself broke and starving in the middle of a famine. At this point, he would have willingly eaten the swine's slop. Finally, he decided to return home even if it meant that he would become a servant rather than a son. As he neared the old homestead, his father saw him coming. His father wasted no time but ran to meet and embrace him. Rather than rebuking his son, the father welcomed him back into his home with a renewed relationship.

DEVOTIONAL THOUGHTS

- **(For children):** God the Father always wants to forgive. In this story, although the son had been very unwise, the father was glad to have his son return home. The son said he was sorry and wanted his father to forgive him. What should we do when we do bad things?
- **(For everyone):** The son wasted his inheritance by living foolishly. When the son returned, what did he own at his father's house? What did his father give him when he returned? How do the father's actions demonstrate compassion?
- This parable is a great picture of what God has done for us in salvation. Think of some things you did before you were saved. Did you deserve the compassion you received? How did you feel once you got saved? Did you realize that you received mercy from the Lord?

PRAYER THOUGHTS

- Ask God to help you rejoice when others receive compassion.
- Ask the Lord to give you strength to draw nearer to Him.

SONG: *ABBA, FATHER, WE APPROACH THEE*

Day 13 (Friday)
Love with Action

> *1 John 3:14 We know that we have passed from death unto life, because we love the brethren. He that loveth not his brother abideth in death.*

15 *Whosoever hateth his brother is a murderer: and ye know that no murderer hath eternal life abiding in him.*

16 *Hereby perceive we the love of God, because he laid down his life for us: and we ought to lay down our lives for the brethren.*

17 *But whoso hath this world's good, and seeth his brother have need, and shutteth up his **bowels of compassion** from him, how dwelleth the love of God in him?*

18 *My little children, let us not love in word, neither in tongue; but in deed and in truth.*

19 *And hereby we know that we are of the truth, and shall assure our hearts before him.*

Introductory Thoughts

The Bible associates love with action. In this passage, the Bible speaks of the believer's love for other believers, relating it to the Lord's crucifixion. If a Christian knows and recognizes the love of God, it should drastically affect his relationships. He cannot deal with others as the world would because the love of God has formed compassion within in his heart. This matter is so important to the Lord that He provided believers with a scenario to help judge their level of compassion. The book of First John says that if a brother has a need, and another brother can help him with his need, yet refuses, he lacks compassion (see also *James 2:15-16*). Therefore, one's deeds, not simply one's words alone, demonstrate true love!

Devotional Thoughts

- **(For children):** We need to do good to all people, but especially to our church family. What are some ways that we can help our pastor, our song leader, our Sunday School teacher, the elderly and those who clean the church, etc?
- **(For everyone):** Compassion requires action. If there is no action attached to one's desires, true love or compassion does not exist. The greatest example was given by Christ when He died on the cross. What are other examples of compassion that come to mind?
- Do you love your brothers and sisters in Christ? What have you done for others to show your love for them? Have you prayed for them? Have you helped them in a time of need?

PRAYER THOUGHTS

- Ask God to provide opportunities for you to show compassion toward others.
- Ask God to help you love others in spite of how they or others may have mistreated you.

SONG: *MORE ABOUT JESUS*

Day 14 (Saturday)
Compassion One of Another

*1 Peter 3:8 Finally, be ye all of one mind, **having compassion one of another**, love as brethren, be pitiful, be courteous:*

9 Not rendering evil for evil, or railing for railing: but contrariwise blessing; knowing that ye are thereunto called, that ye should inherit a blessing.

INTRODUCTORY THOUGHTS

Every word of God is pure, but the Bible contains words of emphasis intending to draw the reader's attention to a specific thought. *1 Peter 3:8-9* begins with the word *finally*, thus signifying that this is the final statement in a list of thoughts. The closing statements on a matter frequently contain crucial truths. Certainly, these two verses offer the believer vital bits of information. They reveal five responsibilities: Believers are to be of one mind. They also are to have compassion one of another, love as brethren, be pitiful (that is, full of pity for others), and be courteous. Verse nine defines *courteous* as not mistreating others even if mistreated. Finally, believers are promised that obedience offers them a great blessing.

DEVOTIONAL THOUGHTS

- **(For children):** Name some of your friends from church. Why do you like them? Is there anyone who doesn't treat you right? How should you treat them?
- **(For everyone):** What would happen if all believers obeyed the commands given in the *1 Peter 3:8-9* passage? What would happen if you obeyed them? How would it benefit the saved and the lost alike?

- Why is this passage so very important for us living in a sinful world? Why should believers have the right relationship with one another? (Hint: Consider **John 13:35**.) How could this help eliminate many of the problems experienced by churches?

Prayer Thoughts

- Ask the Lord to help you obey the commands of **1 Peter 3:8-9**.
- Ask God to work in your heart to love others like you should.

SONG: *BLEST BE THE TIE THAT BINDS*

Notes: _____

_____

_____

_____

_____

_____

_____

Quotes from the next volume

(VOLUME 2, WEEK 2)

Subject: Backbiting

The words that so flippantly slip from our tongues are often used by the Devil as weapons to wound others.

Many believers have quit attending the house of God and given up on serving the Lord because Christians have allowed their words to devour and consume.

A good healthy angry countenance can serve as the best remedy to keep people from backbiting others while in your presence.

3

Contentment

Occurrences: The root word of contentment (*content*) is found sixteen times in the Bible.

Variations: content, contentment, discontented

First usage: *Genesis 37:27* (content)

Last usage: *3 John 10* (content)

Defined: *Content* and *contentment* infer a mind at peace; being satisfied with life's present conditions.

Interesting fact: Though the Bible usually refers to contentment as a godly trait, **Mark 15:15** reveals that Pilate contented the people with ungodly actions.

Bible study tip: Dictionaries are a great resource; however, they sometimes hinder Bible study by giving preconceived ideas concerning the meaning of a word in the Bible. Context always determines meaning and the Bible's built-in dictionary generally defines words.

Sunday, Day 15—Church Day (no devotional)
Monday, Day 16—*What is Contentment?*
Tuesday, Day 17—*The Lord Gives and He Takes Away*
Wednesday, Day 18—Church Night (no devotional)

Thursday, Day 19—*A Caring Father*
Friday, Day 20—*Thou Hast Lacked Nothing*
Saturday, Day 21—*Trust God with the Balance*

Day 15: Church Day

Hebrews 13:5 *Let your conversation be without covetousness; and* **be content** *with such things as ye have: for he hath said, I will never leave thee, nor forsake thee.*

Day 16: (Monday)
What is Contentment?

Philippians 4:10 *But I rejoiced in the Lord greatly, that now at the last your care of me hath flourished again; wherein ye were also careful, but ye lacked opportunity.*

11 Not that I speak in respect of want: for I have learned, in whatsoever state I am, **therewith to be content.**

12 I know both how to be abased, and I know how to abound: every where and in all things I am instructed both to be full and to be hungry, both to abound and to suffer need.

INTRODUCTORY THOUGHTS

The words *content* and *contentment* infer that one is satisfied with life's present conditions *(Genesis 37:27; Exodus 2:21)*. Living contently is the opposite of wanting *(Philippians 4:11)* and covetousness *(Hebrews 13:5)* and is strongly associated with godliness *(1 Timothy 6:6)*. Interestingly, contentment is a learned behaviour that believers must put into practice on a consistent basis throughout life. No one is born into the world content. Yet, once learned and practiced consistently, Christians will experience contentment in spite of any circumstance faced. Unfortunately, far too often, Christians exhibit no more contentment than non-Christians. In fact, believers seem to desire and covet the things of the world more and more with each passing year. This covetousness combined with a lack of contentment amongst Christians results in less godliness and a closer association with worldly pleasures.

Devotional Thoughts

- **(For children):** God wants us to be happy with those things with which He has blessed us. Name some things you have that you really like. Are you happy with these things or do you find yourself always wanting more stuff? How could you learn to be more content? Why and how would this please the Lord and your parents?
- **(For everyone):** Ponder for a moment your life. Are you satisfied with your conditions and possessions or do you find yourself increasingly dissatisfied?
- Meditate for a moment on the things God has provided for you that are not directly associated with money. Can you name some specific examples of things that God has taken away from you that would have been harmful to you or others you love?

Prayer Thoughts

- Take some time to thank God for His manifold blessings upon your life.
- Ask God to give you a greater desire to willingly sacrifice and to be zealously content.

SONG: *'TIS BY THE FAITH OF JOYS TO COME*

Day 17: (Tuesday)
The Lord Gives and He Takes Away

Job 1:20 Then Job arose, and rent his mantle, and shaved his head, and fell down upon the ground, and worshipped,

*21 And said, Naked came I out of my mother's womb, and naked shall I return thither: **the LORD gave, and the LORD hath taken away;** blessed be the name of the LORD.*

22 In all this Job sinned not, nor charged God foolishly.

Introductory Thoughts

Seemingly, Job possessed many of man's most treasured possessions: health, wealth, and a strong family unit. Suddenly, he lost them all. Job lost his health, his possessions, and his children. He also lost the esteem and approbation of his wife and friends. These events very easily could have devastated and embittered him. Yet, rather than expressions of doom and gloom, Job's words offer a profound glimpse into the depths of his contentment. In the midst of his heartache, Job exhibited an extremely important truth. A Christian's material and physical blessings, all of which are completely within the Lord's control, should never influence one's relationship with the Lord or others. Job also pointed out that man will depart this world in the same condition in which he entered: without one shred of material wealth. Ultimately, a Christian's possessions or the lack thereof reflect God's provisions; therefore, a lack of contentment reflects an unwillingness to trust in the Lord.

DEVOTIONAL THOUGHTS

- **(For children):** What is your favorite toy? If you were asked to give that particular toy away, how would you react? How would the Lord want you to behave? Why is it so very important for us to do what God wants us to do?
- **(For everyone):** If God is responsible for all that we have or do not have, what does complaining about our current possessions or conditions reflect about us?
- In the midst of the many things he lost, Job also lost his children. Through it all he was still able to reflect contentment. Can you imagine how difficult things would be if the Lord allowed something like this in your life? Why do you think Job was able to lose so much and still serve the Lord? Could you have continued to serve Him?

PRAYER THOUGHTS

- Ask the Lord to teach you how to be satisfied with what you have.
- Ask God to meet your needs according to His timing and will.

SONG: *ALL THE WAY MY SAVIOUR LEADS ME*

Day 18: Church Night

*1 Timothy 6:6 But **godliness with contentment** is great gain.*

7 For we brought nothing into this world, and it is certain we can carry nothing out.

8 And having food and raiment let us be therewith content.

Day 19: (Thursday)
A Caring Father

*Romans 8:28 And we know that **all things work together for good** to them that love God, to them who are the called according to his purpose.*

INTRODUCTORY THOUGHTS

Since God is responsible for man's possessions or the lack thereof, some Christians question why God gives a man some things while He withholds from others. ***Romans 8:28*** contains one of the answers as it points out that *"all things work together for good."* This does not imply that everything in the believer's life is enjoyable or good. It means that everything combined results in good. God works in every piece of a believer's life. He combines all things so that even the supposed bad things result in what is "good" according to the will of God. So long as God is at the controls, contentment teaches man how to be satisfied. Man's conditions, circumstances, and possessions are appropriate because God has worked everything together for the good of that man.

DEVOTIONAL THOUGHTS

- **(For children):** Most children like to play out in the street. Why would parents not allow their children to play on a busy street? Why would Dad insist on his son only using a sharp knife when he is supervised? Girls love to help their moms cook, yet why do moms insist on removing the food from the oven themselves? These actions reflect the nature of God; He allows or doesn't allow things for our good and well-being.
- **(For everyone):** Knowing that God is your Father and that He cares for you, how do you think He feels when a Christian displays discontentment?
- Look back over your life and think about some of the things that you have desired but never received. Would all of those things have been good for you? What would have happened if God gave them all to you?

PRAYER THOUGHTS

- Ask God to help you yield every aspect of your life to His care.
- Ask God to help you be content in the areas in which you struggle.

SONG: *WITH CHRIST, I SMILE AT THE STORM*

Day 20: (Friday)
Thou Hast Lacked Nothing

Deuteronomy 2:7 For the LORD thy God hath blessed thee in all the works of thy hand: he knoweth thy walking through this great wilderness: these forty years the LORD thy God hath been with thee; ***thou hast lacked nothing.***

Introductory Thoughts

Far too many times, the list of the average person's wants is unending. Yet, an honest child of God recognizes that he has never lacked anything of necessity. Evidence of this truth exists in **Deuteronomy 2:7** as the Lord expressed His care for Israel during the forty years of their wilderness wanderings. Very few people would consider the wilderness a place of plenty, yet the wilderness was the place where God furnished Israel *"a table"* **(Psalm 78:19)**, *"brought streams also out of the rock"* **(Psalm 78:16)**, and kept their shoes and clothes from deteriorating **(Deuteronomy 29:5)**. God could honestly say to His people, though they wandered in a barren land, they *"lacked nothing"* **(Deuteronomy 2:7)**.

Devotional thoughts

- **(For children):** We have enough food to eat, shoes and clothes to wear, and a house in which to live. Let's thank the Lord for being so good to us.
- **(For everyone):** Think about all the good things God has given to you. What necessity do you lack? Is there anything that you have really needed that God failed to provide a means for you to obtain it?
- Think about times in life when it seemed as if all hope was lost. Do you remember the joy you sensed when God provided for your need? Did you take the time then to thank Him for His provision? If not, let's do so right now.

Prayer Thoughts

- Ask the Lord to help align your wants with His will.
- Thank God for His bountiful provisions for you.

SONG: *COUNT YOUR BLESSINGS*

Day 21: (Saturday)
Trust God with the Balance

Proverbs 30:7 *Two things have I required of thee; deny me them not before I die:*

8 Remove far from me vanity and lies: **give me neither poverty nor riches**; *feed me with food convenient for me:*

9 Lest I be full, and deny thee, and say, Who is the LORD? or lest I be poor, and steal, and take the name of my God in vain.

INTRODUCTORY THOUGHTS

A balanced life should be the quest of every believer, especially as it relates to material possessions. ***Proverbs 30:7-9*** describes the heartfelt desire of avoiding extremes. The man expresses his two requests to the Lord: not to be rich and not to be poor. Most people have no desire for the latter but would love to be showered in riches with need of nothing. Yet, Agur in the book of Proverbs provides wise reasons for desiring neither extreme. He feared that being rich would tempt him to forget the Lord. Yet, being poor might cause him to steal and thus take the name of God in vain. His desire focused rather on one necessity and that involved feeding him with food convenient for him.

DEVOTIONAL THOUGHTS

- **(For children):** What would happen if your mom or dad gave you too little or too much to eat? We trust our parents to give us what is just right. We need to trust God that same way. He will give us just what we need. Do you trust the Lord every day?
- **(For everyone):** Who knows best what is convenient for you in this life? Why do you think we fret about things that are so obviously within the Lord's control? What actions should true faith produce?
- Do you find yourself spending more time expressing thankfulness or more time complaining? If honesty compels you to answer complaining, do you see that the problem is a matter of lacking faith and contentment?

PRAYER THOUGHTS

- Ask God for the faith you need to trust Him more and more each day.
- Ask God to help you be content with the balance He provides for you.

SONG: *JESUS, I AM RESTING, RESTING*

Notes: _____

_____

_____

_____

_____

_____

_____

_____

_____

_____

_____

_____

_____

_____

_____

_____

_____

_____

_____

_____

Quotes from the next volume

(VOLUME 2, WEEK 3)

Subject: Benevolence

The Bible offers specific guidance as to when to assist others
who have fallen on hard times.

4

Contentment (con't)

Occurrences: found only one time in the Bible.

First usage in the New Testament: *Mark 15:15* (content)

Last usage in the Old Testament: *Proverbs 6:35* (content)

Interesting fact: *1 Timothy 6:6* is the single use of *content-ment* in the Bible pointing out *"But godliness with content-ment is great gain."*

Bible study tip: When studying a word or biblical concept, consider words found in scripture used to compare or contrast your subject.

Sunday, Day 22—Church Day (no devotional)
Monday, Day 23—*Better Is Little*
Tuesday, Day 24—*Having Food and Raiment*
Wednesday, Day 25—Church Night (no devotional)
Thursday, Day 26—*Take No Thought*
Friday, Day 27—*I Have Learned to Be Content*
Saturday, Day 28—*Without Covetousness*

Day 22: Church Day

*Philippians 4:11 Not that I speak in respect of want: for I have learned, in whatsoever state I am, therewith to be **content**.*

Day 23: (Monday)
Better Is Little

*Proverbs 15:16 **Better is little** with the fear of the LORD than great treasure and trouble therewith.*

*17 **Better is** a dinner of herbs where love is, than a stalled ox and hatred therewith.*

INTRODUCTORY THOUGHTS

Most people have heard the familiar cliché that *"money can't buy you happiness."* In fact, the greatest treasures of life cannot be purchased at all. Yet, accumulating treasures and eating the finest of foods are the prized possessions of life for far too many people. The Bible says that these things fade away in comparison to the spiritual blessings derived from a life devoted to the Lord. In fact, nothing in this world compares to a healthy, biblical fear of the Lord. The love and peace possessed by faithful Christians offers lasting fulfillment while the combined riches of the world simply flee away. When a man fears God, combined with the love of those around him, a dinner of herbs (unsatisfying to the discontented) satisfies his appetite while the blessings of God satisfy him wholly. The Bible repeatedly declares spiritual blessings far superior to any worldly possessions. Men would be wise to choose God's blessings over the world's accolades.

DEVOTIONAL THOUGHTS

- **(For children):** With whom would you rather play: a friend who has lots of the newest toys, but treats you mean or one who only has a couple of toys, but is very nice to you?
- **(For everyone):** Do you find yourself constantly complaining about the things that others possess but you don't have? What are the most important things in this life? Do you have those things? If not, what could you do to obtain them?
- If you knew you could, would you want to be wealthy? What if you knew that by becoming rich, you would lose much of the love and joy you now experience? Would you still want that wealth regardless of the cost?

PRAYER THOUGHTS

- Ask the Lord to help you to be content.

- Ask God to help you ask for only the things God wants you to have.

SONG: *FADE, FADE, EACH EARTHLY JOY*

Day 24: (Tuesday)
Having Food and Raiment

*1 Timothy 6:6 But **godliness with contentment** is great gain.*

7 For we brought nothing into this world, and it is certain we can carry nothing out.

*8 And having **food and raiment** let us be therewith **content**.*

INTRODUCTORY THOUGHTS

True contentment only flourishes within the lives of committed followers of God's word. Three important truths aid in fully comprehending scriptural contentment: (1) Man was born into this world with nothing *(1 Timothy 6:7)*, (2) Upon death, man leaves this earth with nothing *(1 Timothy 6:7)*, and (3) God declares that man should be content when provided with food and raiment (clothing) *(1 Timothy 6:8)*. Understanding and accepting these three truths helps cultivate a true sense of godliness and contentment. This is why the Bible defines godliness combined with contentment as *"great gain"* and warns those who will be rich that they fall victim to temptations, snares, and many foolish and hurtful lusts *(1 Timothy 6:9)*. Interestingly, the Bible warns the covetous man that all of his earthly possessions during a lifetime of accumulation will be left behind for someone else to enjoy *(Ecclesiastes 2:17-21)*. Contrariwise, the contented man with few possessions has his possessions enlarged into *"great gain."*

DEVOTIONAL THOUGHTS

- **(For children):** Name a few things that you have eaten today. Are you wearing shoes or socks or a shirt right now? Let's take time to thank God for giving us these necessary things.
- **(For everyone):** Has God blessed you with food and raiment? Has God blessed you with more than simply food and raiment? Why do you think that even with these necessities, we tend to murmur for more things?
- What things do you most desire? Will you take these things with you once you die? How long do people generally live? Compare that to the

length of eternity. Should your time, strength, and life focus on things that will last a few years or those that will last forever? (Meditate for a moment on the eternal rewards in heaven and the souls of men, women, boys, and girls on earth.)

PRAYER THOUGHTS

- Ask God to help you spend time labouring for the eternal rewards.
- Thank the Lord for your food and clothing.

SONG: *I SING THE ALMIGHTY POWER OF GOD*

Day 25: Church Night

Proverbs 30:7 *Two things have I required of thee; deny me them not before I die:*

8 Remove far from me vanity and lies: **give me neither poverty nor riches**; *feed me with food convenient for me:*

9 Lest I be full, and deny thee, and say, Who is the LORD? or lest I be poor, and steal, and take the name of my God in vain.

Day 26: (Thursday)
Take No Thought

Matthew 6:25 *Therefore I say unto you,* **Take no thought** *for your life, what ye shall eat, or what ye shall drink; nor yet for your body, what ye shall put on. Is not the life more than meat, and the body than raiment?*

26 Behold the fowls of the air: for they sow not, neither do they reap, nor gather into barns; yet your heavenly Father feedeth them. Are ye not much better than they?

27 Which of you by taking thought can add one cubit unto his stature?

28 And why take ye thought for raiment? Consider the lilies of the field, how they grow; they toil not, neither do they spin:

29 And yet I say unto you, That even Solomon in all his glory was not arrayed like one of these.

30 Wherefore, if God so clothe the grass of the field, which to day is, and to morrow is cast into the oven, shall he not much more clothe you, O ye of little faith?

*31 Therefore **take no thought**, saying, What shall we eat? or, What shall we drink? or, Wherewithal shall we be clothed?*

32 (For after all these things do the Gentiles seek:) for your heavenly Father knoweth that ye have need of all these things.

33 But seek ye first the kingdom of God, and his righteousness; and all these things shall be added unto you.

*34 **Take therefore no thought** for the morrow: for the morrow shall take thought for the things of itself. Sufficient unto the day is the evil thereof.*

INTRODUCTORY THOUGHTS

The gospel according to Matthew points to the fowls of the air and the lilies of the field as examples of God's supernatural provisions for His creation. God in His goodness feeds the fowls and clothes the lilies. How much more will He do for man? Since God provides for the lesser things, He tells man not to worry about what he will have to eat, drink, or how he will be clothed. Instead of focusing on one's needs, man should direct his thoughts toward God's kingdom and His righteousness. God provides man with food and raiment and instructs him to be content with such things. The scripture also rebukes the faithless by encouraging men to trust God for their necessary provisions. It is important to note that God's supernatural provisions do not advocate laziness or condone an unwillingness to work *(2 Thessalonians 3:10)*. He simply expects man to trust Him fully and completely.

DEVOTIONAL THOUGHTS

- **(For children):** What do birds eat? Who gives them their food? Who gives the flowers their pretty colors? The Bible says that people are more important to God than birds and flowers. How does God care for you?
- **(For everyone):** Meditate upon the two examples of provision in this passage. Does God provide for the birds and the flowers? Do the birds fret about obtaining more possessions or do flowers strain to flaunt their beauty? If the birds can trust the Lord, how ought we to behave?
- What are the spiritual and physical effects of devoting your time and efforts toward worrying about obtaining more possessions? Does it draw you closer to God? Does it bring joy and peace into your life? If it produces the opposite results, why do people spend so much time and effort worrying?

- Ask God to build your faith so you can trust in Him and His provisions for you.
- Ask the Lord to help you think on eternal rewards rather than temporal pleasures.

SONG: *HIS EYE IS ON THE SPARROW*

Day 27: (Friday)
I Have Learned to Be Content

Philippians 4:10 *But I rejoiced in the Lord greatly, that now at the last your care of me hath flourished again; wherein ye were also careful, but ye lacked opportunity.*

*11 Not that I speak in respect of want: for **I have learned**, in whatsoever state I am, therewith **to be content**.*

12 I know both how to be abased, and I know how to abound: every where and in all things I am instructed both to be full and to be hungry, both to abound and to suffer need.

13 I can do all things through Christ which strengtheneth me.

INTRODUCTORY THOUGHTS

Contentment is a learned virtue, not one with which man is born. If it were natural and easily accepted, every man would be content. Instead, it requires much effort and sacrifice on the individual's part. The apostle Paul learned how to be content by not allowing his circumstances to control or adversely influence him. If he found himself abased (brought low) or if he abounded (overflowed), he knew how to remain contented. He considered both situations to be completely within the will of God. He believed that his circumstances were not to determine his satisfaction levels. So it should be with Christians today. Whether a Christian *abounds* in wealth or *wants* in poverty, he should rejoice for God's provision. This will only result from a supreme love for God.

DEVOTIONAL THOUGHTS

- **(For children):** Think of five of your favorite toys. What if you only had two of those? God wants you to be happy with many or with few.

- **(For everyone):** Are you living with plenty or do you find yourself in need? Can you pinpoint where your current condition reflects the will of God? Are you content or discontent with your current situation?
- Are you striving to learn to be more content? What are some of the steps that you think could help you to learn to be more content with the things you have? From reading *Isaiah 29:24*, do you see where complaining hinders your spiritual development?

PRAYER THOUGHTS

- Ask God to help you to become more grateful for His provisions.
- Ask the Lord to help you learn the truth of *Philippians 4:13*. Ask Him to reveal the depth of how this verse applies to contentment. Are you willing to be content because He strengthens you?

SONG: *HOW FIRM A FOUNDATION*

Day 28: (Saturday)
Without Covetousness

Hebrews 13:5 Let your conversation be without covetousness; and **be content with such things as ye have**: *for he hath said, I will never leave thee, nor forsake thee.*

INTRODUCTORY THOUGHTS

A man's conversation should consistently exhibit a high level of individual contentment. Defining *conversation* and *covetousness* will help to better understand **Hebrews 13:5**. A man's *conversation* in the Bible sometimes refers to more than the words he speaks. It frequently refers to his entire way of life. One who lives *covetously* desires things not belonging to him. The Bible stresses the seriousness of covetousness by connecting it to the sin of idolatry. Combining these two simple truths shows that man should never live his life chasing after things not belonging to him. Why is it so important for a Christian to live a life of contentment? Since God promises to never leave or forsake His own, a discontented Christian lacks a trust in His Creator. Understanding these simple truths should bring great contentment to the believer.

DEVOTIONAL THOUGHTS

- **(For children):** Look around the room and name something you see. Can this be taken away from us? God promises He will never leave us. Can anyone take God away from you or you from God?
- **(For everyone):** Contentment is the opposite of covetousness. A Christian cannot be simultaneously content and covetous. Which does your life portray?
- Explain what it means to you that God will never leave you? Does this truth help you to be more content? If not, what does this mean about your heart condition?

PRAYER THOUGHTS

- Ask God to reveal your covetous thoughts and desires.
- Ask the Lord to help you to be satisfied with His presence in your life.

SONG: *TAKE THE WORLD, BUT GIVE ME JESUS*

Notes: _____

_____

_____

_____

_____

_____

Quotes from the next volume

(VOLUME 2, WEEK 4)

Subject: Bitterness

Bitterness always begins on the inside of an individual and, as we will learn, eventually works its way to the outside for others to see.

The solution for bitterness can be likened to the removal of a plant by its roots. Bitterness continues to grow unless removed at its source from the roots.

5

Courage

Occurrences: found in nineteen Old Testament verses but only once in the New Testament (courage only)

Variations: courage, courageous, courageously, discourage, discouraged, encourage, encouraged

First usage: *Numbers 13:20* (courage)

Last usage: *Colossians 3:21* (discouraged)

Defined: *Courage* reflects the strength of heart. Godly courage is based upon faith, hope, and a trust in the Lord.

Interesting fact: Of the nineteen times the Old Testament refers to *courage*, "good" courage occurs sixteen of those times.

Bible study tip: Consider the prefixes and suffixes added to the word you are studying and how they alter the meaning of your root word. These compound words are crucial to your overall understanding of a Bible word.

Sunday, Day 29—Church Day (no devotional)
Monday, Day 30—*What Is Courage?*
Tuesday, Day 31—*Godly Courage*
Wednesday, Day 32—Church Night (no devotional)

Thursday, Day 33—*Ungodly Courage*
Friday, Day 34—*Be Strong and of a Good Courage*
Saturday, Day 35—*Biblical Heart Failure*

Day 29: Church Day

*Deuteronomy 31:6 **Be strong and of a good courage**, fear not, nor be afraid of them: for the LORD thy God, he it is that doth go with thee; he will not fail thee, nor forsake thee.*

Day 30: (Monday)
What Is Courage?

*Joshua 2:11 And as soon as we had heard these things, our hearts did melt, **neither did there remain any more courage** in any man, because of you: for the LORD your God, he is God in heaven above, and in earth beneath.*

INTRODUCTORY THOUGHTS

Courage originates within the heart of the individual. Two chief witnesses testify to this truth: (1) The English word *courage* comes from a word plainly connected to the heart, and (2) Multiple Bible passages associate courage with the heart *(Numbers 32:7, 9; Deuteronomy 1:28; Psalm 27:14; Psalm 31:24)*. The scripture declares in our passage that the hearts of the people melted as they lost courage (i.e., they lost strength). Other Bible passages associate courage with the strengthening of the heart *(Psalm 27:14; Psalm 31:24)*. These truths illustrate that courage reflects strength of heart and that courage is based upon faith, hope, and trust in God.

DEVOTIONAL THOUGHTS

- **(For children)**: What are some of the feelings you have when you are afraid? The Bible describes this as our hearts melting. It's a sinking feeling. Many times we want to run away from things that make us afraid. However, when we have courage, our hearts feel strong inside as if we could do anything because of God's help.
- **(For everyone)**: Knowing that courage means the strengthening of the heart, do you think courage is always a good thing? Are there times when a strong heart could trigger a rebellious spirit toward God?

- Would you consider yourself to be a courageous person? What do you think would help you to have the right type of attitude in this matter?

PRAYER THOUGHTS

- Christians should display courage to the world and to other believers. Ask God to strengthen your heart so that you have a courageous spirit.
- Ask the Lord to show you things in your life that would help to build godly courage as well as things that might be destroying your courage.

SONG: *WE REST ON THEE*

Day 31: (Tuesday)
Godly Courage

*Numbers 13:20 And what the land is, whether it be fat or lean, whether there be wood therein, or not. **And be ye of good courage**, and bring of the fruit of the land. Now the time was the time of the firstripe grapes.*

INTRODUCTORY THOUGHTS

Yesterday's study focused on the fact that *courage* involves strength of the heart. Our passage today reveals the first of sixteen times that the Bible uses the phrase "***good courage***." Each instance reveals someone trying to encourage a fellow believer and demonstrates the need for a godly courage within the life of every believer. Moses' words to the twelve spies being sent to search out the land of Canaan (the land promised to Israel by God) encouraged these men to be *"of good courage"* while stressing the importance of completing the task set before them. Moses knew that it would take *"good courage"* to fully follow the will of God since most of these men did not seem accustomed to showing courage in the face of overwhelming adversity. Courage must rely upon the power of God and not upon man's wisdom or one's own abilities.

DEVOTIONAL THOUGHTS

- **(For children):** Godly courage is doing right even if your friends are doing wrong. If someone wants to steal, should you steal? If they want to run in church, throw toys, talk when someone else is praying, should you? If they are mean to others, should you be mean too?

- **(For everyone):** Do you struggle finding the courage to obey the Lord? Do you have a hard time witnessing to others? Do you find it difficult to take a stand for the things of God when others around seem to care so little about obeying God?
- Do most of your actions exemplify a godly or an ungodly courage? Do you find it easier to obey or disobey the Lord?

PRAYER THOUGHTS

- Ask God to help you discern the difference between godly and ungodly courage. Ask Him to show you the kind of courage you have within your life.
- Ask God to help you obey His word, even in the midst of a world that takes pride in its disobedience toward God and authority.

SONG: *NEVER BE AFRAID*

Day 32: Church Night

Joshua 10:25 *And Joshua said unto them, Fear not, nor be dismayed, **be strong and of good courage**: for thus shall the LORD do to all your enemies against whom ye fight.*

Day 33: (Thursday)
Ungodly Courage

Psalm 64:1 *Hear my voice, O God, in my prayer: preserve my life from fear of the enemy.*

2 Hide me from the secret counsel of the wicked; from the insurrection of the workers of iniquity:

3 Who whet their tongue like a sword, and bend their bows to shoot their arrows, even bitter words:

4 That they may shoot in secret at the perfect: suddenly do they shoot at him, and fear not.

*5 **They encourage themselves in an evil matter**: they commune of laying snares privily; they say, Who shall see them?*

6 They search out iniquities; they accomplish a diligent search: both the inward thought of every one of them, and the heart, is deep.

INTRODUCTORY THOUGHTS

Our previous study explored godly courage. Yet, the Bible also teaches that courage can be used for ungodly purposes. David described the fear he endured because of his enemies. His testimony provides insight as to the dangerous nature of his enemies. David goes on to confess that his enemies *"encouraged themselves in an evil matter."* Christians are to encourage themselves in the work of God. Unfortunately, those determined to work iniquity frequently are encouraged by their friends and associates to behave even more wickedly. Even David failed in this manner when he told a messenger to "encourage" Joab following the murder of Uriah *(2 Samuel 11:25)*. Godly courage is a righteous act blessed of the Lord. Ungodly courage, on the other hand, can many times be used to hinder the work of God.

DEVOTIONAL THOUGHTS

- **(For children):** Some people have courage that does not please God. Can you name someone who is brave to do wrong? A bank robber, a bully, or someone who breaks into your home may be brave, but God doesn't want us to be brave doing wicked things that go against His word.
- **(For everyone):** Is it easy for you to do evil or bad things? Are you more consistent at obeying or disobeying God's word? What does that tell you about your courage of heart?
- Many times, crowds encourage themselves to act wickedly. Do you find it easier to go along with a crowd or stand alone no matter the pressure? What kind of encouragement are you receiving? Are you following the crowd or the word of God?

PRAYER THOUGHTS

- Ask God to reveal to you the kind of courage you are receiving.
- Ask the Lord to identify any rebellion in your heart.

SONG: *WE GATHER TOGETHER*

Day 34: (Friday)
Be Strong and of a Good Courage

Joshua 1:1 Now after the death of Moses the servant of the LORD it came to pass, that the LORD spake unto Joshua the son of Nun, Moses' minister, saying,

2 *Moses my servant is dead; now therefore arise, go over this Jordan, thou, and all this people, unto the land which I do give to them, even to the children of Israel.*

3 *Every place that the sole of your foot shall tread upon, that have I given unto you, as I said unto Moses.*

4 *From the wilderness and this Lebanon even unto the great river, the river Euphrates, all the land of the Hittites, and unto the great sea toward the going down of the sun, shall be your coast.*

5 *There shall not any man be able to stand before thee all the days of thy life: as I was with Moses, so I will be with thee: I will not fail thee, nor forsake thee.*

6 ***Be strong and of a good courage**: for unto this people shalt thou divide for an inheritance the land, which I sware unto their fathers to give them.*

7 *Only **be thou strong and very courageous**, that thou mayest observe to do according to all the law, which Moses my servant commanded thee: turn not from it to the right hand or to the left, that thou mayest prosper whithersoever thou goest.*

8 *This book of the law shall not depart out of thy mouth; but thou shalt meditate therein day and night, that thou mayest observe to do according to all that is written therein: for then thou shalt make thy way prosperous, and then thou shalt have good success.*

9 *Have not I commanded thee? **Be strong and of a good courage**; be not afraid, neither be thou dismayed: for the LORD thy God is with thee whithersoever thou goest.*

Introductory Thoughts

The Bible reveals that Moses was one of Israel's greatest leaders. To be the leader of the nation of Israel after Moses would have been a daunting task. Yet, this was exactly what God called Joshua to do. Immediately following the death of Moses, the Lord spoke to Joshua and twice instructed him to *"be strong and of a good courage" **(Joshua 1:6, 9)**.* He also admonished him to *"be thou strong and very courageous" **(Joshua 1:7)**.* Without godly courage, Joshua would have shied away from the great responsibilities thrust upon him. If he lacked courage, how could he admonish others to trust God and have great courage? Only courageous people can truly lead others during times when courage is necessary.

DEVOTIONAL THOUGHTS

- **(For children):** Are you fearful? Are you afraid to sing out loud, or to quote a Bible verse, or shake hands with others? Of what are you afraid? God will help you to have courage in these things if you learn to trust Him for strength.
- **(For everyone):** Do you have some difficult tasks set before you? Are there things you need to do that are currently making you afraid? God commanded Joshua to be courageous and He expects no less of His children. Courage is a matter of faith and trust in the Lord. Will you trust Him to help you become more courageous?
- Are you afraid to serve God or commit to His will for your life? You are not the first person to be afraid, but it is important that you trust Him and take courage.

PRAYER THOUGHTS

- Ask God to help you obey His word regardless of your fears.
- Pray God will help you see the rewards of eternity more clearly than the fears of this world.

SONG: *A CHARGE TO KEEP I HAVE*

Day 35: (Saturday)
Biblical Heart Failure

Psalm 27:14 *Wait on the LORD:* **be of good courage***, and he shall strengthen thine heart: wait, I say, on the LORD.*

INTRODUCTORY THOUGHTS

As we have seen, courage comes from a strength of heart. On the contrary, the Bible likens discouragement (the opposite of courage) to a melted heart *(Joshua 2:11)*. In other words, discouragement takes place when a man's heart loses strength. The Bible reveals that discouragement comes through various avenues of life. Men become discouraged because of *"the way"* (i.e., the circumstances of life) *(Numbers 21:4)*. Discouragement also results from fear and unbelief *(Deuteronomy 1:28)* and the magnitude of a task *(1 Chronicles 28:20)*. Ultimately, discouragement rears its ugly head as a result of a lack of faith in God and His word. Since discouragement and a lack of faith go hand in hand, a discouraged man cannot please God *(Hebrews 11:6)*.

DEVOTIONAL THOUGHTS

- **(For children):** David faced a giant without fear because he knew God was with him. Let's ask God to help us not to be afraid of the things He wants us to do.
- **(For everyone):** Are you discouraged? What caused you to become so discouraged? Has your faith been replaced by doubt? Is the Lord pleased with your courage?
- Is discouragement hindering your service to God? Are you willing to allow His word to strengthen your heart once more?

PRAYER THOUGHTS

- Ask God to shield you from the enemies of courage.
- Ask the Lord to help you to see signs of discouragement in your life before becoming consumed by it.

SONG: *WHAT A FRIEND WE HAVE IN JESUS*

Notes: _____

_____

_____

_____

_____

Quotes from the next volume

(VOLUME 2, WEEK 5)

Subject: Carnality

A Christian's carnality hinders his true potential for service to the Lord. Additionally, carnal living also prohibits the future spiritual growth God intends for every Christian to experience.

When we give our minds over to the flesh, we die spiritually. We also miss out on the things that tend toward life and peace *(Romans 8:6)*.

6

Courage (con't)

Occurrences: The Old Testament refers to *courageous* five times and *courageously* one more time.

First usage in the New Testament: *Acts 28:15* (courage)

Last usage in the Old Testament: *Amos 2:16* (courageous)

Interesting fact: *Acts 28:15* shows the one instance of *courage* in the New Testament when Paul took courage when other believers visited him while imprisoned.

Bible study tip: When studying a subject, consider the connotation (an idea or feeling resulting from the manner of a word's usage). For instance, does the word always refer to something good or can it also be evil? Remember that the context always helps to differentiate between the two uses.

Sunday, Day 36—Church Day (no devotional)
Monday, Day 37—*Encourage Yourself*
Tuesday, Day 38—*Encourage Others*
Wednesday, Day 39—Church Night (no devotional)
Thursday, Day 40—*The Spirit of Fear*
Friday, Day 41—*Our Enemy of Unbelief*
Saturday, Day 42—*The Path to Courage*

Day 36: Church Day

*Joshua 23:6 **Be ye therefore very courageous** to keep and to do all that is written in the book of the law of Moses, that ye turn not aside therefrom to the right hand or to the left;*

7 That ye come not among these nations, these that remain among you; neither make mention of the name of their gods, nor cause to swear by them, neither serve them, nor bow yourselves unto them:

8 But cleave unto the LORD your God, as ye have done unto this day.

Day 37: (Monday)
Encourage Yourself

1 Samuel 30:1 And it came to pass, when David and his men were come to Ziklag on the third day, that the Amalekites had invaded the south, and Ziklag, and smitten Ziklag, and burned it with fire;

2 And had taken the women captives, that were therein: they slew not any, either great or small, but carried them away, and went on their way.

3 So David and his men came to the city, and, behold, it was burned with fire; and their wives, and their sons, and their daughters, were taken captives.

4 Then David and the people that were with him lifted up their voice and wept, until they had no more power to weep.

5 And David's two wives were taken captives, Ahinoam the Jezreelitess, and Abigail the wife of Nabal the Carmelite.

*6 And David was greatly distressed; for the people spake of stoning him, because the soul of all the people was grieved, every man for his sons and for his daughters: but **David encouraged himself** in the LORD his God.*

INTRODUCTORY THOUGHTS

God's people have a solemn responsibility to encourage one another. Helping to build another's godly courage remains one of the most effective ways to influence others. Unfortunately, far too many times, close acquaintances fail to encourage (and all too often discourage) one another. In these times, it is especially important that the individual learns to encourage himself in the Lord. In our passage, David returned to Ziklag only to find it burned with fire. The welfare of the women and children seemed hopeless as the Amalekites had taken them all captive. No doubt it was one of David's most challenging times. David and his men were greatly distressed and in need of courage. Unfortunately, the men closest to David turned against him rather than supporting their leader during the most trying time. David's only hope was to encourage *"himself in the LORD his God."* Believers today need to follow David's example. We cannot always depend upon others to receive courage, but we can always depend upon the Lord.

DEVOTIONAL THOUGHTS

- **(For children):** During times when you feel afraid or alone, remember God says He will always be with us and He loves us with an everlasting love. Will you sing "Jesus Loves Me" out loud to encourage yourself right now?
- **(For everyone):** Are there times when you are discouraged? Are there times when there is nobody around offering words of encouragement? How do you react during those times? Who should you blame for remaining in a discouraged state of mind?
- How did David encourage himself? What are some ways that you could encourage yourself?

PRAYER THOUGHTS

- Ask God to help you find ways to encourage yourself. Ask Him to teach you how to avoid the things that will bring discouragement so that you can learn to avoid them.
- Ask God to show you when your courage is growing weaker. Ask Him to help make you a true encourager.

SONG: *BLESSED ASSURANCE*

Day 38: (Tuesday)
Encourage Others

Deuteronomy 3:21 *And I commanded Joshua at that time, saying, Thine eyes have seen all that the LORD your God hath done unto these two kings: so shall the LORD do unto all the kingdoms whither thou passest.*

22 Ye shall not fear them: for the LORD your God he shall fight for you.

23 And I besought the LORD at that time, saying,

24 O Lord GOD, thou hast begun to shew thy servant thy greatness, and thy mighty hand: for what God is there in heaven or in earth, that can do according to thy works, and according to thy might?

25 I pray thee, let me go over, and see the good land that is beyond Jordan, that goodly mountain, and Lebanon.

26 But the LORD was wroth with me for your sakes, and would not hear me: and the LORD said unto me, Let it suffice thee; speak no more unto me of this matter.

27 Get thee up into the top of Pisgah, and lift up thine eyes westward, and northward, and southward, and eastward, and behold it with thine eyes: for thou shalt not go over this Jordan.

*28 But charge Joshua, and **encourage him, and strengthen him**: for he shall go over before this people, and he shall cause them to inherit the land which thou shalt see.*

29 So we abode in the valley over against Bethpeor.

INTRODUCTORY THOUGHTS

In Deuteronomy, Moses rehearsed the events that led up to God's denying him entry into the promised land though he was Israel's leader at the time. The Lord instructed Moses, as he stood upon Mt. Pisgah, to encourage and strengthen Joshua. Moses could have offered numerous excuses for not wanting to encourage Joshua. Instead, Moses determined to obey God by strengthening and encouraging his successor. He knew that Joshua as Moses' replacement was about to face some of the greatest trials of his life. There would be times of fear along with battles and obstacles, small and great. The Lord knew Joshua desperately needed courage to make it through these trials. He, therefore, enlisted Moses and instructed His children to encourage the new leader during this difficult transition *(Deuteronomy 1:38)*.

DEVOTIONAL THOUGHTS

- **(For children):** Has someone you know been hurt or fallen sick? What could you do to help make them feel better (pray, send a card or visit)?

- **(For everyone):** Joshua needed encouragement because he was going to face some difficult times. Can you think of anyone who might be going through some difficult circumstances? What have you done to encourage them? Have you spoken encouraging words to them?
- The Lord expected Moses and the people to encourage Joshua. Moses could have responded, *"I can't because I'm about to die."* The people could have said, *"We can't because we too are afraid."* Yet, God expected obedience. Do you ever make excuses for not encouraging others? Do your excuses satisfy the Lord's expectations of you?

PRAYER THOUGHTS

- Ask God to help you see others who need encouragement.
- Ask the Lord to show you when your actions or words begin to discourage others.

SONG: *MARCHING TO ZION*

Day 39: Church Night

Psalm 31:24 Be of good courage, and he shall strengthen your heart, all ye that hope in the LORD.

Day 40: (Thursday)
The Spirit of Fear

2 Timothy 1:6 Wherefore I put thee in remembrance that thou stir up the gift of God, which is in thee by the putting on of my hands.

7 For God hath not given us the spirit of fear; but of power, and of love, and of a sound mind.

8 Be not thou therefore ashamed of the testimony of our Lord, nor of me his prisoner: but be thou partaker of the afflictions of the gospel according to the power of God;

INTRODUCTORY THOUGHTS

Fear and discouragement are effective weapons in Satan's arsenal which he uses to discourage the people of God from fulfilling the will of God for their lives. Fear is not all bad. The fear of God is good and holy, but the fear of the world withstands faith and brings the believer into bondage *(Proverbs 29:25)*. Fear and faith are foes as are fear and courage. In *2 Timothy 1:6-8*, the Bible points out that the Lord is not the instigator of fear in the life of the believer. In the place of fear, God gives men power, love, and a sound mind. God wants men to be courageous and full of faith. Yet, the fear of man exhibits a lack of courage. It frequently hinders believers from doing the Lord's work and gives the impression that believers are ashamed of the Lord and His people.

DEVOTIONAL THOUGHTS

- **(For children):** Memorize *Isaiah 41:10a*, *"Fear thou not; for I am with thee."* When God wants you to give someone a tract, invite him to attend church, or tell him what Jesus did for him, try to remember this promise from God.
- **(For everyone):** Do fears overcome you when trying to serve God? Do you fear telling others that you are a Christian? Who tries to keep you from doing these things for the Lord?
- Think for a moment: have you ever noticed how talking about the weather, sports, or work seems easier than talking about spiritual matters? Do you become scared when God impresses upon your heart to talk to someone about the Lord? Which of these subjects is most likely to help others? How do you think those other subjects can help you to talk to others about the Lord?

PRAYER THOUGHTS

- What are some of your fears in serving the Lord? Ask Him to help you overcome those fears and take courage in doing His work.
- Ask the Lord to direct your path toward someone in need of hearing the gospel this week. Ask Him to give you the words to say. Pray that this person will have the courage to trust Christ as his or her Saviour.

SONG: *ANYWHERE WITH JESUS*

Day 41: (Friday)
Our Enemy of Unbelief

Deuteronomy 1:19 And when we departed from Horeb, we went through all that great and terrible wilderness, which ye saw by the way of the mountain of the Amorites, as the LORD our God commanded us; and we came to Kadeshbarnea.

20 And I said unto you, Ye are come unto the mountain of the Amorites, which the LORD our God doth give unto us.

21 Behold, the LORD thy God hath set the land before thee: go up and possess it, as the LORD God of thy fathers hath said unto thee; fear not, neither be discouraged.

22 And ye came near unto me every one of you, and said, We will send men before us, and they shall search us out the land, and bring us word again by what way we must go up, and into what cities we shall come.

23 And the saying pleased me well: and I took twelve men of you, one of a tribe:

24 And they turned and went up into the mountain, and came unto the valley of Eshcol, and searched it out.

25 And they took of the fruit of the land in their hands, and brought it down unto us, and brought us word again, and said, It is a good land which the LORD our God doth give us.

26 Notwithstanding ye would not go up, but rebelled against the commandment of the LORD your God:

27 And ye murmured in your tents, and said, Because the LORD hated us, he hath brought us forth out of the land of Egypt, to deliver us into the hand of the Amorites, to destroy us.

28 Whither shall we go up? our brethren have discouraged our heart, saying, The people is greater and taller than we; the cities are great and walled up to heaven; and moreover we have seen the sons of the Anakims there.

29 Then I said unto you, Dread not, neither be afraid of them.

30 The LORD your God which goeth before you, he shall fight for you, according to all that he did for you in Egypt before your eyes;

31 And in the wilderness, where thou hast seen how that the LORD thy God bare thee, as a man doth bear his son, in all the way that ye went, until ye came into this place.

*32 Yet in this thing **ye did not believe the LORD your God**,*

Introductory Thoughts

As Moses recounted Israel's time in the wilderness, he reminded God's people of the reasons for their failure to enter into the land of promise. He rehearsed how it was the people who approached him requesting that spies first be sent into the land to explore it. If the people had trusted God, surveying the land would have been unnecessary. Yet, the people doubted God's provisions so Moses sent in the spies. When they returned, they expressed stories of giants and walled cities that made the people fear to carry out God's will. The spies' report "discouraged" *(Deuteronomy 1:28)* the hearts of the people. This loss of courage yielded an unbelief in the people *(Deuteronomy 1:32)*, greatly displeasing the Lord *(Hebrews 3:17-19)*.

DEVOTIONAL THOUGHTS

- **(For children)**: God created the world and everything in it by simply speaking it into existence. Do you believe that He is powerful enough to help you do what He wants you to do?
- **(For everyone)**: Do you struggle with being courageous? Do you wish you could better understand the reason for this weakness? Start by evaluating your faith in God's word.
- Our passage shows that if Israel had trusted God, they would not have needed spies. Are there some things that you can recall that would be different in your life if you had simply trusted God? Has your lack of faith ever produced a lack of courage?

PRAYER THOUGHTS

- Ask God to help you avoid the evil sin of unbelief.
- Ask God to surround you with people who believe and trust in His word. Pray that God will give you strength to believe even when others choose not to believe.

SONG: *GUIDE ME, O THOU GREAT JEHOVAH*

Day 42: (Saturday)
The Path to Courage

*James 4:7 **Submit** yourselves therefore to God. **Resist** the devil, and he will flee from you.*

8 Draw nigh to God, and he will draw nigh to you. Cleanse your hands, ye sinners; and purify your hearts, ye double minded.

INTRODUCTORY THOUGHTS

The Devil loves to hinder the spiritual blessings that believers possess in Christ. His most effective means is by destroying the believer's faith in God's word and keeping the saint from laying up rewards in heaven. By destroying a believer's courage, the Devil wins the battle. *James 4:7-8* sketches a simple yet effective plan for victory in such times of attack. The believer must first submit to God and His word by submitting his will to the will of God. Next, the saint of God must resist the Devil. When the believer submits to God and resists the Devil, the Devil flees rather than sticking around to watch defeat. When the Devil returns later with renewed attempts to discourage, the believer need only repeat the same scriptural strategy.

DEVOTIONAL THOUGHTS

- **(For children):** The Devil is our enemy. He lies to us and wants to create fear in our hearts. We must pray and do what God tells us to do. Remember the Bible stories in which God helped others—the Red Sea, the walls of Jericho, David and Goliath, Elijah on Mt. Carmel, etc.
- **(For everyone):** Do you feel like the Devil all too often keeps you from doing what you ought to do? Why do you think you fail? Is it your submission to God or your failure to resist the Devil? You must do both, but submitting to God comes first.
- Have you surrendered to do the Lord's will in your life no matter the cost? If not, the Devil will continue to discourage you. Take courage now and trust God!

PRAYER THOUGHTS

- Ask God to help you surrender to His known will for your life.
- Ask God to show you areas of your life in which you do not trust Him. Ask Him to give you victory in those areas.

SONG: *GOD MOVES IN A MYSTERIOUS WAY*

Notes: _____

_____

_____

_____

_____

_____

_____

_____

_____

_____

_____

_____

Quotes from the next volume

(VOLUME 2, WEEK 6)

Subject: Communication

The two disciples on the road to Emmaus did not expect the Lord Jesus to show up in the midst of their communication, but He did! Would your communication be any different if you believed Christ could "show up" in the midst of your discussion?

The Devil has convinced many Christians that the content of their daily conversations has no bearing on their spiritual walk with the Lord.

Christians who desire to serve the Lord and please Him can easily be derailed by choosing to surround themselves by those using evil communications.

7

Wise Decisions

Occurrences: Including the variations mentioned below, this truth occurs over 200 times in scripture.

Variations: choose, choosest, chooseth, choosing, chose, chosen, decided, decision

First usage: *Genesis 6:2* (chose)

Last usage: *Revelation 17:14* (chosen)

Defined: to select or to take by preference

Interesting fact: Abraham found God's choice of land by allowing Lot to make his choice and then taking what was remaining. The Bible tells us that Lot chose all the plain of Jordan which left Abraham with the land of promise *(Genesis 13:9-11)*. Thus, Lot's wrong choice led to Abraham's blessed decision.

Bible study tip: *"All scripture is given by inspiration of God, and is profitable for **doctrine**, for **reproof**, for **correction**, and for **instruction in righteousness"** (2 Timothy 3:16).* Some of the most enthusiastic Bible students emphasize one truth from a list of truths to the exclusion of the others, for example, doctrine. However, Bible study should never be solely or even primarily focused upon one aspect over the others. The simplest solution involves asking God to allow your Bible study to reprove, correct, and instruct you in righteousness.

Sunday, Day 43—Church Day (no devotional)
Monday, Day 44—*Double Mind Double Heart*
Tuesday, Day 45—*Evil Choices Bad Results*
Wednesday, Day 46—Church Night (no devotional)
Thursday, Day 47—The *Foundation for Wise Choices*
Friday, Day 48—*Difficult Decisions*
Saturday, Day 49—*Wise Decisions involving Eternal Consequences*

Day 43: Church Day

Deuteronomy 30:19 *I call heaven and earth to record this day against you, that I have set before you life and death, blessing and cursing: therefore **choose** life, that both thou and thy seed may live:*

Day 44: (Monday)
Double Mind Double Heart

James 1:5 *If any of you lack wisdom, let him ask of God, that giveth to all men liberally, and upbraideth not; and it shall be given him.*

6 But let him ask in faith, nothing wavering. For he that wavereth is like a wave of the sea driven with the wind and tossed.

7 For let not that man think that he shall receive any thing of the Lord.

*8 A **double minded man** is unstable in all his ways.*

INTRODUCTORY THOUGHTS

Decision making is an important element of everyday life. The Bible has many clear guidelines in this area. Every Christian must learn how to make decisions and then trust God with the results. Some decisions involve life changing outcomes, yet every decision must be based on biblically sound principles. The book of James, when referring to prayer, warns the reader of the dangers of indecisive and faithless living. This particular prayer pertains to wisdom, but the principle involves a broader application. A man who struggles with indecisiveness is said to be *"double minded"* reflecting instability in all his ways *(James 1:8)*. A few chapters later the Bible instructs the *"double minded"* believer to purify his heart *(James 4:8)*. Believers must learn to make decisions with God's help and stick with those decisions until the Lord directs otherwise.

DEVOTIONAL THOUGHTS

- **(For children):** Imagine a stormy sea with a ship trying to remain afloat. What happens to the passengers and the ship's contents when the waves get really rough? The Bible likens us to that ship when we fail to heed God's instructions.
- **(For everyone):** How many decisions do you make on a daily basis? How important is it to make spiritually sound decisions? How many wrong decisions does it take to get you into trouble? Would it be better to never make a decision for fear of making the wrong one?
- People sometimes think they would rather avoid making any decision, but making no decision is a decision in itself. Do you find yourself erring in either direction? Are you quick to decide or do you waver with each new decision?

PRAYER THOUGHTS

- Ask the Lord for help in making the right decisions, and then stick by those decisions trusting God's help.
- Pray that God will give you wisdom and show you when you are becoming unstable in your decision making.

SONG: *CONFLICTING FEELINGS*

Day 45: (Tuesday)
Evil Choices Bad Results

Matthew 27:18 For he knew that for envy they had delivered him.

19 When he was set down on the judgment seat, his wife sent unto him, saying, Have thou nothing to do with that just man: for I have suffered many things this day in a dream because of him.

20 But the chief priests and elders persuaded the multitude that they should ask Barabbas, and destroy Jesus.

*21 The governor answered and said unto them, **Whether of the twain will ye that I release unto you?** They said, Barabbas.*

*22 Pilate saith unto them, **What shall I do then with Jesus which is called Christ?** They all say unto him, Let him be crucified.*

*23 And the governor said, **Why, what evil hath he done?** But they cried out the more, saying, Let him be crucified.*

24 When Pilate saw that he could prevail nothing, but that rather a tumult was made, he took water, and washed his hands before the multitude, saying, I am innocent of the blood of this just person: see ye to it.

25 Then answered all the people, and said, His blood be on us, and on our children.

INTRODUCTORY THOUGHTS

Every choice in life can yield eternal consequences, some vastly significant, some of lesser importance. No clearer demonstration exists than the many decisions surrounding Christ's crucifixion. The Jews had unjustly delivered Jesus to the governor. As a gesture to the people at the Roman feast, Pilate frequently released to them a prisoner. In this instance, he gave the Jews a choice between two prisoners—a vile man or the innocent Son of God. Barabbas was justly imprisoned as a robber **(John 18:40)** and murderer **(Mark 15:7)**. This simple decision turned quite complex for the Jews. The people rejected the sinless Son of God and chose to release a guilty man. With evil hearts and wicked intentions, they cried out for the release of Barabbas. Making matters worse, they demanded that Jesus be crucified though He had done nothing worthy of death. The people became pawns of Satan though they were unaware that Jesus was born to die. He was brought to this point to bear the very sin they just committed, along with the sins of the whole world.

DEVOTIONAL THOUGHTS

- **(For children):** What is likely to happen when mom or dad ask you to pick up your toys and get ready for bed and you choose to keep on playing? How does the Lord feel about this kind of a decision?

- **(For everyone):** It is important to be a decision maker, but equally important to make the right decisions. What were the wrong decisions made by those in our passage?
- In this passage, the decisions made by the people showed that they rejected Jesus. Are there times when your decisions reflect the same type of behaviour? What can you do to avoid making these decisions?

PRAYER THOUGHTS

- Ask the Lord to help you avoid making evil decisions. Ask Him to help you understand the consequences of these choices.
- Pray that the Lord will show you how your evil decisions have an affect on you, others around you, and God too.

SONG: *ALMOST PERSUADED*

Day 46: Church Night

*Joshua 24:15 And if it seem evil unto you to serve the LORD, **choose you this day** whom ye will serve; whether the gods which your fathers served that were on the other side of the flood, or the gods of the Amorites, in whose land ye dwell: but as for me and my house, we will serve the LORD.*

Day 47: (Thursday)
The Foundation for Wise Choices

*Proverbs 1:20 **Wisdom** crieth without; she uttereth her voice in the streets:*

21 She crieth in the chief place of concourse, in the openings of the gates: in the city she uttereth her words, saying,

*22 How long, **ye simple ones**, will ye love simplicity? and the scorners delight in their scorning, and fools hate **knowledge**?*

*23 Turn you at my **reproof**: behold, I will pour out my spirit unto you, I will make known my words unto you.*

24 Because I have called, and ye refused; I have stretched out my hand, and no man regarded;

*25 But ye have set at nought all my counsel, and would none of my **reproof**:*

26 I also will laugh at your calamity; I will mock when your fear cometh;

27 When your fear cometh as desolation, and your destruction cometh as a whirlwind; when distress and anguish cometh upon you.

28 Then shall they call upon me, but I will not answer; they shall seek me early, but they shall not find me:

*29 **For that they hated knowledge, and did not choose the fear of the LORD:***

*30 They would none of my counsel: they despised all my **reproof**.*

31 Therefore shall they eat of the fruit of their own way, and be filled with their own devices.

32 For the turning away of the simple shall slay them, and the prosperity of fools shall destroy them.

33 But whoso hearkeneth unto me shall dwell safely, and shall be quiet from fear of evil.

INTRODUCTORY THOUGHTS

In our passage today, the Bible identifies three gifts from God intended to enable believers to make right decisions. These three gifts are knowledge, wisdom, and reproof. *Knowledge* involves factual information that enables the believer to possess details before making a decision. The Lord rebukes the simple by pointing out that *"they hated knowledge" (Proverbs 1:29)*. Because they hated knowledge, the people failed to choose the fear of the Lord. *Wisdom,* on the other hand, involves the proper use of the knowledge provided by God for the individual. Wisdom takes the facts obtained and uses them to make the right choices. The last of the three gifts completes the package. *Reproof* entails the enlightenment of error. Knowledge, wisdom, and reproof work together to enable believers to choose wisely and properly.

DEVOTIONAL THOUGHTS

- **(For children):** Learn everything you can about God and His word. He will help you make the right choices for any decision you face. Learn why mom and dad say "no" to things and be grateful they love you enough to stop you from making some bad decisions.
- **(For everyone):** Knowledge turns out to be the most foundational of the three things mentioned in the passage. Where do you think you

can obtain true knowledge? What are you doing to obtain that knowledge?

- How you accept reproof reveals much about your heart. How do you respond when your errors are pointed out to you by those who love you? How do you react? Do you fix the problems or give excuses and continue in them?

PRAYER THOUGHTS

- Wisdom is a necessity for the believer. According to the Bible, God will give wisdom to those who ask *(James 1:5)*. Ask God to give you the wisdom necessary to make wise choices.
- Ask God to help you understand the importance of making wise choices and to help in making them more frequently.

SONG: *HOLY BIBLE, BOOK DIVINE*

Day 48: (Friday)
Difficult Decisions

Numbers 16:1 Now Korah, the son of Izhar, the son of Kohath, the son of Levi, and Dathan and Abiram, the sons of Eliab, and On, the son of Peleth, sons of Reuben, took men:

2 And they rose up before Moses, with certain of the children of Israel, two hundred and fifty princes of the assembly, famous in the congregation, men of renown:

*3 **And they gathered themselves together against Moses and against Aaron**, and said unto them, Ye take too much upon you, seeing all the congregation are holy, every one of them, and the LORD is among them: wherefore then lift ye up yourselves above the congregation of the LORD?*

4 And when Moses heard it, he fell upon his face:

5 And he spake unto Korah and unto all his company, saying, Even to morrow the LORD will shew who are his, and who is holy; and will cause him to come near unto him: even him whom he hath chosen will he cause to come near unto him.

6 This do; Take you censers, Korah, and all his company;

*7 And put fire therein, and put incense in them before the LORD to morrow: and **it shall be that the man whom the LORD doth choose, he shall be holy**: ye take too much upon you, ye sons of Levi.*

8 And Moses said unto Korah, Hear, I pray you, ye sons of Levi:

9 Seemeth it but a small thing unto you, that the God of Israel hath separated you from the congregation of Israel, to bring you near to himself to do the service of the tabernacle of the LORD, and to stand before the congregation to minister unto them?

10 And he hath brought thee near to him, and all thy brethren the sons of Levi with thee: and seek ye the priesthood also?

11 For which cause both thou and all thy company are gathered together against the LORD: and what is Aaron, that ye murmur against him?

12 And Moses sent to call Dathan and Abiram, the sons of Eliab: which said, We will not come up:

13 Is it a small thing that thou hast brought us up out of a land that floweth with milk and honey, to kill us in the wilderness, except thou make thyself altogether a prince over us?

14 Moreover thou hast not brought us into a land that floweth with milk and honey, or given us inheritance of fields and vineyards: wilt thou put out the eyes of these men? we will not come up.

15 And Moses was very wroth, and said unto the LORD, Respect not thou their offering: I have not taken one ass from them, neither have I hurt one of them.

16 And Moses said unto Korah, Be thou and all thy company before the LORD, thou, and they, and Aaron, to morrow:

17 And take every man his censer, and put incense in them, and bring ye before the LORD every man his censer, two hundred and fifty censers; thou also, and Aaron, each of you his censer.

18 And they took every man his censer, and put fire in them, and laid incense thereon, and stood in the door of the tabernacle of the congregation with Moses and Aaron.

19 And Korah gathered all the congregation against them unto the door of the tabernacle of the congregation: and the glory of the LORD appeared unto all the congregation.

20 And the LORD spake unto Moses and unto Aaron, saying,

21 **Separate yourselves from among this congregation, that I may consume them in a moment.**

22 And they fell upon their faces, and said, O God, the God of the spirits of all flesh, shall one man sin, and wilt thou be wroth with all the congregation?

23 And the LORD spake unto Moses, saying,

24 Speak unto the congregation, saying, Get you up from about the tabernacle of Korah, Dathan, and Abiram.

25 And Moses rose up and went unto Dathan and Abiram; and the elders of Israel followed him.

26 And he spake unto the congregation, saying, **Depart, I pray you, from the tents of these wicked men, and touch nothing of theirs, lest ye be consumed in all their sins.**

27 So they gat up from the tabernacle of Korah, Dathan, and Abiram, on every side: and Dathan and Abiram came out, and stood in the door of their tents, and their wives, and their sons, and their little children.

28 And Moses said, Hereby ye shall know that the LORD hath sent me to do all these works; for I have not done them of mine own mind.

29 If these men die the common death of all men, or if they be visited after the visitation of all men; then the LORD hath not sent me.

30 **But if the LORD make a new thing, and the earth open her mouth, and swallow them up, with all that appertain unto them, and they go down quick into the pit; then ye shall understand that these men have provoked the LORD.**

31 And it came to pass, as he had made an end of speaking all these words, that the ground clave asunder that was under them:

32 And the earth opened her mouth, and swallowed them up, and their houses, and all the men that appertained unto Korah, and all their goods.

33 They, and all that appertained to them, went down alive into the pit, and the earth closed upon them: and they perished from among the congregation.

INTRODUCTORY THOUGHTS

As Moses led Israel out of Egypt and on their journey toward the land of promise, he faced almost constant opposition. Numbers chapter 16 chronicles one such instance in great detail. Korah openly questioned and opposed Moses' leadership forcing him to bring the matter before Almighty God. The Lord said He would answer this challenge directly and reveal His choice between Moses and Korah. Not only did God choose Moses, but He also indicated that Korah would be judged by the earth opening up and swallowing him alive. Before the arrival of God's judgment, the people were instructed to choose by separating from Korah. Judgment fell as the earth opened up, swallowing alive those who followed Korah along with all their possessions. The earth simply closed back up. Interestingly, a brief Bible study (for instance, *Psalm 88*) reveals that *the sons of* Korah chose to obey God by separating from their father. Several subtitles in the book of Psalms like that found in *Psalm 88* indicate these sons followed God and His servant and survived God's judgment. The Devil presents few choices more difficult than choosing between God and family.

DEVOTIONAL THOUGHTS

- **(For children):** Unfortunately, some children have parents that do not love God. These parents ask their children to lie or steal for them. They even may make fun of them for going to church. What should the children do if they love God and truly want to serve Him?
- **(For everyone):** Do you think it was easy for the sons of Korah to walk away from their father and stand against what was wrong? What thoughts might have crossed their minds as they made this choice between their father and God?
- What kind of choices might you one day be forced to make similar to the choice of the sons of Korah? Could you trust God enough to make such a difficult choice?

PRAYER THOUGHTS

- Ask God to help you choose right despite the cost or opposition.
- Pray that God will give you faith to trust Him and especially during difficult times and trials.

SONG: *WHO IS ON THE LORD'S SIDE?*

Day 49: (Saturday)
Wise Decisions Involving Eternal Consequences

Ruth 1:1 *Now it came to pass in the days when the judges ruled, that there was a famine in the land. And a certain man of Bethlehemjudah went to sojourn in the country of Moab, he, and his wife, and his two sons.*

2 And the name of the man was Elimelech, and the name of his wife Naomi, and the name of his two sons Mahlon and Chilion, Ephrathites of Bethlehemjudah. And they came into the country of Moab, and continued there.

*3 **And Elimelech Naomi's husband died**; and she was left, and her two sons.*

*4 And they took them wives of the women of Moab; the name of the one was Orpah, and the name of the other **Ruth**: and they dwelled there about ten years.*

*5 **And Mahlon and Chilion died also both of them**; and the woman was left of her two sons and her husband.*

6 Then she arose with her daughters in law, that she might return from the country of Moab: for she had heard in the country of Moab how that the LORD had visited his people in giving them bread.

7 Wherefore she went forth out of the place where she was, and her two daughters in law with her; and they went on the way to return unto the land of Judah.

8 And Naomi said unto her two daughters in law, Go, return each to her mother's house: the LORD deal kindly with you, as ye have dealt with the dead, and with me.

9 The LORD grant you that ye may find rest, each of you in the house of her husband. Then she kissed them; and they lifted up their voice, and wept.

10 And they said unto her, Surely we will return with thee unto thy people.

11 And Naomi said, Turn again, my daughters: why will ye go with me? are there yet any more sons in my womb, that they may be your husbands?

12 Turn again, my daughters, go your way; for I am too old to have an husband. If I should say, I have hope, if I should have an husband also to night, and should also bear sons;

13 Would ye tarry for them till they were grown? would ye stay for them from having husbands? nay, my daughters; for it grieveth me much for your sakes that the hand of the LORD is gone out against me.

*14 And they lifted up their voice, and wept again: and **Orpah kissed her mother in law; but Ruth clave unto her.***

15 And she said, Behold, thy sister in law is gone back unto her people, and unto her gods: return thou after thy sister in law.

*16 And Ruth said, Intreat me not to leave thee, or to return from following after thee: **for whither thou goest, I will go; and where thou lodgest, I will lodge: thy people shall be my people, and thy God my God:***

17 Where thou diest, will I die, and there will I be buried: the LORD do so to me, and more also, if ought but death part thee and me.

*18 **When she saw that she was stedfastly minded to go with her, then she left speaking unto her.***

INTRODUCTORY THOUGHTS

The book of Ruth tells the story of a family torn apart by death and how God miraculously worked behind the scenes. Ruth, a Moabite, married a Jew who was the son of Elimelech and his wife Naomi. Over time while they resided in Moab, Naomi's husband and both of her sons died. After their deaths, Naomi determined to return to the land of Judah. She discouraged both Ruth and Orpah (her daughters-in-law) from returning with her since she felt that she had nothing to offer them. Each had to decide whether to go with Naomi or stay with their families in the land of Moab and serve their false gods. Orpah decided to stay, while Ruth chose to go with Naomi. At the time, Ruth's decision seemed senseless. Yet, all those who read the book of Ruth know the blessings associated with this one wisely crafted decision. Ruth came to Bethlehem at the right time *(Ruth 1:22)*, married a great man named Boaz *(Ruth 4:13)*, and God allowed her to become part of the lineage of King David and the Lord Jesus Christ *(Ruth 4:17; Matthew 1:5)*. Wow! Now, that is where the phrase "happy ending" was truly coined.

DEVOTIONAL THOUGHTS

- **(For children):** Every day, missionaries leave their friends and family to travel to faraway lands simply to tell people about the Lord. These are very difficult decisions and not everyone agrees with them. What good can come from such a decision?
- **(For everyone):** Do you think that Ruth's decision to go was easier than Orpah's decision to stay? Why or why not? Which one made the right choice? What happened to Orpah after she decided to stay? What happened to Ruth?
- What would Ruth have missed had she decided to stay in Moab? Is it possible that you will miss some blessings if you fail to make wise choices and correct decisions?

PRAYER THOUGHTS

- Ask God to help you see the long-term effects of your present decisions.
- Pray that He will give you the wisdom to make the right choices, even when they are difficult to make.

SONG: *O! SAY, BUT I'M GLAD*

Notes: _____

_____

_____

_____

_____

_____

_____

_____

_____

_____

_____

Notes: _____

_____

_____

_____

_____

_____

_____

_____

_____

_____

_____

_____

_____

_____

_____

_____

_____

_____

Quotes from the next volume

(VOLUME 2, WEEK 7)

Subject: Confession

Confession involves much more than simply receiving the Lord's forgiveness; it involves making wrongs right.

When we confess our sins to the Lord, we are telling God that we desire His fellowship more than we desire the pleasures of sin (*Hebrews 11:25*).

8

Faithfulness

Occurrences: found 111 times in 107 verses in its various forms

Variations: faithful, faithfully, faithfulness, unfaithful, unfaithfully

First usage: *Number 12:7* (faithful)

Last usage: *Revelation 22:6* (faithful)

Defined: firm in duty or commitment, dependable, able to be trusted

Interesting fact: The Bible shows that John Mark was not dependable in the ministry. Fortunately, he transitioned into a man whom Paul later wrote was *"profitable to me for the ministry" (2 Timothy 4:11)*. John Mark had previously shown himself to be unfaithful *(Acts 15:38)*, but his repaired testimony has become an encouraging witness for all future generations.

Bible study tip: The Bible often teaches spiritual truths using earthly pictures *(John 3:3-12)*. Bible study should include the study of the earthly pictures to discover the deeper spiritual truths.

Sunday, Day 50—Church Day (no devotional)
Monday, Day 51—*A Broken Tooth and a Foot Out of Joint*
Tuesday, Day 52—*I Know Him*
Wednesday, Day 53—Church Night (no devotional)
Thursday, Day 54— *The Demise of Sodom*
Friday, Day 55— *Faithful Philippians*
Saturday, Day 56—*Confident in Thy Obedience*

Day 50: Church Day

*Psalm 12:1 Help, LORD; for the godly man ceaseth; for the **faithful** fail from among the children of men.*

Day 51: (Monday)
A Broken Tooth and a Foot Out of Joint

*Proverbs 25:19 **Confidence in an unfaithful man** in time of trouble is like a broken tooth, and a foot out of joint.*

INTRODUCTORY THOUGHTS

Dependability seems to be a diminishing virtue in each succeeding generation. Sealing a deal with a handshake and the saying "my word is my bond" are no longer dependable means of transacting business. Unfortunately, even God's people are less dependable today than in previous generations. The Bible describes the painful experience of dealing with unfaithful people by likening them to a broken tooth or a foot out of joint. A broken tooth exposes raw nerves and makes eating excruciatingly painful. A foot out of joint makes movement hopeless without assistance. The Bible warns believers not to place confidence in a broken tooth, a foot out of joint, or an unfaithful man. Believers should stand apart from the world in this regard by becoming more like God.

DEVOTIONAL THOUGHTS

- **(For children):** If dad promised to fix your broken toy but never did, how would this make you feel? When you make a promise to do something for someone, do you keep your promise? How do you think they feel when you don't keep your promise?

- **(For everyone):** Have you ever experienced anything like a broken tooth or a foot out of joint? What kind of pain would be involved? What kind of daily activities are hindered by both of these problems? Why do you think that God chose these two problems to describe the pains caused by an unfaithful man?
- Can people depend upon you on a daily basis? Would those to whom you consider yourself closest consider you dependable? Why?

PRAYER THOUGHTS

- Pray and ask the Lord to help you see the importance of being dependable.
- Ask the Lord to show you the pains involved when others cannot count on you to be dependable.

SONG: *HOLD THE FORT*

Day 52: (Tuesday)
I Know Him

Genesis 18:16 And the men rose up from thence, and looked toward Sodom: and Abraham went with them to bring them on the way.

17 And the LORD said, Shall I hide from Abraham that thing which I do;

18 Seeing that Abraham shall surely become a great and mighty nation, and all the nations of the earth shall be blessed in him?

*19 For **I know him**, that he will command his children and his household after him, and they shall keep the way of the LORD, to do justice and judgment; that the LORD may bring upon Abraham that which he hath spoken of him.*

INTRODUCTORY THOUGHTS

Every devoted believer treasures the thought that one day God will say to him, *"Well done, thou good and faithful servant" (**Matthew 25:21**).* Abraham was such a man who exhibited faithfulness. In fact, it was God who commended Abraham for his faithful life though living in a very wicked world. The Lord came to visit Abraham in the plains of Mamre while on His way to bring judgment upon Sodom and Gomorrah. As the visit was coming to an end, the Lord remained with Abraham as the two angels journeyed toward Sodom. Interestingly, the Bible reveals the mind of the Lord as He contemplated whether or not to tell Abraham about the judgment coming to Sodom. Why would the Lord consider it necessary to tell Abraham? The Bible provides insight when the Lord said, *"I know him."* God told Abraham because Abraham showed himself faithful *(Amos 3:7)*.

DEVOTIONAL THOUGHTS

- **(For children):** God sees everything we do and how we act at home, at church and everywhere else. Can He count on you to obey your parents at home? Does He hear you asking for prayer and joining the class while singing in Sunday School? Would He praise you for listening to the Bible story, sharing your toys with others, and keeping your hands to yourself?
- **(For everyone):** Why do you think the Lord knew He could depend on Abraham to obey Him? Can you think of any reasons why the Lord would think He can count on you?
- God said He knew Abraham, and He knows you too! What does God know about you? Can He count on you to do the right things? Can your family depend upon you?

PRAYER THOUGHTS

- Ask the Lord to reveal the true level of your dependability.
- Ask the Lord to help you to become more dependable today and in the future. Ask God for the right opportunities to be faithful.

SONG: *I NEVER WILL CEASE TO LOVE HIM*

Day 53: Church Night

*1 Corinthians 4:2 Moreover it is required in stewards, that a man be found **faithful**.*

Day 54: (Thursday)
The Demise of Sodom

*Genesis 18:22 And the men turned their faces from thence, and went toward **Sodom**: but Abraham stood yet before the LORD.*

23 And Abraham drew near, and said, Wilt thou also destroy the righteous with the wicked?

24 Peradventure there be fifty righteous within the city: wilt thou also destroy and not spare the place for the fifty righteous that are therein?

25 That be far from thee to do after this manner, to slay the righteous with the wicked: and that the righteous should be as the wicked, that be far from thee: Shall not the Judge of all the earth do right?

26 And the LORD said, If I find in Sodom fifty righteous within the city, then I will spare all the place for their sakes.

27 And Abraham answered and said, Behold now, I have taken upon me to speak unto the Lord, which am but dust and ashes:

28 Peradventure there shall lack five of the fifty righteous: wilt thou destroy all the city for lack of five? And he said, If I find there forty and five, I will not destroy it.

29 And he spake unto him yet again, and said, Peradventure there shall be forty found there. And he said, I will not do it for forty's sake.

30 And he said unto him, Oh let not the Lord be angry, and I will speak: Peradventure there shall thirty be found there. And he said, I will not do it, if I find thirty there.

31 And he said, Behold now, I have taken upon me to speak unto the Lord: Peradventure there shall be twenty found there. And he said, I will not destroy it for twenty's sake.

32 And he said, Oh let not the Lord be angry, and I will speak yet but this once: **Peradventure ten shall be found there. And he said, I will not destroy it for ten's sake.**

33 And the LORD went his way, as soon as he had left communing with Abraham: and Abraham returned unto his place.

INTRODUCTORY THOUGHTS

Abraham's nephew, Lot, lived in the wicked city of Sodom. Because of the city's vile nature, God determined to pour out His wrath. After the Lord told Abraham about the impending judgment, he pleaded for the Lord to spare the city. Abraham's conversation with the Lord ended with God agreeing to spare the city if He found only ten righteous people within the city of Sodom. Interestingly, Abraham started with the number fifty but stopped when he reached ten. Abraham obviously believed that at ten people he had gone low enough to spare the city? Abraham believed that Lot and his family (his wife, married daughters, sons-in-law and unmarried daughters) would provide the number necessary to escape God's pronounced judgment. Abraham believed he could depend upon Lot to instruct his family in righteousness which would then prevent the impending doom. Surely God would find ten righteous, even if He looked no further than Lot's family. In the end, the city of Sodom was destroyed and only Lot and two daughters escaped alive. The inhabitants of the city and the rest of Lot's family were destroyed. Sin brought God's attention upon Sodom, but an unreliable Lot sealed their fate.

DEVOTIONAL THOUGHTS

- **(For children):** Have you ever felt uncomfortable when you were around people that you did not know? Imagine that a new family with children your age visits church. Would you smile at them, maybe shake hands and tell them your name? Would you invite them to come with you to your Sunday School and sit by them? Would this friendliness encourage them to feel welcome and maybe come visit again?
- **(For everyone):** How would the Bible story of Sodom be different if Lot had been dependable with teaching his family about the Lord? How would the fate of others be different if you were more dependable?
- Many people lost their lives in Sodom. How important was it for Lot to be dependable and to be a good witness for the Lord? What did Lot's unfaithfulness cost him personally?

PRAYER THOUGHTS

- Ask God to help you value the importance of being dependable.
- Pray that the Lord will give you a burden to be able to help those who are counting on you.

SONG: *BRINGING IN THE SHEAVES*

Day 55: (Friday)
Faithful Philippians

Philippians 4:15 Now ye Philippians know also, that in the beginning of the gospel, when I departed from Macedonia, no church communicated with me as concerning giving and receiving, **but ye only.**

16 *For even in Thessalonica* **ye sent once and again unto my necessity.**

INTRODUCTORY THOUGHTS

Paul served the Lord in a capacity similar to what missionaries and evangelists do today. He traveled extensively to tell everyone and anyone about Christ's saving grace. Holding a regular job to earn money would have been impossible due to Paul's manner of life in addition to his recurring travels. However, the Bible tells us that he worked as a tentmaker when the need presented itself *(Acts 18:1-3)*. Most of the time, however, he did not have personal income to provide for himself and his ministry. How would he live during those times? The Bible says that faithful churches provided for his necessities. The church at Philippi served as one such group of believers. Paul refers to a time when he departed from Macedonia. At that time, no church helped him; yet, the believers at Philippi sacrificially provided for his needs. These same believers faithfully helped Paul again in Thessalonica. Paul knew he could depend upon them because they understood the importance of distributing to those who had surrendered to the ministry.

DEVOTIONAL THOUGHTS

- **(For children):** God expects our church family to help one another. How are ways that you could help if someone was sick, hurt, scared, sad, or in need of food or clothing?
- **(For everyone):** Are there people who depend upon you? Are they often disappointed or noticeably encouraged by you? How could you improve and grow in this area?
- Do your brothers and sisters in Christ consider you dependable? Does anyone seem surprised if you are not at church or not involved in ministries? What can you do to be more dependable and increasingly involved?

PRAYER THOUGHTS

- Ask God to reveal to you people who need you to be faithful.
- Ask God to make you a dependable Christian willing to help others.

SONG: *IF JESUS GOES WITH ME*

Day 56: (Saturday)
Confident in Thy Obedience

Philemon 21 Having confidence in thy obedience *I wrote unto thee, knowing that thou wilt also do more than I say.*

INTRODUCTORY THOUGHTS

The epistle of Paul to Philemon was written to address the return of Philemon's servant Onesimus to his master after he had been unfaithful in the past. Paul and Onesiumus spent time together in prison. While in bonds together, Paul was able to lead Onesimus to a saving knowledge of Jesus Christ. After Onesimus got saved and learned the truth, he became a profitable servant of the Lord and a tremendous help to Paul and his ministry. Paul thought it wise to send him back to his master Philemon with a personal letter. Paul asked Philemon to receive him back, not merely as a servant, but as a brother in Christ *(Philemon 15-16)*. Paul requested that anything owed by Onesimus to Philemon should be charged to Paul's account. This was a difficult request, yet Paul knew he could count on Philemon to do right. In fact, Paul trusted Philemon to go well beyond his requests in the letter.

DEVOTIONAL THOUGHTS

- **(For children):** Older children sometimes do not realize how much their actions are carefully watched by the younger children. Can your example be trusted to show the younger children how to behave and follow the rules in church? Are you polite, obedient, and respectful? Do you put things back where they belong and never throw trash on the floor?
- **(For everyone):** When explaining Philemon's dependability, Paul chose words like *confidence* and *trust*. What kind of words would be used to describe your dependability?

- Paul asked Philemon for some difficult things and trusted him to obey. Can you be trusted in tough situations to do the right thing?

PRAYER THOUGHTS

- Ask the Lord to help you to be strong so that others will know that they can count on you.
- Ask the Lord to show you ways to be supportive of other believers.

SONG: *LIVING FOR JESUS (CHISHOLM)*

Notes: _____

_____

_____

_____

_____

_____

_____

_____

_____

_____

_____

_____

_____

_____

_____

_____

_____

_____

_____

Notes: _____

_____

_____

_____

_____

_____

_____

_____

_____

_____

_____

_____

_____

Quotes from the next volume

(VOLUME 2, WEEK 8)

Subject: Conversation

Before meeting the Lord on the road to Damascus, Paul's conversation or lifestyle involved vehemently persecuting the church (**Galatians 1:13**). In his new life with Christ, he immediately began preaching the very faith he once destroyed (**Galatians 1:23**). When a person truly places his faith for salvation in the finished work of Christ, his conversation will change accordingly.

This world, though it consistently fails to recognize and know the Lord, should consistently recognize Christ's conversation through the life of the believer.

9

Faithfulness (con't)

Occurrences: found fifty-six times in the Old Testament and fifty-five times in the New Testament in its various forms

First usage in the New Testament: *Matthew 24:45* (faithful)

Last usage in the Old Testament: *Hosea 11:12* (faithful)

Interesting fact: Moses is the first man the Bible identifies as faithful *(Numbers 12:7)* and the only one specifically identified as faithful by both testaments *(Hebrews 3:2, 5)*. The Bible recognizes his faithfulness despite the fact that Moses was not allowed to enter the Promised Land due to his failure in sanctifying the Lord before the eyes of the people *(Numbers 27:14)*. Fortunately, God considers the overall testimony of a man's life rather than dwelling on a single success or failure.

Bible study tip: Effective Bible study could be equated to good detective work. The best answers are only derived from asking the appropriate questions. In preparation for study, take some time to write a list of questions that you need answered and then use the scripture to answer those questions.

Sunday, Day 57—Church Day (no devotional)
Monday, Day 58—*Pay Your Vows*

Tuesday, Day 59—*Tarry, Watch, and Pray with Me*
Wednesday, Day 60—Church Night (no devotional)
Thursday, Day 61—*We Need Not to Speak*
Friday, Day 62—*From Undependable to Profitable*
Saturday, Day 63—*A Faithful High Priest*

Day 57: Church Day

Proverbs 20:6 *Most men will proclaim every one his own goodness: but **a faithful man** who can find?*

Day 58: (Monday)
Pay Your Vows

Ecclesiastes 5:4 *When thou vowest a vow unto God, defer not to pay it; for he hath no pleasure in fools: pay that which thou hast vowed.*

5 Better is it that thou shouldest not vow, than that thou shouldest vow and not pay.

6 Suffer not thy mouth to cause thy flesh to sin; neither say thou before the angel, that it was an error: wherefore should God be angry at thy voice, and destroy the work of thine hands?

7 For in the multitude of dreams and many words there are also divers vanities: but fear thou God.

INTRODUCTORY THOUGHTS

Scripturally speaking, a vow involves a solemn promise made to another individual or to God Himself. In our passage, *vow* is used both as a verb and a noun. *Vowing* a *vow* is analogous to someone *promising* a *promise*. Men are to keep their word by keeping their promises; or, in other words, men are to be faithfully dependable. When a man makes a promise to God or to another person, he should do everything within his power to keep that promise. The Bible warns against a man allowing his mouth to cause his flesh to sin by making promises with no intention of keeping them. Those who vow a vow to the Lord and fail to perform it are called *"fools"* and the Lord *"hath no pleasure in fools."* Before making any promise, one should first count the cost to determine whether or not making the vow will simply cause him to sin.

DEVOTIONAL THOUGHTS

- **(For children):** You promise to set the table and promise to clean your room. Which is more important? In God's eyes, both are important because God expects you to do what you say you will do.
- **(For everyone):** Are you always quick to say "yes"? Do you find yourself over obligated by promises you make? The Bible speaks strongly about keeping your word, or being dependable. What actions could you take to help you become more dependable?
- Do you make promises to others and fail to keep them? Would others classify you as a dependable person? What steps can you incorporate into your life that will show others that they can always count on you?

PRAYER THOUGHTS

- Ask God to give you wisdom to only promise those things that you can keep.
- Ask the Lord to show you necessary steps to become more dependable for those who need to depend upon you.

SONG: *O JESUS, I HAVE PROMISED*

Day 59: (Tuesday)
Tarry, Watch, and Pray with Me

Matthew 26:36 *Then cometh Jesus with them unto a place called Gethsemane, and saith unto the disciples, Sit ye here, while I go and pray yonder.*

37 *And he took with him Peter and the two sons of Zebedee, and began to be sorrowful and very heavy.*

38 *Then saith he unto them, My soul is exceeding sorrowful, even unto death:* **tarry ye here, and watch with me.**

39 *And he went a little further, and fell on his face, and prayed, saying, O my Father, if it be possible, let this cup pass from me: nevertheless not as I will, but as thou wilt.*

40 *And he cometh unto the disciples, and findeth them asleep, and saith unto Peter, What, could ye not* **watch with me** *one hour?*

41 **Watch and pray,** *that ye enter not into temptation: the spirit indeed is willing, but the flesh is weak.*

42 He went away again the second time, and prayed, saying, O my Father, if this cup may not pass away from me, except I drink it, thy will be done.

43 And he came and found them asleep again: for their eyes were heavy.

44 And he left them, and went away again, and prayed the third time, saying the same words.

45 Then cometh he to his disciples, and saith unto them, Sleep on now, and take your rest: behold, the hour is at hand, and the Son of man is betrayed into the hands of sinners.

46 Rise, let us be going: behold, he is at hand that doth betray me.

Introductory Thoughts

As the Lord's crucifixion drew nigh, He took His disciples to Gethsemane to pray. He asked them to tarry and watch with Him as He separated from them to pray to the Father. Upon returning, He found the disciples asleep so He said to them, *"Could ye not watch with me one hour?"* The Lord went away two more times only to find His disciples asleep both times He returned. He had given His disciples a simple task to tarry, watch, and pray. He quickly saw that He could not depend upon them for support. It comes as no surprise that they would be scattered from Him shortly at His betrayal *(Matthew 26:31, 56)*. These men were not strangers; they were the ones who sat at Christ's feet for three years. Now, they could not be trusted for one hour to watch and pray.

Devotional Thoughts

- **(For children):** If someone asks you to do something and you agree to do it, always try to do the task as soon possible. If you wait, what will the person think if he has to ask you a second or a third time?
- **(For everyone):** Do you think the Lord knew His disciples were unreliable? If so, why did He ask them to watch and pray? Could He have been trying to teach them how much better it would be to obey the Lord and show themselves dependable?
- Do you think things would have been different if you had been one of the disciples? Could the Lord depend upon you during a crucial time? Can He depend upon you to pray to Him and witness to others?

PRAYER THOUGHTS

- Ask the Lord to reveal to you how dependable you really are.
- Ask God to give you strength to mature and grow in this area and show yourself as dependable.

SONG: *FOOTPRINTS OF JESUS*

Day 60: Church Night

*2 Peter 3:17 Ye therefore, beloved, seeing ye know these things before, beware lest ye also, being led away with the error of the wicked, **fall from your own stedfastness.***

Day 61: (Thursday)
We Need Not to Speak

1 Thessalonians 1:1 Paul, and Silvanus, and Timotheus, unto the church of the Thessalonians which is in God the Father and in the Lord Jesus Christ: Grace be unto you, and peace, from God our Father, and the Lord Jesus Christ.

2 We give thanks to God always for you all, making mention of you in our prayers;

*3 Remembering without ceasing your **work of faith**, and **labour of love**, and **patience of hope** in our Lord Jesus Christ, in the sight of God and our Father;*

4 Knowing, brethren beloved, your election of God.

5 For our gospel came not unto you in word only, but also in power, and in the Holy Ghost, and in much assurance; as ye know what manner of men we were among you for your sake.

6 And ye became followers of us, and of the Lord, having received the word in much affliction, with joy of the Holy Ghost:

*7 So that **ye were ensamples to all that believe** in Macedonia and Achaia.*

*8 For **from you sounded out** the word of the Lord not only in Macedonia and Achaia, but also in every place **your faith to God-ward** is spread abroad; so that **we need not to speak any thing.***

9 For **they themselves shew of us what manner of entering in we had unto you**, and how ye turned to God from idols to serve the living and true God;

10 And to wait for his Son from heaven, whom he raised from the dead, even Jesus, which delivered us from the wrath to come.

Introductory Thoughts

This Pauline epistle is addressed to believers in Thessalonica. It opens with an expression of joy and thanksgiving for their work and labour. Paul then reminded them how they came to be followers of him and of the Lord after they received the word through much affliction. Paul praised them for their faithful example to those in Macedonia and Achaia. In fact, they were so faithful that Paul said when He arrived in Macedonia and Achaia, he did not need to speak a word because of the example of the Thessalonian believers. Their testimony spread to these locations, as well as in *"every place."* Paul knew he could trust these saints to be dependable witnesses of the gospel. What an incredible relief and wonderful blessing this must have been for the apostle Paul.

Devotional Thoughts

- **(For children):** A younger child sees you listening to the preaching. He also notices you joining in singing during the entire song service. He truly wants to be just like you. By showing him the right way, his mother and father might not have to correct him so often and the Lord will reward you one day for your faithfulness.
- **(For everyone):** Paul frequently traveled into cities unfamiliar to the gospel. How did the Thessalonian believers make Paul's task so much easier as he entered a new area? What had changed about these believers that convinced many in Macedonia and Achaia of their genuine conversion?
- What kind of testimony do you have with those around you? If someone knocked on the door of your extended family and invited everyone to church, would the task be harder or easier because of you?

Prayer Thoughts

- Can the Lord depend upon you to lead people to the truth? Ask Him to help you be a brighter light for the truth of the gospel.

- Ask God to reveal the effect that you have upon others. Ask Him to help you change when you see yourself setting the wrong example.

SONG: *MUST I GO, AND EMPTY HANDED?*

Day 62: (Friday)
From Undependable to Profitable

Acts 15:36 *And some days after Paul said unto Barnabas, Let us go again and visit our brethren in every city where we have preached the word of the Lord, and see how they do.*

*37 And **Barnabas determined to take with them John**, whose surname was **Mark**.*

38 But Paul thought not good to take him with them, who departed from them from Pamphylia, and went not with them to the work.

39 And the contention was so sharp between them, that they departed asunder one from the other: and so Barnabas took Mark, and sailed unto Cyprus;

40 And Paul chose Silas, and departed, being recommended by the brethren unto the grace of God.

41 And he went through Syria and Cilicia, confirming the churches.

INTRODUCTORY THOUGHTS

Paul and Barnabas functioned similar to pioneer church planters who travel into unreached areas with the gospel. As they traveled, they faithfully preached the gospel and started churches with the goal of returning later to strengthen the believers. As Paul and Barnabas were planning their return to these areas, a conflict arose between them concerning who would accompany them on their journey. Barnabas desired to take a young man named John Mark, but Paul adamantly refused. Mark had accompanied them on the first trip, but departed from them and *"went not with them to the work."* Paul felt as though he could no longer depend upon John Mark because of his earlier failure. The contention was so strong that Paul and Barnabas parted company and went their own separate ways. This is a sad narrative should it end here; however, there is much more to the story. Praise God that Paul later remarked of John Mark that *"he is profitable to me for the ministry" (**2 Timothy 4:11**).*

DEVOTIONAL THOUGHTS

- **(For children):** Pretend that Tom and John ask if they can come to a work day at church. They agree to pick up garbage, paper, and sticks around the yard. Tom does what he agreed to do, but John ends up playing. Which one would more likely be asked to come back to another work day? What could John do to be allowed to come back?
- **(For everyone):** Why did Paul not want to take Mark with him on the trip to check on the churches? Do others feel the same way about serving the Lord with you?
- What did Mark do to change Paul's opinion of him? Do others have confidence in your faithfulness right now? What can you do to change that so that you could be "profitable" in the ministry?

PRAYER THOUGHTS

- Ask God to reveal to you your level of dependability.
- Ask God for the wisdom to fix areas of your life where you fail Him and others.

SONG: *ALL THAT I WAS*

Day 63: (Saturday)
A Faithful High Priest

Hebrews 2:10 For it became him, for whom are all things, and by whom are all things, in bringing many sons unto glory, to make the captain of their salvation perfect through sufferings.

*11 For both **he that sanctifieth** and they who are sanctified are all of one: for which cause he is not ashamed to call them brethren,*

12 Saying, I will declare thy name unto my brethren, in the midst of the church will I sing praise unto thee.

13 And again, I will put my trust in him. And again, Behold I and the children which God hath given me.

*14 Forasmuch then as the children are partakers of flesh and blood, he also himself likewise took part of the same; that **through death he might destroy him that had the power of death, that is, the devil;***

15 And deliver them who through fear of death were all their lifetime subject to bondage.

16 For verily he took not on him the nature of angels; but he took on him the seed of Abraham.

*17 Wherefore in all things it behoved him to be made like unto his brethren, that he might be a **merciful and faithful high priest** in things pertaining to God, to make reconciliation for the sins of the people.*

INTRODUCTORY THOUGHTS

The world's perfect example of dependability is the Lord Jesus Christ. The New Testament records many instances of His faithfulness, but none more expressive than the faithful manner in which He performs His duties as the believer's high priest. According to today's passage, Christ faithfully sanctifies believers. Through His death, He destroys the Devil and the power he exerts over death. The Christian's high priest also remains faithful to deliver and reconcile all who come to Him in faith. Most importantly, Christ is a *"merciful and faithful high priest"* making reconciliation for sin. A high priest goes to God on behalf of the people. As the believer's high priest, the Lord Jesus faithfully hears the believer's prayers and presents them to the Father in His own Name. Never has there been someone so faithful as our high priest!

DEVOTIONAL THOUGHTS

- **(For children):** You promise to take out the trash every week. When would mom really need you to do this the most, when she is well or when she is sick? Practice keeping your promises at all times so when difficult times come, others will know they can fully depend upon you.
- **(For everyone):** Have you ever thought what it would be like to go to the Lord in prayer and realize that He was no longer listening? What a terrible notion! How different would your life be if that really happened to you?
- At all times, the Lord shows Himself dependable! Could the same be said of you? Do others know they can always count on you when times are tough?

PRAYER THOUGHTS

- Ask the Lord to show you the depth of His dependability.
- Ask God to make you more reliable and dependable—more like Him.

SONG: *BEFORE THE THRONE OF GOD ABOVE*

Notes: _____

_____

_____

_____

_____

_____

_____

_____

_____

_____

_____

_____

_____

_____

_____

_____

_____

_____

_____

Quotes from the next volume

(VOLUME 2, WEEK 9)

Subject: Counsel

Though God does not speak to us audibly, we are not left to our own devices. We find a more sure word of consultation through His written word.

Christians should not be surprised when the Devil sends people into our lives who offer counsel contrary to God's will.

10

Diligence

Occurrences: found sixty-two times in sixty-one verses

Variations: diligence, diligent, diligently

First usage: *Exodus 15:26* (diligently)

Last usage: *Jude 3* (diligence)

Defined: steady application, constant effort, and due attention to accomplish what is undertaken without unnecessary delay or sloth

Interesting fact: The book of Proverbs incorporates diligence more than any other book, using it eleven times. Proverbs incorporates diligence in a mostly practical nature suggesting that a man needs diligence in his daily activities.

Bible study tip: Consider the part(s) of speech for the word you are studying. Each part of speech has a purpose and should be considered in your study.

Sunday, Day 64—Church Day (no devotional)
Monday, Day 65—*What Is Diligence?*
Tuesday, Day 66—*Giving All Diligence*
Wednesday, Day 67—Church Night (no devotional)
Thursday, Day 68—*Take Heed unto Thyself*

Friday, Day 69—*Diligently Heed His Word*
Saturday, Day 70—*Diligently Seek Him*

Day 64: Church Day

*Proverbs 21:5 **The thoughts of the diligent** tend only to plenteousness; but of every one that is hasty only to want.*

Day 65: (Monday)
What Is Diligence?

*Proverbs 12:24 **The hand of the diligent** shall bear rule: but the slothful shall be under tribute.*

*27 The slothful man roasteth not that which he took in hunting: but **the substance of a diligent man** is precious.*

INTRODUCTORY THOUGHTS

Sometimes a Bible word is best defined by first establishing what the word does *not* mean. Biblical *diligence* is such a case in point. A diligent man is one who is *not* slothful or lazy according to **Proverbs 12:24**. **Proverbs 10:4** bears witness to this fact by contrasting the diligent with those who are slack or careless. According to **Proverbs 13:4**, a diligent man is not a sluggard. Yet, the Bible also points out that the diligent are to be properly balanced by not hastily rushing through work **(Proverbs 21:5)**. Each of these truths concerning diligence reveals that diligence involves working hard, but with great care and concern. In a world filled with those who choose either quantity or quality of work, God counsels His children to be concerned with both. This is diligence!

DEVOTIONAL THOUGHTS

- **(For children):** When we have a job to do, God wants us to do our very best. When you are asked to do a job at home or at church, do you hurry through it or take enough time to make sure that it is done right?
- **(For everyone):** Look up and read each of the verses mentioned above. What are the benefits associated with being diligent? Do those benefits make sense now that you understand the definition of diligence?

- Consider the words *slothful*, *sluggard*, and *hasty*. Do those words better describe your work ethic? Do they describe your service to God? Do they describe your relationship to God?

PRAYER THOUGHTS

- Ask God to help you to be diligent in everything you do and in every area of your life.
- Ask God to show you any slothfulness in your life so that you can repent of this sin and determine to never allow it again.

SONG: *WE'LL WORK TILL JESUS COMES*

Day 66: (Tuesday)
Giving All Diligence

*2 Peter 1:5 And beside this, **giving all diligence**, add to your faith virtue; and to virtue knowledge;*

6 And to knowledge temperance; and to temperance patience; and to patience godliness;

7 And to godliness brotherly kindness; and to brotherly kindness charity.

8 For if these things be in you, and abound, they make you that ye shall neither be barren nor unfruitful in the knowledge of our Lord Jesus Christ.

INTRODUCTORY THOUGHTS

Christians should first and foremost focus on their walk with the Lord. As such, believers are instructed to add virtue, knowledge, temperance, patience, godliness, brotherly kindness, and charity to their faith. However, notice that every believer is to be *"giving all diligence"* (with great effort, but without haste). Of all these graces mentioned, *faith* seems to be the most foundational of them all. Unfortunately, far too many believers never grow beyond faith, making them unable to put forth much diligence in adding the other graces. Believers should be growing in grace daily (like those listed above) and in the knowledge of our Lord and Saviour *(2 Peter 3:18)*. The word of God remains the only viable source from whence this diligent growth springs forth *(1 Peter 2:2)*.

DEVOTIONAL THOUGHTS

- **(For children)**: God wants you to put forth your best in living for Him. Ask Him to help you to get better at sharing, being kind to others, obeying immediately, and not always wanting your own way.
- **(For everyone)**: List your priorities in life on a sheet of paper. Where do you rank your walk with God on that list? Are you giving diligence to it? Are you striving to draw nigh to God daily?
- Think back over the past few years of your Christian life. In what areas can you pinpoint spiritual growth? In what areas have you wandered away from the Lord? What are you doing to fix the areas that need your attention?

PRAYER THOUGHTS

- Ask God to reveal to you His viewpoint of your Christian life. In doing so, beg of God not to allow your pride and prejudice to get in the way.
- Ask God to strengthen you as you become more diligent in His service.

SONG: *OUR BEST*

Day 67: Church Night

*Proverbs 22:29 Seest thou **a man diligent in his business**? he shall stand before kings; he shall not stand before mean men.*

Day 68: (Thursday)
Take Heed unto Thyself

*1 Timothy 4:16 **Take heed unto thyself**, and unto the doctrine; continue in them: for in doing this thou shalt both save thyself, and them that hear thee.*

INTRODUCTORY THOUGHTS

A godly mother and grandmother helped raise Timothy by teaching him the truths of God's word *(2 Timothy 1:5; 2 Timothy 3:15)*. Paul wrote to Timothy specifically warning him in 1 Timothy chapter 4 concerning the dangers of the last days (i.e., the doctrines of devils, fables, and unedifying quarrels). In the midst of these warnings, Paul reminded Timothy to *take heed unto himself*. Timothy needed to guard against troubles from without while diligently taking care of his own walk with Christ. The Old Testament further reinforces these truths. The children of Israel were told to keep their souls diligently *(Deuteronomy 4:9)* and Solomon instructed his son to keep his heart *"with all diligence"* *(Proverbs 4:23).* Every Christian should carefully and zealously guard his walk with the Lord.

DEVOTIONAL THOUGHTS

- **(For children):** *Psalm 119:11* reveals how to keep from doing wrong. Do you desire to learn and memorize scripture so that you can live right and escape sin?
- **(For everyone):** Are you keeping your heart right? Are you daily seeking to fill your mind and heart with the words of God? Do you consistently pray for strength to resist Satan and his attacks?
- Do you find that you worry about the spirituality of others? Do you find that you often compare yourself with others? Are these thoughts beneficial or detrimental to your walk with Christ?

PRAYER THOUGHTS

- Ask God to show you the condition of your heart. Ask Him to reveal the level of diligence with which you are keeping your heart.
- Pray that the Lord will give you the wisdom to know when worldly attacks are waged against your heart.

SONG: *NOTHING BETWEEN (TINDLEY)*

Day 69: (Friday)
Diligently Heed His Word

*Deuteronomy 11:13 And it shall come to pass, **if ye shall hearken diligently unto my commandments** which I command you this day, to love the LORD your God, and to serve him with all your heart and with all your soul,*

14 That I will give you the rain of your land in his due season, the first rain and the latter rain, that thou mayest gather in thy corn, and thy wine, and thine oil.

15 And I will send grass in thy fields for thy cattle, that thou mayest eat and be full.

16 *Take heed to yourselves, that your heart be not deceived, and ye turn aside, and serve other gods, and worship them;*

17 *And then the LORD'S wrath be kindled against you, and he shut up the heaven, that there be no rain, and that the land yield not her fruit; and lest ye perish quickly from off the good land which the LORD giveth you.*

18 *Therefore shall ye lay up these my words in your heart and in your soul, and bind them for a sign upon your hand, that they may be as frontlets between your eyes.*

19 *And ye shall teach them your children, speaking of them when thou sittest in thine house, and when thou walkest by the way, when thou liest down, and when thou risest up.*

20 *And thou shalt write them upon the door posts of thine house, and upon thy gates:*

21 *That your days may be multiplied, and the days of your children, in the land which the LORD sware unto your fathers to give them, as the days of heaven upon the earth.*

22 *For if ye shall **diligently keep all these commandments** which I command you, to do them, to love the LORD your God, to walk in all his ways, and to cleave unto him;*

23 *Then will the LORD drive out all these nations from before you, and ye shall possess greater nations and mightier than yourselves.*

INTRODUCTORY THOUGHTS

The Lord desired a special relationship with the nation of Israel choosing to bless them both spiritually and physically above all other nations. One such blessing involved bringing them safely into the land of Canaan. However, many of these blessings were dependent upon Israel maintaining the right type of relationship with the Lord. He, therefore, issued several commandments for the Israelites to carefully keep (i.e., Deuteronomy chapter 11). The Lord desired for Israel to *"hearken diligently" (**Deuteronomy 11:13**)* and *"diligently keep" (**Deuteronomy 11:22**)* these commandments. He wanted His people to carefully listen when He spoke, giving God their full attention (listening to every word). He also wanted them to attentively obey what they heard. He always desired for His people to listen to and obey Him. God speaks today through the Bible. He still wants men to diligently hear and obey.

DEVOTIONAL THOUGHTS

- **(For children):** *James 1:22* says, *"Be ye doers of the word, and not hearers only."* When God tells us to do something, what should we do? When we hear what mom or dad tell us to do, what should we do?
- **(For everyone):** Have you ever been speaking to someone and noticed that they are not listening to you? How does that make you feel? Do you desire to continue speaking to them or just stop? How important is it to God that we listen to Him? Are you diligently hearkening unto His words?
- Are you putting forth the right effort to hear the words of God? Are you putting forth the right amount of effort to obey what you hear?

PRAYER THOUGHTS

- Ask God to strengthen your desire to hear and to obey His words.
- Ask God to give you a love for His word as found in *Psalm 119*.

SONG: *DARE TO BE A DANIEL*

Day 70: (Saturday)
Diligently Seek Him

*Hebrews 11:6 But without faith it is impossible to please him: for he that cometh to God must believe that he is, and that he is a rewarder of them that **diligently seek him**.*

INTRODUCTORY THOUGHTS

The eleventh chapter of Hebrews has been appropriately labeled as the *"Hall of Faith."* It speaks of the great feats of faith of some Old Testament Bible characters like Noah, Abraham, Joseph and Moses. In the midst of this faith chronicle, the Lord reveals a great truth concerning faith itself. Without faith, no one can please God. In addition to this, the Lord indicates that an important aspect of faith is to *"diligently seek him."* God promises to reward all those who continually and carefully seek for Him. He is not pleased when Christians fail to pray or read His word regularly. Instead, He wants men to seek Him with diligence!

DEVOTIONAL THOUGHTS

- **(For children):** One verse of the song *Fishers of Men* says, *"Read your Bible, pray every day, and you'll grow, grow, grow."* By reading God's word and praying on a regular basis, you will grow closer to God and learn that He is your best Friend caring for you like no one else.

- **(For everyone):** Do you believe that God rewards those who diligently seek Him? How diligent is your prayer life? Do you give up praying when you do not receive the answers you desire? How is your Bible reading? Do you tire after a few days of reading? Is this diligently seeking Him?
- What hinders us from diligently seeking the Lord? What benefits do we lose from not seeking Him in the manner He desires?

PRAYER THOUGHTS

- Ask God to help you be more diligent in your relationship with Him.
- Ask God to strengthen your faith. Pray that He will give you the desire to seek Him with great diligence.

SONG: *FAIREST LORD JESUS*

Notes: _____

_____

_____

_____

_____

_____

_____

_____

Quotes from the next volume

(VOLUME 2, WEEK 10)

Subject: Contending for the Faith

Far too many Christians have turned a blind eye toward evil and lost any desire to be valiant for the truth. The church and the rest of the world desperately need faithful Christians similar to the prophet Jeremiah who contended for the truth with a heart burdened for the work.

11

Diligence (con't)

Occurrences: found thirty-eight times in the Old Testament and twenty-four times in the New Testament

First usage in the New Testament: *Matthew 2:7* (diligently)

Last usage in the Old Testament: *Zechariah 6:15* (diligently)

Interesting fact: Deuteronomy mentions *diligence* ten times, second only to Proverbs. One's daily spiritual walk should focus on the implementation of diligence.

Bible study tip: Some people struggle with gaining additional biblical understanding by failing to obey current scriptural knowledge *(Psalm 119:100)*. If you are struggling with gaining new understanding, consider whether or not you have obeyed what you presently understand.

Sunday, Day 71—Church Day (no devotional)
Monday, Day 72—*The Benefits of Diligence*
Tuesday, Day 73—*The Sin of Procrastination*
Wednesday, Day 74—Church Night (no devotional)
Thursday, Day 75—*Consider the Ant*
Friday, Day 76—*There Is a Lion in the Way*
Saturday, Day 77—*I Have Finished My Course*

Day 71: Church Day

Proverbs 13:4 *The soul of the sluggard desireth, and hath nothing: but **the soul of the diligent** shall be made fat.*

Day 72: (Monday)
The Benefits of Diligence

Proverbs 12:24 *The **hand of the diligent** shall bear rule: but the slothful shall be under tribute.*

Proverbs 12:27 *The slothful man roasteth not that which he took in hunting: but the substance of a **diligent man** is precious.*

INTRODUCTORY THOUGHTS

Doing the right thing is always the right thing to do and yields great benefits. For instance, consider what the Bible has to say about *diligence*. God's word promises that *diligence* brings an increase of substance *(Proverbs 10:4; Proverbs 13:4; Proverbs 21:5)* and promotion *(Proverbs 12:24; Proverbs 22:29)*. In other words, as the saying goes, *hard work pays off*. It is not difficult to prove that these benefits manifest themselves in the lives of God's people who are diligent. Joseph and Daniel are two great examples of those who were diligent and their diligence brought them obvious promotion. Abraham and Job are great examples of diligent men who experienced a great increase of substance. A word of caution might be appropriate here. Men are not to be diligent merely for the sake of reaping its inherent benefits, but should be diligent for the sake of the One who called them to be diligent.

DEVOTIONAL THOUGHTS

- **(For children):** Do you like to hear mom, dad, the preacher, or your Sunday school teacher say, *"Good job"*? It makes you feel good about what you've done. Simply do your best in everything you do. Others will notice and the Lord will too *(Proverbs 15:3)*.
- **(For everyone):** Do you find favour with people for whom you work? Do you find that you are consistently praised for your efforts in the home or at work? If not, you may be suffering from a lack of diligence in your tasks.
- Do you always try to give your best on the job? Do you always strive to give your best at home? What about school? The Bible tells us, *"Whatsoever thy hand findeth to do, **do it with thy might"** (Ecclesiastes 9:10).*

PRAYER THOUGHTS

- Ask God to reveal how diligent you are in every area of your life.
- Ask God to bring to light the dreadful results of a life lacking diligence.

SONG: *TO THE WORK*

Day 73: (Tuesday)
The Sin of Procrastination

John 4:35 Say not ye, There are yet four months, and then cometh harvest? behold, I say unto you, Lift up your eyes, and look on the fields; for they are white already to harvest.

INTRODUCTORY THOUGHTS

The context of our passage shows the disciples gathering some food while the Lord dealt with a Samaritan woman alone. When the disciples returned, the woman left to tell others she had found the Christ. The disciples were confused when they saw the Lord talking with a Samaritan woman. They immediately seemed to focus on His physical needs and begged Him to eat. To their shock, the Lord suggested that He had meat to eat that they knew not of. What was this meat to which He referred? His meat was to do the will of His Father (i.e., mend broken lives). The Lord instantly turned the disciples' attention toward the harvest, only the harvest involved the souls of men rather than earthly sustenance. Christ pointed out that the time to labour was not some future date, but here and now. The fields were already white to harvest. There was no time for excuse or delay. Now was the time for diligence!

DEVOTIONAL THOUGHTS

- **(For children):** Do you put off learning your Bible memorization until the day before you are supposed to say it? What usually happens when you do this? Wouldn't it be better to practice a little every day and be diligent in your efforts?
- **(For everyone):** Do you constantly find yourself making excuses for why something cannot be done today? Do you find that you put things off so long that things pile up and you run out of time? The Lord is calling you to diligence!

- Like a wheat or corn harvest, the work of God has a time and a season associated with it. We only have so much time on this earth before our time is finished. What are you doing to serve the Lord today?

PRAYER THOUGHTS

- Ask God to help you appropriately prioritize the things in your life.
- Ask God to give you a sense of urgency concerning your service to Him.

SONG: *LITTLE IS MUCH WHEN GOD IS IN IT*

Day 74: Church Night

Hebrews 12:14 Follow peace with all men, and holiness, without which no man shall see the Lord:

*15 **Looking diligently** lest any man fail of the grace of God; lest any root of bitterness springing up trouble you, and thereby many be defiled;*

Day 75: (Thursday)
Consider the Ant

*Proverbs 6:6 Go to the ant, thou sluggard; **consider her ways,** and be wise:*

7 Which having no guide, overseer, or ruler,

8 Provideth her meat in the summer, and gathereth her food in the harvest.

9 How long wilt thou sleep, O sluggard? when wilt thou arise out of thy sleep?

10 Yet a little sleep, a little slumber, a little folding of the hands to sleep:

11 So shall thy poverty come as one that travelleth, and thy want as an armed man.

INTRODUCTORY THOUGHTS

God created the animals and points to them as examples for men to humbly consider. By considering these lessons, Christians can grow in their service as well as their knowledge of God's expectations. Bible students can discover several references to animals and the specific lessons taught by them. Our passage is one such example. Proverbs admonishes the sluggard (a lazy person) to go to the ant and consider her ways *(Proverbs 6:6)*. The ant needs no supervision, for she knows what to do and does it without instruction, supervision, or a king *(Proverbs 6:7)*. The ant works with the future in sight so not to be lacking in times of need *(Proverbs 6:8)*. All of this is accomplished by the ant in spite of a pure physical handicap—*"the ants are a people not strong"* *(Proverbs 30:25)*.

DEVOTIONAL THOUGHTS

- **(For children)**: Read *Colossians 3:23* and witness what it means concerning doing things to always please the Lord. Practice putting your toys away without mom or dad making you do it or watching over you.
- **(For everyone)**: Do you require supervision? Do you find that you put forth inconsistent effort on the job, at school, or at home unless someone is watching over you? Do you change your behaviour when around saved people versus times when you think no Christians are around? Do you dramatically change your behaviour in front of the preacher to put on a good show? If so, you need diligence.
- Is your life in a general upheaval because you always wait until the last minute to get a job done? Are you always stressed at deadlines because you have procrastinated far too long? If so, you are not working ahead and need to be more diligent.

PRAYER THOUGHTS

- Ask God to give you a work ethic more like that of the ant. Ask Him to help you do the right things with or without supervision.
- Pray that God will help you work with the future in mind. Ask Him to remind you of the rewards that can be gained or lost based on the effort we put forth in this life.

SONG: *LOYALTY TO CHRIST (CASSEL)*

Day 76: (Friday)
There Is a Lion in the Way

*Proverbs 26:13 The slothful man saith, **There is a lion in the way;** a lion is in the streets.*

14 As the door turneth upon his hinges, so doth the slothful upon his bed.

15 The slothful hideth his hand in his bosom; it grieveth him to bring it again to his mouth.

16 The sluggard is wiser in his own conceit than seven men that can render a reason.

INTRODUCTORY THOUGHTS

The previous few devotions have shown that diligence and laziness are opposing traits. In this passage, the Bible explores further into the unsavoury traits of a slothful man. *Proverbs 26:13* refers to the slothful man mentioning a lion in the streets. Interestingly, a lazy man is not truly concerned about the lion, but looking for any type of an excuse to stay in bed rather than to perform his duties for the day. He claims that the lion will slay him should he leave the house *(Proverbs 22:13)*. Since the slothful does not consider work an option, he retreats to his bed. There he is found like a door swinging on the hinges *(Proverbs 26:14)*. As a door simply swings back and forth, so the slothful man's main activity involves rolling from one side to the other with excuse piled upon excuse for his laziness.

DEVOTIONAL THOUGHTS

- **(For children):** God wants us to be good dependable workers. Shoving your toys, shoes, clothes, books, etc., under the bed is not straightening your room. It is being lazy (slothful). Where do these things belong in your room?
- **(For everyone):** Are you constantly looking for an excuse not to do the things that you ought to do? Do you look for reasons not to go to work, school, or church? Do you look for excuses not to serve the Lord, especially when it involves work? Do you, like the slothful man, always assume the worst in a situation?
- What is your overall work ethic? Are you sloppy and always looking for shortcuts? If so, you need to consider whether others would consider you slothful or diligent and change your ways to please the Lord.

PRAYER THOUGHTS

- Ask God to show you the difference between genuine grounds for not working and when you are making excuses to avoid it. The Lord in the day of judgment will accept no excuses.

• Ask the Lord to give you a sincere desire to work hard for Him.

SONG: *I WANT THAT MOUNTAIN*

Day 77: (Saturday)
I Have Finished My Course

2 Timothy 4:1 I charge thee therefore before God, and the Lord Jesus Christ, who shall judge the quick and the dead at his appearing and his kingdom;

*2 **Preach the word**; be instant in season, out of season; reprove, rebuke, exhort with all longsuffering and doctrine.*

3 For the time will come when they will not endure sound doctrine; but after their own lusts shall they heap to themselves teachers, having itching ears;

4 And they shall turn away their ears from the truth, and shall be turned unto fables.

*5 But watch **thou in all things, endure afflictions**, do the work of an evangelist, make full proof of thy ministry.*

6 For I am now ready to be offered, and the time of my departure is at hand.

*7 I have fought a good fight, **I have finished my course**, I have kept the faith:*

INTRODUCTORY THOUGHTS

This passage provides some of the last recorded words from Paul to Timothy. In it, Paul charged Timothy to *"preach the word"* **(2 Timothy 4:2)**, *"watch thou in all things, endure afflictions,"* and *"make full proof"* of his ministry **(2 Timothy 4:5).** Paul then focused Timothy's attention toward Paul's departure from this world. The three statements in *2 Timothy 4:7* point to Paul's life of diligence. Paul had fought the fight, finished his course, and kept the faith. He certainly could be viewed by none as a lazy man. In fact, Paul was far from slothful, warning others day and night *(Acts 20:31)*. Before salvation, Paul worked hard to destroy Christians and Christianity. After he learned the truth, he determined to give his best to the Lord and His work.

DEVOTIONAL THOUGHTS

- **(For children):** Determine to always do your best for the Lord, starting right now throughout your entire life. Don't give up just because the task seems hard. The Lord will reward your work *(2 Chronicles 15:7)*.
- **(For everyone):** If your life ended today, what would you leave undone? Would you leave those things undone because you did not put forth the effort or because you lacked opportunity? Have you given your all to the work of the Lord Jesus?
- In what areas of life do you put forth the greatest effort? Should these areas control your heart? Have you given as much effort to the Lord's work as you have your job, your hobbies, or pleasurable activities?

PRAYER THOUGHTS

- Ask God to give you a heartfelt desire to serve Him.
- Pray that the Lord will always give you a view of the brevity of life. Ask Him to reveal what He means by likening life to a vapour *(James 4:14)*.

SONG: *SAIL ON!*

Notes: _____

_____

_____

_____

_____

Quotes from the next volume

(VOLUME 2, WEEK 11)

Subject: Edification

Christians should focus on consciously building others in the faith. Consistently edifying others takes thorough planning and direction; whereas, destructive behaviour frequently takes place haphazardly.

12

Discernment

Occurrences: found twenty-five times in twenty-three verses (sixteen times in the Old Testament and seven times in the New Testament)

Variations: discern, discerned, discerner, discerneth, discerning

First usage: *Genesis 27:23* (discerned)

Last usage: *Hebrews 5:14* (discern)

First usage in the New Testament: *Matthew 16:3* (discern)

Last usage in the Old Testament: *Malachi 3:18* (discern)

Defined: the power or faculty of the mind by which it distinguishes one thing from another, as truth from falsehood, virtue from vice; acuteness of judgment; power of perceiving differences of things or ideas, and their relations and tendencies

Interesting fact: Hebrews mentions discernment twice: first, that the word of God can *discern* the thoughts and intents of the heart *(Hebrews 4:12)* and secondly, that a Christian's senses are to be exercised to *discern* both good and evil *(Hebrews 5:14)*.

Bible study tip: When studying a word repeatedly found in scripture, consider the words frequently associated with your word of study. These other words often provide additional understanding on the studied subject.

Sunday, Day 78—Church Day (no devotional)
Monday, Day 79—*Discerning Discernment*
Tuesday, Day 80—*A Garden Void of Discernment*
Wendsday, Day 81—Church Night (no devotional)
Thursday, Day 82—*The Foundation for Discernment*
Friday, Day 83—*Discerning the Things of God*
Saturday, Day 84—*Exercised for Discernment*

Day 78: Church Day

*Ecclesiastes 8:5 Whoso keepeth the commandment shall feel no evil thing: and **a wise man's heart discerneth** both time and judgment.*

Day 79: (Monday)
Discerning Discernment

*Ezekiel 44:23 And they shall teach my people the difference between the holy and profane, and cause them to **discern between the unclean and the clean.***

INTRODUCTORY THOUGHTS

Far too many Christians fail to ever achieve an extensive working knowledge of biblical terminology. Biblical *discernment* is a case in point. Fortunately, God provides a simple solution for those willing to put forth the effort. Because the Bible generally defines its own vocabulary, searching the word of God remains the most useful means of ascertaining accurate definitions for Bible words. *Ezekiel 44:23* begins by stating that the Levites were to teach the people of God the difference between what is holy and what is profane. The second phrase in the verse indicates that teaching people the difference between the holy and profane enables them to *"discern between the unclean and the clean."* Once the people are taught the difference between holy and profane, they can then cultivate their ability to discern. People who learn to *discern* make choices between good and evil and right and wrong. It is important to note that the knowledge of right and wrong is never the end all; the believer also must become proficient in the ability to discern.

DEVOTIONAL THOUGHTS

- **(For children):** What example can you give of something that you think is good? How about something bad? God wants you to learn to always choose the good and reject the bad.
- **(For everyone):** Before you can nurture your ability to discern, you must recognize how your choices stack up to what is right and wrong. What effort are you putting forth to learn the difference between good and evil and right and wrong?
- How many choices do you think you make every day? Upon what are your decisions based? Are you improving at your ability to discern right from wrong? Are you able to distinguish between God's will for your life and your own fleshly desires?

PRAYER THOUGHTS

- Ask God to give you the wisdom you need in order to discern right from wrong.
- Ask God to show you when you have not discerned properly.

SONG: *OPEN MY EYES, THAT I MAY SEE*

Day 80: (Tuesday)
A Garden Void of Discernment

Genesis 3:1 Now the serpent was more subtil than any beast of the field which the LORD God had made. And he said unto the woman, Yea, hath God said, Ye shall not eat of every tree of the garden?

2 And the woman said unto the serpent, We may eat of the fruit of the trees of the garden:

3 But of the fruit of the tree which is in the midst of the garden, God hath said, Ye shall not eat of it, neither shall ye touch it, lest ye die.

4 And the serpent said unto the woman, Ye shall not surely die:

5 For God doth know that in the day ye eat thereof, then your eyes shall be opened, and ye shall be as gods, knowing good and evil.

6 And when the woman saw that the tree was good for food, and that it was pleasant to the eyes, and a tree to be desired to make one wise, she took of the fruit thereof, and did eat, and gave also unto her husband with her; and he did eat.

7 And the eyes of them both were opened, and they knew that they were naked; and they sewed fig leaves together, and made themselves aprons.

*8 And they heard the voice of the LORD God walking in the garden in the cool of the day: and **Adam and his wife hid themselves** from the presence of the LORD God amongst the trees of the garden.*

Introductory Thoughts

The garden in Eden was a trouble-free environment for its inhabitants, a literal earthly paradise. Adam and Eve were given one basic commandment to obey. They were told not to eat of the tree of the knowledge of good and evil. Interestingly, up until this point, they only knew good. The Devil knew this and deviously crept into the garden. He wanted to tempt Eve with the fruit from this forbidden tree. He convinced her that that tree would enable her to know both good and evil. Eve already had the ability to discern, though severely limited based on the limited number of choices available. She certainly could have refused the temptation choosing rather to obey the Lord. God had given Adam and Eve everything needed to be successful in the garden including the ability to do right. Eve's desire to know good and evil prompted her to overlook the fact that she already had been given the gift of discernment.

Devotional Thoughts

- **(For children):** Making wrong choices produces bad results. In addition to getting in trouble, what else could happen if you disobediently run in your home or at church, jump on furniture, or talk ugly to someone?
- **(For everyone):** What were the consequences resulting from Adam and Eve not using their God-given ability to discern? Are there consequences for us today when we fail to use discernment? What might they be?
- Do you make choices without using godly discernment? Do you rush to a decision without thinking through the potential consequences? What changes could you make in order to use discernment?

PRAYER THOUGHTS

- Ask God to show you the importance of godly discernment.
- Ask God to clearly reveal the times when you are not discerning as you ought.

SONG: *YIELD NOT TO TEMPTATION*

Day 81: Church Night

*Hebrews 4:12 **For the word of God** is quick, and powerful, and sharper than any twoedged sword, piercing even to the dividing asunder of soul and spirit, and of the joints and marrow, and is **a discerner of the thoughts and intents of the heart.***

Day 82: (Thursday)
The Foundation for Discernment

1 Kings 3:5 In Gibeon the LORD appeared to Solomon in a dream by night: and God said, Ask what I shall give thee.

6 And Solomon said, Thou hast shewed unto thy servant David my father great mercy, according as he walked before thee in truth, and in righteousness, and in uprightness of heart with thee; and thou hast kept for him this great kindness, that thou hast given him a son to sit on his throne, as it is this day.

7 And now, O LORD my God, thou hast made thy servant king instead of David my father: and I am but a little child: I know not how to go out or come in.

8 And thy servant is in the midst of thy people which thou hast chosen, a great people, that cannot be numbered nor counted for multitude.

*9 **Give therefore thy servant an understanding heart to judge thy people, that I may discern between good and bad:** for who is able to judge this thy so great a people?*

10 And the speech pleased the Lord, that Solomon had asked this thing.

*11 And God said unto him, Because thou hast asked this thing, and hast not asked for thyself long life; neither hast asked riches for thyself, nor hast asked the life of thine enemies; but **hast asked for thyself understanding to discern judgment;***

12 Behold, I have done according to thy words: lo, I have given thee a wise and an understanding heart; so that there was none like thee before thee, neither after thee shall any arise like unto thee.

INTRODUCTORY THOUGHTS

This passage from First Kings offers the reader keen insights into one of the most enlightening prayer requests found in the Bible. King Solomon's prayer was in response to God's offer in advance to supernaturally answer his requests. Solomon knew that he would be completely dependent upon God's help to be the right type of king. His humility greatly pleased the Lord and God lovingly answered his request and more. Solomon's prayer demonstrated his recognition concerning the importance of *discernment* as he asked for an understanding heart to discern matters of judgment. Without this understanding concerning proper discernment, Solomon would fall short as king. Where could the king find such help? *Psalm 119:104* says that understanding comes through God's precepts (His teachings found in scripture). *Psalm 119:130* teaches that the entrance of God's word into the heart provides understanding to even those who are "simple." *Proverbs 2:6* further reveals that knowledge and understanding come from God's mouth.

DEVOTIONAL THOUGHTS

- **(For children):** As a child, God wants you to learn to choose good and also refuse evil. What is the book that teaches us the difference of right and wrong? Who on earth can help you learn this? On whom do they depend to teach them how to teach you?
- **(For everyone):** Are you able to discern right and wrong? Do you have understanding? If not, what steps are you taking to help you make wiser choices in the future?
- Are you spending quality time in the word of God? Are you spending quality time in prayer? If not, do not expect to have understanding. Do not expect to consistently discern the right things in your life.

PRAYER THOUGHTS

- Ask God to help you evaluate your walk with Him. Ask Him to help you realistically examine your Bible study and prayer life.
- Pray that God will give you understanding in His word as you read. Ask Him to open your eyes to any evil within your own heart.

SONG: *O WORD OF GOD INCARNATE*

Day 83: (Friday)
Discerning the Things of God

*1 Corinthians 2:14 But the **natural man receiveth not the things of the Spirit of God**: for they are foolishness unto him: neither can he know them, because they are spiritually discerned.*

15 But he that is spiritual judgeth all things, yet he himself is judged of no man.

16 For who hath known the mind of the Lord, that he may instruct him? But we have the mind of Christ.

INTRODUCTORY THOUGHTS

There has never been, nor ever will be, a book like the Bible. Unfortunately, some people who desire to learn its contents simply take the wrong approach. It cannot be studied like a textbook or read like a magazine or novel. It must be approached prayerfully with the help of God's Spirit with total dependence upon Him for illumination. According to today's passage, an unsaved man cannot fully understand the word of God because he lacks the spiritual discernment necessary to grasp its full truths. No one can approach the Bible with a fleshly mindset; it must always be approached with faith, believing that it is truly God's word. Only then can the student with the Spirit's help rightly discern the things intended to be understood. An improper approach has led many people to believe the Bible, like all other books, contains contradictions and errors. God graciously affords man the necessary spiritual discernment increasing a man's faith leading him to take God at His word. When man rejects discernment, he increases his darkness.

DEVOTIONAL THOUGHTS

- **(For children)**: Learn this poem: *"When I have a question, Here's what I'll do, I'll open my Bible for Thy word is true."* Now read **Psalm 119:160, "Thy word is true** *from the beginning."*
- **(For everyone)**: Do you have trouble making sense of the word of God? Write down some of your thoughts about the Bible including why you struggle with understanding it. Do you truly believe the Bible to be the perfect words of Almighty God? Do you approach the Bible with a spiritual or fleshly mindset?
- Since the Bible is the foundation for discernment, how important is your faith when approaching it? Do you think it is possible to receive the knowledge and understanding you desire from something you do not fully trust?

PRAYER THOUGHTS

- Ask God to give you a believing heart when you study His word.
- Ask God to allow His word to work in your heart so that you can fully receive what He has just for you (and your family).

SONG: *BREAK THOU THE BREAD OF LIFE*

Day 84: (Saturday)
Exercised for Discernment

Hebrews 5:12 *For when for the time ye ought to be teachers, ye have need that one teach you again which be the first principles of the oracles of God; and are become such as have need of milk, and not of strong meat.*

*13 For **every one that useth milk is** unskilful in the word of righteousness: for he is **a babe.***

*14 But **strong meat** belongeth to them that are of full age, even those **who by reason of use have their senses exercised to discern both good and evil.***

INTRODUCTORY THOUGHTS

The Bible likens a mature Christian to one who exercises. Exercise involves work for it to be most profitable. Many people start exercising with exuberance and zeal, yet quit when the workout begins to get difficult. This too unfortunately applies to those who start out wanting to live a godly life. Too many Christians quit simply because spiritual growth takes a lot of hard work and effort. Today's passage contrasts the difference between a babe in Christ and a believer enjoying the meat of God's word. The babe enjoys the milk of God's word (the basic truths) but the milk limits the extent of his growth; whereas, the mature Christian wants to grow stronger through learning the truths that babes cannot yet handle. The strong Christian exercises his senses enabling him to discern between good and evil. He works hard. He does not quit though times get tough. He keeps reading his Bible. He keeps praying. He keeps obeying the Lord. When he stumbles, he simply picks himself back up, brushes himself off, and keeps moving forward, onward, and upward. So get up and go!

DEVOTIONAL THOUGHTS

- **(For children):** Younger children watch the older ones ride their bikes and effortlessly tie their shoes. How did they learn to ride so well or tie so fast? They kept practicing. Each of them wanted to grow and learn and not remain a baby. God does not want us to remain babies in our Christian lives. We grow by practicing His ways.
- **(For everyone):** What do you expect of the Christian life? Do you expect it to be easy and almost effortless? Do you think the Lord should make choosing the right and never the wrong a mindless process? When the Lord forces you to exercise your senses, do you think He has your best interests in mind?
- What are you doing to exercise your senses to know the difference between good and bad, right and wrong? Are you becoming more consistent in these matters? If exercising inconsistently never achieves the athlete's goals, what makes you think that inconsistency will work in your Christian life?

PRAYER THOUGHTS

- Ask God to make you more consistent in your walk with Him.
- Ask God to enable you to endure the difficulties of serving Him.

SONG: *DWELLING IN BEULAH LAND*

Notes: _____

_____

_____

_____

_____

_____

_____

_____

_____

_____

_____

_____

_____

_____

_____

Quotes from the next volume

(VOLUME 2, WEEK 12)

Subject: Fasting

Fasting should play a prominent role in the life of a Christian. Just as believers ought to pray, witness, study, and give, we should also fast. In fact, the Lord's words assumed the Christian would fast when He said, "when ye fast" (**Matthew 6:16**), not if ye fast.

Fasting involves much more than merely opposing the flesh. Fasting directly afflicts, chastens, and humbles the soul.

13

Discretion

Occurrences: found thirteen times in the Bible (eleven times in the Old Testament and two times in the New Testament)

Variations: discreet, discreetly, discretion

First usage: *Genesis 41:33* (discreet)

Last usage: *Titus 2:5* (discreet)

First usage in the New Testament: *Mark 12:34* (discreetly)

Last usage in the Old Testament: *Jeremiah 10:12* (discretion)

Defined: decision making based upon the cooperative efforts of knowledge, wisdom, and understanding

Interesting fact: The Lord implemented discretion when He stretched out the heavens *(Jeremiah 10:12)*.

Bible study tip: When studying a specific virtue, determine the people groups admonished to seek the virtue. Ask yourself why this virtue would be specifically important for these certain people groups.

Sunday, Day 85—Church Day (no devotional)
Monday, Day 86—*Discernment's Sister*

Tuesday, Day 87—*Discretion in Creation*
Wednesday, Day 88—Church Night (no devotional)
Thursday, Day 89—*A Golden Jewel in a Swine's Snout*
Friday, Day 90—*Joseph: A Man Discreet and Wise*
Saturday, Day 91—*Discretion Shall Preserve Thee*

Day 85: Church Day

Psalm 112:5 A good man sheweth favour, and lendeth: **he will guide his affairs with discretion.**

Day 86: (Monday)
Discernment's Sister

Proverbs 5:1 My son, attend unto my wisdom, and bow thine ear to my understanding:

2 **That thou mayest regard discretion,** *and that thy lips may keep knowledge.*

INTRODUCTORY THOUGHTS

Last week's subject covered the matter of *discernment*, but this week focuses on another closely related subject—*discretion*. The word of God uses three forms of *discretion*: discreet, discretion, and discreetly. A simplistic definition would be to gain knowledge on matters before making a decision and then using wisdom to make the right decision. According to today's passage, discretion cannot be implemented without attending unto wisdom and bowing one's ear to understanding. Only through God's word can one hope to attain understanding, wisdom, or discretion. An individual must make decisions based on God's word in order to be discreet.

DEVOTIONAL THOUGHTS

- **(For children):** God wants you to think before making a decision. When would be the best time of the day to play outside? Where would be the best place to toss a ball with a friend? . . . to speak softly? . . . to run?

- **(For everyone):** Are you sometimes so hasty to make a decision that you fail to weigh all the options? How often do you consult God in prayer over your decisions (whether large or small)?
- Do you make many of your decisions simply based on emotion? Do you ever find that your emotions mislead you? What would be the wisest foundation for your decisions?

PRAYER THOUGHTS

- Ask God to help you to remember to pray before making decisions.
- As you study His word, ask God for wisdom in decision making.

SONG: *O BLESSED WORD*

Day 87: (Tuesday)
Discretion in Creation

Jeremiah 10:10 But the LORD is the true God, he is the living God, and an everlasting king: at his wrath the earth shall tremble, and the nations shall not be able to abide his indignation.

11 Thus shall ye say unto them, The gods that have not made the heavens and the earth, even they shall perish from the earth, and from under these heavens.

*12 He hath made the earth by his power, he hath **established the world by his wisdom**, and hath **stretched out the heavens by his discretion**.*

13 When he uttereth his voice, there is a multitude of waters in the heavens, and he causeth the vapours to ascend from the ends of the earth; he maketh lightnings with rain, and bringeth forth the wind out of his treasures.

INTRODUCTORY THOUGHTS

The Bible proclaims that creation was not some type of random accident. Though proponents of the evolutionary theory vehemently disagree, the Bible indicates that creation involved wisdom and great carefulness by a benevolent Creator. Even scientific evidence reveals the truth of order in our world and the universe. For instance, the sun and the moon work perfectly together. The solar system runs its course without catastrophic misadventures. The heavens provide water for the earth and the earth cycles it back to the heavens. This system, far from haphazard, works together in harmony. What did the Lord do in order to ensure this type of perfection? According to today's passage, the Lord *"stretched out the heavens by his discretion."* To claim otherwise is to depict the Bible as false and God as a liar. God wants His people to use *discretion* in making decisions and clearly reveals that decisions made with discretion yield great benefits for those involved.

DEVOTIONAL THOUGHTS

- **(For children):** What would happen when you jumped into the air, if you didn't come back down? God thought about how the world would work before He made it. We too should think before we do anything.
- **(For everyone):** Do you find yourself frequently making decisions that have to be corrected with more decisions? Do you use wisdom to ensure that your decisions result in the right outcomes?
- Do you get tired of bringing troubles upon yourself? Do you find that most of your decisions bring unwelcomed troubles? Could it be possible that you are not using discretion during the decision-making process?

PRAYER THOUGHTS

- Ask God to help you think about the outcome of your decisions before you make them.
- Ask God to show you the importance of each decision you make.

SONG: *IMMORTAL, INVISIBLE, GOD ONLY WISE*

Day 88: Church Night

Proverbs 19:11 The discretion of a man deferreth his anger; and it is his glory to pass over a transgression.

Day 89: (Thursday)
A Golden Jewel in a Swine's Snout

*Proverbs 11:22 As a jewel of gold in a swine's snout, so is **a fair woman which is without discretion.***

INTRODUCTORY THOUGHTS

Most women who receive gold and jewelry consider them treasured gifts. In fact, gold and some jewels increase in value with some being of inestimable value. These treasures have many uses whereby their owners can benefit. Yet, imagine the reaction when a jewel of gold is mounted in a swine's snout rather than in an appropriate decorative setting. No matter the perceived value of the item, its appeal significantly decreases. The Bible likens this scenario to a fair (beautiful) woman who is void of *discretion*. The world values outward beauty more than inward beauty though the Bible cautions against this. Today's passage equates a beautiful woman *without discretion* to a jewel of gold in a pig's snout. Discretion is of such importance that God instructed the aged women to teach the younger women to be discreet in *Titus 2:5*. The problem began where the Bible began – with a story about a woman in the garden in Eden who partook of the fruit based on what she saw and felt. All of God's people, including ladies, should make their decisions with *discretion*.

DEVOTIONAL THOUGHTS

- **(For children):** What if mom never felt like washing clothes, and dad never felt like going to work? What if you never felt like cleaning your room? God wants us to do what is right, not just what we feel like doing.
- **(For everyone):** What are the most important things in life? Would you agree that the style of your clothing is much less important than gaining wisdom? Is the amount of money you have more important than the right relationship with God? Are your looks more important to you than cultivating discretion?
- Why is it important for ladies to use discretion? If a lady is a wife and mother, her decisions affect more than just herself. Who else do they affect? Do these same truths apply for men? What should both men and women do to ensure that they are leading others in the right direction?

PRAYER THOUGHTS

- Ask God to show you how to order your priorities in a God-pleasing fashion. Ask Him for the grace to change what needs to be changed and accept the things that cannot be changed.

• Pray that the Lord will help you make decisions based upon truth rather than feelings and emotions.

SONG: *WHOLLY THINE* (HAWKS)

Day 90: (Friday)
Joseph: A Man Discreet and Wise

Genesis 41:33 *Now therefore let Pharaoh look out **a man discreet and wise**, and set him over the land of Egypt.*

34 Let Pharaoh do this, and let him appoint officers over the land, and take up the fifth part of the land of Egypt in the seven plenteous years.

35 And let them gather all the food of those good years that come, and lay up corn under the hand of Pharaoh, and let them keep food in the cities.

36 And that food shall be for store to the land against the seven years of famine, which shall be in the land of Egypt; that the land perish not through the famine.

37 And the thing was good in the eyes of Pharaoh, and in the eyes of all his servants.

*38 And Pharaoh said unto his servants, Can we find such a one as this is, **a man in whom the Spirit of God is**?*

*39 And Pharaoh said unto Joseph, Forasmuch as God hath shewed thee all this, **there is none so discreet and wise** as thou art:*

40 Thou shalt be over my house, and according unto thy word shall all my people be ruled: only in the throne will I be greater than thou.

INTRODUCTORY THOUGHTS

Joseph went through so many trials and tribulations that at times he must have questioned if he had been forsaken of God. Our passage picks up the story with Joseph unjustly imprisoned. Pharaoh had a dream and called the wise men of the land together for the interpretation. All of Egypt's wise men could not interpret the dream, but Joseph could. God revealed to Joseph the impending famine with detailed information on how to prepare for it. He instructed Pharaoh on how to gather during the time of plenty to prepare for the famine. These guidelines would allow Egypt to survive and even increase throughout the period of famine. Joseph also counselled Pharaoh to set a man over the land of Egypt who was *"discreet and wise."* Pharaoh told his servants that Joseph was the only one who could adequately do the task because he was *"a man in whom the Spirit of God"* resided. Joseph's acts of discretion not only led Egypt through the famine but also provided for Joseph's family when they too would come to Egypt in need of food (see Genesis chapter 42).

DEVOTIONAL THOUGHTS

- **(For children):** God wants us to always think of ways we can help others. Sometimes simple things are most helpful. How would taking off your muddy shoes at the door help mom? How would getting your toys out of the driveway help dad? How could you help if a younger child was crying or needed help to get a drink of water?
- **(For everyone):** Who gave Joseph both wisdom and discretion? Does God want to give you both wisdom and discretion? Are you willing to ask the Lord for help? *James 1:5* says, *"If any of you lack wisdom, let him ask of God, that giveth to all men liberally, and upbraideth not; and it shall be given him."*
- Who received the benefits from Joseph's discretion? Who might receive benefit if you were discreet in your decisions? Are you concerned about those around you enough to live with discretion?

PRAYER THOUGHTS

- Ask God to show you the effect your choices have on others.
- Ask God to give you wisdom to make the right choices in life.

SONG: *SOLDIERS OF CHRIST, ARISE*

Day 91: (Saturday)
Discretion Shall Preserve Thee

*Proverbs 2:10 When **wisdom** entereth into thine heart, and **knowledge** is pleasant unto thy soul;*

*11 **Discretion** shall preserve thee, understanding shall keep thee:*

*12 **To deliver thee from the way of the evil man**, from the man that speaketh froward things;*

13 Who leave the paths of uprightness, to walk in the ways of darkness;

14 Who rejoice to do evil, and delight in the frowardness of the wicked;

15 Whose ways are crooked, and they froward in their paths:

*16 **To deliver thee from the strange woman**, even from the stranger which flattereth with her words;*

17 Which forsaketh the guide of her youth, and forgetteth the covenant of her God.

18 For her house inclineth unto death, and her paths unto the dead.

19 None that go unto her return again, neither take they hold of the paths of life.

*20 **That thou mayest walk in the way of good men**, and keep the paths of the righteous.*

21 For the upright shall dwell in the land, and the perfect shall remain in it.

22 But the wicked shall be cut off from the earth, and the transgressors shall be rooted out of it.

INTRODUCTORY THOUGHTS

The Bible links together wisdom, knowledge, and discretion to help the Bible student comprehend God's truths. Today's passage provides insight into the composition of this connection. When *wisdom* enters the heart and *knowledge* is pleasant to the soul, then *discretion* preserves the believer. *Preserve* can mean to protect from harm as the context of this passage shows. Those who use discretion are protected from being ensnared by those who have little regard for God or the things of God. Verse 12 indicates that discretion protects the individual from the way of evil men. Verse 16 further reveals how discretion delivers from the strange woman. Discretion implements wisdom and knowledge to keep the believer from unnecessary difficulties that trouble those who fail to abide by biblical principles.

DEVOTIONAL THOUGHTS

- **(For children):** Thinking through things before doing them will help to keep you from trouble and harm. If you decide to pick a fight with someone, or run into a busy street, what could happen to you? Ask God to help you think before you act.
- **(For everyone):** Do you frequently find yourself in trouble? Does each day seem to bring a new set of problems into your life? Do you all

too frequently find yourself in dangerous situations? If these scenarios describe your life, you are most likely lacking in the area of discretion. Why not seek the Lord for wisdom and knowledge and implement them into your life?

- Do you find that you repeatedly commit the same sins? Sin does not happen by accident. It is a deliberate act. Fortunately, in every temptation, God provides a way of escape. When we sin, we refuse to use discretion.

PRAYER THOUGHTS

- Ask God to preserve you from sin.
- Ask God to show you when you make a wrong choice before it is too late to take corrective actions.

SONG: *BE THOU MY VISION*

Notes: _____

_____

_____

_____

_____

_____

_____

_____

_____

_____

_____

_____

_____

_____

_____

Notes: _____

_____

_____

_____

_____

_____

_____

_____

_____

_____

_____

_____

Quotes from the next volume

(VOLUME 2, WEEK 13)

Subject: Fear

Fear introduced is faith attacked.

The fear of God is so vital in the life of the believer that the Bible refers to it as the whole duty of man.

Worldly fear brings bondage and hinders Christian service, yet godly fear encourages the believer to serve the Lord in righteousness.

The fear of the Lord points forward to a time of judgment and reward. A man who refuses to fear God will never serve God with a sincere heart and pure motives.

14

Endurance

Occurrences: found ninety-nine times in ninety-seven verses

Variations: endure, endured, endureth, enduring

First usage: *Genesis 33:14* (endure)

Last usage: *1 Peter 2:19* (endure)

Defined: to last, remain, and abide in the same state without perishing and without yielding; also to suffer without resistance

Interesting fact: *Endurance* in its various forms is found predominantly in the book of Psalms, utilizing it fifty-five times. Psalm 136 contains twenty-six of those occurrences wherein each verse in this Psalm says, *"for his mercy endureth for ever."*

Bible study tip: Many Bible verses naturally break down into smaller parts. During a verse study, begin by applying the study principle of *"rightly dividing the word of truth" (2 Timothy 2:15)*. Oftentimes, you can only truly gain an understanding of a verse by independently understanding the individual parts.

Sunday, Day 92—Church Day (no devotional)
Monday, Day 93—*What Does It Mean to Endure?*
Tuesday, Day 94—*The Enduring God*
Wednesday, Day 95—Church Night (no devotional)
Thursday, Day 96—*Why Don't We Endure?*
Friday, Day 97—*Seeing Him Who Is Invisible*
Saturday, Day 98—*Enduring Sound Doctrine*

Day 92: Church Day

Hebrews 6:15 *And so, after he had **patiently endured,** he obtained the promise.*

Day 93: (Monday)
What Does It Mean to Endure?

Job 8:15 *He shall lean upon his house, but it shall not stand: he shall hold it fast, but **it shall not endure.***

INTRODUCTORY THOUGHTS

Today's study begins by considering how the Bible defines words and specifically how it defines this week's subject: *endurance.* Scriptural interpretation and Bible definitions are often found by dividing passages into their component parts. Today's verse contains four parts: (1) *"The hypocrite shall lean upon his house,"* (2) *"but it shall not stand:"* (3) *"he shall hold it fast,"* (4) *"but it shall not endure."* The next step begins by associating the various phrases together to gain insight into how the Bible interprets itself and defines words. Combining the first section with the third section and the second section with the fourth section reveals the intent of the passage along with the definitions and context of the word *endure.* In this passage, the hypocrite leaning upon his house is analogous to him holding it fast. Secondly, the fact that it does not stand means that it does not *endure.* **Psalm 102:26** offers further confirmation by revealing that *endure* is the opposite of *perish.* Based upon the scripture, one can deduce that the word *endure* means to remain firmly in the present condition. This technique allows the Bible student to study scripture independent of dictionaries and commentaries that frequently contain man's philosophies and wisdom.

DEVOTIONAL THOUGHTS

- **(For children):** A good soldier does not run during battle but remains in the fight. God wants every Christian to live as a good soldier of Jesus Christ. That means to stick with what you're supposed to do, even when it seems far too difficult to handle.
- **(For everyone):** Do you know people in your life who have strength in the area of endurance? How do you feel about those people? Do you desire to emulate them in this area?
- Begin thinking about areas of life in which you ought to be able to endure. Do you think that endurance is a strong aspect of your life? If not, are you willing to allow the Lord to develop this trait in you?

PRAYER THOUGHTS

- Ask God to use this study to further develop your endurance.
- Ask God to show you your tendencies, whether you are prone to endure or to quit, to fight for Him or to run when trouble arises.

SONG: *AWAKE! FOR THE TRUMPET IS SOUNDING!*

Day 94: (Tuesday)
The Enduring God

*Ecclesiastes 3:14 I know that, **whatsoever God doeth, it shall be for ever**: nothing can be put to it, nor any thing taken from it: and God doeth it, that men should fear before him.*

INTRODUCTORY THOUGHTS

Christians are supposed to strive to be Christlike. For this reason, today's lesson will involve searching the scriptures to learn about the nature of God. One constant theme concerning the Lord's nature is that He *endures*. The Bible not only proclaims that the LORD will personally *endure for ever* **(Psalm 9:7; Psalm 102:12)**, but the scripture declares forty-two times that His mercy *"endureth for ever."* God's enduring mercy means that man does not always receive the bad that he deserves. The Bible also proclaims that many other things directly associated with God will endure. These include God's *"goodness"* **(Psalm 52:1)**, *"name"* **(Psalm 135:13)**, *"truth"* **(Psalm 100:5)**, *"glory"* **(Psalm 104:31)**, *"righteousness"* **(Psalm 111:3)**, *"dominion"* **(Psalm 145:13)**, and *"word"* **(1**

Peter 1:25). In other words, the God of the Bible and all things directly associated with Him will *endure for ever.*

DEVOTIONAL THOUGHTS

- **(For children):** You are playing outside with some close friends. Your mother calls and says it's time to come in and get ready for church. Your friends want you to stay and play a little more, but you leave immediately. How have you helped them and truly been a good friend?
- **(For everyone):** As children of God, we are to be like our Father. The changing world does not change who and what God is and how He interacts with others. Could the same be said of you?
- God's endurance enables us to consistently depend upon Him. He provides for us an anchor on which we can rest in troublesome times. What kind of an effect does your endurance or lack of endurance have upon others?

PRAYER THOUGHTS

- Ask God to help you to be the same regardless of your changing surroundings.
- Ask God to strengthen your level of endurance especially as the world's morals continue to deteriorate.

SONG: *PRAISE TO THE LORD, THE ALMIGHTY*

Day 95: Church Night

*James 5:11 Behold, **we count them happy which endure.** Ye have heard of the patience of Job, and have seen the end of the Lord; that the Lord is very pitiful, and of tender mercy.*

Day 96: (Thursday)
Why Don't We Endure?

*1 Corinthians 13:7 Beareth all things, believeth all things, hopeth all things, **endureth all things.***

INTRODUCTORY THOUGHTS

Today's verse deals with charity, the enabler for enduring all things. Christians tend to realize the importance of endurance but all too often fail in its implementation. For this reason, it is important to identify those things that hinder an individual's endurance. Most people tend to focus on surface traits like strength, courage, and wisdom. Truly, the absence of these would be unfavourable, yet the scripture identifies *charity* as the key component for enduring *"all things."* In other words, a lack of endurance surfaces as a result of the absence of charity in the Christian's life. Therefore, failing to have fervent charity will eventually result in a lack of resolve. This is why the Bible says *charity never faileth* **(1 Corinthians 13:8).**

DEVOTIONAL THOUGHTS

- **(For children):** Jesus remained on the cross to fulfil His Father's will. He also displayed His unfailing love for us through the sacrifice of Himself. He could have come down off the cross but chose to remain because He put others first. We should do the same thing.
- **(For everyone):** Do you find that you have trouble enduring various things that seem to come at you from every side? Who or what do you normally blame for your shortcomings? What is the real root of your problem?
- Is your labour for the Lord constantly starting and stopping? Do you struggle to make it through life's trials and troubles? If so, you may need to focus on the fact that the root of the problem has to do with charity. Never forget what Jesus said as He faced the cross: *"Thinkest thou that I cannot now pray to my Father, and he shall presently give me more than twelve legions of angels?" **(Matthew 26:53).*** He did not endure because of a lack of options, but because love constrained Him to do so.

PRAYER THOUGHTS

- Ask God for a special love for Him and for others so that you will endure the difficulties of life.
- Pray that the Lord will work in your heart, building you up to endure life's manifold trials.

SONG: *MY JESUS, I LOVE THEE*

Day 97: (Friday)
Seeing Him Who Is Invisible

Hebrews 11:27 *By faith he forsook Egypt, **not fearing the wrath of the king: for he endured, as seeing him who is invisible.***

INTRODUCTORY THOUGHTS

At the age of forty, Moses fled Egypt in fear for his life *(Exodus 2:11-15; Acts 7:20-29)*. It is not hard to imagine the degree of fear sensed by Moses as he ran from the most powerful man who ruled the most powerful nation on earth during his day. Today's verse reveals that Moses yet again departed from Egypt, forty years later this time, not fearing the wrath of the king. What made the difference? How did Moses keep from losing his mind during such a difficult time of trial? How did he endure the troubles associated with leaving Egypt? He endured because he saw *"him who is invisible."* He saw God! He did not see the Lord simply with his physical eyes, but rather through the eye of faith. Moses endured for one reason, the Lord was with him and he knew it. Endurance becomes possible as the believer learns to acknowledge the presence of the Almighty in his or her life.

DEVOTIONAL THOUGHTS

- **(For children):** God was certainly with Moses. Our Bible tells us that He is always with us too. He knows everything and is more powerful than anything we can imagine and everyone on earth. Our God is able and willing to help us do anything He desires for us to do.
- **(For everyone):** Do you recognize the Lord's presence on a daily basis? Do you live your life with the Lord's presence in mind? Does God's presence strengthen you to persevere?
- When you are met with a new trial, do you think first about yourself or others? What happens to your problems when you direct your focus upon yourself? What happens when you instead direct your focus toward the Lord?

PRAYER THOUGHTS

- Ask God to become more real to you as the trials appear.
- Pray that the Lord will help you to be selfless during these times of trouble.

SONG: *TURN YOUR EYES UPON JESUS*

Day 98: (Saturday)
Enduring Sound Doctrine

*2 Timothy 4:3 For the time will come when they will not **endure** **sound doctrine**; but after their own lusts shall they heap to themselves teachers, having itching ears;*

INTRODUCTORY THOUGHTS

Life throws many obstacles in the believer's path. Oftentimes, these obstacles cause people to stumble and err from the truth. In fact, the Bible prophesies of the absence of people who are able to endure sound doctrine during the last days. Unfortunately, this is a major stumbling block and a lofty hurdle for modern Christianity to overcome. The typical Christian deems the Bible too difficult. He is more at ease avoiding it like the plague. In truth, the Bible is a difficult book. Yet, it is difficult not because of hard words, but because of the hard truths contained within its pages. The Bible is not likened to a sword in vain—it pierces the heart and reveals man's deepest and darkest secrets. The sword does its most efficient work through Bible reading, Bible preaching, and Bible teaching. Yet, regardless of the path truth travels, believers must be able to *endure sound doctrine.*

DEVOTIONAL THOUGHTS

- **(For children):** When mom says, *"It's time for bed,"* the Bible clearly instructs how you should react. The Bible says, *"Children, obey your parents in all things."* Ask God to help you love Him, love His word, and obey your parents.
- **(For everyone):** Are you constantly offended by the truths of God's word? Are you angry when the preacher preaches against things you know are personally contrary to God's word and will for your life? Do you find that being shown Bible verses contrary to your lifestyle annoys you?
- Do you treasure the scripture? Do you find joy in learning from its pages? Are you willing to let the Bible change you?

PRAYER THOUGHTS

- Ask God to give you a love for His word like that of the one who penned Psalm 119.

• Ask God to soften your heart to the truths of His word.

SONG: *I'LL NOT GIVE UP THE BIBLE*

Notes: _____

_____

_____

_____

_____

_____

_____

_____

_____

_____

_____

_____

Quotes from the next volume

(VOLUME 2, WEEK 14)

Subject: Fellowship

There is great wisdom attained through the right kind of fellowship with other like-minded believers. When one believer wavers during times of temptation, his "fellow" believer will encourage him to stay faithful to the Lord's work. When one of the saints struggles in times of uncertainty, his fellow believers can remind him of God's faithfulness.

Fellowship suggests an agreement amongst the involved parties.

15

Endurance (con't)

Occurrences: found seventy-three times in the Old Testament and twenty-six times in the New Testament

Variations: endure, endured, endureth, enduring

First usage in the New Testament: *Matthew 10:22* (endureth)

Last usage in the Old Testament: *Ezekiel 22:14* (endure)

Interesting fact: The Bible specifically mentions endurance ninety-nine times. It is found forty-one times within the phrase *"his mercy endureth for ever."*

Bible study tip: Similar to any other task, the right tools for Bible study are imperative. Consider investing in a concordance or Bible study software. These tools will help you find a word in scripture along with all of its uses. Get into the habit of reading all of the verses where the word appears before drawing any conclusions as to its meaning or applications.

Sunday, Day 99—Church Day (no devotional)
Monday, Day 100—*A Good Soldier of Jesus Christ*
Tuesday, Day 101—*Persecutions and Tribulations*
Wednesday, Day 102—Church Night (no devotional)

Thursday, Day 103—*Suffering Wrongfully*
Friday, Day 104—*Endure Chastening*
Saturday, Day 105—*Enduring Temptation*

Day 99: Church Day

*Psalm 136:1 O give thanks unto the LORD; for he is good: for **his mercy endureth for ever**.*

*2 O give thanks unto the God of gods: for **his mercy endureth for ever**.*

*3 O give thanks to the Lord of lords: for **his mercy endureth for ever**.*

Day 100: (Monday)
A Good Soldier of Jesus Christ

*2 Timothy 2:3 Thou therefore **endure hardness**, as a good soldier of Jesus Christ.*

INTRODUCTORY THOUGHTS

Prior military personnel know the difficulties associated with functioning as a good soldier. Their training focuses on teaching them how to endure physical and emotional hardships unique to their service. They learn how to follow and obey their chain of command and frequently do things commanded without always understanding the how and why. Paul's letter to Timothy relates the Christian life to that of a soldier. Timothy, as well as every other faithful Christian, is challenged with difficulties based solely on the fact that he is a follower of the Lord Jesus Christ. Paul instructed Timothy how to react during those times when the difficulties arise. According to Paul, Timothy was to *"endure hardness, as a good soldier of Jesus Christ."* The Christian life is not supposed to be a life of ease. Fortunately, with Christ in focus, things take on a clearer focus with a notable purpose and plan. The Christian life contains "hardness" but submission to the true Commander in Chief helps the suffering seem like a *light affliction (2 Corinthians 4:17)*. Like the good soldier, the faithful Christian needs to learn how to *endure hardness* in order to avoid bitterness and bewilderment during life's battles.

DEVOTIONAL THOUGHTS

- **(For children):** You will never enjoy every chore you are asked to do, but a bad attitude can make it harder to handle. Complaining while cleaning your room will make the task seem longer and harder. The task will seem lighter if while you are working you sing, pray, quote scripture, or focus on how good God and your parents have been to you.
- **(For everyone):** Can you think of any *"hardness"* faced as a result of others knowing that you are trying to live the Christian life? How did you handle this adversity? Did you want to give up? Did you actually quit? If not, what made you endure?
- In the midst of a battle, do you think it helps the morale of others when soldiers focus on the "hardness" and begin complaining? What about you? Do you spend time complaining about the "hard" things in your life? Does complaining offer you comfort or accentuate the difficulty?

PRAYER THOUGHTS

- Ask God to help you learn how to endure "hardness" that comes from living a godly Christian life in this world.
- Ask God to help you see the Christian life as the life of a soldier in a spiritual battle.

SONG: *AM I A SOLDIER OF THE CROSS?*

Day 101: (Tuesday)
Persecutions and Tribulations

2 Thessalonians 1:3 We are bound to thank God always for you, brethren, as it is meet, because that your faith groweth exceedingly, and the charity of every one of you all toward each other aboundeth;

*4 So that we ourselves glory in you in the churches of God for **your patience and faith in all your persecutions and tribulations that ye endure:***

5 Which is a manifest token of the righteous judgment of God, that ye may be counted worthy of the kingdom of God, for which ye also suffer:

6 Seeing it is a righteous thing with God to recompense tribulation to them that trouble you;

INTRODUCTORY THOUGHTS

The Thessalonian believers chose to willingly trust Christ as Saviour and to obediently become His followers. According to Paul's account, these believers endured great difficulties because of their faithfulness to the Lord. Paul commended them for their patience and faith for enduring these persecutions and tribulations. Unfortunately, far too many Christians today are unwilling to live godly *(2 Timothy 3:12)* for fear that living the Christian life will bring persecution and ridicule. These believers in Thessalonica understood what it was like to have people scoff at them for their boldness in the faith. They understood what it felt like to be mocked and cursed for their unwillingness to compromise. This is why Paul praised them. They endured the persecutions and tribulations with patience and faith. The world needs more Thessalonian type believers in the church today.

DEVOTIONAL THOUGHTS

- **(For children):** Your friends at school or your neighbours laugh at you for believing the creation story found in the Bible. They do this because schools today teach that a big explosion made the world and God did not create it. Who is right: your friends or God's word? Believe God, pray for them, and glorify God that He has counted you worthy to suffer for His sake *(Philippians 1:29, 1 Peter 3:14).*
- **(For everyone):** Have you ever had someone mock you for being a Christian or living your scriptural convictions? How did you respond when they gave you a hard time? It is not just worldly unbelievers that give Christians a hard time. Unfortunately, sometimes other believers are the Christian's worst adversaries.
- Has the Lord dealt with you about making changes to your life? Have you refused fearing the persecution that may follow? Consider this: would you rather deal with the mockery of men now or face the displeasure of Almighty God?

PRAYER THOUGHTS

- Ask God to make you more bold. Ask Him to help you overcome your fear of persecution.

• Ask God to teach you to trust in Him and show you that the *"fear of man bringeth a snare"* **(Proverbs 29:25)**.

SONG: *PARDON ME, O MY GOD,*

Day 102: Church Night

*1 Corinthians 15:58 Therefore, my beloved brethren, **be ye stedfast, unmoveable**, always abounding in the work of the Lord, forasmuch as ye know that your labour is not in vain in the Lord.*

Day 103: (Thursday)
Suffering Wrongfully

*1 Peter 2:19 For this is thankworthy, if a man for conscience toward God **endure grief, suffering wrongfully.***

*20 For what glory is it, if, when ye be buffeted for your faults, ye shall take it patiently? but if, when ye do well, and suffer for it, ye **take it patiently**, this is acceptable with God.*

*21 For even hereunto were ye called: because Christ also suffered for us, leaving us an example, that ye should **follow his steps**:*

22 Who did no sin, neither was guile found in his mouth:

*23 Who, **when he was reviled, reviled not again**; when **he suffered, he threatened not**; but committed himself to him that judgeth righteously:*

24 Who his own self bare our sins in his own body on the tree, that we, being dead to sins, should live unto righteousness: by whose stripes ye were healed.

25 For ye were as sheep going astray; but are now returned unto the Shepherd and Bishop of your souls.

INTRODUCTORY THOUGHTS

Most people naturally want to be understood, loved, and accepted by others. Yet, sometimes no matter how hard one tries, some people will never accept those who replace the worldly pleasures of this life with a sacrificial service for the Saviour. Worldly people hate those who want to do right and live right. This makes the heartache and anguish resulting from the spreading of falsehoods sometimes difficult to bear. Yet, how should a Christian respond when wrongfully attacked for simply trying to do right? According to the Bible, it is admirable to suffer when wrongly accused. Again, the Bible provides Christ as the perfect example of wrongfully suffering. There was no sin in the Saviour, nor was there guile found in His mouth. Yet, He endured more grief than anyone who has ever lived. How did He handle it? When He was reviled, He did not respond accordingly. When He suffered, He did not threaten those who caused His pain. Believers are called to follow the steps of the Saviour. When people falsely accuse believers, they must endure, considering the great miscarriage of justice endured by Christ.

DEVOTIONAL THOUGHTS

- **(For children):** A friend lies to his mother blaming you for breaking his new toy. The mother believes him even though you politely say you did not do it. You feel hurt, but instead of arguing with the boy's mother, ask God to help the boy to admit that what he did was not true. Always remember that God knows the truth.
- **(For everyone):** Have you ever had someone say things about you that are not true? How did it make you feel? Did you want to immediately defend yourself and say some harsh things back? Or have you learned to leave much of your defense in the hands of the Lord?
- Why do you think we feel it is so important to defend ourselves? Is it possible that pride makes us do such things? Was our Saviour wrong in the things in which He was accused? Why didn't He fight to clear His name?

PRAYER THOUGHTS

- Ask God to help you to trust Him in times when people spread false things about you.
- Ask the Lord to keep you humble.

SONG: *MUST JESUS BEAR THE CROSS ALONE?*

Day 104: (Friday)
Endure Chastening

Hebrews 12:4 Ye have not yet resisted unto blood, striving against sin.

5 And ye have forgotten the exhortation which speaketh unto you as unto children, **My son, despise not thou the chastening of the Lord,** *nor faint when thou art rebuked of him:*

6 **For whom the Lord loveth he chasteneth,** *and scourgeth every son whom he receiveth.*

7 If ye **endure chastening,** *God dealeth with you as with sons; for what son is he whom the father chasteneth not?*

8 But if ye be without chastisement, whereof all are partakers, then are ye bastards, and not sons.

9 Furthermore we have had fathers of our flesh which corrected us, and we gave them reverence: shall we not much rather be in subjection unto the Father of spirits, and live?

10 For they verily for a few days chastened us after their own pleasure; but **he for our profit, that we might be partakers of his holiness.**

11 Now no chastening for the present seemeth to be joyous, but grievous: nevertheless **afterward it yieldeth the peaceable fruit of righteousness** *unto them which are exercised thereby.*

INTRODUCTORY THOUGHTS

Contrary to today's all-inclusive teachings, no one comes into this world as a child of God. In fact, the Bible plainly teaches that God becomes the Father of only those who trust Christ as personal Saviour. This new relationship between the Father and His children results from a personal, conscious, willing decision. As the Father of His children, God at times finds it necessary to chasten (or correct) believers. No chastening is enjoyable, especially that from an all-knowing Father. Unfortunately, when God begins administering His corrective hand, far too many Christians quit. Consequently, those who quit on the Lord never experience the by-product of God's chastening—*"the peaceable fruit of righteousness."* Christians should never take the grace of God in vain by thinking that simply being saved pleases the Lord. God wants and expects much more. His chastening hand confirms the believer's wrongdoing and directs him in the right direction. When God cares enough to correct a man's wrongdoing, it is an uncaring response to quit. The believer who loves the Lord will accept the correction and grow in the grace and knowledge of Christ.

DEVOTIONAL THOUGHTS

- **(For children):** Taking something that doesn't belong to you without permission is wrong. The Bible says, *"Thou shalt not steal."* Mom and dad love you enough to teach you these truths now. A thief who gets caught may end up standing before the judge and will sometimes end up in jail. God teaches us the rules and guidelines necessary to keep us out of trouble.
- **(For everyone):** Can you think of anything lately that the Lord has personally had to correct in your life? How did you feel when the Lord convicted you concerning this sin? What did you do when He chastened you?
- Do you get upset when someone points out as wrong something that you are doing? Do you get defensive when someone proves from the scriptures that you are wrong?

PRAYER THOUGHTS

- Ask God to soften your heart toward His chastening hand so that you are more easily corrected.
- Ask God to give you a willingness to change based upon the truth found in His precious word.

SONG: *AFFLICTIONS DO NOT COME ALONE*

Day 105: (Saturday)

Enduring Temptation

James 1:12 Blessed is the man that endureth temptation: *for when he is tried, he shall receive the crown of life, which the Lord hath promised to them that love him.*

13 Let no man say when he is tempted, I am tempted of God: for God cannot be tempted with evil, neither tempteth he any man:

*14 But **every man** is tempted, when he is **drawn away of his own lust**, and enticed.*

*15 Then when **lust** hath **conceived**, it **bringeth forth sin:** and sin, when it is finished, bringeth forth death.*

INTRODUCTORY THOUGHTS

God created Lucifer as a perfect, holy being. Unfortunately, when Lucifer willfully chose to rebel against his Creator, his actions eventually severed the relationship for all of God's creation. As a result of Lucifer's rebellion, he became God's archenemy as well as the enemy of all of God's saints too. This is why Satan uses every tool in his spiritual arsenal to lure the believer into sin and rebellion. It is important to understand how a simple temptation leads to some dire consequences. A man's lust draws him away from God and tempts him to fulfil his lustful desires. When lust is fully conceived, it brings forth sin. Repeatedly sinning hardens the heart and lessens the believer's resolve. God always makes a way of escape according to *1 Corinthians 10:13*. The child of God need only look for that way out because it will always be there. Like the Lord Jesus in Matthew chapter 4, the believer ought to respond to temptation with the word of God. If the Christian submits to God and resists the Devil, the Devil will flee rather than face defeat *(James 4:7)*.

DEVOTIONAL THOUGHTS

- **(For children):** It's close to suppertime so mom tells you, "No cookies." The Devil will try to convince you to take one anyway. Surely, mom won't miss just one. She will never know. No matter what mom knows or finds out, God will know.
- **(For everyone):** Do you constantly find yourself defeated as a result of the sins that you allow in your life? Do you allow Satan's temptations to direct your thoughts and actions? If so, you are not enduring temptation.
- Do you know the joys of overcoming temptation? When is the last time you remember the "blessed" feeling of enduring some temptation hurled at you by the Devil?

PRAYER THOUGHTS

- Ask God to keep you in His word so that you can endure temptation and withstand Satan's fiery darts.
- Ask God to give you a resolve to live a clean life for Him.

SONG: *YIELD NOT TO TEMPTATION*

Notes: _____

_____

_____

_____

_____

_____

_____

_____

_____

_____

_____

_____

_____

_____

_____

_____

_____

_____

_____

_____

_____

Quotes from the next volume

(VOLUME 2, WEEK 15)

Subject: Flattery

If you have trusted the Lord Jesus Christ as your Saviour, you are no longer appointed to God's wrath *(1 Thessalonians 5:9)*; however, it helps to fully understand God's hatred for sin.

16

Equity

Occurrences: found ten times in the Bible, exclusively in the Old Testament.

First usage: *Psalm 98:9* (equity)

Last usage: *Malachi 2:6* (equity)

Defined: the impartial distribution of justice; doing what is right

Interesting fact: Similar to the word *equity* suggesting a judging with equality, *requite* indicates a recompensing with equality: *"as I have done, so God hath requited me" (Judges 1:7).*

Bible study tip: The English language places importance upon every facet of a particular word, even down to the letters making up the word. It is often helpful to look at the letter groupings in your word to see if other words in the Bible might share those letter groupings. This search can often yield sister words that greatly aid your original study.

Sunday, Day 106—Church Day (no devotional)
Monday, Day 107—*What Is Equity?*
Tuesday, Day 108—*The Righteous Judge*

Wednesday, Day 109—Church Night (no devotional)
Thursday, Day 110—*A Foundation for Equity*
Friday, Day 111—*A Good Path*
Saturday, Day 112—*Perverting All Equity*

Day 106: Church Day

Psalm 98:9 *Before the LORD; for he cometh to judge the earth:* **with righteousness shall he judge the world, and the people with equity.**

Day 107: (Monday)
What Is Equity?

Isaiah 59:14 *And judgment is turned away backward, and justice standeth afar off: for truth is fallen in the street, and* **equity cannot enter.**

INTRODUCTORY THOUGHTS

Some Bible words are more difficult than others to define in the strictest sense; *equity* is one such word. Yet, the Lord provides enough information for any diligent student willing to compare spiritual things with spiritual *(1 Corinthians 2:13)*. In *Isaiah 59:14*, the word *equity* relates to *judgment, justice,* and *truth.* The fact that the word *equity* occurs only *ten times* in scripture links it indirectly with the Ten Commandments. Within those ten occurrences, the word basically involves judging with equality based upon a just standard. Additionally, *Judges 1:7* and *2 Chronicles 6:23* reveal that the related word *requite* means *to get even* or *to return evenly.* The Lord will prove in the future that this is the standard by which He judges *(Psalm 98:9)*. Since believers are to be Christlike, this too should be true of His faithful followers.

DEVOTIONAL THOUGHTS

- **(For children):** God wants you to always try to do right. You see your best friend grab a toy away from another child who was playing with it first. After they start arguing, the adult asks you what happened. What should you say when you are asked who had the toy first?
- **(For everyone):** Where are some places that equity would be beneficial (i.e., government, schools, homes, etc.)? What would be the benefits of practicing equity in your life?

- Do you practice equity daily in your life? What kind of troubles do you face that could be easily solved with equity?

PRAYER THOUGHTS

- Ask God to help you to become more equitable in your judgment.
- Ask God to teach you the benefits of judging others based on an equal standard that is according to scripture.

SONG: *BLESS, O MY SOUL, THE LIVING GOD*

Day 108: (Tuesday)
The Righteous Judge

*2 Timothy 4:8 Henceforth there is laid up for me a crown of righteousness, which the Lord, **the righteous judge**, shall give me at that day: and not to me only, but unto all them also that love his appearing.*

INTRODUCTORY THOUGHTS

Imagine one day standing before *"the righteous judge"* of the universe who knows every action, thought, and motive. One day, this will become the reality for all those who have ever lived. The Son of God is that judge because the Father committed all judgment to Him *(John 5:22)*. He will judge the world with righteousness and the people with *equity (Psalm 98:9)*. His Father gave Him full authority to mete out this judgment. As the judge, He incorporates an equal standard in every ruling. The scripture testifies of this judgment when it says the Lord has a crown for Paul. Fortunately, this crown is not limited to Paul only, *"but unto **all** them also that love his [Christ's] appearing."* It is important to note that the word of God stands as the standard by which all truth is judged. The Lord Jesus Christ remains the righteous judge by which all is judged. Unfortunately, far too many judges pervert judgment by incorporating a changing standard into their decisions.

DEVOTIONAL THOUGHTS

- **(For children):** A judge decides if a person has done right or wrong. At times, he lets a bad person go unpunished because he likes him and a good person gets punished because the judge does not like him. Yet,

God plays no favourites. He will always be right and fair in deciding if a person has done right or wrong. His rule book is the Bible.

- **(For everyone):** Have you ever been judged unfairly? Were you judged guilty although you were innocent? Christ will never judge inaccurately or with any hidden agenda.
- Have you ever felt wronged due to an unjust judgment? How did it affect you? What does it mean to you that the Lord judges with equity?

PRAYER THOUGHTS

- Take time to thank God for being equitable in judgment.
- Ask the Lord to make you more equitable in your judgment of others.

SONG: *HOLY, HOLY, HOLY*

Day 109: Church Night

*Proverbs 1:1 **The proverbs of Solomon** the son of David, king of Israel;*

2 To know wisdom and instruction; to perceive the words of understanding;

*3 **To receive** the instruction of wisdom, justice, and judgment, and **equity**;*

4 To give subtilty to the simple, to the young man knowledge and discretion.

Day 110: (Thursday)
A Foundation for Equity

*John 7:24 Judge not according to the appearance, but **judge righteous judgment**.*

INTRODUCTORY THOUGHTS

One of the most misunderstood, misquoted, and abused truths of scripture revolves around whether or not a person should judge. Contrary to popular teaching, all believers are instructed to judge all things *(1 Corinthians 2:15)*. Yet, how a person judges makes the judgment scriptural or unscriptural. Judging with *equity* involves incorporating an unwavering standard by which to judge. When emotion, modern thought, and one's educational attainments form the foundational basis for how someone judges, the standards are ever changing and never consistently applied. They rarely yield an equitable outcome. Therefore, it is important to consult an unwavering standard concerning every decision and matter. This standard must be something perfect without possibility of corruption. Only one standard consistently fits this mold, and, of course, it is the Bible. The word of God remains the standard by which the saints will be judged and the only viable source by which all things should and must be judged while on earth *(John 12:48)*.

DEVOTIONAL THOUGHTS

- **(For children):** The Bible always has been and always will be pure and true *(Psalm 119:140, 160)*. For this reason, we can always trust the Bible to judge our decisions revealing whether they are right or wrong.
- **(For everyone):** What is your primary standard for making correct judgments? Does your standard for judgment frequently waver? Would you say that it is a safe standard that generally leads to godly judgment?
- How often do you make decisions only to later question them? Why does that happen to you? What is your ultimate authority for making judgments?

PRAYER THOUGHTS

- Ask the Lord to give you a desire to judge based upon His word rather than your emotions or any other wavering foundation.
- Pray that God gives you a boldness to judge on the truth alone.

SONG: *O LORD, 'TIS MATTER OF HIGH PRAISE*

Day 111: (Friday)
A Good Path

Proverbs 2:6 For the LORD giveth wisdom: out of his mouth cometh knowledge and understanding.

7 He layeth up sound wisdom for the righteous: he is a buckler to them that walk uprightly.

8 He keepeth the paths of judgment, and preserveth the way of his saints.

9 Then shalt thou understand righteousness, and judgment, and equity; yea, every good path.

INTRODUCTORY THOUGHTS

The last few lessons revealed how equity should always be linked to judgment. The passage today reiterates this truth, suggesting that righteousness, judgment, and equity are not only closely associated, but inseparable. Verse 8 reveals that it is the Lord who **"keepeth the paths of judgment."** Verse 9 points out that righteousness, judgment, and equity are said to be the *"good"* paths. These good paths stand in stark contrast to those paths that seem right to the world, but in the end are *"the ways of death" (Proverbs 14:12; Proverbs 16:25)*. The saint of God has a clear choice. He can do things his own way resulting in an untimely death, or he can follow after God's plan and find that God *"preserveth the way of his saints."* The choice is simple: choose God's good path and not the well trodden path travelled by the world. God's plan or path is for a man to judge with righteousness and equity.

DEVOTIONAL THOUGHTS

- **(For children):** If the lights went out in your house, how would a flashlight help you not to stumble or trip over things? *Psalm 119:105* tells us that God's word shows us the good path in life (how to have the right relationship with the Lord and with others, along with how to get to heaven and how to stay on the right path).
- **(For everyone):** Are you stubborn when shown the error of your ways? Do you find that you insist on doing things your own way? Do you frequently struggle to follow the "good path" revealed by God in His word?
- Is your judgment based on righteousness and equity? If your judgment is not characterized by these traits, you are no different than those in the world who judge based on wicked biases.

PRAYER THOUGHTS

- Ask God to give you light to follow the "good path" and never presume upon the goodness and grace of God.
- Ask God to show you the importance of sound judgment during your decision-making process.

SONG: *WHO WOULD TRUE VALOUR SEE*

Day 112: (Saturday)
Perverting All Equity

Micah 3:8 *But truly I am full of power by the spirit of the LORD, and of judgment, and of might, to declare unto Jacob his transgression, and to Israel his sin.*

9 *Hear this, I pray you, ye heads of the house of Jacob, and princes of the house of Israel, that abhor judgment, and* **pervert all equity***.*

10 ***They build up Zion with blood***, *and Jerusalem with iniquity.*

11 *The heads thereof* **judge for reward***, and the priests thereof* **teach for hire***, and the prophets thereof* **divine for money***: yet will they lean upon the LORD, and say, Is not the LORD among us? none evil can come upon us.*

12 ***Therefore shall Zion*** *for your sake* **be plowed** *as* **a field***, and* **Jerusalem shall become heaps***, and the mountain of the house as the high places of the forest.*

INTRODUCTORY THOUGHTS

Incorporating equity within one's judgment processes remains crucial at every level, whether concerning a nation, a community, a church, or a home. The book of Micah describes what happens when leaders pervert equity. **Micah 3:11** declares that they *"judge for reward,"* *"teach for hire,"* and *"divine for money."* One might assume this perversion of equity would immediately send a nation into destruction; but **Micah 3:10** points out that they *"**build up** Zion with blood."* No matter how successful and prosperous an individual or group may seem, in the end, the Lord will bring judgment. In this case, Zion shall *"be plowed as a field, and Jerusalem shall become heaps" (Micah 3:12).* When a nation, community, church, or family perverts equity, God brings judgment when He deems the time appropriate. **Proverbs 14:34** clearly points out that *"Righteousness exalteth a nation: but sin is a reproach to any people."* Those who judge success through worldly means rather than by using biblical standards will fail to see God's judgment coming until it becomes too late.

DEVOTIONAL THOUGHTS

- **(For children):** Your friend throws a ball and breaks a lamp in his house. He says he will give you five dollars if you tell his mother the dog knocked the lamp over and broke it. What would the Lord expect you to say to your friend?

- **(For everyone):** How do you feel when the leaders of your nation pervert equity? How do you think God feels when we pervert equity? How do you think your family feels when you pervert equity?
- How long will we continue to judge falsely before the Lord gains our attention? How many trials are we willing to bring upon ourselves because of a lack of balance in our judgment?

PRAYER THOUGHTS

- Ask God to open your eyes to the standards by which you judge.
- Ask God to help you to incorporate equity in every judgment you make.

SONG: *COME, LET OUR SOULS ADORE THE LORD*

Quotes from the next volume

(VOLUME 2, WEEK 16)

Subject: Flattery (con't)

The Devil is both very subtle and sly. He knows that being patient in his attacks against the truth can result in his ultimate victory as he wears down the saints.

Christians need their self-confidence replaced with a greater confidence and trust in the Lord.

It is difficult for new Christians to fully comprehend sin's effects. From God's perspective, every facet of sin involves a vile act. However, from man's viewpoint, though sin can be extremely harmful, the temporary pleasures *(Hebrews 11:25)* distract from sin's injurious nature.

In a day when seminary students are more schooled on the finer arts of secular humanism than biblical doctrines, the church desperately needs a remnant of men standing in the pulpits unapologetically preaching the truth.

17
Faith

Occurrences: found 247 times in 231 verses (only twice in the Old Testament)

Variations: faith, faithless (Note: Faithfulness was previously covered.)

First usage: *Deuteronomy 32:20* (faith)

Last usage: *Revelation 14:12* (faith)

Defined: Pertaining to scripture, faith involves trusting what God has said.

Interesting fact: *"Faith"* is only found twice in the Old Testament and the first time it refers to those in whom there is *"no faith"* *(Deuteronomy 32:20)*. However, Hebrews chapter eleven, often called the faith chapter, utilizes faith twenty-three times in forty verses with the vast majority alluding back to the faith of Old Testament saints. Although the word *faith* was almost completely nonexistent from the Old Testament writings, Hebrews paints a more complete picture of faith before Christ's incarnation.

Bible study tip: A previous tip encouraged breaking down compound words into their component parts by pointing out that a prefix or suffix added to a root word merely modifies the root.

With every rule there are exceptions. Be sure to consider that the prefix or suffix sometimes modifies the root but at other times presents an entirely new concept.

Sunday, Day 113—Church Day (no devotional)
Monday, Day 114—*What Is Faith?*
Tuesday, Day 115—*The Importance of Faith*
Wednesday, Day 116—Church Night (no devotional)
Thursday, Day 117—*The Source of Faith*
Friday, Day 118—*The Outcome of Faith*
Saturday, Day 119—*Ask in Faith*

Day 113: Church Day

*Galatians 5:6 For in Jesus Christ neither circumcision availeth any thing, nor uncircumcision; but **faith which worketh by love**.*

Day 114: (Monday)
What Is Faith?

*Hebrews 11:1 Now **faith is the substance of things hoped for, the evidence of things not seen**.*

2 For by it the elders obtained a good report.

3 Through faith we understand that the worlds were framed by the word of God, so that things which are seen were not made of things which do appear.

INTRODUCTORY THOUGHTS

The Bible refers to *faith* in a couple of different ways: (1) it speaks of *"the faith,"* which generally signifies faith as a body of doctrine, and (2) it speaks of faith as *trusting God*. This study focuses on the latter of the two uses, one's personal faith distinguished from *the faith*. Simply put, one who has *faith* takes God at His word. This faith refuses information, regardless of how seemingly reliable, that deters one from fully accepting the words of God as true. It is not a mystical feeling to be sought or the proverbial "blind faith." Instead, the scripture describes faith as *"substance"* and *"evidence" (Hebrews 11:1)*. It is real and it is a choice. Faith is the very thing that carries a man to heaven for eternity and determines the outcome of the rewards received at the judgment. Every man must decide whether or not to take God at His word or continue in unbelief and faithlessness.

DEVOTIONAL THOUGHTS

- **(For children):** You ask a younger child to jump into a wagon so that you can pull him around the yard. Yet, he refuses to get in because he is scared. You assure him that there is nothing to fear, but he doesn't believe you. Likewise, God wants us to believe His word and do what He tells us, fully trusting in Him.
- **(For everyone):** The Bible has much to say about having weak faith. God uses this description of faithlessness far too often to describe the faith of His own people. What type of faith do you possess?
- Do you take God at His word? What about times when His word is contrary to what your flesh wants? Do you still trust Him even during those times when your mind and body say no?

PRAYER THOUGHTS

- Ask God to give you a desire to increase in faith.
- Ask God to soften your heart so that you might believe His word even more assuredly.

SONG: *TRUSTING JESUS (STITES)*

Day 115: (Tuesday)
The Importance of Faith

*Hebrews 11:6 But **without faith it is impossible to please him**: for he that cometh to God must believe that he is, and that he is a rewarder of them that diligently seek him.*

INTRODUCTORY THOUGHTS

Any person who suggests that Christianity is simply an easy way to avoid the trials of life speaks as a fool or a liar. In actuality, the Christian life involves an ongoing, outward battle along with a constant inner struggle. Perhaps the greater of the two is the struggle which exists within a believer. Part of the Christian (called the new man) wants to do right, while the other part delights in doing wrong and following the old ways (the old man). Faith in God's word and God's plan is a primary means of assuring one's spiritual success. Today's passage focuses on the absolute necessity for personal faith within the life of a Christian. The book of Hebrews says, *"without faith it is impossible to please him [God]."* Hence, the Bible repeatedly states that unbelief displeases God. In fact, faith is so crucial to pleasing God that He devoted an entire Bible chapter pointing to the lives of those who exemplified faith. Since God spent the time, space, and effort to chronicle the faith of those of the past, He surely places no less emphasis on the faith of those living today.

DEVOTIONAL THOUGHTS

- **(For children):** David believed God. Read *1 Samuel 17:34-37*. Why did David believe he could kill the giant Goliath? Similar to the example of David, God is well pleased when we believe in Him, His word, and His plan for us.
- **(For everyone):** The Lord is not going to add any names to Hebrews chapter 11, but He continues to keep track of those whose lives exemplify a life of faith. Are you concerned with making such a list by living a life of faith?
- Do you desire to live a life pleasing to God? What are you doing in order to achieve this goal? When is the last time you can remember exemplifying a great measure of faith?

PRAYER THOUGHTS

- Ask God to mold you into a person known for strong faith.
- Ask God to open your eyes to the importance of taking Him at His word.

SONG: *MY FAITH HAS FOUND A RESTING PLACE*

Day 116: Church Night

Psalm 27:13 I had fainted, unless I had believed to see the goodness of the LORD in the land of the living.

Day 117: (Thursday)
The Source of Faith

Romans 10:17 So then faith cometh by hearing, and hearing by the word of God.

INTRODUCTORY THOUGHTS

The Bible repeatedly teaches that faith is of paramount importance in the life of every believer. Furthermore, the Bible clearly specifies the origin of faith as *"the word of God."* Unfortunately, most Christians understand little about the singular source of true faith. The Bible teaches that the believer's faith increases only in proportion to his hearing of God's words. Man may see things in this life that lead him toward doubt and dismay, yet the hearing of God's word shrinks these doubts by building and strengthening faith. For instance, reading about the working of God in the lives of men like Moses, Joseph, and David, and women like Ruth, Hannah, and Sarah increases faith in God. These imperfect men and women displayed great faith because of God and His word. Remember that faith is a choice, but there is little opportunity for choice without the hearing of God's word.

DEVOTIONAL THOUGHTS

- **(For children):** To be able to believe God, you have to know what He says. To please God, you have to know what He expects. What book did God give us that tells us about Him, His promises, and what He wants us to do?
- **(For everyone):** Do you devote a sufficient amount of time for reading your Bible? Do you realize that too much time spent separated from the Bible feeds unbelief? Your lack of faith and inconsistency may mean that you need more Bible time.
- How does Bible reading build your faith? How can learning about the lives of Moses, Paul, David, and Abraham strengthen your faith today?

PRAYER THOUGHTS

- Ask God to help you make time every day to read your Bible.
- Ask God to strengthen you in times of unbelief by reminding you of His work in the lives of men and women of the past.

SONG: *THE OLD BOOK AND THE OLD FAITH*

Day 118: (Friday)
The Outcome of Faith

*James 2:17 Even so **faith, if it hath not works, is dead, being alone**.*

*18 Yea, a man may say, Thou hast faith, and I have works: shew me thy faith without thy works, and **I will shew thee my faith by my works.***

19 Thou believest that there is one God; thou doest well: the devils also believe, and tremble.

*20 But wilt thou know, O vain man, that **faith without works is dead**?*

INTRODUCTORY THOUGHTS

Most Christians think of faith as something mysterious—unable to be defined, seen, or proven. The average person might claim to have faith, but scripture provides a definitive test where an individual can know if he possesses scriptural faith. The fact is that true faith ALWAYS moves people to action. This truth is manifested throughout scripture but nowhere more emphatically as Hebrews chapter 11. BY FAITH . . . Abel **offered** *(Hebrews 11:4)*, Abraham **obeyed** *(Hebrews 11:8)*, Isaac **blessed** *(Hebrews 11:20)*, Moses **refused** to be called the son of Pharaoh's daughter *(Hebrews 11:24)*, and so forth. True faith always moves people to action. Consider this practical application. If someone cries out in a crowded building that the building is on fire, the response of the hearers will demonstrate their faith or the lack thereof. Those who remain testify that they do not believe the report; those who act upon what they have heard demonstrate their faith in that report. How's your faith?

DEVOTIONAL THOUGHTS

- **(For children):** *Ephesians 6:1-3* instructs children to obey their parents. The results of faithful obedience are found in verse 3. If you have faith that God means what He says, you will act upon that belief by obeying the Bible.
- **(For everyone):** What has faith moved you to do lately? Has it moved you to witness? Has it moved you to give more for the work of the Lord? Has it moved you to pray more? If it hasn't moved you, it is because you don't have the faith that you should.
- What do you think the Lord would have you to do? What stops you from doing it? What is hindering your obedience? Will you forsake your unbelief and take God at His word?

PRAYER THOUGHTS

- Ask God to show you if you lack true faith.
- Ask God to increase your faith so that you can obey and please Him.

SONG: *'TIS BY THE FAITH OF JOYS TO COME*

Day 119: (Saturday)
Ask in Faith

James 1:5 If any of you lack wisdom, let him ask of God, that giveth to all men liberally, and upbraideth not; and it shall be given him.

6 But let him ask in faith, nothing wavering. For he that wavereth is like a wave of the sea driven with the wind and tossed.

7 For let not that man think that he shall receive any thing of the Lord.

8 A double minded man is unstable in all his ways.

INTRODUCTORY THOUGHTS

God wants to answer prayer. As a loving, compassionate Father, God wants to regularly hear from His children. Prayer is a matter of life and death for believers. Yet, sin hinders prayers and operates as the enemy to getting prayers answered. Though several sins are identified as hindrances, unbelief stands as prayer's chief opponent. Believers should approach God's throne of grace with boldness *(Hebrews 4:16)* knowing that God can and will reward the diligent seeker *(Hebrews 11:6)*. In today's passage, the believer is challenged to come to God in faith without wavering. A man who comes to the Lord with a wavering heart should realize that his double minded ways hinder his prayers and directly impact his relationship to the Lord *(James 1:7)*. Ask and receive in faith.

DEVOTIONAL THOUGHTS

- **(For children):** Ask several people you highly respect to give you an example of God answering their prayers. Likewise, God wants to answer your prayers too. He loves to hear from you and finds joy in answering your prayers to Him.
- **(For everyone):** Are you frequently getting your prayers answered? Reflect upon your faith when you approach the Lord. Do you pray ex-

pecting God to answer, or do you wonder if He even hears you when you speak?

- Do you find that you approach the Lord in prayer with little faith that He can or will move on your behalf? Why is that? Has the Lord given you any definite reason to doubt His faithfulness?

PRAYER THOUGHTS

- Ask God to remind you of all the answered prayers in your past.
- Ask God for the faith necessary to pray without wavering.

SONG: *SWEET HOUR OF PRAYER*

Notes: _____

_____

_____

_____

_____

_____

Quotes from the next volume

(VOLUME 2, WEEK 17)

Subject: Forgiveness

God's character demands righteous judgment; therefore, man cannot sin with impunity.

Because of God's complete forgiveness, sins can never and will never affect a man's position in Christ. However, those same sins can adversely hinder one's fellowship with the Lord.

True forgiveness also forgets the transgression. To claim that someone is forgiven and still remains accountable for a wrongdoing suggests that they were never actually forgiven.

Forgiving others because you have been forgiven illustrates God's mercy to others.

18
Faith (con't)

Occurrences: *Faithless* is found four times (all in the New Testament).

First usage in the New Testament: *Matthew 6:30* (faith)

Last usage in the Old Testament: *Habakkuk 2:4* (faith)

Interesting fact: The Bible points to those who have *"no faith" (Deuteronomy 32:20)*, *"little faith" (Matthew 6:30)*, and *"great faith" (Matthew 8:10)*, and yet the Lord promised His disciples that *"faith as a grain of mustard seed"* could remove mountains *(Matthew 17:20)*.

Bible study tip: Some Bible passages indicate progressive Christian growth processes. Take heed to the order in which each virtue appears in a list and consider the sequence within the overall series. Frequently, effective spiritual growth occurs in the order listed. For instance, consider *2 Peter 1:5-7* and *James 1:2-4*.

Sunday, Day 120—Church Day (no devotional)
Monday, Day 121—*The Shield of Faith*
Tuesday, Day 122—*The Family of Faith*
Wednesday, Day 123—Church Night (no devotional)
Thursday, Day 124—*The Foundation of Great Things*

Friday, Day 125—*I Know Thy Faith*
Saturday, Day 126—*A Little Faith Goes a Long Way*

Day 120: Church Day

James 1:1 *James, a servant of God and of the Lord Jesus Christ, to the twelve tribes which are scattered abroad, greeting.*

2 My brethren, count it all joy when ye fall into divers temptations;

*3 Knowing this, that **the trying of your faith worketh patience.***

Day 121: (Monday)
The Shield of Faith

Ephesians 6:10 *Finally, my brethren, be strong in the Lord, and in the power of his might.*

*11 **Put on the whole armour of God**, that ye may be able to stand against the wiles of the devil.*

12 For we wrestle not against flesh and blood, but against principalities, against powers, against the rulers of the darkness of this world, against spiritual wickedness in high places.

13 Wherefore take unto you the whole armour of God, that ye may be able to withstand in the evil day, and having done all, to stand.

14 Stand therefore, having your loins girt about with truth, and having on the breastplate of righteousness;

15 And your feet shod with the preparation of the gospel of peace;

*16 **Above all, taking the shield of faith**, wherewith ye shall be able to quench all the fiery darts of the wicked.*

17 And take the helmet of salvation, and the sword of the Spirit, which is the word of God:

18 Praying always with all prayer and supplication in the Spirit, and watching thereunto with all perseverance and supplication for all saints;

INTRODUCTORY THOUGHTS

Christians in every age have faced varied battles ranging from small skirmishes to life-ending combat. God's word tells the believer to equip himself as a good soldier of Jesus Christ *(2 Timothy 2:3)* by putting on *"the whole armour of God."* This armour enables those engulfed in the battle to *"stand against the wiles of the devil."* The apostle Paul identifies this armour and the importance of every element. Interestingly, as he refers to *"the shield of faith,"* he suggests taking it *"above all."* Faith, though often overlooked, remains a crucial element within the saint's spiritual arsenal. The Bible drives home this truth by pointing out that the shield of faith can *"quench all the fiery darts of the wicked."* Without faith, the believer stands exposed and vulnerable. It is utterly impossible to *"be strong in the Lord"* apart from a steadfast faith in God and His word. While the sword (the Bible) works on the offense, faith protects and shields.

DEVOTIONAL THOUGHTS

- **(For children):** Jesus quoted Bible back to the Devil when he tried to get Him to do wrong. What Bible verse could you use if the Devil sought to get you to disobey mom or dad? (See **Colossians 3:20.**)
- **(For everyone):** Today's passage likens faith to a shield. In what ways do you think faith works like a shield in the life of a believer? A shield held by a warrior protects him from external and internal injuries. How does the shield of faith protect the believer?
- Can you think of times when you were wounded in spiritual battle? Did your faith at that time tend to strengthen or weaken your resolve? Does that explain why you were wounded?

PRAYER THOUGHTS

- Ask God to build your faith, enabling supernatural protection during battle.
- Ask God to clearly reveal the dangers of the spiritual battle we face.

SONG: *FAITH IS THE VICTORY!*

Day 122: (Tuesday)
The Family of Faith

2 Timothy 1:1 Paul, an apostle of Jesus Christ by the will of God, according to the promise of life which is in Christ Jesus,

2 To Timothy, my dearly beloved son: Grace, mercy, and peace, from God the Father and Christ Jesus our Lord.

3 I thank God, whom I serve from my forefathers with pure conscience, that without ceasing I have remembrance of thee in my prayers night and day;

4 Greatly desiring to see thee, being mindful of thy tears, that I may be filled with joy;

*5 When I call to remembrance the **unfeigned faith** that is in thee, which dwelt first in thy grandmother Lois, and thy mother Eunice; and I am persuaded that in thee also.*

INTRODUCTORY THOUGHTS

An *epistle (**Colossians 4:16**)* is a letter from one person, or a group of people, to another. The epistle of Second Timothy was from Paul to a preacher named Timothy. Timothy was a young man *(**1 Timothy 4:12**)* but possessed a strong love for the Lord. Paul testified of this truth repeatedly and today's passage shows Paul commenting on Timothy's *"unfeigned faith."* There was something refreshingly genuine about Timothy's walk with the Lord. Though Paul was speaking specifically about Timothy's faith, he made mention that this faith did not start with Timothy. This faith had been passed from his grandmother Lois to his mother Eunice, and then on to Timothy. In fact, he was being taught scripture from the time he was a child *(**2 Timothy 3:15**)*. This type of upbringing yielded a young man of *"unfeigned faith"* who further matured into adulthood with spiritual fortitude worthy of emulation.

DEVOTIONAL THOUGHTS

- **(For children):** The most important decision you will ever make revolves around trusting Christ as your Saviour. Ask dad and mom how they learned to believe in God and when they came to trust in Him. The next most important thing you can do is to learn the Bible. Do you think Timothy sat quietly and listened during his family Bible study time?
- **(For everyone):** Do you consider your family a family of faith? Are you taking the time to instill faith in the hearts of your children? Have you made it a matter of priority to teach your children that God can be trusted?
- What role did scripture play in building Timothy's family's faith? Does your family spend the time necessary to help insure that faith will be built in the life of each family member?

PRAYER THOUGHTS

• Ask God to build a hedge of faith around your family.
• Ask God to teach you how to begin building faith in the lives of everyone in your home.

SONG: *GOD, GIVE US CHRISTIAN HOMES*

Day 123: Church Night

1 Thessalonians 5:8 But let us, who are of the day, be sober, **putting on the breastplate of faith** *and love; and for an helmet, the hope of salvation.*

Day 124: (Thursday)
The Foundation of Great Things

2 Peter 1:5 And beside this, giving all diligence, **add to your faith virtue***; and to virtue knowledge;*

6 And to knowledge temperance; and to temperance patience; and to patience godliness;

7 And to godliness brotherly kindness; and to brotherly kindness charity.

8 For if these things be in you, and abound, they make you that ye shall neither be barren nor unfruitful in the knowledge of our Lord Jesus Christ.

INTRODUCTORY THOUGHTS

Every mature Christian knows that physical strength remains incapable of scaling the spiritual heights of the Christian life. Yet, far too many Christians spend enormous efforts in trying to live the Christian life in their own power. Sooner or later, they all experience the sheer futility of such an endeavour. The Christian life is to be lived and developed in the spiritual realm, never the physical one. Spiritual maturity comes as building blocks that are placed one upon another. Interestingly, when a man begins walking in the power of the Spirit, God opens his eyes to each new area of life in need of attention, correction, and growth. Today's passage refers to several of these attributes. Each characteristic builds upon the previous ones; things like virtue, knowledge, temperance, patience, godliness, brotherly kindness, and charity. Every believer ought to strive to exemplify these, yet the Bible identifies one as foundational to them all. According to *2 Peter 1:5*, *faith* remains foundational as the first grace to which believers are to add all others. Those who neglect faith have nothing upon which to build.

DEVOTIONAL THOUGHTS

- **(For children):** When you build with blocks, you have to start with one block on the bottom to hold and support the others. Building your life starts by believing the truth of God's word. As you continue to learn what the Bible says, by building one block on top of the other, you can do what it says to do.
- **(For everyone):** Since faith is foundational to the other spiritual characteristics, how would you say you are doing with your building? Does your foundation need additional attention? Are you trying to work on things like patience without the proper foundation?
- It can be impossible and definitely unwise to build upon a weak foundation. Are you constantly trying to rebuild facets of your crumbling life? Pinpointing the problem might simply be a foundational lack of faith.

PRAYER THOUGHTS

- Ask God to build your faith strong so you can grow in your walk with the Lord.
- Ask God to reveal the strength of your faith on a daily basis.

SONG: *LIVING BY FAITH*

Day 125: (Friday)
I Know Thy Faith

Revelation 2:18 *And unto the angel of the church in Thyatira write; These things saith the Son of God, who hath his eyes like unto a flame of fire, and his feet are like fine brass;*

19 *I know thy works, and charity, and service, and faith, and thy patience, and thy works; and the last to be more than the first.*

INTRODUCTORY THOUGHTS

God knows everything about everything, yet Christians sometimes act as though He has some debilitating limitations. Once again, the Bible shines the light of truth upon the matter. It reveals that He is great, *"and of great power:* **his understanding is infinite"** *(Psalm 147:5).* In fact, His eyes *"are in every place, beholding the evil and the good"* **(Proverbs 15:3).** In other words, there is nothing that escapes the knowledge and attention of God. This includes the good and the bad! The Son of God proclaimed to the church at Thyatira that He knew their *works, charity, service, faith, and patience.* He too knows about the level of a man's faith! He knows the content, strength, and reality of that faith. A man can and will fool others and frequently even deceives himself *(Jeremiah 17:9),* but he has no capacity to mislead God. The Lord knows those who believe and accept His word as the perfect word of God and He is not unrighteous to forget *(Hebrews 6:10).*

DEVOTIONAL THOUGHTS

- **(For children):** *Jeremiah 16:17* says our ways are not hid from God's face. He sees what we are doing even when we think no one else sees us. We need to believe God's word and do right at all times because He sees everything all the time.
- **(For everyone):** One day, all those who are saved will stand at the judgment seat of Christ to give an account of their lives. Perhaps one aspect of this account will address our level of faith toward the words of God. How will you fair under the Almighty's scrutiny?
- Does it bother you to know that God knows your level of faith? Does this realization make you want to increase in faith in order to please Him?

PRAYER THOUGHTS

- Ask God to give you a realistic view of your faith.
- Pray that God will help you to have a real, strong, and lasting faith in Him.

SONG: *O, FOR A FAITH THAT WILL NOT SHRINK*

Day 126: (Saturday)
A Little Faith Goes a Long Way

*Matthew 17:20 And Jesus said unto them, Because of your unbelief: for verily I say unto you, If ye have **faith as a grain of mustard seed**, ye shall say unto this mountain, Remove hence to yonder place; and it shall remove; and nothing shall be impossible unto you.*

INTRODUCTORY THOUGHTS

Our recent studies have revealed the importance of faith within the believer's life along with his walk with the Lord. Yet, this study on faith can be overwhelming considering the emphasis placed upon it by God's word. Fortunately, the Bible also teaches that even the smallest amount of faith produces some of the most remarkable outcomes for the glory of God. Though our passage directly centers on the Lord's dealings through the apostles, the same principle applies to all—a little faith goes a long way. The believer should always ask for increased faith, yet never neglect the faith he now possesses. Daily, the Christian ought to pray in faith, read the Bible in faith, and witness in faith, while incorporating faith into every other aspect of his life and service. Take note that the believer does not benefit from waiting upon greater faith while failing to exercise the faith with which he has already been blessed.

DEVOTIONAL THOUGHTS

- **(For children):** Have you ever planted a tiny seed and watched it grow into a tall plant? God makes it grow. When you give a tract or quote a Bible verse to others, the Bible likens this to planting a tiny seed in their hearts. Through prayer, God makes that seed grow so that the people can choose whether or not they want to hear and know more.
- **(For everyone):** It takes faith to get saved. If you are saved, then you have at least some level of faith. Are you daily allowing that faith to lead you to follow the Lord?
- Are you worried by thoughts that you do not have enough faith? Do you pray and witness, but wonder if your faith was strong enough? Don't forget that a little faith goes a long way and ultimately the outcomes are dependent upon the Lord.

PRAYER THOUGHTS

- Ask God to encourage you to exercise the faith you currently possess.
- Pray and ask God to take the faith that you have and build it up so that you can be more pleasing to Him.

SONG: *I KNOW WHOM I HAVE BELIEVED*

Notes: _____

_____

_____

_____

_____

_____

_____

_____

_____

_____

_____

_____

_____

_____

_____

_____

_____

_____

_____

_____

_____

_____

Notes: _____

_____

_____

_____

_____

_____

_____

_____

_____

_____

_____

_____

_____

_____

_____

_____

_____

_____

_____

_____

Quotes from the next volume

(VOLUME 2, WEEK 18)

Subject: Frugal

A fool watches as his substance departs with no benefits to show for the loss, but a strong man sets aside money and wisely preserves what the Lord has entrusted to him.

19

Forgiveness

Occurrences: found 123 times in 105 verses

Variations: forgave, forgavest, forgive, forgiven, forgiveness, forgivenesses, forgiveth, forgiving

First usage: *Genesis 50:17* (forgive)

Last usage: *1 John 2:12* (forgiven)

Defined: overlook or not impute an offense and treat the offending party as not guilty

Interesting fact: The first instance of forgiveness involves men asking for forgiveness from Joseph, the most prominent type of Christ in the word of God. The last occurrence shows up when John writes about those who have had their sins forgiven in the name of Christ.

Bible study tip: The Bible admonishes believers to study to show themselves *"approved unto God . . . rightly dividing the word of truth" (2 Timothy 2:15)*. The fact that the Bible can be rightly divided infers that it too can be wrongly divided. To avoid this pitfall, consider a few questions when studying the scripture: (1) to whom is the passage addressed? (2) in what time period was the passage written (i.e., before the cross or after the cross)? (3) did the Lord ever change the pattern? Keep in mind that God remains the same, but His dealings with men are at times demonstrably different.

Sunday, Day 127—Church Day (no devotional)
Monday, Day 128—*What Is Forgiveness?*
Tuesday, Day 129—*Who Can Forgive Sins?*
Wednesday, Day 130—Church Night (no devotional)
Thursday, Day 131—*Why Do We Forgive?*
Friday, Day 132—*How Often Should We Forgive?*
Saturday, Day 133—*Forgiveness Breeds Love*

Day 127: Church Day

Daniel 9:9 To the Lord our God belong mercies and forgivenesses, though we have rebelled against him;

Day 128: (Monday)
What Is Forgiveness?

Psalm 32:1 Blessed is he whose transgression is forgiven, whose sin is covered.

2 Blessed is the man unto whom the LORD imputeth not iniquity, and in whose spirit there is no guile.

INTRODUCTORY THOUGHTS

The subject of *forgiveness* would fill volumes yet never exhaust the depths of its meaning. The study for the next two weeks will provide the reader with a deeper understanding and greater appreciation concerning the necessity for forgiveness in the Christian life. We embark on this study by offering a basic meaning for the word *forgiveness*. Three scripture passages reveal the association of forgiveness to *covering (Psalm 32:1; Psalm 85:2; Romans 4:7)*. The first passage further reveals that the covering of *sin* is directly connected to forgiving of *transgression*. The second two verses connect the covering of sin to the forgiving of *iniquity*. With these truths in mind, the act of forgiving someone involves the act of cancelling the penalty for wrongdoing. As the wrongdoing is forgiven, whether it be sin, transgression, or iniquity, the offense is *cov-*

ered as it is forgiven. This covering does not suggest placing a covering over the wrongdoing to hide it, but the act of taking care of its penalty.

DEVOTIONAL THOUGHTS

- **(For children):** Read *Psalm 38:18*. When we are truly sorry for the wrong things that we do and ask God to forgive us, He forgives. He chooses to forget them. We should react the same way toward those who have done us wrong by forgiving them.
- **(For everyone):** What does it mean to you when you really think about the fact that God has forgiven you of your sins? Did you deserve to be forgiven? Meditate on the goodness of God for forgiving you.
- How ready are you to forgive others who have hurt you? Ask the Lord to teach you more about the wonders of His forgiveness and how you can and should forgive others.

PRAYER THOUGHTS

- Ask God to continue working on your heart about forgiving others.
- Take time to thank God for His complete forgiveness through Christ and the continual daily forgiveness.

SONG: *ARISE, MY SOUL, ARISE*

Day 129: (Tuesday)
Who Can Forgive Sins?

Luke 5:20 *And when he saw their faith, he said unto him, Man,* **thy sins are forgiven thee***.*

21 And the scribes and the Pharisees began to reason, saying, Who is this which speaketh blasphemies? **Who can forgive sins, but God alone?**

22 But when Jesus perceived their thoughts, he answering said unto them, What reason ye in your hearts?

23 Whether is easier, to say, **Thy sins be forgiven thee***; or to say, Rise up and walk?*

24 But that ye may know that the Son of man hath **power upon earth to forgive sins***, (he said unto the sick of the palsy,) I say unto thee, Arise, and take up thy couch, and go into thine house.*

25 And immediately he rose up before them, and took up that whereon he lay, and departed to his own house, glorifying God.

26 And they were all amazed, and they glorified God, and were filled with fear, saying, We have seen strange things to day.

INTRODUCTORY THOUGHTS

Everyone should and must learn how and when to forgive others. However, forgiveness has some inherent limitations. True forgiveness **of sins** comes only from Almighty God. People may and should forgive others for things in which they have been wronged, but only God has the capacity to forgive transgressions against Himself and His word. Once an individual has trusted Christ as Saviour, he has been forgiven of all trespasses and the shed blood of Christ serves as the sole basis for that forgiveness *(Ephesians 1:7; Colossians 1:14)*. Though it is important to seek forgiveness from others whom you may have wronged, everyone must still go directly to the Lord to seek the forgiveness for sins. The forgiveness offered by others cancels the conflict amongst and between them; however, the conflict caused by sin between God and man may still remain even after reconciliation has taken place between individuals.

DEVOTIONAL THOUGHTS

- **(For children):** The Bible commands you to honour your father and mother, yet you talk back to them. Not only do you need to tell your parents that you are sorry, but you also need to tell God that you are sorry for disobeying His word.
- **(For everyone):** Do you remember a time in your life when you realized that you were lost and you came to the Lord with a sincere heart asking Him to forgive you of your sins? Failure to seek forgiveness for your sin will lead to an eternity spent in the lake of fire.
- Do you often seek other's forgiveness, but fail to seek the forgiveness from the Lord? Are there things right now that you need to take to the Lord and seek His forgiveness? Do it now!

PRAYER THOUGHTS

- Think about the sins you have committed and ask God to forgive you for each and every one of them.

• Ask the Lord to bring to mind the sins for which you have never sought His forgiveness.

SONG: *GRACE GREATER THAN OUR SIN*

Day 130: Church Night

*1 John 1:9 If we confess our sins, **he is faithful and just to forgive us our sins**, and to cleanse us from all unrighteousness.*

Day 131: (Thursday)
Why Do We Forgive?

*Ephesians 4:32 And be ye kind one to another, tenderhearted, **forgiving one another**, even as God for Christ's sake hath forgiven you.*

INTRODUCTORY THOUGHTS

The study of why men ought to forgive others may seem obvious, but it is actually quite complex without some thorough Bible study. On several occasions, the Lord told His disciples that they needed to forgive in order to be forgiven *(Matthew 6:14-15; Matthew 18:34-35; Mark 11:25-26; Luke 6:37)*. As a result of these statements, many Christians live in fear that they will not receive God's forgiveness unless and until they have forgiven all those who have wronged them. Two things need to be understood contextually: (1) these commandments from the Gospels were given prior to Christ's sacrificial death upon the cross and (2) He was speaking specifically to His Jewish people. Diligent Bible study always involves asking to whom God is speaking in any particular text. Epistles written specifically to and for the church following Christ's sacrifice reveal that those who are saved are already forgiven on the basis of Christ's payment on the cross. Today, men do not forgive to be forgiven; they should forgive others because they have already been forgiven *(Colossians 3:13)*.

DEVOTIONAL THOUGHTS

• **(For children):** A friend worked hard building a house with blocks. You knock it down, feel badly about it, and tell him that you are sorry. He says, "That's OK." A different friend knocks down your blocks and says he's sorry. You get angry and hit him. You should treat people like you want to be treated. God forgives us when we ask.

- **(For everyone):** Have you been forgiven? If so, why do you struggle to forgive others when they wrong you? What would it be like if the Lord held grudges like we do? Are you willing to forgive others as the Lord has forgiven you?
- Do you continually punish others for the wrongs for which you supposedly had forgiven them? Is this the way the Lord works? Does He hold things against you that you have previously asked Him to forgive?

PRAYER THOUGHTS

- Ask God to help you forgive others as you have been forgiven.
- Ask the Lord to soften your heart so that you will be ready and quick to forgive.

SONG: *THE GATE AJAR FOR ME*

Day 132: (Friday)
How Often Should We Forgive?

*Matthew 18:21 Then came Peter to him, and said, Lord, **how oft shall** my brother sin against me, and **I forgive him?** till seven times?*

22 Jesus saith unto him, I say not unto thee, Until seven times: but, Until seventy times seven.

INTRODUCTORY THOUGHTS

The Lord is gracious and merciful and ready to forgive, but how ready to forgive should Christians be? Simon Peter pondered this question as He asked the Lord about it. The Bible records the Lord's response to Peter for all future generations to consider. Peter wanted specifics; what are to be the limitations of one's forgiveness? Like many of us, He wanted boundaries and limitations. He specifically wanted to know how many times he needed to forgive those who had wronged him. The Lord answered Peter's inquiry by saying that he shouldn't just forgive seven times (the amount Peter asked about), but seventy times seven. Some of those reading the Lord's response have concluded incorrectly that the Lord was simply placing a much higher limitation upon one's willingness to forgive others. Yet, the Lord intended to convey something without limitation. Men ought to forgive those who have wronged them every time an offender comes in true repentance (meaning he is sorry for what he has done) *(Luke 17:3-4)*.

DEVOTIONAL THOUGHTS

- **(For children):** Your friend tears a page in your favorite book, breaks some crayons, and breaks one of your toys. Each time, he says he is truly sorry and will try to be more careful with your things. Will you let him play with your toys again? God wants you to give your friend another chance because he is more important than your things.
- **(For everyone):** Do you have a point at which you stop forgiving others? Does it become increasingly difficult to forgive others when they wrong you? Do you think the Lord struggles to forgive you for repeatedly failing Him on a second, third, or fourth offense?
- The people closest to you generally wrong you the most. Do you struggle to forgive your family and closest friends? Has bitterness taken the place of forgiveness? If so, you need to repent and get this right with God.

PRAYER THOUGHTS

- Ask God to give you a forgiving heart toward others.
- Ask God to help you give others the same chances that God has given to you when you wrong Him.

SONG: *O TO BE LIKE THEE!*

Day 133: (Saturday)
Forgiveness Breeds Love

Luke 7:36 And one of the Pharisees desired him that he would eat with him. And he went into the Pharisee's house, and sat down to meat.

37 And, behold, a woman in the city, which was a sinner, when she knew that Jesus sat at meat in the Pharisee's house, brought an alabaster box of ointment,

38 *And stood at his feet behind him weeping, and began to wash his feet with tears, and did wipe them with the hairs of her head, and kissed his feet, and anointed them with the ointment.*

39 *Now when the Pharisee which had bidden him saw it, he spake within himself, saying, This man, if he were a prophet, would have known who and what manner of woman this is that toucheth him: for she is a sinner.*

40 *And Jesus answering said unto him, Simon, I have somewhat to say unto thee. And he saith, Master, say on.*

41 *There was a certain creditor which had two debtors: the one owed five hundred pence, and the other fifty.*

42 *And when they had nothing to pay, **he frankly forgave them both.** Tell me therefore, **which of them will love him most?***

43 *Simon answered and said, **I suppose that he, to whom he forgave most.** And he said unto him, Thou hast rightly judged.*

44 *And he turned to the woman, and said unto Simon, Seest thou this woman? I entered into thine house, thou gavest me no water for my feet: but she hath washed my feet with tears, and wiped them with the hairs of her head.*

45 *Thou gavest me no kiss: but this woman since the time I came in hath not ceased to kiss my feet.*

46 *My head with oil thou didst not anoint: but this woman hath anointed my feet with ointment.*

47 *Wherefore I say unto thee, **Her sins, which are many, are forgiven; for she loved much: but to whom little is forgiven, the same loveth little.***

48 *And he said unto her, Thy sins are forgiven.*

INTRODUCTORY THOUGHTS

Luke chapter seven records the story of Christ eating at the house of a Pharisee named Simon. A woman, who knew Jesus was visiting Simon, entered into the house with a box of ointment and a determination to outwardly shower the Lord with her love for Him. She anointed His feet and wiped them with the hairs of her head, all the while weeping. This event greatly troubled Simon because of the woman's unsavoury past. Christ knew Simon's inward thoughts questioning how the Lord could allow this *sinner* to make such a fuss over Him. Did He not know her sordid reputation? Christ used this opportunity to teach some important truths concerning forgiveness by putting Simon to a test. Christ questioned this Pharisee about who would love most: a person forgiven of little or one forgiven of much. The answer was obvious to Simon—a person forgiven of much possessed a natural capacity to love more than one who had been forgiven for less. In other words, those who have been forgiven the most by the Lord often display a greater, more fervent love toward the Lord than those who have been forgiven to a lesser degree.

DEVOTIONAL THOUGHTS

- **(For children):** We often fail God by talking back, whining, throwing fits, and failing to immediately obey when told to do something. Yet, our parents still love us and want us to be their children. Because God is God, He loves us more than even our parents. We should be very thankful for Him.
- **(For everyone):** Have you been forgiven of much by the Lord? Do you find that you love Him more when you think of the sins for which He has forgiven you? Does His forgiveness toward you help you to forgive others?
- Why do you fail to forgive others? Is it their fault, or is it a lack of love on your part? Whom do you need to forgive right now? If you put it off again, you may never do it! Do it now even if it means a special trip or call.

PRAYER THOUGHTS

- Ask God to remind you of your life before you met Christ.
- Ask the Lord to give you a heart to rejoice when others are forgiven.

SONG: *THERE IS A FOUNTAIN FILLED WITH BLOOD*

Notes: _____

_____

_____

_____

_____

_____

Notes: _____

_____

_____

_____

_____

_____

_____

_____

_____

_____

_____

_____

_____

Quotes from the next volume

(VOLUME 2, WEEK 19)

Subject: Giving

God does not need anything from man yet finds great pleasure in receiving gifts from those whom He loves.

Giving by faith requires giving God the firstfruits of one's increase.

Giving to God's work is not a magical formula guaranteeing personal enrichment. In fact, a Christian who sacrificially gives to the Lord may lose his job. He may give to the Lord only to incur some major unexpected expense. Yet, the Christian can be sure that he will never give to the Lord without receiving a resultant blessing from God.

20

Forgiveness (con't)

Occurrences: found fifty-four times in the Old Testament and sixty-nine times in the New Testament

First usage in the New Testament: *Matthew 6:12* (forgive)

Last usage in the Old Testament: *Amos 7:2* (forgive)

Interesting fact: The believer's forgiveness is never based upon his own worthiness but granted unto the believer for *"Christ's sake" (Ephesians 4:32).*

Bible study tip: The Bible often defines terms by restating a thought but incorporating a new word or phrase in the restatement. Pay close attention to the context of a verse or phrase, especially immediately following the subject verse. Often, God's word clearly defines a word or concept by restating the same concept using alternate terminology. For example, *Genesis 11:30* defines barren: *"But Sarai was barren; she had no child."*

Friday, Day 139—*Ye Ought Rather to Forgive*
Saturday, Day 140—*Forgive Me This Wrong*

Day 134: Church Day

Ephesians 1:7 *In whom we have redemption through his blood, **the forgiveness of sins**, according to the riches of his grace;*

Day 135: (Monday)
A Foundation for Forgiveness

Psalm 78:31 *The wrath of God came upon them, and slew the fattest of them, and smote down the chosen men of Israel.*

32 For all this they sinned still, and believed not for his wondrous works.

33 Therefore their days did he consume in vanity, and their years in trouble.

34 When he slew them, then they sought him: and they returned and inquired early after God.

35 And they remembered that God was their rock, and the high God their redeemer.

36 Nevertheless they did flatter him with their mouth, and they lied unto him with their tongues.

37 For their heart was not right with him, neither were they stedfast in his covenant.

*38 But **he, being full of compassion, forgave their iniquity**, and destroyed them not: yea, many a time turned he his anger away, and did not stir up all his wrath.*

39 For he remembered that they were but flesh; a wind that passeth away, and cometh not again.

INTRODUCTORY THOUGHTS

Psalm 78 provides remarkable insights into God's dealings with His people, the nation of Israel. His interactions with them differ considerably from His dealings with the Church today. Regardless, the individual's natural man has remained unchanged for 6,000 years now. The Old Testament records many examples of men rebelling against God in spite of God's goodness. Following God's corrective hand, men sometimes exhibit faithfulness. Yet all too often, this faithfulness is short-lived as the individual returns to the folly that will again require God's corrective actions. Regardless, man seems to repeat the never ending cycle of folly and forgiveness. Knowing this makes one wonder why God continues to forgive. His forgiveness originates from His innate compassion for His creation. God's word says that the Lord forgives because He is *full of compassion (Psalm 78:38)*. In other words, the Lord forgives man because He *suffers with* man as man continues his cycle of inconsistent living. Praise God for His compassionate forgiveness.

DEVOTIONAL THOUGHTS

- **(For children)**: A younger child grabs a toy away from you just because he wants to play with it. How do you feel toward him? Have you ever done something like that to others? We should forgive one another and not remain angry with anyone.
- **(For everyone)**: Are you slow to forgive others for sins for which you also seek forgiveness? How would learning how to be more compassionate compel you to be more forgiving toward others?
- How does the first coming of Christ aid in the Father's forgiveness? How could we better associate with others so that we may forgive them when they wrong us?

PRAYER THOUGHTS

- Take time to thank God for His compassion toward you.
- Ask God to give you a genuine compassion toward others.

SONG: *THE KING OF LOVE MY SHEPHERD IS*

Day 136: (Tuesday)
Be Ready to Forgive

Psalm 86:1 *Bow down thine ear, O LORD, hear me: for I am poor and needy.*

2 Preserve my soul; for I am holy: O thou my God, save thy servant that trusteth in thee.

3 Be merciful unto me, O Lord: for I cry unto thee daily.

4 Rejoice the soul of thy servant: for unto thee, O Lord, do I lift up my soul.

*5 For thou, Lord, art good, and **ready to forgive**; and plenteous in mercy unto all them that call upon thee.*

INTRODUCTORY THOUGHTS

This psalm, like many of the others, records a prayer of David. David expressed how he desperately wanted God's attention and ear. He begins by boldly proclaiming God's preserving power and mercy and then pleading for a restoration of the joy he once had but had now lost. This psalm clearly reveals David's single hope—the fact that the Lord remains *"ready to forgive."* When a believer approaches God confessing his sins, he finds an ear ready to hear his petitions and pleas. Man needs only come and seek the forgiveness with a sincere heart because God remains ready and waiting to grant that forgiveness. The Lord stands watching for His people to come to Him in true repentance (similar to the father of the wandering son in Luke chapter 15).

DEVOTIONAL THOUGHTS

- **(For children):** Mom sees you break one of her favorite dishes. In her heart, she still loves you even before you tell her that you are sorry. God is that way with us. We should be that way with others.
- **(For everyone):** If we are to be like our Father, it stands to reason we ought to be seeking for opportunities to forgive others even before they approach us seeking our forgiveness. Do you have a desire to offer forgiveness toward those who have offended you?
- The Lord's readiness to forgive goes along with His swiftness to forget. Do you claim to be ready to forgive, yet hold on to the memories and bitterness toward those who have wronged you?

PRAYER THOUGHTS

- Ask God to give you a heart that is ready and willing to forgive others.
- Ask the Lord to help you forgive others before they even ask.

SONG: *LEAD ME TO CALVARY*

Day 137: Church Night

Psalm 25:18 *Look upon mine affliction and my pain; and **forgive all my sins**.*

Day 138: (Thursday)
The Blessing of Forgiveness

Romans 4:6 Even as David also describeth the blessedness of the man, unto whom God imputeth righteousness without works,

*7 Saying, **Blessed are they whose iniquities are forgiven**, and whose sins are covered.*

8 Blessed is the man to whom the Lord will not impute sin.

INTRODUCTORY THOUGHTS

The Christian life is a life of continual blessings, though it also contains many experiences in life's difficulties. The believer is blessed by God's provisions in the past and offered hope through God's promised future provisions. *Psalm 68:19* proclaims that the Lord *"daily loadeth us with benefits."* These benefits include both spiritual and physical blessings of salvation, answered prayers, good health, and family. However, David specifically described the blessedness of a man imputed righteousness apart from his works. Our passage records his words as he proclaimed, *"Blessed are they whose iniquities are forgiven."* Though forgiven of past, present, and future sin, man's capacity for sinning remains unabated within his natural body. Every faithful Bible student knows never to minimize forgiveness of one's sin as one of the greatest blessings of all!

DEVOTIONAL THOUGHTS

- **(For children):** Name some things that dad and mom do for you on a daily basis. We disappoint them when we don't act right and refuse to do what we're told. Yet, no matter our failings, they keep on doing wonderful things for us. God is good to us even though we don't deserve it.
- **(For everyone):** Imagine owing someone a large debt. What if that person came to you and told you the debt was forgiven. How would you react to such news? How have you received the news that your sins have been forgiven?
- How often do you thank God for the *benefits* that He loads upon you? Are you truly grateful for His provision of forgiveness? Do you know the blessings of having your sins forgiven?

PRAYER THOUGHTS

- Ask God to remind you of His goodness in forgiving your debt of sin.
- Ask the Lord to help you to be grateful for His benefits.

SONG: *SAVED BY THE BLOOD (HENDERSON)*

Day 139: (Friday)
Ye Ought Rather to Forgive

2 Corinthians 2:5 But if any have caused grief, he hath not grieved me, but in part: that I may not overcharge you all.

6 Sufficient to such a man is this punishment, which was inflicted of many.

7 So that contrariwise ye **ought** *rather to forgive him,* **and comfort him,** *lest perhaps such a one should be swallowed up with overmuch sorrow.*

8 Wherefore I beseech you that ye would confirm your love toward him.

INTRODUCTORY THOUGHTS

The two epistles addressed to the Corinthian church clearly highlight many of the problems associated with the carnal church of Corinth. Today's passage specifically deals with the restoration of those who had fallen into sin. All church discipline, though frequently neglected, should initially focus on the restoration of the individual rather than his simple condemnation. In fact, *Galatians 6:1* instructs spiritual believers to consider themselves by restoring *"such an one in the spirit of meekness."* Unfortunately, people oftentimes seem to glory in the judgment aspect of discipline while diminishing or completely neglecting the joys involved with the restoration of the individual into fellowship. Careful attention to the wording of *2 Corinthians 2:7* reveals two important aspects of this church discipline: believers *"ought"* to forgive; and additionally believers ought *"rather"* to forgive. Unlike those who are quick to condemn, the Bible emphasizes forgiveness **rather** than the punishment aspects of discipline.

DEVOTIONAL THOUGHTS

- **(For children):** A playmate is taking your crayons and breaking them by not holding them right while he colors. Instead of getting angry, would you be willing to show him the proper way to hold and use the crayons?
- **(For everyone):** Do you find joy in carrying around bitterness toward others? Do you hold onto grudges even after you have been asked to forgive? What joys do you miss by not offering forgiveness to those who have wronged you?
- How do you deal with those who have done you wrong? Do you avoid them even after they seek your forgiveness? Do you let them know of your desire to restore them? Do you allow them to be restored when they have sought restoration?

PRAYER THOUGHTS

- Ask the Lord to show you the joy of truly forgiving others.
- Ask God to help you restore in the spirit of meekness those who have fallen.

SONG: *FOOTPRINTS OF JESUS*

Day 140: (Saturday)
Forgive Me This Wrong

2 Corinthians 12:11 I am become a fool in glorying; ye have compelled me: for I ought to have been commended of you: for in nothing am I behind the very chiefest apostles, though I be nothing.

12 Truly the signs of an apostle were wrought among you in all patience, in signs, and wonders, and mighty deeds.

13 For what is it wherein ye were inferior to other churches, except it be that I myself was not burdensome to you? forgive me this wrong.

INTRODUCTORY THOUGHTS

The church of God at Corinth offered the apostle Paul some type of support which he refused to receive from them. The Bible does not tell us whether Paul's actions toward this church were appropriate. However, we do know that Paul admitted the possibility that he could have been wrong and asked for their forgiveness in the matter. We are not informed exactly why he asked for their forgiveness, but the Bible simply states that he might have wronged these believers. Paul wrote more books of the Bible than anyone else and was not *"behind the very chiefest apostles" (2 Corinthians 12:11)*. Yet, he did not use his vaunted position or noted authority to avoid responsibility for his actions. Instead, he sought forgiveness from these carnal Corinthians. Believers today should likewise follow the apostle Paul's example of seeking forgiveness from those whom they have wronged or even those possibly wronged. Who is right or wrong lacks relevance when it comes to one's relationship with fellow believers no matter the position or station in life!

DEVOTIONAL THOUGHTS

- **(For children)**: When we treat someone wrong, mom or dad usually makes us tell that person that we're sorry. The Lord would like for us to learn to say we're sorry without having to be told to do so.
- **(For everyone)**: Are you full of pride? Do you struggle to apologize to those you have wronged? Do you need to apologize to your spouse, your children, your friends, or someone else? Seek their forgiveness and seek it now!
- Have you ruined relationships in the past because of your pride? Humble yourself and seek the forgiveness of those you have wronged.

PRAYER THOUGHTS

- Ask God to bring to mind those you may have wronged.
- Ask God to humble you to seek their forgiveness.

SONG: *DID YOU THINK TO PRAY?*

Notes: _____

_____

Quotes from the next volume

(VOLUME 2, WEEK 20)

Subject: Giving (con't)

Giving must be purposeful and does not happen by accident. Before giving to the Lord, the Christian must first purpose in his heart to willingly give.

21

Friendship

Occurrences: found 107 times in ninety-nine verses

Variations: friend, friendly, friends, friendship

First usage: *Genesis 26:26* (friends)

Last usage: *3 John 14* (friends)

Defined: mutual attachment and care shared between two or more individuals

Interesting fact: The Bible uses the word *friend* as a designation associated to a best man at a wedding *(Judges 14:20; John 3:29)*.

Bible study tip: Pay close attention to the minutia. That which seems at first insignificant could prove to be the very key to opening your understanding of a truth. Write out all the things that seem to be of interest concerning your study. If the point proves crucial, you may have discovered another factor involved in diligent Bible study. Always keep in mind the fact that you are studying the very words of God!

Sunday, Day 141—Church Day (no devotional)
Monday, Day 142—*A Friend That Sticketh Closer*
Tuesday, Day 143—*A Friend Loveth at All Times*

Wednesday, Day 144—Church Night (no devotional)
Thursday, Day 145—*Shew Yourself Friendly*
Friday, Day 146—*Getting Friends the Wrong Way*
Saturday, Day 147—*Two Are Better Than One*

Day 141: Church Day

***Proverbs 27:10** Thine own friend, and thy father's friend, forsake **not**; neither go into thy brother's house in the day of thy calamity: for better is a neighbour that is near than a brother far off.*

Day 142: (Monday)
A Friend That Sticketh Closer

Proverbs 18:24** A man that hath friends must shew himself friendly: and **there is a friend that sticketh closer than a brother.

INTRODUCTORY THOUGHTS

Some people seem unable to function without daily interaction with friends. Yet, others think such attachments overbearing and far too demanding. Unfortunately, the world frequently misconstrues what constitutes true friendship. Additionally, far too many times, friends abuse this important relationship. Social media sites even refer to one's mere acquaintances as *"friends."* No wonder the world remains so confused concerning the essence of true biblical friendship. Regardless of one's perspective on these matters, the Bible points out that there is One friend that man cannot do without and He is *"a friend that sticketh closer than a brother" (**Proverbs 18:24**).* This could simply refer to people who have friends more loyal than those in one's own family, but likely references the Lord. His level of commitment causes Him to be a friend to those deemed unlovable by the world. Simply consider what the Bible says about His sacrifice. Christ died on the cross for His *enemies (**Romans 5:10**)* so that they could become His *friends (**John 15:13-15**).* Truly, He is that *"friend that sticketh closer than a brother."*

DEVOTIONAL THOUGHTS

- **(For children):** Name some of your closest friends. God loves you more than they do. Jesus died on the cross for us even though He knew we would be disobedient. Our friends would not and could not have done that for us.

- **(For everyone):** What comes to mind when you think of the Lord's faithfulness as a friend to mankind? Can you name some of His traits as a friend that He exemplifies best?
- There is no other friend like the Lord Jesus. He stays by your side regardless of your faithfulness to Him. Have you thanked Him today for being such a friend to you? Have you rejoiced in the blessings of knowing Him personally?

PRAYER THOUGHTS

- Ask God to show you ways in which He has been a friend to you.
- Thank the Lord for being a faithful friend.

SONG: *NO, NOT ONE!*

Day 143: (Tuesday)
A Friend Loveth at All Times

Proverbs 17:17 A friend loveth at all times, and a brother is born for adversity.

INTRODUCTORY THOUGHTS

Unfortunately, true lasting friendships seem increasingly difficult to cultivate and nurture in today's fast paced world. Yet, the interactions associated to true friendships remain important and healthy. There are many traits that define true friendships. Today's passage points out one of the primary features that constitute a true friend: *"A friend loveth at all times."* This love is not to be confused with being dishonest in hopes of protecting the feelings of a friend. In fact, a true friend will offer a needed rebuke. This is why the Bible says, *"faithful are the wounds of a friend" (Proverbs 27:6).* True friends never allow current circumstances to determine the level of commitment to a relationship. A true friend will remain faithful when all others have betrayed or departed. This test of friendship has been the proving ground for many friends throughout the history of mankind. One need look no further than the prodigal son for evidence of such *(Luke 15:11-24).*

DEVOTIONAL THOUGHTS

- **(For children):** Imagine that you are playing with a puzzle and another child wants to help finish it with you. You say, *"No, it's mine!"* Your teacher tells you to be kind and share. That teacher is acting like a true friend. She cares enough about you to show you the way the Lord would want you to play.
- **(For everyone):** Do you know a friend that *"loveth at all times"*? Is there someone in your life that loves you unconditionally? If you are saved, the Lord is that kind of friend to you.
- While thinking on friendship, examine the friendship you offer to others. Are you the kind of friend that loves at all times? Do you love others enough to offer a faithful rebuke when it is necessary? Are you a true friend?

PRAYER THOUGHTS

- Ask the Lord to give you some true friends in this life.
- Ask God to help you to be the kind of friend He would want you to be.

SONG: *I'VE FOUND A FRIEND*

Day 144: Church Night

Psalm 119:63 I am a companion of all them that fear thee, and of them that keep thy precepts.

Day 145: (Thursday)
Shew Yourself Friendly

Proverbs 18:24 A man that hath friends must shew himself friendly: and there is a friend that sticketh closer than a brother.

INTRODUCTORY THOUGHTS

Very few people understand the simplicity involved in cultivating true friendships. In fact, far too many people emphasize the wrong factors when considering how to make friends. They look at one's appearance or charisma and attribute it as the key to making friends. Yet, the Bible points out a simple process as the key for gaining true friends. The one who makes friends simply must first *"shew himself friendly."* Unapproachable people remain lonely and tend to miss out on much of what life has to offer. Those who struggle making friends should examine themselves to see whether or not they truly display themselves as friendly or more standoffish. People generally refuse to put forth the extra effort to get to know those who come across unwelcoming. People want to make friends with those who are approachable and there is no better way to make yourself approachable than to show yourself friendly. If a man does not appear to be friendly, others will pass him in their quest to cultivate lasting relationships.

DEVOTIONAL THOUGHTS

- **(For children):** If you see someone with whom you would like to be friends, you may have to be the first one to say, *"Hello"*; to extend your hand for a handshake; to sit by him or her in church or Sunday School. Don't wait for that person to come to you. Be the first to be friendly!
- **(For everyone):** Do you generally try to make friends with people who seem unfriendly? Do you think others feel the same way about making friends? Are there some people you would like to get to know better? Have you presented yourself friendly toward them?
- Are you easy to get along with? Do you treat others nicely? Are you kind and considerate in their presence? Do you make yourself available as a friend?

PRAYER THOUGHTS

- Ask God to show you the way in which you conduct yourself with others.
- Ask the Lord to help you to be friendly to those who need a friend.

SONG: *GOD BE WITH YOU TILL WE MEET AGAIN*

Day 146: (Friday)
Getting Friends the Wrong Way

Proverbs 19:4 Wealth maketh many friends; but the poor is separated from his neighbour.

*Proverbs 19:6 Many will intreat the favour of the prince: and **every man is a friend to him that giveth gifts.***

INTRODUCTORY THOUGHTS

Many people have so-called friends, but oftentimes these friendships are built upon weak support structures. Yet, testing the true depths of one's friendships can be quite challenging. The previous lesson pointed to the ease of making friends by showing yourself friendly. Yet, too many people focus on using material means to gain friendships. Money can buy friends but there remains that doubt concerning the true foundation of those relationships. The Bible teaches that *"wealth maketh many friends" (Proverbs 19:4)*. This truth is further emphasized in *Proverbs 14:20* where the Bible says, *"the rich hath many friends."* This fact remains ever more prevalent as the days go on. Those who are rich will have many *"friends,"* while those who are poor have far fewer close associations. Unfortunately, *"Every man is a friend to him that giveth gifts" (Proverbs 19:6)*. As long as there is money or gifts to be given, people will have *"friends";* but as soon as the money runs out, the *"friends"* will be gone too. True friendships, however, may be gained by showing yourself friendly and will be cultivated through righteousness.

DEVOTIONAL THOUGHTS

- **(For children):** You want to play with some children, but they don't want you to play with them. You leave and come back with some candy. They decide to let you play if you will share your candy. These children are not acting as your true friends.
- **(For everyone):** Take a moment and think about those you call friends. Why are they your friends? What made them like you in the first place? Would they still be your friends if you did not have any money or nice things to give them?
- Why are you friends with the people with whom you are friends? Do they feel obligated to buy things in order to keep your friendship? If so, this is an unrighteous relationship and one that rarely lasts.

PRAYER THOUGHTS

- Ask the Lord to help you examine the nature of your friendships.
- Ask God to give you godly friends and show you how to be a godly friend toward others.

SONG: *HAVE COURAGE TO SAY NO!*

Day 147: (Saturday)
Two Are Better Than One

Ecclesiastes 4:7 Then I returned, and I saw vanity under the sun.

*8 **There is one alone**, and there is not a second; yea, he hath neither child nor brother: yet is there no end of all his labour; neither is his eye satisfied with riches; neither saith he, For whom do I labour, and bereave my soul of good? This is also vanity, yea, it is a sore travail.*

*9 **Two are better than one**; because they have a good reward for their labour.*

*10 **For if they fall, the one will lift up his fellow**: but woe to him that is alone when he falleth; for he hath not another to help him up.*

INTRODUCTORY THOUGHTS

Life presents many troubles that at times make it difficult to stand strong in the Christian walk. Standing alone makes it seem nigh impossible. Perhaps this is why God created friendships. The most precious times amongst spiritually-minded friends often take place when one of them finds himself in need. Far too many Christians stumble and fall spiritually because they have no one offering support and encouragement. True Christian friends are a help when those troublesome times arise. A true Christian friend encourages and strengthens his friend before he hits his lowest point and contemplates quitting. The heartbeat of *Ecclesiastes 4:7-10* reveals that it is hard to serve the Lord alone. Yet serving Him with Christian friends provides extra strength in times of weakness and despair. A friend may be there to lift his brother up one day only to find the act of kindness reciprocated on another occasion.

DEVOTIONAL THOUGHTS

- **(For children):** You want to hand someone a tract or speak to someone new at church, but you are afraid to do so. Your friend says, *"I'll go with you and help."* Friends can help us do what the Lord wants us to do.
- **(For everyone):** What kind of friends do you have? Are they friends that help you in your service for God? Would they help you get back on your feet if you fell during your Christian walk?
- Are you the kind of friend that godly Christians would seek out for a relationship? Are you the kind of person that encourages others who

have fallen to rise back to their feet and go forward in their service with the Lord?

PRAYER THOUGHTS

- Ask God for friends who have a strong desire to serve Him.
- Ask the Lord to help you to be a godly friend to others.

SONG: *BLEST BE THE TIE THAT BINDS*

Notes: _____

_____

_____

_____

_____

_____

_____

Quotes from the next volume

(VOLUME 2, WEEK 21)

Subject: Hate

God hates! For those enamored by the teachers who strictly emphasize the love of God, this fact may be difficult to appreciate. Yet, it is both true and scriptural. In fact, the truth becomes even more peculiar when considering that God's hatred is founded within His love.

The truths of God's word naturally divide believers from those in the world.

God will look even more favourably upon His children as the world refuses, rejects, and abuses them. Though disdained by the heathen and mocked of men for the Lord's sake, God will never allow those forsaken by the world to be isolated from His blessings.

22

Friendship (con't)

Occurrences: the various forms appear twice as many times in the Old Testament than in the New Testament

First usage in the New Testament: *Matthew 11:19* (friend)

Last usage in the Old Testament: *Zechariah 13:6* (friends)

Interesting fact: The last reference to *friend* in the Old Testament *(Zechariah 13:6)* is a prophecy concerning the crucifixion of Christ in the house of His friends. The first reference to *friend* in the New Testament *(Matthew 11:19)* suggests that the publicans and sinners were accounted as Christ's *friends*.

Bible study tip: Be careful never to simply assume that the modern usage of a word defines the word's usage in the Bible. Its scriptural usage can differ considerably. Modern dictionary definitions are often derived from how the words are most commonly used at the time of the dictionary's publication. The English language has been on a continual decline for approximately four centuries.

Sunday, Day 148—Church Day (no devotional)
Monday, Day 149—*A Friend to the Afflicted*
Tuesday, Day 150—*If Thy Friend Entice Thee*

Wednesday, Day 151—Church Night (no devotional)
Thursday, Day 152—*The Friendship of Pilate and Herod*
Friday, Day 153—*Go Tell Thy Friends*
Saturday, Day 154—*The Friend of God*

Day 148: Church Day

Proverbs 27:17 Iron sharpeneth iron; so **a man sharpeneth the countenance of his friend.**

Day 149: (Monday)
A Friend to the Afflicted

Job 6:14 To him that is afflicted pity should be shewed from his friend; *but he forsaketh the fear of the Almighty.*

INTRODUCTORY THOUGHTS

Few men, if any, have been afflicted like Job. His troubles involved the catastrophic loss of family members as well as physical ailments beyond most people's ability to endure. During the depths of these difficult trials, Job's three *"friends" (Job 2:11)* visited him. They showed up to comfort him but instead turned out to be additional sources of grief. Each word spoken by his friends seemed to compound his already miserable condition and circumstances. Job did not consider this to be the work of a friend and told them that, *"To him that is afflicted pity should be shewed from his friend."* Later in the same chapter, Job said that his friends dug a pit for him *(Job 6:27)*. Job's friends should have shown him pity during his troublesome times instead of scorning *(Job 16:20)* and abhorring him *(Job 19:19)*. True friends know how to comfort and console their friends as they experience trouble and pain in life. They certainly do not unrighteously judge and condemn.

DEVOTIONAL THOUGHTS

- **(For children):** This Sunday, look around your Sunday School class. Who is missing? Were they sick? Did their family have car trouble, etc? Will you let them know you missed them and are praying that they can make it the next Sunday?
- **(For everyone):** Do your friends ever suffer through tough times? What do you do when they go through such times? Do you show

them any sympathy or do you rebuke them without even knowing why such things are taking place?

- As Christian friends, there are times when a rebuke is necessary. Yet, there are other times when our friends need an understanding ear and shoulder. Are you balanced in this area?

PRAYER THOUGHTS

- Ask God to help you find a godly balance with your friends.
- Ask the Lord to help you learn how to be both comforting and supportive of your friends.

SONG: *IS THY CRUSE OF COMFORT WASTING?*

Day 150: (Tuesday)
If Thy Friend Entice Thee

Deuteronomy 13:6 *If thy brother, the son of thy mother, or thy son, or thy daughter, or the wife of thy bosom, or thy **friend**, which is as thine own soul, **entice thee secretly, saying, Let us go and serve other gods**, which thou hast not known, thou, nor thy fathers;*

7 Namely, of the gods of the people which are round about you, nigh unto thee, or far off from thee, from the one end of the earth even unto the other end of the earth;

8 Thou shalt not consent unto him, nor hearken unto him; neither shall thine eye pity him, neither shalt thou spare, neither shalt thou conceal him:

9 But thou shalt surely kill him; thine hand shall be first upon him to put him to death, and afterwards the hand of all the people.

*10 And **thou shalt stone him with stones, that he die; because he hath sought to thrust thee away from the LORD thy God**, which brought thee out of the land of Egypt, from the house of bondage.*

INTRODUCTORY THOUGHTS

Good friends are a tremendous blessing to be nurtured and treasured. Yet, friendships are to have certain God-ordained limitations. The wrong kinds of friends and inappropriate associations have led many people away from the truth and astray from God. The Bible provides detailed instructions to help people avoid any relationship that tends to lead to rebellion against God. Although these instructions were explicitly given while Israel remained under the Law of God, they forever reveal God's feelings toward those who would lead someone away from Him. Just as it was instructed of the Israelites, men today should never consent nor hearken to those who seek to lure them astray *(Deuteronomy 13:8)*. In refusing to listen to those individuals, a believer should never feel guilt or pity the so-called friend, but rather find joy from making the right decision.

DEVOTIONAL THOUGHTS

- **(For children):** A friend asks you to go to the mountains for a picnic on Sunday morning with him and his family. God wants us to set aside that day to go to church to praise Him and learn of Him. What will you choose? A true friend will want you to obey God first.
- **(For everyone):** How do you choose your friends? What kind of traits do you look for in a friend? Do you merely look for common interests, or are there other things for which you look?
- What should you do if a friend asked you to do something that you know would displease the Lord? Should you continue to spend time around this person?

PRAYER THOUGHTS

- Ask God for wisdom and discernment when choosing friends.
- Ask the Lord to give you friends who sincerely love Him.

SONG: *CLOSE TO THEE*

Day 151: Church Night

Philippians 1:3 *I thank my God upon every remembrance of you,*

4 Always in every prayer of mine for you all making request with joy,

*5 For **your fellowship in the gospel** from the first day until now;*

Day 152: (Thursday)
The Friendship of Pilate and Herod

Luke 23:12 *And the same day **Pilate and Herod were made friends together:** for before they were at enmity between themselves.*

INTRODUCTORY THOUGHTS

Friendships generally develop around some type of common ground or linked association. These activities can be either good or bad, righteous or wicked. Pilate and Herod are prime examples of the wrong kind of relationship nurtured through a sinful association. Before they joined forces against the Son of God, they *"were at enmity between themselves."* The word *enmity* reveals that they not only were not friends, but actually disdained each other to the point of being enemies. Nothing could repair this breach until they joined together in the trial of the Saviour. Standing together against Jesus Christ repaired this relationship and created an unholy association. On that day, they found common ground by uniting together in mockery of the Son of God. The Bible speaks of a future time when, *"The kings of the earth set themselves, and the rulers take counsel together, against the LORD" (Psalm 2:2).* Earthly kings rarely get along unless they find a common interest or benefit. Far too often, these rulers find themselves in an unholy alliance rather than a holy one.

DEVOTIONAL THOUGHTS

- **(For children):** Are there some boys and girls you don't like? Why don't you like them? What makes you like those you call your friends? The best answer you can give is that you love God and so do they.
- **(For everyone):** What common ground do you have with your friends? What draws you to them and them to you? Do they have a love for the Saviour? If not, what does this say for you?
- Do your friends aid you in your service to God, or do they tempt you to go astray? Do they appreciate you for your love for the Lord Jesus? Do you appreciate their faithfulness to the Lord?

PRAYER THOUGHTS

- Ask the Lord to open your eyes to the true spiritual nature of your friendships.
- Ask God about each friendship and whether or not He approves.

SONG: *HAVE COURAGE TO SAY NO!*

Day 153: (Friday)
Go Tell Thy Friends

Mark 5:15 And they come to Jesus, and see him that was possessed with the devil, and had the legion, sitting, and clothed, and in his right mind: and they were afraid.

16 And they that saw it told them how it befell to him that was possessed with the devil, and also concerning the swine.

17 And they began to pray him to depart out of their coasts.

18 And when he was come into the ship, he that had been possessed with the devil prayed him that he might be with him.

19 Howbeit Jesus suffered him not, but saith unto him, **Go home to thy friends, and tell them** *how great things the Lord hath done for thee, and hath had compassion on thee.*

20 And he departed, and began to publish in Decapolis how great things Jesus had done for him: and all men did marvel.

Introductory Thoughts

The Lord healed many people during His earthly ministry. Today's passage speaks of a particular man who had been delivered from devil possession. What a relief he must have experienced! However, the people in his community did not rejoice that the Lord had performed such a wonderful miracle. In fact, they turned against the Saviour and wanted Him to depart from their coasts. The Lord complied with their demands; however, the man delivered of the devils wanted to travel with the Lord. He loved the Lord so much that he wanted to stay close to Him. However, as the healed man sought to enter the ship, Christ told him to return to his home and tell his friends what had happened to him. The Lord knew that this man was in the best position to reach out to his friends with the truth. He knew this man's testimony concerning the truth was what they needed to hear and believe. Christians should always be prepared and ready for times when opportunities arise to tell their friends about the truth. Acts chapter 10 records another example when Cornelius called his friends together expecting to hear Simon Peter preach the truth of the gospel. Real friends insure that their friends are put into a position to hear the truth and never squander spiritual opportunities.

DEVOTIONAL THOUGHTS

- **(For children):** Do your closest friends go to church and love the Lord? If they don't, ask mom and dad if you can invite them. Give them some gospel tracts, quote them a Bible verse that you know well, or tell them your favorite Bible story. A true friend tells his friends about the Lord.
- **(For everyone):** Nobody can reach your friends like you can. Do you have any friends that do not know the Lord as personal Saviour? Have you taken the time to tell them about their need to be saved?
- Have you invited your friends to come to church? Have you told them about the great things the Lord has done for you and is doing in your life? Have you encouraged them to read their Bible, pray, and attend church?

PRAYER THOUGHTS

- Ask the Lord to give you boldness to tell a friend about Jesus.
- Ask the Lord to give you a burden for the salvation of your unsaved friends.

SONG: *RESCUE THE PERISHING*

Day 154: (Saturday)
The Friend of God

John 15:12 This is my commandment, That ye love one another, as I have loved you.

*13 **Greater love hath no man than this, that a man lay down his life for his friends.***

*14 **Ye are my friends, if ye do whatsoever I command you.***

*15 Henceforth I call you not servants; for the servant knoweth not what his lord doeth: but **I have called you friends**; for all things that I have heard of my Father I have made known unto you.*

16 Ye have not chosen me, but I have chosen you, and ordained you, that ye should go and bring forth fruit, and that your fruit should remain: that whatsoever ye shall ask of the Father in my name, he may give it you.

17 These things I command you, that ye love one another.

INTRODUCTORY THOUGHTS

Even since the Garden in Eden, God never intended for man to consider Him to be distant or unapproachable. In fact, the Bible repeatedly points out the opposite scenario. God's word proclaims that the Lord did not merely claim His followers as servants, but referred to them as His friends! He specifically referred to Abraham as the *"friend of God" (2 Chronicles 20:7; James 2:23)*. He spoke to Moses *"face to face, as a man speaketh unto his friend" (Exodus 33:11)*. These are not the actions of a God who desires separation from His creation. Though this intimate association with God seems remote and only expressed on a few occasions, John points out that we too can be God's friends (if we obey Him). This friendship must be based on mutual grounds because those who love the Lord are never lovers of the world. *James 4:4* points out that *"friendship of the world is enmity with God."* Though it appears that few people were called the friend of God, John chapter 15 suggests that this honour is much more prevalent than would appear. Christ told His followers, *"Ye are my friends, if ye do whatsoever I command you" (John 15:14)*. Furthermore, Christ laid down His life for His friends *(John 15:13)*.

DEVOTIONAL THOUGHTS

- **(For children):** Do you like to play with those who are mean or those who are nice, those who disobey or those who follow the rules? God says we can be His friend by doing what the Bible says. It's exciting to know that the Creator of the universe who simply spoke the world into existence wants to be friends with us.
- **(For everyone):** Being called a friend of God remains one of the highest honours God conveys upon His creation. Can you honestly say that you are a friend of God?
- You cannot serve two masters. You cannot simultaneously be a friend of God and a friend of the world. Whom do you want to claim as your friend? God? or the world?

PRAYER THOUGHTS

- Ask God to give you a desire to walk with Him like never before.
- Thank the Lord for the opportunity to be called His friend.

SONG: *JESUS! WHAT A FRIEND FOR SINNERS*

23

Kindness

Occurrences: found sixty-two times in fifty-seven verses

Variations: kind (verb), kindly, kindness

First usage: *Genesis 20:13* (kindness)

Last usage: *2 Peter 1:7* (kindness)

Defined: disposed to do good to others and contribute to the happiness of others; having tenderness or goodness of nature; benevolent

Interesting fact: Only four of the forty-five instances of the word *kind* refer to the act of being kind as opposed to the other uses of the term. For instance, *Genesis 1:11* talks about the tree yielding fruit after his kind (of the same family or sort). This application sheds light on our present study by showing that *kindness* manifests itself when we treat other as though they are family.

Bible study tip: The Bible is not like any other book and its study must be reverential. It can never be approached with a critical eye. God has always blessed those who believe and obey what they read by giving them additional light on scriptural truths.

Sunday, Day 155—Church Day (no devotional)
Monday, Day 156—*Brotherly Kindness*
Tuesday, Day 157—*The Kindness and Love of God Appeared*
Wednesday, Day 158—Church Night (no devotional)
Thursday, Day 159—*The Kindness of David*
Friday, Day 160—*Smitten in Kindness*
Saturday, Day 161—*A Desire Is Kindness*

Day 155: Church Day

Psalm 117:2 For **his merciful kindness is great toward us**: and the truth of the LORD endureth for ever. Praise ye the LORD.

Day 156: (Monday)
Brotherly Kindness

2 Peter 1:5 And beside this, giving all diligence, add to your faith virtue; and to virtue knowledge;

6 And to knowledge temperance; and to temperance patience; and to patience godliness;

7 And to godliness **brotherly kindness;** and to brotherly kindness charity.

8 For if these things be in you, and abound, they make you that ye shall neither be barren nor unfruitful in the knowledge of our Lord Jesus Christ.

INTRODUCTORY THOUGHTS

God's choice of the word *kindness* reveals a compound word clearly defined within scripture. When studying a compound word, it helps to first consider the root word definition. *Kindness* contains the root word *kind*. A cursory look might reveal this study as quite simplistic, but a good Bible student exposes the spiritual depths of any particular truth. He first considers other uses of the word *kind* and then examines the words containing the same root word. For example, the Bible refers to something reproducing *"after his kind."* The context of this phrase reveals that it refers to those belonging to the same family. Likewise, the compound word *kindred* incorporates the same root word *kind* and means to be within the same family. This truth is further confirmed by our subject passage referring to *"brotherly kindness" (2 Peter 1:7)*. These truths indicate that a man demonstrates kindness as he treats other people as though they are a treasured part of his own family.

DEVOTIONAL THOUGHTS

- **(For children):** Your mom, dad, sisters, brothers, grandparents, aunts, uncles, and cousins are all members of your family. Because you love them very much, you treat them in a special way. God wants you to treat other people just as though they were members of your family.
- **(For everyone):** If kindness is treating people like family (though they are not family), can you think of anyone who has treated you with kindness?
- Name a few specific instances where the Lord showed a special kindness toward you. What are some ways in which kindness could be showed to others?

PRAYER THOUGHTS

- As we study kindness, ask the Lord to give you a willing heart.
- Ask the Lord to help you exemplify true biblical kindness toward others.

SONG: *BELOVED, NOW ARE WE*

Day 157: (Tuesday)
The Kindness and Love of God Appeared

Titus 3:3 For we ourselves also were sometimes foolish, disobedient, deceived, serving divers lusts and pleasures, living in malice and envy, hateful, and hating one another.

*4 But after that **the kindness and love of God** our Saviour toward man **appeared**,*

5 Not by works of righteousness which we have done, but according to his mercy he saved us, by the washing of regeneration, and renewing of the Holy Ghost;

6 Which he shed on us abundantly through Jesus Christ our Saviour;

7 That being justified by his grace, we should be made heirs according to the hope of eternal life.

INTRODUCTORY THOUGHTS

Our previous study revealed that kindness refers to treating someone as a cherished member of the family. The Bible proclaims that God is great in *kindness (Nehemiah 9:17)*. It also reveals that kindness is marvellous *(Psalm 31:21)* and full of mercy *(Psalm 117:2)*. Believers should be thrilled to know that God demonstrates this kindness toward His beloved creation. By nature, men are the children of wrath *(Ephesians 2:3)*. Yet, each person has the opportunity to be treated like a beloved member of God's family as a result of Christ's sacrifice on the cross *(Titus 3:4)*. Those who have trusted Christ as Saviour have been granted the inestimable privilege of being *"heirs"* of God *(Titus 3:7)* and *"joint-heirs"* with Christ *(Romans 8:17)*. This blessing, generally intended for and limited to family, is extended to those whom God counts as family.

DEVOTIONAL THOUGHTS

- **(For children):** Have you ever lied or disobeyed your mom or dad? That is sin and God cannot allow anyone with unforgiven sin to enter into heaven. Yet, He wants us to be with Him there. He sent His Son to die on the cross for our sins. Isn't God kind to us?
- **(For everyone):** Meditate on the kindness of God for a moment. What does it mean to you? What are some benefits of His kindness?
- Have you done anything to merit the kindness of God? Did He see something in you that caused His kindness to fall upon you? How did you receive the Lord's kindness?

PRAYER THOUGHTS

- Take time to thank the Lord for His kindness toward you.
- Ask the Lord to help you see His kindness on a daily basis.

SONG: *THE LOVE OF GOD*

Day 158: Church Night

Psalm 31:21 Blessed be the LORD: for he hath shewed me his marvellous kindness in a strong city.

Day 159: (Thursday)
The Kindness of David

2 Samuel 9:1 *And David said, Is there yet any that is left of the house of Saul,* ***that I may shew him kindness*** *for Jonathan's sake?*

2 *And there was of the house of Saul a servant whose name was Ziba. And when they had called him unto David, the king said unto him, Art thou Ziba? And he said, Thy servant is he.*

3 *And the king said, Is there not yet any of the house of Saul,* ***that I may shew the kindness of God unto him****? And Ziba said unto the king, Jonathan hath yet a son, which is lame on his feet.*

4 *And the king said unto him, Where is he? And Ziba said unto the king, Behold, he is in the house of Machir, the son of Ammiel, in Lodebar.*

5 *Then king David sent, and fetched him out of the house of Machir, the son of Ammiel, from Lodebar.*

6 *Now when Mephibosheth, the son of Jonathan, the son of Saul, was come unto David, he fell on his face, and did reverence. And David said, Mephibosheth. And he answered, Behold thy servant!*

7 *And David said unto him, Fear not: for* ***I will surely shew thee kindness for Jonathan thy father's sake, and will restore thee all the land of Saul thy father; and thou shalt eat bread at my table continually.***

8 *And he bowed himself, and said, What is thy servant, that thou shouldest look upon such a dead dog as I am?*

9 *Then the king called to Ziba, Saul's servant, and said unto him, I have given unto thy master's son all that pertained to Saul and to all his house.*

10 *Thou therefore, and thy sons, and thy servants, shall till the land for him, and thou shalt bring in the fruits, that thy master's son may have food to eat: but* ***Mephibosheth thy master's son shall eat bread alway at my table.*** *Now Ziba had fifteen sons and twenty servants.*

11 *Then said Ziba unto the king, According to all that my lord the king hath commanded his servant, so shall thy servant do. As for* ***Mephibosheth, said the king, he shall eat at my table, as one of the king's sons.***

12 *And Mephibosheth had a young son, whose name was Micha. And all that dwelt in the house of Ziba were servants unto Mephibosheth.*

13 *So* **Mephibosheth dwelt in Jerusalem: for he did eat continually at the king's table**; *and was lame on both his feet.*

INTRODUCTORY THOUGHTS

The Bible records Jonathan and David's strikingly close friendship like that of siblings. Regardless of this cherished relationship, Jonathan's father, king Saul, feared and despised David. Both king Saul and his son died during battle, thus paving the way for David to ascend to the throne of Israel. Once David became king, he sought for an opportunity to show *kindness* to any of Jonathan's remaining family members. After searching through the land, it was discovered that Saul and Jonathan had one remaining descendent (Mephibosheth). David sent for Mephibosheth and told him his intentions of showing him the *kindness* normally reserved for a member of the king's family. This act of kindness included the restoration of his family's property. David's kindness also made provision for Mephibosheth to eat at the king's table *(2 Samuel 9:7)*, *"as one of the king's sons" (2 Samuel 9:11)*. David's kindness meant that Mephibosheth would be viewed and treated as a son. This demonstration of kindness illustrates God's act of kindness toward His beloved children through Christ Jesus.

DEVOTIONAL THOUGHTS

- **(For children):** The Bible tells us that God is kind to everyone. He gives them sunshine and rain and many other good things. We should be like God and be kind toward others.
- **(For everyone):** If Saul had done right as the king, it is possible that Mephibosheth as his grandson could have sat on the throne. Instead, he was lame (crippled) and likely poor and without a throne. What do you think that the kindness of David meant to him?
- This study again displayed the connection between kindness and family. How did David's kindness show that he was willing to treat Mephibosheth as family?

PRAYER THOUGHTS

- Ask the Lord to put some people in your life to whom you can show kindness.

• Ask the Lord to teach you how to show kindness toward others.

SONG: *JESUS LOVES EVEN ME*

Day 160: (Friday)
Smitten in Kindness

Psalm 141:5 Let the righteous smite me; it shall be a kindness: and let him reprove me; it shall be an excellent oil, which shall not break my head: for yet my prayer also shall be in their calamities.

INTRODUCTORY THOUGHTS

Far too many of today's pundits sanction giving others whatever they want in an attempt to display true love. Parents have become increasingly trapped in this dilemma being convinced that they fail their children unless they give them every new gadget. The husbands thought to love the most are the ones who shower their wives with the most, the best, and do so frequently. The average person may find these scenarios reasonable, but they remain completely contrary to the word of God. In fact, the Bible expresses just the opposite. Today's passage reveals that a righteous man could actually smite someone with his words in *kindness*. A righteous man will always offer a rebuke (or correction) to those heading in the wrong direction. The intention of such a rebuke is to set the person back on the right track; true biblical kindness at work. Proverbs extols the virtues of those wounds gained when offered in the spirit of kindness and friendship *(Proverbs 27:6)*. Kindness is never demonstrated by simply telling others what they want to hear but often confirmed through *open rebuke (Proverbs 27:5)*.

DEVOTIONAL THOUGHTS

• **(For children):** Do you like to be sick? Ask Mom why she doesn't let you eat all the cookies and candy that you want. Do you like to get hurt? Ask Dad why he doesn't let you help with certain power tools. They say "no" because they love you.
• **(For everyone):** Do you have people in your life who love you enough to let you know when you are wrong? Do you listen, or do you try to ignore them and push them away?
• Do you enjoy being corrected by others? Do you understand the blessings found in being rebuked by those who love and care for you? Have

you ever considered that a rebuke offered in love is a manifestation of kindness?

PRAYER THOUGHTS

- Ask the Lord to give you people who care enough to tell you the truth when you are wrong.
- Ask God to give you a receptive heart towards righteous rebukes.

SONG: *AFFLICTIONS DO NOT COME ALONE*

Day 161: (Saturday)
A Desire Is Kindness

Proverbs 19:22 The desire of a man is his kindness: and a poor man is better than a liar.

INTRODUCTORY THOUGHTS

Most sincere people, seeking opportunities to show kindness toward others, will generally have more opportunities than means. In fact, some instances will arise when helping others remains practically impossible. This is especially true when a financial need arises beyond the person's capacity to help. Does this mean kindness does not exist or that the individual lacks genuineness? No! Today's passage teaches a profound principle, *"the desire of a man is his kindness."* Kindness is exemplified where there is a present desire to be kind toward others even though the individual may be without means to fulfil his desire to help. The passage ends by stating that *"a poor man is better than a liar."* A man who desires to help but cannot do so is better than those who lie or deceive others about their true heart's intent to show kindness. Thankfully, God does not simply look at the outward act but can always see the heart's true desire, purpose, and motive!

DEVOTIONAL THOUGHTS

- **(For children):** A dog chews your friend's ball and ruins it. You wish you could get him another ball but can't because you don't have any money. God knows your thoughts of kindness. He is pleased that you wanted to help even though you were unable.
- **(For everyone):** Do you have a genuine desire to show the kindness of God to others? Do you pretend to care when you really do not?

- Kindness is obviously a matter of the heart. Have you showed kindness to anyone lately? If not, why not? Is it possible that your heart has become hardened because of sin?

PRAYER THOUGHTS

- Ask God for a genuine desire to show kindness toward others.
- Ask the Lord to give you a burden to pray and help others as opportunities arise.

SONG: *IS YOUR ALL ON THE ALTAR?*

Notes: _____

_____

_____

_____

_____

_____

_____

_____

_____

_____

_____

_____

_____

_____

_____

_____

_____

_____

_____

Notes: _____

_____

_____

_____

_____

_____

_____

_____

_____

_____

_____

_____

_____

_____

_____

_____

_____

Quotes from the next volume

(VOLUME 2, WEEK 23)

Subject: Jesting

Laughter seems much more enjoyable than sorrow, yet life's lessons are learned much faster from sorrow than they are from amusement.

God is gracious, merciful, and longsuffering. The Lord will never laugh at the difficulties of any to whom He has not first offered refuge and deliverance.

24

Kindness (con't)

Occurrences: found fifty-one times in the Old Testament and eleven times in the New Testament

First usage in the New Testament: *Luke 6:35* (kind)

Last usage in the Old Testament: *Jonah 4:2* (kindness)

Interesting fact: Just as David looked for an opportunity to show kindness to Mephibosheth for Jonathan's sake *(2 Samuel 9:1, 3, 7)*, God the Father demonstrates kindness toward us for Christ's sake *(Ephesians 4:32)*.

Bible study tip: The Bible points to the Holy Ghost as the Christian's ultimate teacher *(John 14:26; 1 Corinthians 2:13)*. He teaches by comparing spiritual things with spiritual. The greatest way to study the Bible involves comparing the Bible with itself: verses with verses and words with words.

Sunday, Day 162—Church Day (no devotional)
Monday, Day 163—*Even Barbarians Can Show Kindness*
Tuesday, Day 164—*Be Kindly Affectioned*
Wednesday, Day 165—Church Night (no devotional)
Thursday, Day 166—*The Law of Kindness*
Friday, Day 167—*Charity Is Kind*
Saturday, Day 168—*His Kindness Toward Us*

Day 162: Church Day

Colossians 3:12 *Put on therefore, as the elect of God, holy and beloved, **bowels of** mercies, **kindness**, humbleness of mind, meekness, longsuffering;*

13 Forbearing one another, and forgiving one another, if any man have a quarrel against any: even as Christ forgave you, so also do ye.

Day 163: (Monday)
Even Barbarians Can Show Kindness

Acts 28:1 *And when they were escaped, then they knew that the island was called Melita.*

*2 And **the barbarous people shewed us no little kindness**: for they kindled a fire, and received us every one, because of the present rain, and because of the cold.*

Introductory Thoughts

Today's passage picks up the narrative as the apostle Paul had just escaped a ship wreck near an island called Melita. The shipwreck and the weather made for some grim conditions. It was cold and rainy and the island contained what the Bible termed as a barbarous people. For most, this frightful scenario would seem hopeless. Yet, "something" or Someone had placed a desire within the hearts of this barbarous people to show kindness toward Paul and those with him. When these strangers showed up on the island, the natives kindled a fire and wholeheartedly welcomed them. The apostle Luke (the penman of Acts) emphasized that the people showed *"no little kindness,"* suggesting that the kindness manifested was considerable. Think about it! These people, ignorant of the Lord and His word, showed kindness to strangers; surely, God's people could do as much.

Devotional Thoughts

- **(For children):** There are many children who don't know God and don't go to church. Yet, they are good to their family and friends. Even though they don't know God, God put that *"want to"* within their hearts to treat others right. If children who don't know God can do that, what do you think God expects of us?

- **(For everyone):** Who do you think put the desire to show kindness within the hearts of these barbarians? Even without God, these people could understand the concept of helping others in need. Why do you suppose Christians fail to consistently show kindness to others?
- Why should we show more kindness than a group of barbarians showed to some strangers? How does this reflect upon our level of commitment if we exhibit less kindness than those who do not know the Lord?

PRAYER THOUGHTS

- Ask the Lord to show you the needs of others.
- Ask God to give you the desire that was in the barbarians to treat even strangers with kindness.

SONG: *MORE LIKE THE MASTER*

Day 164: (Tuesday)
Be Kindly Affectioned

Romans 12:10 Be kindly affectioned one to another with brotherly love; in honour preferring one another;

INTRODUCTORY THOUGHTS

Our previous studies revealed that the word *kind* is connected to a term suggesting family relationships. Therefore, today's passage associating *kindly* with *brotherly love* makes perfect sense. The book of Romans instructs believers to be *"kindly affectioned one to another."* By being kindly affectioned, believers will naturally exhibit *"brotherly love"* toward each other. The Bible reveals God as the Christian's Father. This relationship indicates that each believer is related as a part of the same family, the family of God. How should family members treat other family members? The context of today's passage reveals that believers should prefer others before themselves *(Romans 12:10)*, distribute to the necessities of other saints *(Romans 12:13)*, and give themselves to hospitality *(Romans 12:13)*. In other words, believers should treat other believers as members of one's family. As many Christians soon find out, the relationships enjoyed between fellow believers will frequently be closer than those enjoyed with blood relatives.

Devotional Thoughts

- **(For children):** Ask dad or mom to read **Galatians 6:10** to you and explain what it means. Jesus commanded His disciples to love one another **(John 13:34)**. Are you treating your church friends right?
- **(For everyone):** Whom do you generally put first: yourself or others? When you fail to put others first, why do you think you fail? Whom should you prefer? What should you do if you are wrong in this matter?
- Do you find it difficult to help others financially? Is it because you are unwilling or unable? Do you enjoy helping others grow spiritually? If not, why?

Prayer Thoughts

- Ask the Lord to give you affection for the people of God.
- Ask God to soften your heart to the needs of others.

SONG: *BRETHREN, WE HAVE MET TO WORSHIP*

Day 165: Church Night

*Joel 2:13 And rend your heart, and not your garments, and turn unto the LORD your God: **for he is** gracious and merciful, slow to anger, and **of great kindness**, and repenteth him of the evil.*

Day 166: (Thursday)
The Law of Kindness

Proverbs 31:26 *She openeth her mouth with wisdom; and **in her tongue is the law of kindness**.*

Introductory Thoughts

Proverbs 31 reveals the attributes of a *virtuous woman (Proverbs 31:10)*. Though a virtuous woman possesses many wonderful traits, perhaps her greatest strength lies in the manner in which she speaks—with wisdom. This God-given wisdom enables her to refrain her lips from foolishness, instead choosing to edify others with her speech. Many people offer others advice and even wisdom, but this woman is said to speak with the *"law of kindness"* in her tongue. Not only does she speak wisely, but she presents this wisdom with the right spirit--the spirit of kindness.

Apparently, when she speaks wisely, her words encourage others to listen and heed what she says. Her hearers want to receive her words and put them into practice. Why? Because she presents her words with this *"law of kindness"* much like those today who are *"speaking the truth in love" (Ephesians 4:15)*.

DEVOTIONAL THOUGHTS

- **(For children):** Sing the songs *"Oh, Be Careful Little Mouth What You Say"* and *"Keep Thy Tongue from Evil."* God wants the words we speak to others to be kind and helpful and never intentionally hurtful.
- **(For everyone):** Do you offer words of wisdom to those who lend you their ears? Do they generally receive what you have to say when you speak to them? If not, is it possible that you do not speak with *the law of kindness*?
- How do you speak to others? Do you tell them the truth? Do you speak the truth in love *(Ephesians 4:15)*? Would your words be better received if you changed your presentation?

PRAYER THOUGHTS

- Ask God to put the law of kindness in your tongue.
- Ask Him to help you speak the truth in love.

SONG: *TAKE MY LIFE, AND LET IT BE*

Day 167: (Friday)
Charity Is Kind

1 Corinthians 13:4 Charity suffereth long, and is kind; charity envieth not; charity vaunteth not itself, is not puffed up,

5 Doth not behave itself unseemly, seeketh not her own, is not easily provoked, thinketh no evil;

6 Rejoiceth not in iniquity, but rejoiceth in the truth;

7 Beareth all things, believeth all things, hopeth all things, endureth all things.

INTRODUCTORY THOUGHTS

Charity is certainly love, but not merely what we would consider a standard type of love and certainly not like today's usage or definition.

Charity is a deeper, fuller, and stronger type of love. In fact, charity remains at the peak of Christianity *(1 Corinthians 13:13; 2 Peter 1:7)* and is to be sought above all else *(Colossians 3:14).* With this in mind, a man would be wise to study the subject of charity in the Bible. After careful consideration, if he finds himself not behaving charitably, he should adjust his actions. The Bible also says that charity suffers long and envies not *(1 Corinthians 13:4).* It rejoices not in iniquity, but in truth *(1 Corinthians 13:6).* Additionally, charity is *kind (1 Corinthians 13:4).* This shows that those behaving charitably treat others like members of their family. Those displaying charity will care for others in the good times as well as the bad. They will rejoice when there is truth, but never in iniquity.

DEVOTIONAL THOUGHTS

- **(For children):** God wants you to have a special love for others and consider that what you do or say may affect them negatively or hurt them greatly. Do you brag to others when you get a new toy? Are you happy for others when they get something new and you don't? Do you share?
- **(For everyone):** Do you have charity? Do you suffer long with others? Do you envy those who get nice things? Do you rejoice when they do right by the Lord?
- Charity is called the bond of perfectness *(Colossians 3:14)* and considered to be the greatest virtue during this age. How important is it to you to have charity? If it is not important to you, why not?

PRAYER THOUGHTS

- Ask God to help you to grow in your walk with Him so that you will learn to be more charitable toward others.
- Pray for a desire to show kindness toward others no matter the circumstances.

SONG: *GOD BE WITH YOU TILL WE MEET AGAIN*

Day 168: (Saturday)
His Kindness Toward Us

Ephesians 2:4 But God, who is rich in mercy, for his great love wherewith he loved us,

5 *Even when we were dead in sins, hath quickened us together with Christ, (by grace ye are saved;)*

6 *And hath raised us up together, and made us sit together in heavenly places in Christ Jesus:*

7 *That in the ages to come he might shew the exceeding riches of his grace in **his kindness toward us** through Christ Jesus.*

INTRODUCTORY THOUGHTS

According to the Bible, before a man trusts Christ as Saviour, he remains the enemy of God *(Romans 5:10; Colossians 1:21).* But God, in His great mercy, saves His enemies as they individually choose to trust in Christ's payment for their sins. Though a Christian has the indwelling Spirit, he never fully comprehends all that the Lord has done for him through salvation. This is why the Bible says that God's love passes all knowledge *(Ephesians 3:19).* However, the more a man draws nigh to God, the more he learns about the kindness God has shown him through Jesus Christ. No matter how much we learn in this life, eternity will continue to reveal to the saints the depths of the kindness of God. No wonder the greatness and marvelous nature of His love is truly beyond comprehension.

DEVOTIONAL THOUGHTS

- **(For children):** Name your favorite food, toy, shoes, etc. These things actually came as blessings from God. Ask your parents to explain how *"Every good gift and every perfect gift is from above" (James 1:17).* Take a moment and contemplate God's kindness.
- **(For everyone):** How long would it take for others to figure out the depth of your kindness toward them? How complex is your kindness? Are you even kind to others?
- Have you considered the kindness of God to us through the death of His Son? What are some things about your salvation that display God's kindness toward you?

PRAYER THOUGHTS

- Ask the Lord to show you different ways in which He has been kind to you through His Son.
- Take time to thank the Lord for what He has done for you.

SONG: *HERE IS LOVE*

Notes: _____

_____

_____

_____

_____

_____

_____

_____

_____

_____

_____

_____

_____

Quotes from the next volume

(VOLUME 2, WEEK 24)

Subject: Judging

Carnal Christians and those who do not know the Lord consider judging others as the greatest of sins. The opposite actually holds true. Believers fail by not judging "righteous judgment."

The Bible is a perfect Book containing perfect laws. Therefore, all judgment should be based upon infallible standards provided by God within His glorious word.

Christians should devote their time to comparing themselves against the precepts of God's word to help correct their shortcomings. In doing so, the time of judgment at His judgment seat would lose much of its dread.

25

Truthfulness

Occurrences: *Truth* is found 318 times. Interestingly, *lies* (in various forms) is found 230 times, and *false* (and its variations) appears another ninety-nine times.

Variations: true, truth

First usage: *Genesis 24:27* (truth)

Last usage: *Revelation 22:6* (true)

Defined: conforming to fact or reality; veracity; purity from falsehood

Interesting fact: The first and last mention of truth (in the forms of truth and true) both testify to God's truth *(Genesis 24:27; Revelation 22:6)*.

Bible study tip: Though Bible study certainly involves the intellect, by far, the student's greatest benefits or most disturbing hindrances result from one's spiritual closeness to the Lord. In fact, the Bible points out that the Lord chooses to hide *"things from the wise and prudent,"* while revealing *"them unto babes" (Matthew 11:25)*. In other words, man's education does not in itself make God's truths more accessible.

Sunday, Day 169—Church Day (no devotional)
Monday, Day 170—*No Lie Is of the Truth*
Tuesday, Day 171—*What God Cannot Do*
Wednesday, Day 172—Church Night (no devotional)
Thursday, Day 173—*The Father of Lies*
Friday, Day 174—*Liars by Nature*
Saturday, Day 175—*They Bend Their Tongue for Lies*

Day 169: Church Day

Proverbs 12:22 Lying lips are abomination to the LORD: but they that deal truly are his delight.

Day 170: (Monday)
No Lie Is of the Truth

*1 John 2:21 I have not written unto you because ye know not the truth, but because ye know it, and that **no lie is of the truth.***

INTRODUCTORY THOUGHTS

People love comparing themselves to those whom they deem less righteous or unspiritual. By finding someone living on a spiritually lower level, any wrong doing can seem quite justified in one's own eyes. Another way to get by with certain character flaws is by distinguishing between what men call big and little sins. As long as someone refuses to commit the big sins, he considers himself decent, upright, and sometimes spiritually superior. One of the most prevalent areas is that of telling lies. Those who err in this area equate some lies as "white lies" (lies deemed less harmful than the big ones). Yet, the Bible doesn't make any such distinction. According to the Bible, truth and lies are at opposite ends of the spectrum. *"No lie is of the truth"* *(1 John 2:21)*. Truth tainted by error or falsehood ceases to be truth. Regardless of how simple a lie may appear, no lie has as its source pure truth. If truth was the basis for a statement, then it would remain truth.

DEVOTIONAL THOUGHTS

- **(For children):** You and a friend draw on the wall with crayons. When asked about it, you say that your friend did it. Is that completely true?

Who always knows the truth even when you don't tell the truth? God says, *"Lie not one to another" (Colossians 3:9a).*

- **(For everyone):** If something is 99.9 percent true, is it really true? How much falsehood is necessary to make truth cease from being the truth?
- What is the origin of all truth? What is the origin of all lies? How much of your life (words, actions, entertainment, etc.) is founded upon truth?

PRAYER THOUGHTS
- Ask the Lord to show you the importance of truth.
- Ask the Lord to help you recognize the lies existing within your life.

SONG: *WE HAVE AN ANCHOR*

Day 171: (Tuesday)
What God Cannot Do

Titus 1:1 Paul, a servant of God, and an apostle of Jesus Christ, according to the faith of God's elect, and the acknowledging of the truth which is after godliness;

*2 In hope of eternal life, which **God, that cannot lie**, promised before the world began;*

INTRODUCTORY THOUGHTS

The Bible describes God as a God of truth. He will not lie *(1 Samuel 15:29)* and cannot lie *(Titus 1:2)*. This attribute of truth is designated to each person of the Trinity or the Godhead. Truth is declared as an attribute of God the Father in *Titus 1:1-2*, of God the Son in *John 14:6*, and of God the Spirit in *John 16:13*. Even the very words of God are ascribed this attribute in *John 17:17* where the Bible says, *"Sanctify them through thy truth: thy word is truth."* Thank God that He is truth and so is His word. A lie to the least extent within the words of God or in God's very nature would incriminate God's expressed deity. Lying is contrary to the nature of God. The scripture says that it is *"impossible"* for God to lie *(Hebrews 6:18)*. Impossible! It would be a different world if men would simply live more like Christ.

DEVOTIONAL THOUGHTS

- **(For children):** God's word is true from the beginning *(Psalm 119:160)*. Whatever God tells us is always right, and whatever He says *"shall come to pass" (Ezekiel 12:25)*. We can always believe Him and believe in Him. Read and take good care of your Bible.
- **(For everyone):** Do you know for sure that you are going to heaven when you die? How do you know for sure? How did you find out what to do in order to go to heaven? How would all of this change if God were not a God of truth?
- How important is it to you to know that God is a God of truth? What are some of the ways that you rely on the truthfulness of God? What things in your life depend upon God's truthfulness?

PRAYER THOUGHTS

- Thank God for His faithfulness in being truthful.
- Ask God to show you how important truthfulness is in your life.

SONG: *GREAT IS THY FAITHFULNESS*

Day 172: Church Night

Proverbs 21:6 *The getting of treasures by a **lying tongue** is a vanity tossed to and fro of them that seek death.*

Day 173: (Thursday)
The Father of Lies

John 8:44 *Ye are of your father the devil, and the lusts of your father ye will do. He was a murderer from the beginning, and abode not in the truth, because there is no truth in him. **When he speaketh a lie, he speaketh of his own: for he is a liar, and the father of it.***

INTRODUCTORY THOUGHTS

The Devil was created perfect in every aspect *(Ezekiel 28:15)* with complete capacity to do right. Yet, he was also created with a free will to choose whether to do right or to do wrong. Sometime in the distant past, he chose to abide *"not in the truth."* This conscious decision to depart from the truth caused him to become the *"father"* of lies. In one form or another, every lie traces back to the work of the Devil. As the enemy of God, Satan wants to deceive God's creation into believing a lie so that rejecting the truth and remaining condemned in darkness *(2 Corinthians 4:4)* seems like the natural thing to do. Satan incorporates every deceptive means at his disposal. One of his main tactics is to convince people that there are many ways to heaven (good works, baptism, church membership, etc.) and many ways to know the truth (feelings, science, circumstances, etc.). Yet, the Bible emphatically proves that God is truth and His word is truth and only through God and His word are we assured of learning and knowing truth.

DEVOTIONAL THOUGHTS

- **(For children):** The Devil is not our friend. He lied to Eve about God's word in *Genesis 3:4*. He wanted Eve to believe him and she believed his lie. Ask mom or dad how this affected Adam and Eve and how it also affects everyone born, including you.
- **(For everyone):** What are some lies you have been led to believe in your lifetime? Where did those lies originate? How can these lies be traced back to the Devil?
- Why does God speak the truth? Why does the Devil speak lies? What motives lie behind the telling of lies? What does this teach us about the difference between the Lord and the Devil?

PRAYER THOUGHTS

- Ask God to protect you from the lies of Satan.
- Ask God to give you a burden for those who have been blinded by the Devil's lies.

SONG: *A MIGHTY FORTRESS IS OUR GOD*

Day 174: (Friday)
Liars by Nature

Psalm 58:1 Do ye indeed speak righteousness, O congregation? do ye judge uprightly, O ye sons of men?

2 Yea, in heart ye work wickedness; ye weigh the violence of your hands in the earth.

3 The wicked are estranged from the womb: **they go astray as soon as they be born, speaking lies.**

INTRODUCTORY THOUGHTS

The Bible plainly teaches that men are, by nature, prone to sinning. As soon as children learn to speak, they purposefully begin to spout out lies. In fact, children do not have to be taught how to lie, but must be taught the importance of telling the truth. Sometimes the lies come naturally as a means of self-preservation, protecting themselves from judgment or punishment for wrongdoing. Every parent remembers occasions when something went wrong at home and as they tried to determine the guilty party, no child would admit to knowing of any wrongdoing. King David understood this truth. He said, *"the wicked are estranged from the womb."* He went on to say, *"they go astray as soon as they be born, speaking lies."* Unfortunately, the most natural thing a man might ever do is to lie. Lying may be natural but truth telling and honesty are thoroughly refreshing and demanded of God. Lying is a habit that must be stopped early in life or immediately after one's new birth into the family of God.

DEVOTIONAL THOUGHTS

- **(For children):** Before babies learn to talk, they express themselves by crying. They cry if they are hungry, hurting, or need changing. They soon learn crying is the way to get what they want or get everyone's attention. Sometimes they cry when nothing is wrong. When they use crying just to get their way, it is a form of lying. Older children sometimes fall into the same trap.
- **(For everyone):** Think back over your life and recall times when you lied to protect yourself. Was this a righteous or unrighteous act? Have you asked the Lord to forgive you for lying and to help you stop?
- Do you remember a time when you were asked a question (i.e., "What are you doing?"); and before you knew it, you had given a lie for the answer (i.e., "Nothing.")? Why do we do things like that? Why does it seem to take so much effort to tell the truth?

PRAYER THOUGHTS

- Ask God to make you conscious of the times when you tell lies.
- Ask God to give you a holy desire to speak the truth at all times.

SONG: *ONLY A SINNER*

Day 175: (Saturday)
They Bend Their Tongue for Lies

Jeremiah 9:3 And they bend their tongues like their bow for lies: but they are not valiant for the truth upon the earth; for they proceed from evil to evil, and they know not me, saith the LORD.

INTRODUCTORY THOUGHTS

The Bible has much to say about the tongue or the words man speaks. The tongue of man is a deadly weapon *(James 3:5-8)*. As such, the scripture likens it to a bow that is bent; only the arrows are the expressed lies *(Jeremiah 9:3)*. A similar thought is found in *Psalm 64:3* where David said of the wicked that they *"whet their tongue like a sword, and bend their bows to shoot their arrows, even bitter words."* Unfortunately, even Christians sometimes make light of how deadly words can be. The old saying, *"sticks and stones may break my bones, but words will never hurt me,"* may sound quaint; but far from the truth. Words do wound. The Bible likens lies to arrows that are shot out of a bow. Relating lies to the arrows conveys the pain caused by the lying. Lies often do bring hurt; sometimes not physical, but in some form or another lies wound others.

DEVOTIONAL THOUGHTS

- **(For children):** The tongue is likened to fire *(James 3:6; Proverbs 16:27)*. What does a real fire do when it goes unchecked? You can hurt other people with your words, especially if your words are not true. Let's ask God to help us with our mouths as David did in *Psalm 141:3*.
- **(For everyone):** Have you spread lies about other people? How could those lies hurt them (either physically, emotionally, or even their testimony, etc.)? Would you willingly shoot a person in the heart with an arrow? If not, why would you allow your lies to do it?
- Have you ever had someone lie about you? How did that make you feel? Did it cause any trouble that you had to later fix? Did it seem as though those lies would crush you?

PRAYER THOUGHTS

- Ask God to help you think before speaking hurtful lies about others.
- Ask God to make you think of your lies as arrows that can hurt others.

SONG: *HIS WAY WITH THEE*

Notes: _____

_____

_____

_____

_____

_____

_____

_____

_____

_____

_____

_____

_____

_____

_____

_____

Quotes from the next volume

(VOLUME 2, WEEK 25)

Subject: Leading

Far too many people allow themselves to accept unbalanced viewpoints. For instance, people focus on the glory of leadership while failing to realize the tremendous responsibility that comes with leadership.

Before a man will ever learn how to be a great leader, he must first learn how to be a dependable follower.

26

Truthfulness (con't)

Occurrences: *Truth* is found 145 times in the Old Testament and 173 times in the New Testament.

First usage in the New Testament: *Matthew 14:33* (truth)

Last usage in the Old Testament: *Malachi 2:6* (truth)

Interesting fact: *Proverbs 6:16-19* identifies seven things that are an abomination to the LORD. Of the seven mentioned, two are specifically identified as *"a lying tongue"* and *"A false witness that speaketh lies."*

Bible study tip: A healthy fear of the Lord is a most resourceful virtue in the study of scripture. A man that fears the Lord will be taught in the way *(Psalm 25:12)*. Additionally, the fear of the Lord is the beginning of knowledge *(Proverbs 1:7)* and wisdom *(Psalm 111:10)* and the Lord pays great attention to those who tremble at His word *(Isaiah 66:2)*. Ask the Lord to give you a healthy respect and fear for the words of God found in scripture.

Sunday, Day 176—Church Day (no devotional)
Monday, Day 177—*God's Lie Detector Test*
Tuesday, Day 178—*A Refuge of Lies*
Wednesday, Day 179—Church Night (no devotional)

Thursday, Day 180—*Wearied with Lies*
Friday, Day 181—*God Hates Lying*
Saturday, Day 182—*Lying to God*

Day 176: Church Day

Colossians 3:9 Lie not one to another, seeing that ye have **put off the old man with his deeds;**

Day 177: (Monday)
God's Lie Detector Test

*Job 6:28 Now therefore be content, **look upon me; for it is evident unto you if I lie.***

INTRODUCTORY THOUGHTS

Honest scientists are increasingly learning truths once deemed unimaginable by those who did not know the scriptures. Some of these truths concern the inner workings of man's mind and body. These relatively recent discoveries reveal that the body emits signals exposing truths intended by men to remain concealed. Sometimes the individual even lies attempting to conceal the facts further. For this reason, people began studying body language in hopes of determining if an individual's movements reveal otherwise hidden truths. Yet, the Bible has included these secrets long before man's scientific discoveries. In fact, the main character found in the oldest book of the Bible understood these principles. Job claimed that the truthfulness of his statements could be seen by simply looking at him. People have long assumed that the conscience is responsible for body language and the scriptures support this claim. **Romans 9:1** confirms this truth as Paul stated, *"I say the truth in Christ, I lie not, **my conscience also bearing me witness** in the Holy Ghost."* The Bible repeatedly shows that the conscience reveals the truth even when man intentionally tries to hide it, lie, or deceive.

DEVOTIONAL THOUGHTS

- **(For children):** No matter how much we try to hide our lies from others, inside we know if what we are saying is right or wrong. People can frequently tell by the way you are acting whether you are telling the truth.

- **(For everyone):** Who created man? God programmed the conscience to testify of a man's truthfulness *(Psalm 139:14)*? Don't you think that this proves how much the Creator is concerned with the truthfulness of your statements?
- Why would God wire man with indicators that express a man's guilt or innocence in what they are saying? Why should we be concerned with remaining always truthful?

PRAYER THOUGHTS

- Ask the Lord to help you see the importance of telling the truth.
- Ask the Lord to give you wisdom when others are lying to you.

SONG: *I SURRENDER ALL*

Day 178: (Tuesday)
A Refuge of Lies

Isaiah 28:14 Wherefore hear the word of the LORD, ye scornful men, that rule this people which is in Jerusalem.

*15 Because ye have said, We have made a covenant with death, and with hell are we at agreement; when the overflowing scourge shall pass through, it shall not come unto us: for **we have made lies our refuge, and under falsehood have we hid ourselves:***

16 Therefore thus saith the Lord GOD, Behold, I lay in Zion for a foundation a stone, a tried stone, a precious corner stone, a sure foundation: he that believeth shall not make haste.

*17 Judgment also will I lay to the line, and righteousness to the plummet: and the **hail shall sweep away the refuge of lies**, and the waters shall overflow the hiding place.*

18 And your covenant with death shall be disannulled, and your agreement with hell shall not stand; when the overflowing scourge shall pass through, then ye shall be trodden down by it.

19 From the time that it goeth forth it shall take you: for morning by morning shall it pass over, by day and by night: and it shall be a vexation only to understand the report.

20 For the bed is shorter than that a man can stretch himself on it: and the covering narrower than that he can wrap himself in it.

Introductory Thoughts

Unfortunately, far too many people today seek to hide the truth behind their lies. This condition is nothing new. In fact, the rulers of Jerusalem claimed to *"have made lies our refuge, and under falsehood have we hid ourselves" (Isaiah 28:15).* The Lord quickly answered their false assumption. He informed them that their lies would not stand when the Lord passed through their midst with judgment *(Isaiah 28:16-19).* In verse 20, God offered an illustration of the manner in which their lies would fail to protect them. He said, *"the bed is shorter than that a man can stretch himself on it: and the covering narrower than that he can wrap himself in it" (Isaiah 28:20).* In other words, no matter how big, well thought out, or cunning a man's lies may be, they will never be enough. Hiding behind lies is useless and fruitless. Lies can neither support a man nor hide him when the trouble arrives.

Devotional Thoughts

- **(For children):** You break a vase in the house. You tell mom you didn't do it (lie #1). You say the dog did it, but he was outside (lie #2). Then you say your little brother did it, but he was taking a nap (lie #3). You may get in trouble for breaking the vase, but you will suffer more trouble for breaking the vase and lying about how it happened. God wants us to tell the truth all of the time.
- **(For everyone):** When you tell a lie, you do so in order to hide the truth. How long do you think the lies will hide the truth? Will there be a time in the future when all your lies will be exposed? What should you do about your lies?
- Sometimes the truth gets us in trouble, but lies will always get us in trouble. Why would it be easier to tell the truth in the beginning? Which one usually yields more trouble?

Prayer Thoughts

- Ask God to help you see the trouble that will come by lying.
- Ask the Lord to show you that you cannot hide behind lies.

SONG: *THE SOLID ROCK*

Day 179: Church Night

Ephesians 4:25 Wherefore putting away lying, speak every man truth with his neighbour: for we are members one of another.

Day 180: (Thursday)
Wearied with Lies

*Ezekiel 24:12 She hath **wearied herself with lies**, and her great scum went not forth out of her: her scum shall be in the fire.*

INTRODUCTORY THOUGHTS

The context of our passage is the sinfulness of God's people, particularly those residing within the city of Jerusalem. The city is said to have *"**wearied** herself with lies."* A similar truth is taught in *Jeremiah 9:5* where the Bible says, *"they have taught their tongue to speak lies, and **weary** themselves to commit iniquity."* The context is different, but the concept remains constant: it requires hard work to tell and sustain lies. Anybody that has ever told a lie knows that it takes much greater effort to sustain a lie than to simply let the truth stand upon its own merit. Among other things, lying takes creativity, calculation, and a good memory. Additionally, lying stresses a person's conscience. Very rarely does one lie suffice within any particular deception, but the original lie often requires additional lies to support it. Lying is hard work and very stressful for those who have not seared their conscience!

DEVOTIONAL THOUGHTS

- **(For children):** Mom notices some cookies are missing from the plate on the counter. You ate them, but when asked, you say that you didn't. Later, as the thought that you lied comes to your mind, you begin to feel bad. Telling the truth the first time will keep you from having such thoughts and bad feelings.
- **(For everyone):** What do you feel like when you lie? At times, do you feel as though you have a heavy load of guilt weighing down upon your shoulders? Do your lies make you grow weary?
- If lying is hard work (and it is), why do you sometimes prefer lying over telling the truth? Why do you allow yourself to bring the burden of guilt upon your shoulders when the burden can be lifted by simply choosing to speak the truth?

PRAYER THOUGHTS

- Ask the Lord to give you the common sense to speak the truth.
- Ask God to show you the extra work that lying requires so that you will speak the truth.

SONG: *TELL IT TO JESUS*

Day 181: (Friday)
God Hates Lying

Proverbs 6:16 These six things doth the LORD hate: yea, seven are an abomination unto him:

*17 A proud look, **a lying tongue,** and hands that shed innocent blood,*

18 An heart that deviseth wicked imaginations, feet that be swift in running to mischief,

*19 **A false witness that speaketh lies,** and he that soweth discord among brethren.*

INTRODUCTORY THOUGHTS

Today's passage provides a list of things that God expressly hates. That list includes those who murder the innocent when it refers to *"hands that shed innocent blood" (Proverbs 6:17)*. It also mentions those whose hearts devise *"wicked imaginations" (Proverbs 6:18)*. In the midst of this list, the Lord twice references lying as it refers to *"a lying tongue" (Proverbs 6:17)* and *"a false witness that speaketh lies" (Proverbs 6:19)*. This should really concern those prone to lying with seeming impunity. God hates lying so much that He is going to judge those who do it. The scripture says, *"he that speaketh lies shall not escape" (Proverbs 19:5)*, but will *"perish" (Proverbs 19:9)*. In fact, liars are listed among the wicked groups that will *"have their part in the lake which burneth with fire and brimstone" (Revelation 21:8)*.

DEVOTIONAL THOUGHTS

- **(For children):** When something is hated, it is extremely disliked. Name some things that you hate. God hates lying no matter who does it and no matter what excuse you might give. Ask Him to help you to please Him by always telling the truth.
- **(For everyone):** Are you prone to lying? How does it make you feel knowing that God hates something that you regularly do? Are you going to continue to lie even though you know that it displeases the Lord?
- Our study shows that lying is included with some of the vilest sins committed. Have you considered that your lies are disgusting in the sight of God and will one day be judged by Him?

PRAYER THOUGHTS

- Ask God to remind you of how He feels about the telling of lies.
- Ask God to give you a sincere desire to be truthful and honest.

SONG: *AT CALVARY*

Day 182: (Saturday)
Lying to God

Acts 5:1 But a certain man named Ananias, with Sapphira his wife, sold a possession,

2 And kept back part of the price, his wife also being privy to it, and brought a certain part, and laid it at the apostles' feet.

*3 But Peter said, Ananias, why hath Satan filled thine heart **to lie to the Holy Ghost**, and to keep back part of the price of the land?*

*4 Whiles it remained, was it not thine own? and after it was sold, was it not in thine own power? why hast thou conceived this thing in thine heart? **thou hast not lied unto men, but unto God**.*

INTRODUCTORY THOUGHTS

The Bible records the fact that Ananias lied to Peter! He told Peter that he and his wife had sold some property for a certain amount of money. Yet, God and His servant knew that he had sold it for more than that indicated to Peter. The Bible teaches that Ananias told these lies to a man but had in fact lied to the Lord *(Acts 5:4)*. Man may not recognize the extent of a lie, but lies told to others are lies told to God. This brings a whole new perspective to the wickedness of lying. Men's lies are not just before and against men, but they appear before and are in conflict with a holy God. No wonder the apostle Paul said, *"Now the things which I write unto you, behold, before God, I lie not" (Galatians 1:20)*. He understood that lying to men would be lying before God, and he did not want to be guilty of that.

DEVOTIONAL THOUGHTS

- **(For children):** You are playing at a friend's house. After he leaves the room, you accidentally break his toy and hide it deep in the toy box. When he finds it later and asks you about it, you say you don't know anything about it. Your friend may never know the truth, but God does *(Proverbs 15:3)*. When you lied to your friend, you also lied to God and you need to tell both of them how sorry you are.

- **(For everyone)**: Have you ever told a lie? Did you consider that the Lord heard you? Not only did He hear you, but did you consider that your lie was a lie to God Himself? Should this fact change your opinion about lying?
- Do you think you would lie if you were standing in the presence of God? If not, then why do you lie just because you are not standing in front of Him? God hears every lie and He will hold us accountable for each and every one of them.

PRAYER THOUGHTS

- Ask God to remind you that He is listening every time you speak.
- Ask the Lord to help you understand that you are not just lying to men, but you are lying to Him.

SONG: *DO NOT I LOVE THEE, O MY LORD?*

Notes: _____

_____

_____

_____

_____

Quotes from the next volume

(VOLUME 2, WEEK 26)

Subject: Love

When God asks us to love, He is asking us to make a choice to love others regardless of our swinging moods or wavering feelings.

When an individual loves someone else, his love is best demonstrated by his sacrifices. This holds true concerning God's demonstrated love for the world. God gave His only begotten Son to die for the sins of the world.

27

Humility

Occurrences: *Humility* (including its various forms) occurs seventy-two times in sixty-five verses.

Variations: humble, humbled, humbledst, humbleness, humbleth, humbly, humiliation, humility

First usage: *Exodus 10:3* (humble)

Last usage: *1 Peter 5:6* (humble)

Defined: free from pride and arrogance; lowliness of mind, deep sense of one's own unworthiness in the sight of God; self-abasement

Interesting fact: Proverbs says that humility precedes honour. The first usage of *humble* involves God rebuking Pharaoh for refusing to humble himself before God *(Exodus 10:3)*.

Bible study tip: The letters of the English language are called *characters* for a reason — they often exhibit personality. Even today, many people still pronounce the word *humble* as though the *h* is silent. Thus, the first letter of the word promotes the meaning of the word. No honest Bible student would consider this simply coincidental.

Sunday, Day 183—Church Day (no devotional)
Monday, Day 184—*What Is Humility?*
Tuesday, Day 185—*He Humbleth Himself*
Wednesday, Day 186—Church Night (no devotional)
Thursday, Day 187—*False Humility*
Friday, Day 188—*A Tender Heart Yields Humility*
Saturday, Day 189—*Humility Moves the Lord*

Day 183: Church Day

Micah 6:8 *He hath shewed thee, O man, what is good; and what doth the LORD require of thee, but to do justly, and to love mercy, and to* **walk humbly with thy God?**

Day 184: (Monday)
What Is Humility?

Isaiah 2:9 *And the mean man boweth down, and* **the great man humbleth himself:** *therefore forgive them not.*

Isaiah 2:11 **The lofty looks of man shall be humbled,** *and the haughtiness of men shall be bowed down, and the LORD alone shall be exalted in that day.*

INTRODUCTORY THOUGHTS

Our previous studies have discussed the Bible's built-in dictionary. Interestingly, the discovery of this method of defining words is not new. In fact, men like King James VI (also known as King James I) commented on God's graciousness concerning His word. He pointed out that the definitions of many Bible words could be found by considering surrounding words. John Eadie explains this in his book: *The English Bible*, vol. 2, London, Macmillan, 1876, p. 191. Our study in *humility* is a case in point. The true riches of this word can only be gleaned when one considers some of the words used in close proximity of the word *humble* (along with its variations). These words include: *croucheth* **(Psalm 10:10)**, *lowly* **(Proverbs 16:19)**, *boweth down* **(Isaiah 2:9)**, *bowed down* **(Isaiah 2:11)**, *brought down* **(Isaiah 5:15)**, *hewn down* **(Isaiah 10:33)**, and *abased* **(Luke 14:11; Luke 18:14)**. God wants the Bible student to understand the depths and riches of His word and words. In this case, He clearly indicated that humility results from one being brought low.

DEVOTIONAL THOUGHTS

- **(For children):** What can you do well? Sing, quote Bible verses, or draw? Do you do these things so others will notice and brag on you? The Lord blesses you with the ability to do certain things so that you can please Him and help others in the process.
- **(For everyone):** The Bible reveals that humility is the opposite of pride. Therefore, no one can be both proud and humble simultaneously. Would you classify yourself as one who has a problem with pride or one who recognizes the importance of humility?
- What are some areas of your life where pride tends to rear its ugly head? What should you do when you sense that you are being overtaken with pride?

PRAYER THOUGHTS

- Ask the Lord to help you focus on areas where you are proud so that you can humble yourself before Him.
- Ask the Lord to begin a work of humility in your heart.

SONG: *IS YOUR ALL ON THE ALTAR?*

Day 185: (Tuesday)
He Humbleth Himself

Psalm 113:4 The LORD is high above all nations, and his glory above the heavens.

5 Who is like unto the LORD our God, who dwelleth on high,

*6 **Who humbleth himself** to behold the things that are in heaven, and in the earth!*

INTRODUCTORY THOUGHTS

The Lord is high above His creation. He *"is high above all nations, and his glory above the heavens" (Psalm 113:4).* He is so exalted that He must humble *"himself to behold the things that are in heaven, and in the earth" (Psalm 113:6).* As strange as it may seem, it humbles God to behold His creation (i.e., the sun, the moon, and the stars). The Bible even declares that *"the stars are not pure in his sight" (Job 25:5).* All of these things were created by God, yet it humbles Him to behold them. Not only is this true of the Father, but God the Son humbled Himself when He was adorned with a body of flesh *(Philippians 2:8)*. God created man, yet it humbled Him to take on a body of flesh like man.

DEVOTIONAL THOUGHTS

- **(For children):** God the Son left heaven's glory (where everything is perfect) to come to this world and take upon Himself a body like ours. He understands what it is like to be hungry, thirsty, and tired. He chose to become a man and did so willingly so that He could die for our sins on the cross.
- **(For everyone):** In what ways could the Lord's beholding His creation be humbling to the Creator? In what ways could the Son have been humbled by taking upon Himself a body of flesh?
- It is important to note that God did not humble Himself because of pride; He humbled Himself for us. If God can humble Himself for us, shouldn't we be willing to humble ourselves for Him?

PRAYER THOUGHTS

- Ask God to help you to be willing to humble yourself.
- Take time to thank God for becoming a man for us.

SONG: *I GAVE MY LIFE FOR THEE*

Day 186: Church Night

*Isaiah 57:15 For thus saith the high and lofty One that inhabiteth eternity, whose name is Holy; I dwell in the high and holy place, with him also that is of a **contrite and humble spirit, to revive the spirit of the humble,** and to revive the heart of the contrite ones.*

Day 187: (Thursday)
False Humility

*Colossians 2:18 Let no man beguile you of your reward in a voluntary humility and worshipping of angels, intruding into those things which he hath not seen, **vainly puffed up by his fleshly mind,***

19 And not holding the Head, from which all the body by joints and bands having nourishment ministered, and knit together, increaseth with the increase of God.

20 Wherefore if ye be dead with Christ from the rudiments of the world, why, as though living in the world, are ye subject to ordinances,

21 (Touch not; taste not; handle not;

22 Which all are to perish with the using;) after the commandments and doctrines of men?

23 Which things have indeed a shew of wisdom in will worship, and humility, and neglecting of the body; not in any honour to the satisfying of the flesh.

INTRODUCTORY THOUGHTS

Though despicable in the eyes of God, humility can be feigned or faked. *Colossians 2:18* touches on this principle. The saints were admonished against demonstrating a *"voluntary humility"* while being *"vainly puffed up"* by their fleshly minds. Humility and being *"puffed up"* are at opposite ends of the spectrum. Yet, these believers pretended to be humble, while they were, in reality, puffed up. *Colossians 2:23* reveals a second clear proof that humility can be false. Here the Bible speaks of things having *"a shew"* of *"humility."* In other words, people can *"shew"* humility while being overtaken with pride. False humility can sometimes convince and satisfy others, but rest assured that God clearly knows the difference.

DEVOTIONAL THOUGHTS

- **(For children):** Picking up trash around your yard or at church is never a pleasant job. Are you willing to pick it up when no one is around to see, or do you only do it when someone is watching? God wants us to be willing to do things for Him when only He is watching.
- **(For everyone):** Can you think of any instance where someone seemed to show humility but was obviously filled with pride? Is God ever fooled by someone trying to deceive others with their feigned humility? Does the individual's *"shew"* please the Lord?
- What is really going on within your heart? Are you full of pride or do you try to stay humble by giving God the glory? You cannot be both prideful and humble simultaneously. Do you make *"a shew"* of humility, knowing that it is feigned? What will you do to seek true humility?

PRAYER THOUGHTS

- Ask the Lord to help you to be real with Him and with others.
- Ask God to give you a genuine humility that pleases Him.

SONG: *ALL THAT I WAS*

Day 188: (Friday)
A Tender Heart Yields Humility

2 Kings 22:19 Because thine heart was tender, and thou hast humbled thyself before the LORD, when thou heardest what I spake against this place, and against the inhabitants thereof, that they should become a desolation and a curse, and hast rent thy clothes, and wept before me; I also have heard thee, saith the LORD.

INTRODUCTORY THOUGHTS

Josiah was a godly king who began his reign at the age of eight years old. Because of his genuine appreciation for the Lord, he would later commission the people to work upon the house of God. It was during this work that the high priest found the book of the law of the Lord. As the scripture was read before Josiah, he rent his clothes recognizing God's wrath was about to come upon His people. Josiah could have become hardened in heart against the Lord; however, he chose not to allow this to happen. Unlike many of his counterparts, Josiah humbled himself. What made Josiah different? His tender heart made all the difference *(2 Kings 22:19)*. Josiah's humility was not feigned; it was the natural outpouring of a heart tender toward the things of God.

DEVOTIONAL THOUGHTS

- **(For children):** When God the Son left heaven's glory and came to earth in order to take upon Himself a body of flesh, He was still God. But He willingly put Himself under God the Father's authority and did everything to please Him. We too should have a heart that wants to be obedient to God every day and in every way.
- **(For everyone):** Do you humble yourself before God when you receive bad news or when you go through a particular trial? Do you find a desire in your heart to murmur or argue with the Lord? If so, your heart needs to be softened by prayer and the word of God.

- When is the last time you humbled yourself before God? Are you full of pride? Are you hard-hearted and stiff-necked?

PRAYER THOUGHTS

- Ask God to soften your heart toward Him.
- Ask God to help you find true humility.

SONG: *I NEED THEE EVERY HOUR*

Day 189: (Saturday)
Humility Moves the Lord

*2 Chronicles 7:14 If my people, which are called by my name, shall **humble themselves**, and pray, and seek my face, and turn from their wicked ways; then will I hear from heaven, and will forgive their sin, and will heal their land.*

INTRODUCTORY THOUGHTS

Humility moves God to action. This common theme runs throughout the Bible; however, our passage reveals some truth otherwise hidden. According to Second Chronicles, the people of God are responsible to humble themselves. While doing so, they must also pray, seek God's face, and turn from their wicked ways. God's use of the word *then* in the passage reveals that God's actions result from the actions of His people. Their humility will move the Lord to action. If, or when, they humble themselves, God hears from heaven, forgives their sin, and heals their land. God takes note when people display humility *(Isaiah 57:15; Isaiah 66:1-2)*. Though some things have changed concerning Israel versus the church, God remains constant and is still looking for humility in the lives of His children.

DEVOTIONAL THOUGHTS

- **(For children):** Consider the word pride. The middle letter is "I." When you are proud, you think first and foremost of yourself. You might think how much better you are than others or how you want your own way and don't care how it affects others. God despises pride. He is pleased when we see our pride and come to Him for help fixing our problem.

- **(For everyone):** Do you need the Lord to do something special in your life? Do you constantly try to impress Him with your efforts? Have you considered that you might need to put away your pride and humble yourself before Him?
- Each of the steps God gave to man in our passage is in opposition to a prideful life. What does this teach us about man's greatest problem? Will you humble yourself, pray, seek God's face, and turn from your wicked ways?

PRAYER THOUGHTS

- Ask God to remove pride from your heart.
- Ask God to help you truly seek to please Him.

SONG: *PRAISE THE SAVIOUR, YE WHO KNOW HIM*

Notes: _____

_____

_____

Quotes from the next volume
(VOLUME 2, WEEK 27)
Subject: Love (con't)

The Bible says, "A friend loveth at all times." This infers that the concept of falling in and out of love is unscriptural. Biblically defined love is not a fleeting emotion controlled by one's feelings. It remains a choice based on the truths of scripture and falls outside the whims of one's emotional passions.

Biblical love forgives and continues to unconditionally forgive regardless of any objectionable response to one's love *(Proverbs 10:12)*.

Christians have a purpose similar to Jacob's determination to serve. At times, service for the Lord may seem filled with great difficulties, but a deep and genuine love for the Saviour will make one's service seem "but a few days."

28

Humility (con't)

Occurrences: *Humility* is found fifty-six times in the Old Testament and sixteen times in the New Testament.

First usage in the New Testament: *Matthew 18:4* (humble)

Last usage in the Old Testament: *Micah 6:8* (humbly)

Interesting fact: A man's true humility captures the Lord's attention. Even the wicked king Ahab found favour with God by choosing to humble himself before the Lord *(1 Kings 21:29)*.

Bible study tip: The Bible will, at times, express inward spiritual virtues through outward visible manifestations. For example, the rending of a garment frequently symbolizes the rending of a man's heart. When studying a subject directly linked to an outward and visible manifestation, study the resulting manifestations in order to gain a clearer understanding of the inward spiritual virtue.

Sunday, Day 190—Church Day (no devotional)
Monday, Day 191—*He Led Thee to Humble Thee*
Tuesday, Day 192—*Humility Precedes Honour*
Wednesday, Day 193—Church Night (no devotional)
Thursday, Day 194—*It Is Better to Be Humble*

Friday, Day 195—*The Humble Shall Be Exalted*
Saturday, Day 196—*Grace unto the Humble*

Day 190: Church Day

Philippians 2:5 *Let this mind be in you, which was also in Christ Jesus:*

6 Who, being in the form of God, thought it not robbery to be equal with God:

*7 But **made himself of no reputation**, and took upon him the form of a servant, and was made in the likeness of men:*

*8 And being found in fashion as a man, **he humbled himself**, and became obedient unto death, even the death of the cross.*

Day 191: (Monday)
He Led Thee to Humble Thee

Deuteronomy 8:1 *All the commandments which I command thee this day shall ye observe to do, that ye may live, and multiply, and go in and possess the land which the LORD sware unto your fathers.*

*2 And thou shalt remember all the way which the LORD thy God led thee these forty years in the wilderness, **to humble thee,** and to prove thee, to know what was in thine heart, whether thou wouldest keep his commandments, or no.*

*3 And **he humbled thee**, and suffered thee to hunger, and fed thee with manna, which thou knewest not, neither did thy fathers know; that he might make thee know that man doth not live by bread only, but by every word that proceedeth out of the mouth of the LORD doth man live.*

INTRODUCTORY THOUGHTS

Careless Bible students often make wrongful assumptions for the purpose of God's interaction with man. One such example involves the reasoning for Israel's wilderness wanderings. Several alternative explanations might be supposed, but the Bible emphasizes one primary purpose, that of *humility*. Moses declared this truth to the people when he said, *"thou shalt remember all the way which the LORD thy God led thee . . . **to humble thee**."* He quickly added that God *"**humbled thee**, and suffered*

thee to hunger, and fed thee with manna." **Deuteronomy 8:16** reempha-
sizes this truth: *"Who fed thee in the wilderness with manna, which thy
fathers knew not, **that he might humble thee**."* The Lord selected Israel's
trials and troublesome path in order to humble them. Truth is frequently
that simple but missed by those who read the Bible with preconceived
philosophies and concepts.

DEVOTIONAL THOUGHTS

- **(For children):** If mom or dad doesn't feel well, you should play quietly and try not to argue with your brothers or sisters. This may seem
  difficult, but God may use these times to test your willingness to obey
  both Him and your parents.
- **(For everyone):** The Lord chose the path of the Israelites in order to
  humble them. Why would people who had just been delivered from
  bondage need to be humbled?
- Is it possible that the Lord allows us to go through trials to keep us
  humble? How can trials, if handled properly, work humility into the
  heart of those afflicted by those troubles?

PRAYER THOUGHTS

- Ask the Lord to lead you in the path that He wants for your life and
  then reveal how much He loves you by allowing these trials to take
  place.
- Ask God to keep you humble in the ways He sees fit.

SONG: *HE LEADETH ME*

Day 192: (Tuesday)
Humility Precedes Honour

Proverbs 15:33 *The fear of the LORD is the instruction of wisdom;
and **before honour is humility**.*

INTRODUCTORY THOUGHTS

It seems that far too many men seek to be honoured by others whether deserved or completely unwarranted. However, few men understand
the proper biblical path for being rightfully honoured. One would naturally think honour comes to those who are confident and proud, but
the Bible reveals the opposite. **Proverbs 15:33** and **Proverbs 18:12** both

declare that *humility* precedes honour. This means that a person desiring to receive honour must first possess the character trait of true humility. Conversely, the Bible points out that a haughty heart precedes the pathway to destruction *(Proverbs 18:12)*. Moreover, the Bible couples humility with the fear of the Lord and shows that it yields riches, honour, and life *(Proverbs 22:4)*. Desiring these good things is only reasonable, yet they are only derived through God's prescribed means and not man's self-styled means.

DEVOTIONAL THOUGHTS

- **(For children):** Some children always want to be first – first in line, first to choose a toy, etc. They blurt out what they want or run ahead of everyone to get their way. However, the Lord remains most pleased when we are willing to put others first.
- **(For everyone):** Do you desire honour? Are you actively seeking honour? What path are you taking to get it? Are you seeking it through pride and a haughty spirit or through genuine humility?
- Do you seek the praise of others by audible request or through your silent actions? Are you constantly explaining your greatness or do you allow your genuine effort to speak for itself?

PRAYER THOUGHTS

- Ask the Lord to give you a genuine humility.
- Ask God to help you find honour His way.

SONG: *BE THOU MY VISION*

Day 193: Church Night

*Proverbs 29:23 A man's pride shall bring him low: but **honour shall uphold the humble in spirit.***

Day 194: (Thursday)
It Is Better to Be Humble

Proverbs 16:19 Better it is to be of an humble spirit with the lowly, than to divide the spoil with the proud.

INTRODUCTORY THOUGHTS

Following the victory of a battle, the victors generally divide the spoil. The soldiers triumphantly go through the enemy camp removing anything they desire. The act of dividing the spoil indicates a time of victory and intense celebration as a result of winning the battle. Yet, the Bible reveals that there is something far better than dividing the spoil with the proud: being *"of an humble spirit with the lowly."* This can only pertain to those looking at life from a godly perspective. Man would naturally rather celebrate a victory with the proud than to be humbled through defeat. The context of the passage quite possibly could indicate that the lowly refers to those who have suffered the defeat; therefore, it is better to be humbled by defeat than to be proud in victory.

DEVOTIONAL THOUGHTS

- **(For children):** When you receive a new toy, do you brag and say, "It's mine and you can't play with it?" Or do you thank the Lord for it and willingly share it with others? Which would please the Lord most? Is your toy more important than treating others with respect and dignity?
- **(For everyone):** What sounds better: victory or defeat? The answer seems obvious unless you look at things from a spiritual perspective. What does this truth teach us about the greatness of humility?
- The most important things in life *to* us are not necessarily the most important things *for* us. Would you say that you possess humility or are you consumed with pride? From our study, do you understand how important it is to be humble?

PRAYER THOUGHTS

- Ask God to show you the importance of humility.
- Ask the Lord to show you the wickedness of pride.

SONG: *WHEN I SURVEY THE WONDROUS CROSS*

Day 195: (Friday)
The Humble Shall Be Exalted

Luke 14:11 *For whosoever exalteth himself shall be abased; and* **he** **that humbleth himself shall be exalted.**

INTRODUCTORY THOUGHTS

The Bible repeatedly emphasizes that honour follows humility! But how does this work? According to our passage, *"whosoever exalteth himself shall be abased; and he that humbleth himself shall be exalted."* Abased means to be brought low, while *exalted* means to be elevated. **Matthew 23:12** and **Luke 18:14** reiterate the truth found in **Luke 14:11**, yet none of the verses expound upon *how* this takes place. What or who is at work behind the scenes to make this principle true? The answer is found in **James 4:10**—*"Humble yourselves in the sight of the Lord, and he shall lift you up."* Man's finite mind-set leads him to think that the way up is up and the way down is down; but according to the Bible, the opposite is true. The way up (to be exalted) is down (through humility) and the way down (to be abased) is up (self-exaltation). Those who seek to be exalted by others will find themselves frustrated through their own efforts; yet those who seek humility will be exalted by God.

DEVOTIONAL THOUGHTS

- **(For children):** The Bible proclaims that David was a man after God's own heart. He strove to follow and obey the Lord. Yet, when he disobeyed, he was sorry for his sin (Psalm 38:18). God elevated this boy who watched sheep and exalted him to become king of Israel.
- **(For everyone):** Do you desire for the Lord to exalt you? How does the Bible teach us to receive this blessing? Are you willing to humble yourself before God?
- Are you willing to live your life according to God's plans or have you determined to do things your own way? Will you humble yourself and allow Him to exalt you?

PRAYER THOUGHTS

- Ask God to soften your heart toward Him.
- Ask the Lord to teach you how to do things His way.

SONG: *ALONE WITH GOD*

Day 196: (Saturday)
Grace unto the Humble

James 4:6 But he giveth more grace. Wherefore he saith, God resisteth the proud, but giveth grace unto the humble.

INTRODUCTORY THOUGHTS

The Bible associates several qualities to the truly humble person. The book of James lists a few of these prominent traits as follows. The humble man submits to the will of God *(James 4:7)*. Additionally, he repents of his sins *(James 4:8)* and mourns over his disobedience *(James 4:9)*. He refuses to speak evil of his brother *(James 4:11)*, but rather chooses to leave judgment to the Lord because He is the righteous Judge *(James 4:12)*. He refuses to boast about what he is doing *(James 4:13-16)* because he knows that his failure to do right is a sin *(James 4:17)*. Yet, the greatest truth concerning the humble man is not what he does or gives for God, but what God gives to him. The Bible says that God gives *grace* to the humble and resists the proud *(1 Peter 5:5-6)*. Think about this profound truth. God gives a man what he needs if that man will simply remain humble.

DEVOTIONAL THOUGHTS

- **(For children):** A friend repeatedly treats you mean. You do not have to continue to play with him, but if you talk badly about him to others, you are trying to hurt him. This behaviour displeases the Lord. Pray for your friend that God will teach him to do right.
- **(For everyone):** Do your actions resemble the qualities of a humble person? Do you quickly repent of your sins and mourn over them? Do you try not to boast of your abilities and efforts? Do you understand that the Lord is righteous in all His doings and knows your heart better than you know it?
- God resists the proud, but gives grace to the humble. Often this world resists the humble while exalting those with a proud spirit. Who are you seeking to please? Would you rather have favour with the Lord or with man?

PRAYER THOUGHTS

- Ask the Lord to keep you humble.
- Ask God to show you the condition of your heart.

SONG: *HE GIVETH MORE GRACE*

Notes: _____

_____

_____

_____

_____

_____

_____

_____

_____

_____

_____

_____

_____

_____

_____

_____

_____

_____

_____

Quotes from the next volume

(VOLUME 2, WEEK 28)

Subject: Meditation

When a believer meditates upon the things of God, those truths become more firmly planted in the heart. Eventually, the contents of the heart become evident from the words that escape the mouth *(Luke 6:45)*.

29

Integrity

Occurrences: found sixteen times in the Old Testament only; primarily in Job, Psalms, and Proverbs

First usage: *Genesis 20:5* (integrity)

Last usage: *Proverbs 20:7* (integrity)

Defined: purity, incorruptness, uprightness, honesty. Integrity involves the whole moral character but especially uprightness in mutual dealings.

Interesting fact: After Job lost everything, God bragged to Satan that Job held fast his *integrity* in spite of his troubles *(Job 2:3)*. Unfortunately, even Job's wife questioned his integrity. She asked him why he retained it and further suggested he should simply curse God and die *(Job 2:9)*.

Bible study tip: When a word appears minimally in the scripture, one must exhaust every possible detail of context in understanding its meaning. Note the part of speech, other words used to compare or contrast, or other words frequently associated with the word that might narrow down its meaning. If still unsuccessful, consider the word's etymology and how it entered the English language.

Sunday, Day 197—Church Day (no devotional)
Monday, Day 198—*What Is Integrity?*
Tuesday, Day 199—*Integrity of Heart*
Wednesday, Day 200—Church Night (no devotional)
Thursday, Day 201—*Walking in Integrity*
Friday, Day 202—*Retain Thine Integrity*
Saturday, Day 203—*The Benefits of Integrity*

Day 197: Church Day

Psalm 41:12 *And as for me, thou* **upholdest me in mine integrity,** *and settest me before thy face for ever.*

Day 198: (Monday)
What Is Integrity?

Genesis 20:1 *And Abraham journeyed from thence toward the south country, and dwelled between Kadesh and Shur, and sojourned in Gerar.*

2 And Abraham said of Sarah his wife, She is my sister: and Abimelech king of Gerar sent, and took Sarah.

3 But God came to Abimelech in a dream by night, and said to him, Behold, thou art but a dead man, for the woman which thou hast taken; for she is a man's wife.

4 But Abimelech had not come near her: and he said, Lord, wilt thou slay also a righteous nation?

5 Said he not unto me, She is my sister? and she, even she herself said, He is my brother: **in the integrity of my heart** *and innocency of my hands have I done this.*

6 And God said unto him in a dream, Yea, I know that thou didst this **in the integrity of thy heart;** *for I also withheld thee from sinning against me: therefore suffered I thee not to touch her.*

INTRODUCTORY THOUGHTS

Men used to be commended for their level of integrity and one's handshake was considered a man's bond. As societies continue to crumble from the pollution of immorality, men of integrity are quickly disappearing. Unfortunately, churches seem far from immune to this moral decline. What is integrity? In a narrow sense, integrity as used in scripture can be difficult to pinpoint. The word integrity occurs sixteen times in scripture. By considering each occurrence, one can discover clues that provide insight as to its meaning. Integrity is contrasted with the words like perverse (Proverbs 19:1) and perverseness (Proverbs 11:3). Conversely, integrity is used in conjunction with words like upright (Job 2:3; Proverbs 11:3) and uprightness (1 Kings 9:4; Psalm 25:21). In our passage, the word integrity is used alongside the word innocency (Genesis 20:5). These facts would lead the believer to realize that integrity speaks of a moral purity and moral correctness.

DEVOTIONAL THOUGHTS

- **(For children):** David said, "I will behave myself wisely in a perfect way" (Psalm 101:2). The Lord wants what we say and do to be correct and right at all times.
- **(For everyone):** If integrity has to do with being morally correct, why is this so very important to us as followers of Christ? What are some instances that showed the Lord Jesus demonstrating integrity while on earth?
- Would people be more likely to describe you as perverse or innocent? How could you change the way people think of you if their view of you is not in accordance with the Bible standards?

PRAYER THOUGHTS

- Ask the Lord to do a work of purification within your heart.
- Ask God to show you the sinfulness of your heart.

SONG: *JESUS, I MY CROSS HAVE TAKEN*

Day 199: (Tuesday)
Integrity of Heart

*1 Kings 9:4 And if thou wilt walk before me, **as David thy father walked, in integrity of heart, and in uprightness**, to do according to all that I have commanded thee, and wilt keep my statutes and my judgments:*

INTRODUCTORY THOUGHTS

The Lord blessed the throne of David and desired to do the same for his posterity. Because the Lord wanted to establish Solomon's rule, He provided some guidelines for Solomon. One prominent issue involved Solomon following in his father's footsteps by living with *integrity of heart*. Integrity is very much a matter of the heart. In fact, four times in scripture *integrity* is associated with the heart. Twice the Bible refers to the integrity of Abimelech's heart *(Genesis 20:5-6)* and another two times it refers to the integrity of David's heart *(1 Kings 9:4; Psalm 78:72)*. Though these men had little else in common, both understood that integrity involved a matter of the heart. A lack of integrity is first and foremost a heart issue.

DEVOTIONAL THOUGHTS

- **(For children):** What we say and do comes from our heart *(Luke 6:45)*. Let's get God's word in our heart so we know to say and do the right things *(Psalm 119:11)*.
- **(For everyone):** Do you have a desire in your heart for moral purity? Do you want to be clean, righteous, upright, and holy in your actions?
- What things are you allowing to creep into your heart? We know the heart is a place where much wickedness finds its origins *(Matthew 15:19)*, but these things get in because we allow them access.

PRAYER THOUGHTS

- Ask the Lord to help you guard your heart from wickedness.
- Ask God to purify your heart.

SONG: *GIVE ME THY HEART*

Day 200: Church Night

Proverbs 11:3 The integrity of the upright shall guide them: but the perverseness of transgressors shall destroy them.

Day 201: (Thursday)
Walking in Integrity

Proverbs 20:7 The just man walketh in his integrity: his children are blessed after him.

INTRODUCTORY THOUGHTS

As this study has shown, integrity is a matter of the heart, yet it also affects every other aspect of a man's life. Though men sometimes try to separate an individual's walk from his true heart's condition, the Bible reveals the futility of such. Testifying to this truth, the Bible speaks of *walking* in integrity *(Psalm 26:1, 11; Proverbs 19:1; Proverbs 20:7)*. The Bible says that *"by their fruits ye shall know them" (Matthew 7:16, 20)* and this principle applies to one's integrity too. Our passage from Proverbs reveals that as the *"just"* man walks in his integrity, his children are likewise blessed because of his walk. The secrets of a person's heart are often unveiled in his walk. Furthermore, a man who walks in his integrity does not fear the judgment of God *(Psalm 26:1)*. Men need integrity of heart, but that integrity must manifest itself in their daily walk.

DEVOTIONAL THOUGHTS

- **(For children):** The Bible says Daniel had already "purposed in his heart" (settled the matter) that he was not going to eat or drink those things that God did not permit, even though it was appointed by the king of Babylon (Daniel 1:5, 8). Daniel wanted to live so that other people could tell that he loved God. We should live like that too.
- **(For everyone):** Do your outward actions display an inward heart of integrity? Do others recognize you as a God-fearing, born-again believer? Do they readily notice that there is something different about you?
- Do your words and actions exhibit righteousness and holiness or perverseness? Do they testify of an innocent heart or one filled with the filth of this world?

PRAYER THOUGHTS

- Ask God to show you that your walk in this world is important.
- Ask God to remind you that your actions speak for your heart.

SONG: *TAKE TIME TO BE HOLY*

Day 202: (Friday)
Retain Thine Integrity

Job 2:7 So went Satan forth from the presence of the LORD, and smote Job with sore boils from the sole of his foot unto his crown.

8 And he took him a potsherd to scrape himself withal; and he sat down among the ashes.

*9 Then said his wife unto him, **Dost thou still retain thine integrity?** curse God, and die.*

10 But he said unto her, Thou speakest as one of the foolish women speaketh. What? shall we receive good at the hand of God, and shall we not receive evil? In all this did not Job sin with his lips.

INTRODUCTORY THOUGHTS

Simply for being a man of integrity, Job suffered greatly. No matter what obstacles Job was forced to overcome, he would not relinquish his integrity. In the midst of Satan's attacks, the Lord commended Job for his integrity when He said that Job *"holdeth fast his integrity" (Job 2:3)*. When Job's wife verbally joined in the attacks, she pressured him to relinquish his integrity. Job wisely responded to her by saying, *"Thou speakest as one of the foolish women speaketh."* Job was not willing to relinquish his integrity. There are things men consider important in life, but few realize the paramount importance of maintaining one's integrity. The Bible repeatedly stresses the importance of integrity: *"Better is the poor that walketh in his integrity, than he that is perverse in his lips, and is a fool" (Proverbs 19:1)*. This passage illustrates that the most important things in life cannot be purchased with money, nor can they be lost due to the absence of wealth.

DEVOTIONAL THOUGHTS

- **(For children):** Shadrach, Meshach, and Abed-nego would not bow down to the king's idol even if it meant their death in the fiery furnace. Daniel refused to stop praying to the living God even though it meant he would be thrown into a den of lions. When troubles come, we too should be willing to live for God no matter the cost.
- **(For everyone):** What are the most important things to you in this life? How much time do you have invested in acquiring things? How

much time are you spending on things that have little to no eternal value?
- Do you think that many people today would handle the pressure put upon Job by someone he loved dearly? Would you have refused to quit and fought hard to retain your integrity? Does your walk with the Lord falter in times of trial?

PRAYER THOUGHTS
- Ask the Lord to give you a longing to protect your integrity.
- Ask God to help you do right, even in times of great testing.

SONG: *I AM RESOLVED*

Day 203: (Saturday)
The Benefits of Integrity

Psalm 25:21 Let integrity and uprightness preserve me; for I wait on thee.

INTRODUCTORY THOUGHTS
It has often been said that ignorance is bliss, meaning that to be wise is folly. Nothing can be further from the truth. As with most areas of life, a man must recognize the benefits of integrity before he will truly find its protection of utmost importance. Our passage describes one benefit of integrity when it says that integrity preserves a person. Preservation can refer to several areas like being kept from trouble or kept from death. Both of these would be considered invaluable. Additionally, the Bible says that integrity upholds the believer *(Psalm 41:12)*. This means that the Lord holds men up in the midst of troublous times. *Proverbs 11:3* declares another benefit: *"The integrity of the upright shall guide them."* Praise God! Integrity guides men in the right way and keeps them from trouble!

DEVOTIONAL THOUGHTS
- **(For children):** Doing and saying the right things from the heart will keep you out of trouble. What happens when you lie, steal, fight, or talk back? Wouldn't you rather have gladness inside (Psalm 97:11)?

- **(For everyone):** Are you constantly getting into trouble? Do you struggle to walk on the right paths of life? When you do, this is likely because of a lack of integrity.
- Do you care about your integrity? Do you strive to live a holy and clean life before the Lord and others? Are you willing to endure hardness and trials simply to retain your integrity? What would it take for you to recognize its importance?

PRAYER THOUGHTS

- Ask the Lord to clean you up both inside and out.
- Ask the Lord to remind you of these benefits on a daily basis.

SONG: *ABLE TO DELIVER*

Notes: _____

_____

_____

_____

_____

_____

_____

_____

_____

_____

Quotes from the next volume

(VOLUME 2, WEEK 29)

Subject: Ministry

Sometimes we forget that the first four letters of the word ministry spell out the word "mini." Ministry is never about becoming popular or famous or lording over others. Ministry involves decreasing while allowing others to increase.

30

Joy

Occurrences: found 216 times in 201 verses

Variations: enjoy, joy, joyed, joyful, joyfully, joyfulness, joy-ing, joyous

First usage: *Leviticus 26:34* (enjoy)

Last usage: *Jude 24* (joy)

Defined: the emotion excited by the acquisition or expectation of good; to enjoy; have or possess with pleasure even if possessions are minimal

Interesting fact: *Joy* is the second aspect of the ninefold fruit of the Spirit mentioned in Galatians chapter 5.

Bible study tip: If a word or concept occurs minimally in a specific section of scripture, try to find out why. The absence could indicate that the doctrinal teaching or truth only applies to a specific group of people. Or it could demonstrate that the book's setting is not conducive to the word or concept you are studying.

Sunday, Day 204—Church Day (no devotional)
Monday, Day 205—*What Is Joy?*

Tuesday, Day 206—*Joy in the Lord*
Wednesday, Day 207—Church Night (no devotional)
Thursday, Day 208—*Joy, a Gift from God*
Friday, Day 209—*Joy in Righteousness*
Saturday, Day 210—*Expressions of Joy*

Day 204: Church Day

Nehemiah 8:10 Then he said unto them, Go your way, eat the fat, and drink the sweet, and send portions unto them for whom nothing is prepared: for this day is holy unto our Lord: **neither be ye sorry; for the joy of the LORD is your strength.**

Day 205: (Monday)
What Is Joy?

Esther 8:15 And Mordecai went out from the presence of the king in royal apparel of blue and white, and with a great crown of gold, and with a garment of fine linen and purple: and the city of **Shushan rejoiced and was glad.**

16 **The Jews had light, and gladness, and joy,** *and honour.*

17 And in every province, and in every city, whithersoever the king's commandment and his decree came, **the Jews had joy and gladness,** *a feast and a good day. And many of the people of the land became Jews; for the fear of the Jews fell upon them.*

Introductory Thoughts

Words always have associative properties with other words; the word *joy* is no exception. When considering a definition of *joy*, many people would assume it is being *happy* or *happiness* in general. However, the Bible does not associate *joy* primarily with being *happy*. God provided another word to enable the Bible student to define the word *joy*. In each of the three verses in our passage, the scripture makes reference to joy, either indirectly: *rejoiced (Esther 8:15)* or directly *(Esther 8:16, 17)*. A careful consideration will identify that joy is associated with the words *glad (Esther 8:15)* and *gladness (Esther 8:16, 17)*. This connection is consistent throughout the Bible *(Psalm 51:8; Psalm 105:43; Isaiah*

16:10) and is specifically connected to *gladness of heart (Deuteronomy 28:47; 1 Kings 8:66; Esther 5:9)*.

DEVOTIONAL THOUGHTS

- **(For children):** Name some things that make you glad. We feel gladness in our hearts when we do something good for others and when we obey the rules set down by those in authority. How do you feel when you disobey?
- **(For everyone):** What kind of terms could be used to describe you: sorrowful or joyful? Do others find joy in spending time with you or do they become increasingly sorrowful as time continues?
- Would you say that you have *gladness of heart*? If not, why? What are the things or situations that hinder you from knowing the *joy* of the Lord?

PRAYER THOUGHTS

- Ask God to show you the condition of your heart.
- Ask the Lord to help you experience lasting joy.

SONG: *COME, CHRISTIANS, JOIN TO SING*

Day 206: (Tuesday)
Joy in the Lord

*Psalm 43:4 Then will I go unto the altar of God, unto **God my exceeding joy**: yea, upon the harp will I praise thee, O God my God.*

INTRODUCTORY THOUGHTS

The Bible provides several sources of man's joy, but each source can in some way be directly traced back to the Lord. In today's passage, **Psalm 43:4** describes God as the psalmist's *"exceeding joy."* According to **Psalm 16:11**, there is *"fulness of joy"* in God's presence. While the Bible indicates that man's soul can be joyful in the Lord *(Psalm 35:9; Isaiah 61:10)*, it also associates joy directly to God's strength *(Psalm 21:1)*. Moreover, God's word provides a source of joy for the saint *(Jeremiah 15:16)*. In the New Testament, the book of Romans identifies God as the saint's source of joy, but specifically, this joy comes *"through our Lord Jesus Christ" (Romans 5:11)*. Perhaps men lack the joy of the Lord because they disregard the Lord of their joy.

DEVOTIONAL THOUGHTS

- **(For children):** David said, *"I will be glad and rejoice in thee" (Psalm 9:2)*. *Habakkuk 3:18* concludes with *"I will joy in the God of my salvation."* How can you be assured of being glad and find joy in the Lord? The answer is simply dwell upon the things He has done for you through the cross.
- **(For everyone):** Do you spend time in prayer daily? Do you set aside the time to read and study the word of God? If not, you are missing some of the most important opportunities to know the joy of the Lord.
- What are your sources for joy? Is your joy irregular? If so, you most likely are looking for joy in the wrong place. When our affections are placed squarely upon the source of joy, it will not falter or waver like those who trust in self.

PRAYER THOUGHTS

- Ask the Lord to help you find your joy in Him and His word.
- Ask God to show you if your sources for finding joy are misleading you.

SONG: *JESUS IS ALL THE WORLD TO ME*

Day 207: Church Night

*John 15:11 These things have I spoken unto you, that my joy might remain in you, and **that your joy might be full.***

Day 208: (Thursday)
Joy, a Gift from the Lord

*Ecclesiastes 2:26 For God giveth to a man that is good in his sight wisdom, and knowledge, and **joy**: but to the sinner he giveth travail, to gather and to heap up, that he may give to him that is good before God. This also is vanity and vexation of spirit.*

INTRODUCTORY THOUGHTS

Today's passage teaches several remarkable truths concerning joy. First, joy is given to man by God--but not indiscriminately given to every man. Apparently, joy is given to those who are not sinners in the sense of wallowing in it. Everyone sins, but this verse speaks to the fact that God does not openly bless the sinner who has no desire for God to help him overcome his sinful ways. Moreover, our passage further reveals that God considers it good in His sight for a man to have joy. This point may seem insignificant, but it emphasizes God's true desire for man. Just as God desires for men to have wisdom and knowledge, He wants men to know the joy that comes only from and through Him. Some may think the source of joy disputable, but *James 1:17* affirms that *"every good gift and every perfect gift is from above."*

DEVOTIONAL THOUGHTS

- **(For children):** Everyone likes receiving gifts; however, most gifts do not last long. Sometimes gifts are broken, stolen, ruined, or worn out. Yet, God's greatest gift to us is the gift of His salvation. This gift will last forever and cannot be broken, stolen, ruined, or worn out. You can always feel joy inside for having accepted God's gift. He wants you to have this gift so that you can go to heaven.
- **(For everyone):** Does God want you to have joy? Is He willing to give you joy? If so, why don't you consistently experience the fulness of joy? Is it possible that some sin in your life hinders the joy that God desires for you?
- Is joy important to God? Is it important to you? Are you willing to put away the things of this world that rob you of the joy that the Lord has for you?

PRAYER THOUGHTS

- Ask the Lord to help you see the importance of having joy.
- Ask God to give you the joy that He wants you to know.

SONG: *JOY UNSPEAKABLE*

Day 209: (Friday)
Joy in Righteousness

Luke 10:17 And the seventy returned again with joy, saying, Lord, even the devils are subject unto us through thy name.

INTRODUCTORY THOUGHTS

We have already learned that our joy is to be found in the Lord and this joy is a special gift from above. With this truth foundational to our study, what are some things that we can do as believers that will bring us lasting joy? Far too many people think joy surfaces once the stresses of life cease or at least begin to diminish. Yet, the Bible teaches that joy can be found only in faithfully serving the Lord. Today's verse reveals that the disciples found joy through what God had done in and through them! Considering a few more scriptural examples of joy should help to solidify our mindset concerning this subject. The Bible records great joy as the people of God willingly sacrificed to the Lord *(1 Chronicles 29:17)*. *Proverbs 21:15* reveals that *"It is joy to the just to do judgment."* The book of Luke tells us that there is joy in heaven when one sinner repents *(Luke 15:7)*. From these and other examples, we know that true joy will be found when we willingly serve the Lord God, but never in the things of this world.

DEVOTIONAL THOUGHTS

- **(For children):** Heaven will be a place full of joy with no sin, sickness, or even sadness, etc. The Bible teaches that in heaven God's servants shall serve Him (Revelation 22:3). We will be serving in heaven, yet true joy on earth right now also comes from doing what God wants us to do.
- **(For everyone):** When is the last time you witnessed to someone you knew was lost? When is the last time you gave financially toward the work of a missionary? These things and similar actions are the things that will bring you lasting joy.
- Would you rather spend time doing your favorite hobby or serving the Lord? Be honest! What does your answer tell you about your heart's condition?

PRAYER THOUGHTS

- Ask God to show you the things in life that bring true lasting joy.
- Ask the Lord to help you get your priorities in order.

SONG: *FADE, FADE, EACH EARTHLY JOY*

Day 210: (Saturday)
Expressions of Joy

*Isaiah 49:13 Sing, O heavens; and **be joyful**, O earth; and break forth into singing, O mountains: for the LORD hath comforted his people, and will have mercy upon his afflicted.*

INTRODUCTORY THOUGHTS

People express joy in distinct ways: some expressions involve tears, some laughter, and some simple words of praise; yet each expression of joy stems from the goodness of God. With all these variations, the Bible repeats a few expressions in conjunction with people having joy. Several times we are told that the people of God rejoiced with great joy *(1 Kings 1:40; Nehemiah 12:43)*. This joy on the part of the people of God generally manifested itself as a vocal expression of praise. Additionally, the Bible also connects joy with music, like the noise of a harp *(Isaiah 24:8)* and singing *(Psalm 95:1-2)*. Though the Bible conveys various types of expressions, true joy cannot be hidden.

DEVOTIONAL THOUGHTS

- **(For children):** Most children who have gone to church really like the song *"Jesus Loves Me."* Think about how different this song would be if everyone singing had a sad face or a sad voice. Would this reflect the true joy that should be in their heart? When your heart is glad, your face will show it and your voice will reveal it.
- **(For everyone):** Do you frequently have a song in your heart? Do you find yourself humming, whistling, or singing some song of praise to God? If so, this generally reflects a person with joy in the Lord. The things that come out of your mouth tell a great deal about what is going on in your heart *(Matthew 12:34)*. What types of things seem to frequently proceed out of your mouth?

PRAYER THOUGHTS

- Ask the Lord to fill your heart with a song of joy.
- Ask God to help you take note of the things that come from your mouth.

SONG: *HEAVENLY SUNLIGHT*

Notes: _____

_____

_____

_____

_____

_____

_____

_____

_____

_____

_____

_____

_____

_____

_____

Quotes from the next volume

(VOLUME 2, WEEK 30)

Subject: Modesty

God's people should conscientiously cover themselves so that the shame of their nakedness does not appear before others.

Man looks on the outward appearance, but God sees both the outward and the inward man. God's word emphasizing the inward man does not reflect a lack of concern for the outward adornments.

31

Joy (con't)

Occurrences: found 143 times in the Old Testament and seventy-three times in the New Testament

First usage in the New Testament: *Matthew 2:10* (joy)

Last usage in the Old Testament: *Zechariah 8:19* (joy)

Interesting fact: Joy occurs only six times in the section commonly called the Minor Prophets, and not at all in Revelation. Yet, it shows up thirty-four times in Psalms.

Bible study tip: According to the scripture, a love for the Saviour is a prerequisite for gaining additional Bible knowledge *(John 14:21)*. This verse further teaches a triangular series of events: he that has the commandments and keeps them loves the Saviour, and he that loves the Saviour will have the Lord manifest Himself to that man.

Sunday, Day 211—Church Day (no devotional)
Monday, Day 212—*Fulness of Joy*
Tuesday, Day 213—*Restore unto Me the Joy*
Wednesday, Day 214—Church Night (no devotional)
Thursday, Day 215—*Joy and Peace*
Friday, Day 216—*Joy and the Holy Ghost*
Saturday, Day 217—*Joyful in All Our Tribulation*

Day 211: Church Day

Isaiah 12:3 Therefore **with joy** *shall ye draw water out of the wells of salvation.*

Day 212: (Monday)
Fulness of Joy

John 15:9 As the Father hath loved me, so have I loved you: continue ye in my love.
10 If ye keep my commandments, ye shall abide in my love; even as I have kept my Father's commandments, and abide in his love.
11 These things have I spoken unto you, **that my joy might remain in you, and that your joy might be full.**

Introductory Thoughts

The Lord wants His children to have joy and that without limitations. He wants Christians to experience the fulness of joy that only comes from right relationships. This fulness only exists in the lives of believers as certain conditions are met. The right relationship involves fellowship with God which in turn evolves into the right kind of fellowship with other believers. According to today's passage, the words of the Lord Jesus bring fulness of joy to the saint of God. Additionally, answered prayer offers fulness of joy *(John 16:24)*. In addition to our fellowship with the Lord, the Bible suggests that fellowship with other believers also yields fulness of joy *(2 John 12)*. Every astute Bible student recognizes that these two fellowships are inextricably linked *(1 John 1:3)*. No dedicated Christian can experience true fellowship with other dedicated believers without first having the right kind of fellowship with God Almighty.

Devotional Thoughts

- **(For children):** The Lord Jesus wants His children to experience the greatest joy inside of us. That can only come from obeying. Jesus offered us the perfect example of obedience to His Father. God wants us to obey Him and His word also.
- **(For everyone):** Do you have the joy of the Lord in your life? Do you know the fulness of joy of which the Bible speaks? If not, what is the cause of the joy missing in your life? Do you have the right kind of fellowship with the Lord? Are you fellowshipping with other believers?

- We all tend to blame circumstances and other people for the problems which arise in our lives. Yet, who is really to blame for our life lacking the joy that God so richly wants us to experience?

PRAYER THOUGHTS

- Ask God to strengthen your fellowship with Him and with His people.
- Ask the Lord to give you fulness of joy.

SONG: *O! SAY, BUT I'M GLAD*

Day 213: (Tuesday)
Restore unto Me the Joy

Psalm 51:7 Purge me with hyssop, and I shall be clean: wash me, and I shall be whiter than snow.
*8 Make me to hear **joy and gladness**; that the bones which thou hast broken may rejoice.*
9 Hide thy face from my sins, and blot out all mine iniquities.
*10 Create in me a **clean heart**, O God; and renew a **right spirit** within me.*
11 Cast me not away from thy presence; and take not thy holy spirit from me.
*12 **Restore unto me the joy of thy salvation**; and uphold me with thy free spirit.*
13 Then will I teach transgressors thy ways; and sinners shall be converted unto thee.

INTRODUCTORY THOUGHTS

Psalm 51 describes some of the dire consequences resulting from David's sin with Bathsheba (see 2 Samuel chapters 11-12). Our passage commences with David's testifying about his desire to be washed *(Psalm 51:7)*. The next verse speaks of his desire to hear *joy and gladness*. David then goes on to express his desire for a *clean heart* and a *right spirit*. David was experiencing the debilitating results of his sin. Sin diminishes the spiritual blessings that God intends. In addition to these lost blessings, David also lost his *joy*. Joy is offered to the people of God, but never unconditionally. The conditions necessary for fulness of joy were discussed in the previous lesson, but it should be noted that the opposite actions yield contrary outcomes.

Devotional Thoughts

- **(For children):** Two children sneak some cookies off the table without permission. When asked about the missing cookies, one child tells the truth and says he is sorry; the other child lies. The truthful child walks away with *joy* in his heart. The other child is miserable because his sin will be *"before him" (Psalm 51:3b)* until he admits it.
- **(For everyone):** Do you rejoice in serving the Lord, or is it more of a burden? Do you find joy in Bible reading and prayer, or do you find it burdensome?
- Have you lost your joy? Look back over your life and consider why you might have lost it? What are you willing to do to seek the Lord concerning its restoration?

Prayer Thoughts

- Ask the Lord to help you see whether or not you have the joy of the Lord in your life daily.
- If joy has been lost, ask the Lord to show you how to restore it in your life.

Song: *LORD, I'M COMING HOME*

Day 214: Church Night

Philippians 4:4 Rejoice in the Lord alway: and again I say, Rejoice.

Day 215: (Thursday)
Joy and Peace

Romans 15:13 Now the God of hope fill you with all joy and peace in believing, that ye may abound in hope, through the power of the Holy Ghost.

Introductory Thoughts

Joy and peace! Any sensible person would readily admit his desire for a life filled with joy. Yet, few people understand the prerequisites for regularly living that way. Previous studies mentioned several of joy's accompanying virtues, but today's passage provides one of joy's unifying properties. According to our passage, *peace* accompanies *joy*. **Proverbs 12:20** also expresses this same relationship: *"Deceit is in the heart of them* *that imagine evil: but* **to the counsellors of peace is joy**." Those who seek peace will often find joy in this life because peace and joy are entwined. *Isaiah 55:12* restates this truth: *"For ye shall go out with* **joy**, *and be led forth with* **peace**." It is important to note that men will not *"go out with joy"* unless they are first *"led forth with peace."* Peace and joy are always inseparable. Those who have the *peace of God* after they are at *peace with God* through salvation will experience *"joy unspeakable"* **(1 Peter 1:8)**.

Devotional Thoughts

- **(For children):** What do you find more enjoyable: fighting with friends or playing nicely? Do you know God wants each of us to be peacemakers? That means you don't always get your own way. You will have more joy in your heart when you try to be kind to others rather than always getting your own way.
- **(For everyone):** Do you realize that you have *"peace with God"* that comes from being saved *(Romans 5:1)*? Why stop there when you can also experience the *"peace of God"* (peace only offered to the saved) ruling in your heart *(Colossians 3:15)*?
- Peace and joy are dependent upon God and not upon outside influences. Have you lost your joy and peace? If so, you cannot blame anyone but yourself.

Prayer Thoughts

- Ask the Lord to ingrain His truths into your heart and especially the connection between having peace and experiencing joy.
- Ask the Lord to help you keep your peace and your joy.

Song: *CONSTANTLY ABIDING*

Day 216: (Friday)
Joy and the Holy Ghost

*Acts 13:52 And the disciples were **filled with joy**, and with the Holy Ghost.*

Introductory Thoughts

As we have previously studied, God is the believer's source of joy. Specifically, God's indwelling presence makes this an accessible virtue. The Lord indwells those who are saved and does so through the person of the Holy Ghost. It should, therefore, come as no surprise that the disciples who were filled with the Holy Ghost were also filled with joy. God identifies the nature of the kingdom of God as *"righteousness, and peace, and **joy in the Holy Ghost***" *(Romans 14:17)*. This is why the Bible includes *joy* and *peace* when it defines the ninefold fruit of the Spirit *(Galatians 5:22)*. This is why the believers in Thessalonica received the word *"with joy of the Holy Ghost" (1 Thessalonians 1:6)*. The more the Holy Ghost has control, the more joy from the Lord a man will experience.

DEVOTIONAL THOUGHTS

- **(For children):** The Holy Ghost is God. He comes to live inside of us the moment we get saved. We can't see Him, yet, He guides us, teaches us, and helps us to remember God's word. Every one of us should obey the Bible so that we can have joy from serving Jesus.
- **(For everyone):** Does God have full access to your life? Are you surrendered to the Lord? Have you given yourself wholly to Him?
- Have you lost your joy? If so, what do you think is lacking in your life and walk? Can you pinpoint why you lack the joy of the Holy Ghost? Do you allow the Lord to have as much of you as He desires?

PRAYER THOUGHTS

- Ask the Lord to guide you into His joy.
- Ask the Lord to consecrate you more to Himself through the inner workings of His Spirit.

SONG: *HAVE THINE OWN WAY, LORD!*

Day 217: (Saturday)
Joyful in All Our Tribulation

*2 Corinthians 7:4 Great is my boldness of speech toward you, great is my glorying of you: I am filled with comfort, **I am exceeding joyful in all our tribulation.***

INTRODUCTORY THOUGHTS

Some people attribute a lack of joy to unfavourable circumstances. They believe joy is attainable only when their circumstances enable them to experience joy. The Bible offers a completely different perspective. Paul testified, *"I am exceeding joyful in all our tribulation."* Paul experienced tribulation and yet was exceeding joyful! He also wrote of the churches of Macedonia abounding in joy though they were *"in a great trial of affliction"* *(2 Corinthians 8:2)*. Furthermore, Paul wrote of the saints of God in Thessalonica that they received the word of God with joy even though they were *"in much affliction"* *(1 Thessalonians 1:6)*. Lastly, believers should *"count it all joy"* when falling into divers temptations *(James 1:2)*. We should understand that our joy as Christians is not dependent upon favourable circumstances.

DEVOTIONAL THOUGHTS

- **(For children):** Jesus left heaven's glory and became a man. He suffered and died on the cross after having taken our sins upon Himself. Would you think that the cross was a joyful time for Jesus? No, yet **Hebrews 12:2** says He had joy. He knew He was doing the Father's will and He was doing something wonderful for us. If someone in your family fell sick, what could you do to help them? Would this not bring joy to you?
- **(For everyone):** Do you have joy in the good times and also in the midst of troubles and trials? What circumstances often lead to the loss of joy in your life?
- Do you find that your joy comes and goes all too easily? Why do you lose your joy? Why do you allow the circumstances of life to rob you of the joy that the Lord has set before you?

PRAYER THOUGHTS

- Ask the Lord to help you have joy in the good times and in the bad.
- Ask God to strengthen your joy in Him in all circumstances.

SONG: *SINGING I GO*

Notes: _____

_____

_____

_____

_____

_____

_____

Notes: _____

_____

_____

_____

_____

_____

_____

_____

_____

_____

_____

_____

_____

Quotes from the next volume

(VOLUME 2, WEEK 31)

Subject: Murmuring

Murmuring is a grievous sin harmful to everyone involved or impacted. When God's people murmur, they do so because their heart is not sufficiently focused upon the Lord.

People murmur as they focus on events within their lives, rather than upon the Lord and His word. Yet, the Christian's life events are ultimately brought to pass, either directly or indirectly, by a loving and caring God.

Life's trials and difficulties are intended to draw people into a deeper knowledge of the Lord. However, murmuring hinders the lessons that result from the trials.

32

Meekness

Occurrences: found thirty-one times in twenty-nine verses

Variations: meek, meekness

First usage: *Numbers 12:3* (meek)

Last usage: *1 Peter 3:15* (meekness)

Defined: not easily provoked or irritated; yielding

Interesting fact: Moses was meek above all men which were upon the face of the earth *(Numbers 12:3)*.

Bible study tip: Pay close attention to those Old Testament passages quoted in the New Testament. The differences in wording usually provide new insights into the meaning of the Old Testament word or passage.

Sunday, Day 218—Church Day (no devotional)
Monday, Day 219—*What Is Meekness?*
Tuesday, Day 220—*The Meekest Man*
Wednesday, Day 221—Church Night (no devotional)
Thursday, Day 222—*The Meekness of Christ*
Friday, Day 223—*Meekness Is Not Weakness*
Saturday, Day 224—*The Sacrifice of the Meek*

Day 218: Church Day

Psalm 147:6 The LORD lifteth up the meek: he casteth the wicked down to the ground.

Day 219: (Monday)
What Is Meekness?

Titus 3:1 Put them in mind to be subject to principalities and powers, to obey magistrates, to be ready to every good work,

*2 To speak evil of no man, to be no brawlers, but gentle, **shewing all meekness unto all men**.*

3 For we ourselves also were sometimes foolish, disobedient, deceived, serving divers lusts and pleasures, living in malice and envy, hateful, and hating one another.

INTRODUCTORY THOUGHTS

What is true scriptural meekness? Is meekness simply humility or does it encompass something more pervasive? Though there is some overlap in meaning, meekness goes far beyond humility. According to scripture, meekness has to do with the way men respond to one another. Today's passage reveals that meekness is best expressed by avoiding both speaking evil of others and brawling. Meekness involves responding to others with a gentle spirit. Two prominent figures, Moses *(Numbers 12:3)* and the Lord Jesus Christ *(Matthew 11:29)*, exemplified meekness in their lives. Both men were known for their meekness. God not only desires humility in the life of the believer, but also wants His people to be known for their meekness.

DEVOTIONAL THOUGHTS

- **(For children):** Would you speak to a tiny baby with a harsh tone or gently? Would you ever hit a baby? God wants us to treat others with gentleness, even those who fail to treat us the same way. Behaving this way is called meekness.
- **(For everyone):** How do you know if you are being meek? When others criticize, how do you respond to their unjust criticisms? Do you seek to defend yourself at all costs no matter the extent to which you must strike back?

- What thoughts come to mind when you think of the character of Moses and the Lord Jesus Christ? What traits displayed their greatness? How would you learn to become meeker?

PRAYER THOUGHTS

- Ask the Lord to teach you how to be meeker each day.
- Ask God to help you learn how to have a meek and quiet spirit.

SONG: *O TO BE LIKE THEE!*

Day 220: (Tuesday)
The Meekest Man

Numbers 12:1 *And Miriam and Aaron spake against Moses because of the Ethiopian woman whom he had married: for he had married an Ethiopian woman.*

2 And they said, Hath the LORD indeed spoken only by Moses? hath he not spoken also by us? And the LORD heard it.

*3 **(Now the man Moses was very meek, above all the men which were upon the face of the earth.)***

INTRODUCTORY THOUGHTS

The Bible reveals many instances of Moses coming under attack for trying to obey God while leading others through the wilderness. His consistent response reveals why God said that he was meeker than any man upon the face of the earth. The vast majority of times, Moses responded to others in the spirit of gentleness. Today's passage reveals one such episode when Aaron and Miriam verbally attacked Moses for marrying an Ethiopian woman. Moses did not respond to their criticisms but instead pleaded for their well-being after the Lord brought judgment upon them. This was not the only instance of a personal attack upon Moses. In fact, it is quite common for God's messengers to be attacked when acting as a spiritual leader of others. Yet, Moses' recurring response is found in **Numbers 16:4**, *"And when Moses heard it, he fell upon his face."* Consistently, Moses prayed on the behalf of his accusers.

DEVOTIONAL THOUGHTS

- **(For children):** Sometimes people in our own home and at church do not treat us right or speak nicely to us. Instead of striking back at them, God wants us to be more like Moses as he prayed for his brother and sister although they were mean to him.
- **(For everyone):** Have you ever been attacked by others simply for doing the right things? How did you respond when they said untrue things about you? How did you want to respond?
- What would you have done if you were in Moses' position? Would and could you have responded like him? Why do you think Moses responded with gentleness? Why did he pray for those who afflicted him?

PRAYER THOUGHTS

- Ask the Lord to give you meekness like that of Moses.
- Ask the Lord to help you respond properly to criticism.

SONG: *DID YOU THINK TO PRAY?*

Day 221: Church Night

*James 1:21 Wherefore lay apart all filthiness and superfluity of naughtiness, and **receive with meekness the engrafted word, which is able to save your souls.***

Day 222: (Thursday)
The Meekness of Christ

*Matthew 21:5 Tell ye the daughter of Sion, Behold, **thy King cometh unto thee, meek,** and sitting upon an ass, and a colt the foal of an ass.*

INTRODUCTORY THOUGHTS

The Bible repeatedly referred to Christ's *meekness* during His interaction with others. Meekness implies a gentle response toward those who attack. Jesus Christ demonstrated meekness to its perfection on the cross of Calvary when He said, *"Father, forgive them; for they know not what they do" (**Luke 23:34**).* Peter emphasized this point when he said of

Christ, *"Who, when he was reviled, reviled not again; when he suffered, he threatened not; but committed himself to him that judgeth righteously"* *(1 Peter 2:23).* Isaiah prophesied of Christ, *"He was oppressed, and he was afflicted, yet he opened not his mouth: he is brought as a lamb to the slaughter, and as a sheep before her shearers is dumb, so he openeth not his mouth" (Isaiah 53:7).* The Bible says that Jesus was mocked, spit on, and struck by His accusers, yet He displayed incomprehensible meekness.

DEVOTIONAL THOUGHTS

- **(For children):** Jesus is God and could have effortlessly destroyed any and all who came against Him. In fact, He could have prayed to His Father and the Bible says He would have sent twelve legions of angels to help Him *(Matthew 26:53).* Yet, on the cross He prayed, "Father, forgive them" as the ultimate example for us to follow.
- **(For everyone):** Nobody in the Bible exemplifies meekness any better than Christ. What can we learn from the way He responded to the afflictions He endured on Calvary?
- The Lord Jesus Christ had every right to respond to those who abused Him. His accusers were wrong and in many cases acted in an evil fashion. Yet, He refused to respond to their taunts. What does this teach us about how we ought to respond when others wrongfully accuse us?

PRAYER THOUGHTS

- Ask the Lord to give you meekness like Christ displayed.
- Ask the Lord to help you respond righteously when others wrongfully attack you.

SONG: *NO, NOT ONE!*

Day 223: (Friday)
Meekness Is Not Weakness

*Proverbs 16:32 He that is **slow to anger** is better than the mighty; and he that **ruleth his spirit** than he that taketh a city.*

INTRODUCTORY THOUGHTS

Many people view meekness as an inherent weakness, yet the Bible corrects this faulty notion. The ability to demonstrate meekness in a time of ridicule or persecution displays strength. Today's passage reveals that a man slow to anger is *"better than the mighty."* In fact, a man that *"ruleth his spirit"* is better than a military conqueror who *"taketh a city."* Rather than a weakness, the ability to demonstrate meekness is a sign of great strength. The Bible declares that the Lord Jesus Christ was meek *(Matthew 11:29)*; yet He simultaneously held the world together *"by the word of His power" (Hebrews 1:3)*. We see that God referred to Moses as meek, yet he had the power through the Lord to part the Red Sea *(Exodus 14:21)* and to open the earth and swallow his enemies *(Numbers 16:28-34)*. Weak individuals respond in anger when attacked; those who are strong exercise meekness.

DEVOTIONAL THOUGHTS

- **(For children):** No one is stronger than God. The Bible says God is slow to anger and of great kindness. It is easy to strike back with our words or hands when someone does us wrong. God says you are strongest when you control those feelings and show kindness instead.
- **(For everyone):** Are you concerned that your meekness may be perceived by others as a weakness? Why does this concern you if it pleases God? Whom do you want to please?
- Do you think of the Lord Jesus as weak? Do you consider Moses to be an example of weakness? Do you think those who lived in their days considered them weak? If not, then why do we think we are weak when we exhibit meekness in our interactions with others?

PRAYER THOUGHTS

- Ask the Lord to show you the strength of meekness.
- Ask God to help you desire to please Him especially when others are treating you badly.

SONG: *COME UNTO ME* (JONES)

Day 224: (Saturday)
The Sacrifice of the Meek

Isaiah 29:19 The meek also shall increase their joy in the LORD, and the poor among men shall rejoice in the Holy One of Israel.

INTRODUCTORY THOUGHTS

In the midst of suffering, Christians can fail to rejoice in future blessings resulting from obedience. Additionally, the trials of life can cause one to lose focus on the unseen future blessings. One such case involves rightfully leaving vengeance to the Lord *(Romans 12:19)*. God's blessings are frequently not seen or realized until much later. The meek who leave vengeance to the Lord have God's promise that *"The LORD lifteth up the meek" (Psalm 147:6)*. Nevertheless, a believer living a meek life may become disheartened by those who take advantage of kindheartedness. In fact, a meek and compassionate believer may appear weak in the eyes of the world necessitating the Lord's deliverance *(Psalm 76:9; Psalm 149:4)*. In the end, the Lord will deliver *(Psalm 76:9)*, lift up *(Psalm 147:6)*, beautify *(Psalm 149:4)*, and bless *(Matthew 5:5)* the meek. It is important to remember that the future blessings following life's temporary trials are worth forgoing the immediate pleasures that might come from taking matters into our own hands.

DEVOTIONAL THOUGHTS

- **(For children):** King Saul was jealous of David and repeatedly tried to kill him although David had done nothing wrong. David could have killed king Saul two different times but chose not to. He believed God would take care of the matter. What happened to king Saul in the end? Who took his place on the throne as king of Israel?
- **(For everyone):** Do you want the blessings of the Lord upon your life or the immediate gratification that comes from knowing that you told that person how it was? Would you rather satisfy the Lord or your own wicked fleshly desires?
- Are you willing to wait upon God's blessings knowing that you have exemplified the meekness of Christ? Do you require present satisfaction in order to do right?

PRAYER THOUGHTS

- Ask God to give you patience when your righteous actions cause others to abuse you.
- Ask the Lord to show you the blessings that come from living meekly.

SONG: *O THAT WILL BE GLORY*

Notes: _____

_____

_____

_____

_____

_____

_____

_____

_____

_____

_____

_____

_____

Quotes from the next volume

(VOLUME 2, WEEK 32)

Subject: Praise

When a man begins to praise himself, he does so in direct rebellion to the words and direction of God *(Proverbs 27:2).*

Praise is the natural overflowing of affection that occurs when one individual views some positive quality in another. Men praise God because they find His attributes and actions worthy of worship.

Though the praise of men can never reach to the height of God's worth, God still chose to inhabit the praises of His people *(Psalm 22:3).*

33

Meekness (con't)

Occurrences: found fifteen times in the Old Testament and sixteen times in the New Testament

First usage in the New Testament: *Matthew 5:5* (meek)

Last usage in the Old Testament: *Zephaniah 2:3* (meek, meekness)

Interesting fact: Only two people are specifically identified in the scripture as meek: Moses *(Numbers 12:3)* and Jesus Christ *(Matthew 11:29)*.

Bible study tip: All scripture is profitable for you, but not all scripture was written directly to you. The Bible identifies three groups of people in *1 Corinthians 10:32*: Jews, Gentiles, and the church of God (made up of both saved Jews and Gentiles). When studying a subject, consider whether this truth might be applied specifically (or exclusively) to each of these distinctive groups. Keep in mind that the majority of scripture was written directly to the Jewish people, not the church.

Sunday, Day 225—Church Day (no devotional)
Monday, Day 226—*The Spirit of Meekness*
Tuesday, Day 227—*The Fruit of the Spirit*

Wednesday, Day 228—Church Night (no devotional)
Thursday, Day 229—*A Meek and Quiet Spirit*
Friday, Day 230—*Instructing in Meekness*
Saturday, Day 231—*The Meek Will He Guide*

Day 225: Church Day

*Ephesians 4:1 I therefore, the prisoner of the Lord, beseech you that ye **walk worthy** of the vocation wherewith ye are called,*

*2 **With all lowliness and meekness**, with longsuffering, forbearing one another in love;*

3 Endeavouring to keep the unity of the Spirit in the bond of peace.

Day 226: (Monday)
The Spirit of Meekness

1 Corinthians 4:17 For this cause have I sent unto you Timotheus, who is my beloved son, and faithful in the Lord, who shall bring you into remembrance of my ways which be in Christ, as I teach every where in every church.

18 Now some are puffed up, as though I would not come to you.

19 But I will come to you shortly, if the Lord will, and will know, not the speech of them which are puffed up, but the power.

20 For the kingdom of God is not in word, but in power.

*21 What will ye? shall I **come unto you** with a rod, or **in love, and in the spirit of meekness**?*

INTRODUCTORY THOUGHTS

The Bible describes the Corinthian Church as carnal. In fact, some of the believers at Corinth had become puffed up that Paul was not personally coming to visit them. Instead, the apostle Paul sent Timothy to the church of God at Corinth with words of warning. Paul informed them that he could come to them with the rod of judgment or *"in love, and in the spirit of meekness."* Paul strongly believed in dealing with wayward believers in the spirit of meekness. He expressed as much in **Galatians 6:1** when he wrote: *"Brethren, if a man be overtaken in a fault, ye which are spiritual, **restore such an one in the spirit of meekness**; considering thyself, lest thou also be tempted."* Paul favoured restoration and believed that responding in love and meekness was generally the best avenue for that restoration. Often, the prideful response of those who should be reacting spiritually toward wayward believers simply drives these believers further away from God.

DEVOTIONAL THOUGHTS

- **(For children):** We all like to hear pleasant words (Proverbs 16:24). When someone does not treat us the right way, God wants us to tell them they are wrong but use gentle and kind words rather than harsh and hateful ones. In fact, by correcting in meekness, they will more likely listen to what you have to say.
- **(For everyone):** How do you deal with fellow believers who have done you wrong? Do you immediately rebuke them in anger or do you patiently try to win them back in the spirit of meekness?
- How do you deal with your family when they have done you wrong? Do you yell and scream at them or do you attempt to restore them in meekness?

PRAYER THOUGHTS

- Ask the Lord to give you a right kind of heart for His people.
- Ask God to help you restore in the spirit of meekness those who have gotten away from the ways of the Lord.

SONG: *COME, YE DISCONSOLATE*

Day 227: (Tuesday)
The Fruit of the Spirit

Galatians 5:19 Now **the works of the flesh are manifest,** *which are these; Adultery, fornication, uncleanness, lasciviousness,*

20 *Idolatry, witchcraft, hatred, variance, emulations, wrath, strife, seditions, heresies,*

21 *Envyings, murders, drunkenness, revellings, and such like: of the which I tell you before, as I have also told you in time past, that they which do such things shall not inherit the kingdom of God.*

22 **But the fruit of the Spirit is** *love, joy, peace, longsuffering, gentleness, goodness, faith,*

23 **Meekness,** *temperance: against such there is no law.*

INTRODUCTORY THOUGHTS

Today's passage contrasts the **works** of the flesh with the **fruit** of the Spirit. The **works** of the flesh are **works** done by man in his own strength and abilities; whereas, the **fruit** of the Spirit is the **natural growth** in the believer's life when surrendered to the leading of God's Spirit. The Bible lists eighteen works of the flesh *(Galatians 5:19-21)* but only one ninefold fruit of the Spirit *(Galatians 5:22-23)*. The fruit of the Spirit includes many wonderful things such as love, joy, and peace. However, *meekness* remains one of most undervalued characteristics in that list. Similar to the other fruit, meekness should naturally mature in the believer's life as he yields to the Lord. When a believer lacks meekness, it is because he is not properly surrendered to God's will.

DEVOTIONAL THOUGHTS

- **(For children)**: When fruit trees are properly cared for, they produce the desired results. Apple, pear, and peach trees produce juicy fruits. A child of God is nurtured much like those trees when he feeds upon the nourishment of God's word. One of the results of this growth is meekness.
- **(For everyone)**: Do you recognize the ninefold fruit of the Spirit maturing within your life? Do you yield to the Spirit of God so that He can accomplish the Father's will in and through your life?
- Are you able to demonstrate meekness when others have mistreated you? Do you find yourself responding vengefully or do you display a supernatural gentleness in the face of adversity?

PRAYER THOUGHTS

- Ask the Lord to help you yield to His Spirit.
- Ask God to grow His ninefold fruit in your life.

SONG: *ETERNAL SPIRIT, WE CONFESS*

Day 228: Church Night

Zephaniah 2:3 *Seek ye the LORD, all ye **meek of the earth,** which have wrought his judgment; seek righteousness, **seek meekness**: it may be ye shall be hid in the day of the LORD'S anger.*

Day 229: (Thursday)
A Meek and Quiet Spirit

1 Peter 3:1 Likewise, ye wives, be in subjection to your own husbands; that, if any obey not the word, they also may without the word be won by the conversation of the wives;

2 While they behold your chaste conversation coupled with fear.

3 Whose adorning let it not be that outward adorning of plaiting the hair, and of wearing of gold, or of putting on of apparel;

*4 But let it be the hidden man of the heart, in that which is not corruptible, even **the ornament of a meek and quiet spirit**, which is in the sight of God of great price.*

INTRODUCTORY THOUGHTS

Most saved women who have an unsaved spouse would testify that their chief concern lies with seeing their husbands come to know Christ as Saviour. The context of today's passage reveals how an unsaved husband can be won to Christ through his wife's actions. Displaying a meek and quiet spirit is paramount in such efforts. This meekness is to be worn and displayed much like an ornament, and such a spirit is of great price in the sight of God. Most women who are married to unsaved men will admit that their husbands tend to treat them with a lessening degree of devotion as the marriage ages. Regardless, the Bible admonishes wives in this situation to respond in meekness toward their husbands with the goal of winning them to Christ. Today's passage specifically applies to wives with unsaved husbands but also has far reaching application to all believers.

DEVOTIONAL THOUGHTS

- **(For children):** Children like to dress up using mom's and dad's clothes. The children do this to look all grown up. Sometimes we focus so much on the outside we fail to realize that God is most concerned with what we look like on the inside. Sometimes the words we say betray us because they reflect what we are on the inside.
- **(For everyone):** A good marriage takes effort and work. What are some ways that a lady married to an unsaved man could respond to bring spiritual conviction in his life when he mistreats her?

- Most people place an undue emphasis on a woman's beauty when the Bible emphasizes more important matters. The Bible declares that a *"meek and quiet spirit"* is an ornament. There are few things that demonstrate the beauty of a woman more than one who has a meek and quiet spirit. How could meekness improve your life?

Prayer Thoughts

- Ask the Lord to give you meekness when dealing with the lost.
- Ask God to give you a desire to respond with meekness to those who mistreat you.

SONG: *HAPPY THE HOME WHEN GOD IS THERE*

Day 230: (Friday)
Instructing in Meekness

*2 Timothy 2:24 And **the servant of the Lord must** not strive; but be gentle unto all men, apt to teach, patient,*

*25 **In meekness instructing those that oppose themselves;** if God peradventure will give them repentance to the acknowledging of the truth;*

26 And that they may recover themselves out of the snare of the devil, who are taken captive by him at his will.

Introductory Thoughts

Every Christian is called to be a servant of the Lord toward others. In this service, God specifically instructs us how to serve in the right way and with the right spirit. The Bible shows us that God's servants should be *"gentle unto all men, apt to teach, patient."* Additionally, believers should instruct in meekness *"those that oppose themselves."* Unfortunately, God's people often struggle with balance and overcompensate or undercompensate in their dealings with the lost or the backslidden. For instance, Christians sometimes allow the wicked to gain control when they fail to respond. Those who do speak up sometimes oppose their adversaries with a vengeful anger. Neither extreme follows God's precepts. As God's servants, we are to respond to others in God's behalf using His methods. God desires to give the lost and the backslidden *"repentance to the acknowledging of the truth"* so *"that they may recover themselves out of the snare of the devil, who are taken captive by him at his will."* We should strive to assist in bringing about God's desired outcomes.

DEVOTIONAL THOUGHTS

- **(For children):** The Bible says, "the sweetness of the lips increaseth learning" (Proverbs 16:21). When others are told what God says to do, they will be more willing to learn because of the kind words used rather than harsh ones. How would you like to be taught?
- **(For everyone):** How do you react when others say things to you in the wrong spirit? Do you respond? If so, do you respond with anger or with gentleness even when others fail to do so with you?
- Why do you think we tend to respond with anger? Are you angry for God's sake or have you taken something personal? How should we respond for God's sake?

PRAYER THOUGHTS

- Ask the Lord to help you see that you are His servant.
- Ask God to give you His heart for those who are wayward.

SONG: *MORE LIKE THE MASTER*

Day 231: (Saturday)
The Meek Will He Guide

Psalm 25:8 *Good and upright is the LORD: therefore will he teach sinners in the way.*

9 *The meek will he guide in judgment: and the meek will he teach his way.*

INTRODUCTORY THOUGHTS

Those who are constantly defending themselves in the midst of wrongdoing find it difficult to receive knowledge and understanding. This is the point of today's passage. Our society increasingly resorts to making excuses as to why they feel it unnecessary to be taught or corrected for wrongdoing. Unfortunately, many Christians are increasingly guilty of this same character flaw. However, the Bible promises to guide the meek in judgment; that is, the meek will be led of the Lord in matters of judgment. In addition to this leading, the Lord will also teach the meek His way. However, when we are quick to defend ourselves when feeling threatened, we will not learn the Lord's lessons. We will not be guided by Him in judgment, nor will we be taught His way.

DEVOTIONAL THOUGHTS

- **(For children):** When you have misbehaved and mom or dad read *Colossians 3:20* to you, how do you feel? Do you feel angry for being corrected with scripture or do you want to obey God more? If you want to learn other truths from the Bible, you need to do what you already know to do first.
- **(For everyone):** How do you respond to the Lord's correction from the scriptures? Do you get offended when corrected by His word? Do you respond in meekness and genuine humility?
- Are you missing out on many of the Lord's blessings because of your unwillingness to be corrected? What lessons have you missed because of your unwise response? What judgments have you made on your own without the Lord's guidance? Are you tired of refusing to receive His correction?

PRAYER THOUGHTS

- Ask God to help you respond in a proper manner toward His correction.
- Ask the Lord to help you repent of stubbornness.

SONG: *PRECIOUS PROMISE*

Quotes from the next volume

(VOLUME 2, WEEK 33)

Subject: Prayer

Simply stated, prayer is talking to God.

Prayer is an act that portrays the greatness of God while testifying to man's inherent frailties.

34

Obedience

Occurrences: found 166 times in 159 verses

Variations: disobedience, disobedient, disobeyed, obedience, obedient, obey, obeyed, obeyedst, obeyeth, obeying

First usage: *Genesis 22:18* (obeyed)

Last usage: *1 Peter 4:17* (obey)

Defined: to hear and comply with commands or instructions; to forbear doing that which is prohibited

Interesting fact: Saul disobeyed God and then offered a sacrifice in the absence of Samuel. Samuel revealed a great truth to us all when he told Saul that *"to obey is better than sacrifice" (1 Samuel 15:22).*

Bible study tip: One of the primary causes of false doctrine results from failing to find the scriptural meaning of a word. For instance, failing to understand the scriptural use of the word *obedience* can lead someone to attribute salvation to a man's works *(Romans 6:17; Romans 10:16; 2 Thessalonians 1:8; Hebrews 5:9; 1 Peter 1:22; 1 Peter 4:17).* Look for the hints and key words that show that the Bible does not specifically identify obedience as a work.

Sunday, Day 232—Church Day (no devotional)
Monday, Day 233—*What Is Obedience?*
Tuesday, Day 234—*The Details of Obedience*
Wednesday, Day 235—Church Night (no devotional)
Thursday, Day 236—*The Importance of Obedience*
Friday, Day 237—*The Blessings of Obedience*
Saturday, Day 238—*The Curse of Disobedience*

Day 232: Church Day

*1 Samuel 15:22 And Samuel said, Hath the LORD as great delight in burnt offerings and sacrifices, as in obeying the voice of the LORD? Behold, **to obey is better than sacrifice**, and to hearken than the fat of rams.*

Day 233: (Monday)
What Is Obedience?

*2 Kings 18:12 Because **they obeyed not the voice of the LORD their God,** but transgressed his covenant, and all that Moses the servant of the LORD commanded, and would not hear them, nor do them.*

INTRODUCTORY THOUGHTS

Diligent Bible study is commanded of God. However, far too many Christians simply fail to comprehend the depths and riches of God's words. For instance, society has distorted the meaning of obey by limiting obedience solely to following a set of commands. Although obedience certainly does involve following the rules, the Bible indicates a much broader application. Today's passage sheds light on obedience and the depth of its meaning. The Bible says that Israel "would not hear them, nor do them" (that is, hear or do the commandments of God). With this context, it is easy to understand that the Bible defines disobedience as the refusal to hear and do the commandments of the Lord. Other similar passages teach this same truth (*1 Samuel 15:22; Proverbs 5:13; Jeremiah 17:23)*. Obedience is twofold: first, the individual must have an attentive ear, and second, he must act by faith.

DEVOTIONAL THOUGHTS

- **(For children):** Parents should incorporate visual demonstrations of obedience. Put three objects on the floor and ask your spouse or an older child to pick them "all" up. (Plan ahead by instructing your participant to only pick up two of the objects.) Explain to the younger children that this behaviour is not obedience.
- **(For everyone):** Hearing and doing only part of what we are told to do is not obedience at all. Saul is an explicit example of this truth *(1 Samuel 28:18)*. He did "obey" in part what God told him to do but the Lord told him, *"thou obeyedst not the voice of the LORD."*
- Are you obedient? Why is it so very important to obey? To whom should we be obedient?

PRAYER THOUGHTS

- Ask the Lord to give you a strong desire to obey.
- Ask the Lord to teach you the true meaning of obedience.

SONG: *FOLLOW ON*

Day 234: (Tuesday)
The Details of Obedience

Numbers 14:39 And Moses told these sayings unto all the children of Israel: and the people mourned greatly.

40 And they rose up early in the morning, and gat them up into the top of the mountain, saying, Lo, we be here, and will go up unto the place which the LORD hath promised: for we have sinned.

41 And Moses said, Wherefore now do ye transgress the commandment of the LORD? but it shall not prosper.

42 Go not up, for the LORD is not among you; that ye be not smitten before your enemies.

*43 For the Amalekites and the Canaanites are there before you, and ye shall fall by the sword: because **ye are turned away from the LORD, therefore the LORD will not be with you.***

44 But they presumed to go up unto the hill top: nevertheless the ark of the covenant of the LORD, and Moses, departed not out of the camp.

45 *Then the Amalekites came down, and the Canaanites which dwelt in that hill, and smote them, and discomfited them, even unto Hormah.*

INTRODUCTORY THOUGHTS

The Lord brought the children of Israel out of their long captivity in Egypt with a mighty hand. God intended to lead them directly into the land of promise; however, the people's disobedience hindered the outcome. Numbers chapter 13 records the people's decision to send spies into the land. These twelve spies, with the exception of Joshua and Caleb, returned with a report of unbelief. Because of the spies' evil report, the Israelites feared to enter the land. Their unilateral decision provoked the Lord so much that He told them that they would die in the wilderness (with the exception of the two faithful witnesses). The people were immediately troubled by God's judgment so they decided to take matters into their own hands. Now they were "ready" to take the land, but the Lord was no longer going to accompany them into battle. This battle, which could have been easily won with the Lord's help, was lost because of disobedience (or delayed obedience). Proper obedience must be done in the proper time and according to God's timetable. The right decision made too late is the wrong decision.

DEVOTIONAL THOUGHTS

- **(For children):** God told Noah to build an ark because He was sending a flood to destroy the world. Noah obeyed. He tried to get others to come into the ark, but they laughed and mocked him. When God shut the door and the rain started, the people wanted to come in, but by then it was too late.
- **(For everyone):** True obedience always has time restrictions. Do you do things when you are supposed to do them or do you try to make excuses as to why you cannot do them at the time appointed?
- People often think that obedience has no time schedule, but this is not true in the Lord's work. A sermon intended by God to meet the people's needs this Sunday may be too late if delayed because of disobedience until the next Sunday. Tomorrow could be too late to witness to the unsaved if God wants it done today.

- Ask God to make you more aware of the timing of obedience.
- Ask the Lord to help you understand the details of obeying.

SONG: *ALMOST PERSUADED*

Day 235: Church Night

Joshua 1:8 *This book of the law shall not depart out of thy mouth; but thou shalt meditate therein day and night,* ***that thou mayest observe to do according to all that is written therein****: for then thou shalt make thy way prosperous, and then thou shalt have good success.*

Day 236: (Thursday)
The Importance of Obedience

Deuteronomy 21:18 *If a man have a stubborn and rebellious son, which will not obey the voice of his father, or the voice of his mother, and that, when they have chastened him, will not hearken unto them:*

19 Then shall his father and his mother lay hold on him, and bring him out unto the elders of his city, and unto the gate of his place;

20 And they shall say unto the elders of his city, This our son is stubborn and rebellious, he will not obey our voice; he is a glutton, and a drunkard.

21 And all the men of his city shall stone him with stones, that he die: so shalt thou put evil away from among you; and all Israel shall hear, and fear.

INTRODUCTORY THOUGHTS

The Old Testament Law sometimes condemned the guilty without remedy and with little mercy for the oft offending party. Our passage explains one such instance. It describes the method by which God's Law punished a disobedient child following repeated attempts made to correct him. Certainly, the method of punishment has changed under grace, but the passage proves the importance of obedience. Though God's method of punishment has changed, His requirement for obedience has remained forever constant. Failing to learn obedience at an early age presents a stumbling block that impedes future growth. Perhaps this is why the Old Testament Law was so strict in punishing offending children. Unfortunately, far too many children in Christian homes think that if they could simply escape the confines of their godly homes they could truly enjoy life. Some of these children simply can't wait to grow up to be finally free to do whatever they want. However, God demands obedience and judges disobedience regardless of one's misconceptions.

DEVOTIONAL THOUGHTS

- **(For children):** Sometimes children think life is unfair because they seem to have so many "bosses." Ask dad and mom if they have anyone whom they must obey. Ask what happens when they don't obey. If you learn to obey dad and mom now, obeying won't be nearly so hard after you have grown up.
- **(For everyone):** What are some of the reasons why it is important to learn obedience at an early age? In what situations must adults obey on a daily basis?
- Do you think that the punishment of disobedient children described in today's passage was simply too strict under the law? Why do you think the judgment was so severe? What can we learn from this punishment?

PRAYER THOUGHTS

- Ask the Lord to help you see the importance of timely obedience.
- Ask God to develop a godly obedience in you before you learn the bad habits of disobedience.

SONG: *WHO LAUGHS AT SIN*

Day 237: (Friday)
The Blessings of Obedience

Deuteronomy 11:26 Behold, I set before you this day a blessing and a curse;

*27 **A blessing, if ye obey the commandments** of the LORD your God, which I command you this day:*

28 And a curse, if ye will not obey the commandments of the LORD your God, but turn aside out of the way which I command you this day, to go after other gods, which ye have not known.

INTRODUCTORY THOUGHTS

The children of Israel had an important decision to make: whether to obey the Lord or unwisely refuse to obey Him. The Lord assured His children that their obedience would pay off with fruitful dividends. He promised to bless their obedience and curse their disobedience. The Bible clearly lists the blessings of obedience *(Deuteronomy 28:1-14)*. Though the blessings of obedience can vary from one person to the next, obedience always yields God's blessing. For instance, Abraham was told that all nations would be blessed in his seed because he obeyed the voice of the Lord *(Genesis 22:18)*. Isaiah told the Israelites that, if they would obey, they would eat the good of the land *(Isaiah 1:19)*. Jeremiah told his audience that their obedience would cause it to be well with their soul and that their souls would live *(Jeremiah 38:20)*. Blessings received from obedience may vary, but the blessings of obedience are well worth any temporary fleshly sacrifice.

DEVOTIONAL THOUGHTS

- **(For children):** Obeying makes us feel good inside. Sometimes it brings rewards – an ice cream cone, a new toy, staying up a little later one night, etc. Yet, the best reward is knowing that what you've done is well pleasing to the Lord (Colossians 3:20).
- **(For everyone):** What are some blessings that a child might receive by obeying his parents? What are some blessings that a worker might receive by obeying his boss? What are some blessings that believers might receive by obeying the Lord?
- How do you feel when you have obeyed when no one is watching? Do you feel a sense of joy or feelings of remorse for doing right? The joy that we feel and the lack of guilt might be an element of the blessings of obedience.

PRAYER THOUGHTS

- Ask God to help you see the blessings resulting from obedience.
- Ask the Lord to help you consider the negative consequences resulting from making a decision to disobey.

SONG: *TRUST AND OBEY*

Day 238: (Saturday)
The Curse of Disobedience

Deuteronomy 11:26 Behold, I set before you this day a blessing and a curse;

27 A blessing, if ye obey the commandments of the LORD your God, which I command you this day:

28 And **a curse, if ye will not obey the commandments** of the LORD your God, but turn aside out of the way which I command you this day, to go after other gods, which ye have not known.

INTRODUCTORY THOUGHTS

The Bible repeatedly addresses the outcomes of obedience and disobedience. It reveals that blessings follow obedience and curses follow disobedience. This truth was plainly explained to the children of Israel on several occasions. In fact, the Bible lists the curses that follow disobedience *(Deuteronomy 28:15-44)*. The curses range from personal judgment to national judgment, but the obvious fact was that disobedience withheld blessings. For instance, disobedience drove Adam and Eve from the garden in Eden *(Genesis 3:22-24)*. Saul's disobedience cost him his kingdom *(1 Samuel 28:18)*. Moses' disobedience meant that he could not enter into the land of promise *(Numbers 20:12)*. The consequences of disobedience may differ today, but every act of disobedience has negative consequences.

DEVOTIONAL THOUGHTS

- **(For children):** Disobedience brings punishment. King David was one of Israel's greatest kings but he too disobeyed God's rules. As a result, he lost three children and his family did not get along very well. We can all learn from the lesson of king David. It's always better to obey.
- **(For everyone):** What kind of punishments can a child receive for disobeying his parents? What could happen to an employee who does not obey his boss? What could happen to a citizen who does not obey the laws of the land?
- Do you enjoy the blessings of God? Would you rather experience the blessings of obedience or the curses of disobedience?

PRAYER THOUGHTS

- Ask God to help you grasp the dire consequences of disobedience.
- Ask the Lord to help you see the importance of obeying.

SONG: *LORD, IF THINE EYES SURVEY OUR FAULTS*

Notes: _____

_____

_____

_____

_____

_____

_____

_____

_____

_____

_____

_____

_____

_____

_____

_____

_____

_____

_____

_____

_____

_____

Notes: _____

_____

_____

_____

_____

_____

_____

_____

_____

_____

_____

_____

_____

_____

_____

_____

_____

_____

_____

Quotes from the next volume

(VOLUME 2, WEEK 34)

Subject: Prayer (con't)

If believers fail to pray for others, who will take up the slack to pray for those in need?

Prayer was meant to give man a means of communicating with the Creator. It is to originate from the depths of the heart and never to be memorized and repeated.

35

Obedience (con't)

Occurrences: found ninety-five times in the Old Testament and seventy-one times in the New Testament

First usage in the New Testament: *Matthew 8:27* (obey)

Last usage in the Old Testament: *Zechariah 6:15* (obey)

Interesting fact: The various uses of obedience only appear six times in the four gospel books. Of those six times, five testify to the obedience of *nature (Matthew 8:27; Mark 1:27; Mark 4:41; Luke 8:25; Luke 17:6)* and one speaks to the disobedience of *man (Luke 1:17)*.

Bible study tip: The Bible never contradicts itself! Look for instances where one account of a particular event sheds additional light on a previously recorded account. Take notice how God at times varies in His dealings with man, yet remains unchanged in His person and character. There are yet other times where God identifies an *if/then* scenario. Obedience falls into the last category. Man is to obey authorities and also obey God. There are times when a man must choose to obey God by disobeying the ruling authorities. Peter's comments to those in authority reveal the priority of obeying God when a conflict arises *(Acts 5:29)*.

Test Sunday, Day 239—Church Day (no devotional)
Monday, Day 240—*The Obedience of a Citizen*
Tuesday, Day 241—*Obedience in the Home*
Wednesday, Day 242—Church Night (no devotional)
Thursday, Day 243—*Obedience in the Workplace*
Friday, Day 244—*Obedience in the Church*
Saturday, Day 245—*A Conflict in Obedience*

Day 239: Church Day

Deuteronomy 6:3 Hear therefore, O Israel, and observe to do it; that it may be well with thee, and that ye may increase mightily, as the LORD God of thy fathers hath promised thee, in the land that floweth with milk and honey.

Day 240: (Monday)
The Obedience of a Citizen

*Titus 3:1 Put them in mind to **be subject to principalities and powers, to obey magistrates,** to be ready to every good work,*

2 To speak evil of no man, to be no brawlers, but gentle, shewing all meekness unto all men.

INTRODUCTORY THOUGHTS

Because political abuses are becoming increasingly common, people have become disillusioned with their governing officials. However, God is very specific concerning His purpose for government. It is empowered by God for the punishment of evil doers and the praise of the righteous *(Romans 13:1-6)*. The Bible refers to rulers as *"God's ministers" (Romans 13:6)* and these ministers are offered as a gift from God to the people. As believers, we are to submit ourselves to the ordinances of man for the Lord's sake *(1 Peter 2:13-17)*. In our passage, Titus was reminded that one of his responsibilities as a preacher was to put the people in mind *"to be subject to principalities and powers"* and to encourage them *"to obey magistrates."* This may sound like a daunting responsibility because governments frequently go beyond the scope of their God-given authority. This is why God has not left Christians without direction when He instructs that is better to obey God than men *(Acts 5:29)*.

Devotional Thoughts

- **(For children):** Discuss what might happen if dad chose to run all stop signs, ignore red lights, and never yield to an ambulance on an emergency call. Laws are made for our protection and God wants us to obey them.
- **(For everyone):** As citizens of a country, we are responsible to obey the laws. Do you obey the laws of the land? If not, who are you really disobeying so long as these laws do not contradict the laws of God?
- As believers, we are to pray for those in authority that we might live a quiet and peaceable life *(1 Timothy 2:1-2)*. Do you pray for the government? Do you pray for your king or president? Do you ask God to give your leaders wisdom?

Prayer Thoughts

- Ask God to give you a love for the country in which you live.
- Ask the Lord to help you be a good testimony by obeying the laws.

SONG: *WHAT WILT THOU HAVE ME TO DO?* (BLISS)

Day 241: (Tuesday)
Obedience in the Home

Colossians 3:18 Wives, submit yourselves unto your own husbands, as it is fit in the Lord.

19 *Husbands, love your wives, and be not bitter against them.*

20 ***Children, obey your parents*** *in all things: for this is well pleasing unto the Lord.*

Introductory Thoughts

The home was God's first institution. God gave specific instructions on how the home was to be ordered. In any home dedicated to God's service, each individual has a responsibility to be accountable in the area of obedience. First and foremost, a father or husband is to be obedient to the headship of Jesus Christ *(1 Corinthians 11:3)*. Second, the mother or wife is accountable to submit to the authority of her husband *(Genesis 3:16; Ephesians 5:22; Colossians 3:18; Titus 2:4-5)*. Lastly, the children are to obey their parents in the Lord *(Ephesians 6:1; Colossians 3:20)*. The home failing to follow God's plan could possibly have some limited success but will ultimately experience great difficulties. Yet, God will faithfully bless the Christian home where each member submits to his or her God-given authorities.

DEVOTIONAL THOUGHTS

- **(For children):** When God says, *"Children, obey your parents,"* to whom is He referring? Some children recognize they must obey dad, but mom seems so kind that they think they do not have to obey her. It is important to realize that when you disobey either of them, you are disobeying God.
- **(For everyone):** What is your role in the home? What could you do to make sure that your home knows the joys that God intended for it?
- Why is it so important that we follow God's plan in our home? What could go wrong if God's order is ignored in your home? Are you doing your best to be faithfully obedient?

PRAYER THOUGHTS

- Ask the Lord to show you the importance of your role in the home.
- Ask God to help you faithfully obey those in authority over you.

SONG: *GOD, GIVE US CHRISTIAN HOMES*

Day 242: Church Night

John 14:21 He that hath my commandments, and keepeth them, he it is that loveth me: and he that loveth me shall be loved of my Father, and I will love him, and will manifest myself to him.

Day 243: (Thursday)
Obedience in the Workplace

Titus 2:9 Exhort servants to be obedient unto their own masters, and to please them well in all things; not answering again;

10 Not purloining, but shewing all good fidelity; that they may adorn the doctrine of God our Saviour in all things.

INTRODUCTORY THOUGHTS

Living the Christian life is not limited in time or place. In fact, the workplace serves as one of the most important places for a Christian to exemplify a testimony for the Lord Jesus. Yet, Christians can fail miserably by being lazy workers or disobedient to employers. According to scripture, servants are to obey their masters *(Titus 2:9)* from the heart *(Colossians 3:22)* with fear and trembling *(Ephesians 6:5-6)*. Not only are Christians responsible to obey godly bosses, but the Bible commands the same respect to be given to those who are froward *(1 Peter 2:18)*. Believers ought to behave beyond the norm in their service in the workplace. The Bible affirms this truth by saying that servants should *"please"* their masters well in all things *(Titus 2:9)*. Many lost people have been led to Christ by Christians who live godly and display an impeccable testimony at work.

DEVOTIONAL THOUGHTS

- **(For children)**: When we do a job for someone, we are to work as if the Lord Himself asked us to do it. We should not need anyone standing over us making sure we do it *(Proverbs 6:6-8)*.
- **(For everyone)**: No matter your age or work experience, it is important to learn how to work right. When somebody asks you to do a job, you should do it heartily to the best of your ability.
- What does the Bible mean when it says that servants should not answer again? What does it mean to say that we should not purloin? How can we work with all good fidelity *(Titus 2:10)*?

PRAYER THOUGHTS

- Ask the Lord to help you be a godly worker.
- · Ask God to give you grace to deal with an ungodly employer so that you can maintain your testimony in such a difficult situation.

SONG: *LIVING FOR JESUS* (CHISHOLM)

Day 244: (Friday)
Obedience in the Church

Hebrews 13:17 Obey them that have the rule over you, and submit yourselves: for they watch for your souls, as they that must give account, that they may do it with joy, and not with grief: for that is unprofitable for you.

INTRODUCTORY THOUGHTS

No matter where we look we see order and authority. Even God's acts of creation reveal this order. The Bible says that the sun was given to rule the day and the moon to rule the night *(Genesis 1:16)*. The Lord gave priests and prophets to the children of Israel in the Old Testament to lead them and show them His truths. Faithful to His nature, God has also given a level of authority within the church. According to our passage, we are to *"obey them that have the rule"* over us. On a couple of different occasions, the word *rule* is used in the job description of a pastor or elder *(1 Timothy 3:5; 1 Timothy 5:17)*. Today's passage also reveals that the man of God watches for the souls of the people and must give an account to God for his watch care. No true God-called leader takes his position lightly.

DEVOTIONAL THOUGHTS

- **(For children):** As children, we are to obey the preacher and teachers at church. Do you listen quietly and intently during the story or sermon? Do you stop running in church or pick up your own trash when asked to do so? Do you bring toys from home and pout when they are taken away?
- **(For everyone):** The man of God is responsible to God for how he leads the people of God within the congregation. We should follow him as he follows the Lord.
- The Lord warns the man of God not to lord over His heritage *(1 Peter 5:3)*; but at the same time, God has given the preacher authority within the body of believers. How seriously do you take the warnings given to you by the preacher? Do you apply the messages heard at church to your life and situation?

PRAYER THOUGHTS

- Ask God to help you listen as the preacher preaches God's word.
- Ask God to give your preacher wisdom to lead the people.

SONG: *THE PREACHER'S LIFE*

Day 245: (Saturday)
A Conflict in Obedience

*Acts 5:29 Then Peter and the other apostles answered and said, **We ought to obey God rather than men.***

INTRODUCTORY THOUGHTS

We previously alluded to the very real probability of conflicting authorities. What happens when the government tells men that they cannot obey the words of God? What should a lady do when her husband tells her to do something clearly contrary to the scriptures? What should employees do when asked by their employer to disobey a clear command found in the word of God? What should a church do when the preacher departs from the truths of the Bible? These are tough questions, but the Lord did not leave us without answers and guidance. When authorities conflict, *"We ought to obey God rather than men."* Man's responsibility in obedience is first and foremost to God. Men should obey those who have been given authority by God so long as those men do not lead contrary to God's precepts.

DEVOTIONAL THOUGHTS

- **(For children):** *Ephesians 6:1* says, *"Children, obey your parents in the Lord."* Some children who love the Lord have parents who do not. Some ungodly parents ask their children to steal. God says that is wrong *(Exodus 20:15)*. Whom should the children always obey?
- **(For everyone):** What are some areas in your life where authorities might conflict? Is there an authority in your life that tries to lead you to disobey the word of God?
- What would you do if the government said you could not read the Bible, pray, or go to church anymore? What would you do if your boss told you to drink alcohol at the company gathering?

PRAYER THOUGHTS

- Ask God to give you wisdom in times when authorities conflict.
- Ask the Lord to give you boldness in such times.

SONG: *DARE TO BE A DANIEL*

Notes: _____

_____

_____

_____

_____

_____

_____

_____

_____

_____

_____

_____

_____

_____

_____

_____

_____

Quotes from the next volume

(VOLUME 2, WEEK 35)

Subject: Teaching

When an individual refuses to have a teachable spirit, he identifies himself as a fool. Every person has much to learn. Be teachable!

It is easy to tell others what to do and how to do it, but very unwise to fail to follow one's own instructions and teachings.

36

Patience

Occurrences: found forty-nine times in forty-six verses

Variations: patience, patient, patiently

First usage: *Psalm 37:7* (patiently)

Last usage: *Revelation 14:12* (patience)

Defined: the suffering of afflictions or provocation with a calm temper; enduring injustice without murmuring or fretfulness. Most often, patience signifies an inability on one's part to change the afflictions or circumstances; he can merely endure them.

Interesting fact: Though God is the giver of patience *(Romans 15:5)*, the attribute itself is never directly assigned to the Lord. The corresponding attribute ascribed to the Lord is that of longsuffering.

Bible study tip: When studying a Bible word, use a computer software program to find every verse where the word or variations of the word occur. Copy the verses into a separate document and print. Develop a symbol system using colored markers to distinguish things found in your study. Make notes as you progress and reexamine your findings the second time through.

Sunday, Day 246—Church Day (no devotional)
Monday, Day 247—*What Is Patience?*
Tuesday, Day 248—*Ye Have Need of Patience*
Wednesday, Day 249—Church Night (no devotional)
Thursday, Day 250—*Tribulation Worketh Patience*
Friday, Day 251—*Fruit with Patience*
Saturday, Day 252—*Be Patient Toward All Men*

Day 246: Church Day

Romans 12:12 *Rejoicing in hope;* **patient in tribulation***; continuing instant in prayer;*

Day 247: (Monday)
What Is Patience?

2 Thessalonians 1:4 *So that we ourselves glory in you in the churches of God for your* **patience and faith in all your persecutions and tribulations** *that ye endure:*

INTRODUCTORY THOUGHTS

Have you ever heard that it is unwise to pray for patience? Since *"tribulation worketh patience" (Romans 5:3)*, it is thought to be dangerous to pray for patience. The idea may be quaint, but it does not make for good advice. The word *patience* is historically connected to the word *passion* which is biblically defined as suffering *(Acts 1:3)*. True to its association, the word *patience* means *to suffer or endure some time of trial.* No wonder doctors and hospitals refer to a person suffering from health issues as a *patient.* The Bible bears further testimony to these truths by associating patience with waiting *(James 5:7)* and enduring *(2 Thessalonians 1:4; James 5:11)*. The Bible also combines *patience* with the word *longsuffering (Colossians 1:11)*. These words may appear the same, but they are not. *Longsuffering* has to do with the *quantity* (or length of time) of endurance, while *patience* has to do with the *quality* of endurance.

DEVOTIONAL THOUGHTS

- **(For children)**: The apostle Paul spent time in jail because of his preaching. Instead of complaining, he sang songs of praise to God, wrote some books of the Bible, and told others about the Lord. Those who wait for something unpleasant to pass without complaining are truly patient.

- **(For everyone):** While in the midst of trials, do you endure those trials without murmuring? Are you able to give God glory through them? Are you patiently trusting the Lord to work in His time or in your time?
- Patience is not merely waiting on something but involves the manner in which we wait. What do you need the Lord to do in your life? Are you patiently praying for wisdom for what you need to learn through the trial?

PRAYER THOUGHTS

- Ask God to show you whether or not you are patient.
- Ask God to build you into an example of patience.

SONG: *DAY BY DAY*

Day 248: (Tuesday)
Ye Have Need of Patience

Hebrews 10:36 For ye have need of patience, that, after ye have done the will of God, ye might receive the promise.

INTRODUCTORY THOUGHTS

Patience functions as an essential attribute in the life of every faithful believer. The Bible clearly points to patience as necessary for the development of experience and hope *(Romans 5:3-5)*. Additionally, patience makes the believer *"perfect and entire, wanting nothing" (James 1:4)*. In fact, Peter's second epistle promises that the believer possessing patience *"shall neither be barren nor unfruitful in the knowledge of our Lord Jesus Christ" (2 Peter 1:5-9)*. Therefore, the Bible seems to emphatically proclaim that men *"have need of patience" (Hebrews 10:36)*. Patience is especially necessary in times of trial and during periods of uncertainty. Patience will not be necessary in eternity, but life on earth presents times that demand the utmost patience.

DEVOTIONAL THOUGHTS

- **(For children):** Do you have trouble waiting in lines at the store? Do you want to do better? Ask the Lord to give you more lines in which to wait. Then practice making the waiting better: practice your Bible verses, talk to other children close by, thank God for the things you are able to purchase.
- **(For everyone):** Do you want hope? Do you want to be more complete in your Christian walk? Do you want to know more of the power of Christ in your life? If so, patience serves as your source for these things.
- Many people have been taught to avoid praying for patience, but the Bible is clear that we need patience. Do you want what God says you need? Will you trust God to work out matters so that patience comes in God's time and His way?

PRAYER THOUGHTS

- Ask God to give you a desire for things that accompany patience.
- Ask God to give you boldness to pray for patience.

SONG: *GOD WILL TAKE CARE OF YOU* (MARTIN)

Day 249: Church Night

Psalm 33:20 Our soul waiteth for the LORD: he is our help and our shield.

Day 250: (Thursday)
Tribulation Worketh Patience

Romans 5:3 And not only so, but we glory in tribulations also: knowing that tribulation worketh patience;

4 And patience, experience; and experience, hope:

5 And hope maketh not ashamed; because the love of God is shed abroad in our hearts by the Holy Ghost which is given unto us.

INTRODUCTORY THOUGHTS

The previous devotion explored the importance of patience in the life of the believer. That study revealed how God's word challenges us to have boldness and to pray for patience. Today's study reveals why Christians are frequently taught not to ask or pray for patience. The scripture points out a four step process by which the believer increases in hope. This process includes wonderful aspects like patience, experience, and hope; however, the step preceding patience troubles most believers. *"Tribulation worketh patience"* *(Romans 5:3)*. Since patience develops through enduring times of difficulty, the difficulties present the best opportunity to gain true patience. James reinforces this truth by stating that *"the trying of your faith worketh patience"* *(James 1:3)*. People should not be discouraged from praying for patience since the inevitable tribulation and trials develop the patience, experience, and hope that God desires in the Christian's life.

DEVOTIONAL THOUGHTS

- **(For children):** Samuel anointed David to be Israel's second king while Saul was still on the throne. David waited for God to remove Saul although Saul repeatedly tried to kill David. When David became king, the trials and tribulations helped him to wait on God when his own son Absalom tried to take his throne away.
- **(For everyone):** *"Ye have need of patience"* *(Hebrews 10:36)*, but do you love God enough to go through tribulations in order to attain to the patience that God would have for you? Are you willing to endure the trials to gain the necessary patience?
- As a believer you will never experience the hope you want without allowing God's process described in *Romans 5:3-5* to develop it in your life. Do you ever wonder why Paul would say that he gloried in tribulations *(Romans 3:5)*?

PRAYER THOUGHTS

- Ask God to help you more fully comprehend the benefits of patience.
- Ask God to give you a heart like Paul's concerning tribulations.

SONG: *'TIS SO SWEET TO TRUST IN JESUS*

Day 251: (Friday)
Fruit with Patience

*Luke 8:15 But that on the good ground are they, which in an honest and good heart, **having heard the word, keep it, and bring forth fruit with patience**.*

INTRODUCTORY THOUGHTS

Hear God's word, keep it, and it will *"bring forth fruit with patience."* Today's passage comes from a series of verses *(Luke 8:11-15)* wherein the Lord explained the interpretation of a parable to His disciples. The Lord's interpretation incorporates another wonderful truth concerning patience. He likens patience to planting a seed and waiting for the fruit of that seed to develop and grow. Of course, the growth and maturation process takes time. A farmer going into the field every day to look for growth shows a lack of patience and wisdom. This truth equally applies to the Christian life; growing in the Lord takes time. Expecting maturity overnight is both unwise and unfruitful. A newly born-again Christian certainly cannot expect to bear the fruit of an established believer in a short period of time. In fact, the Lord promises that fruit will be brought forth only with patience. Consider the truth taught concerning the husbandman who *"waiteth for the precious fruit of the earth, and hath long patience for it" (James 5:7)*. We must all patiently wait for the seeds of life to develop into fruit in the Lord's time.

DEVOTIONAL THOUGHTS

- **(For children):** A baby drinks milk for a period of time after birth. Eventually, his teeth develop and he can eat meat. Likewise, the Bible is food for the child of God. He first learns the easier parts which the Bible calls milk. As he grows and matures, he will be able to understand the harder parts called meat.
- **(For everyone):** Do you know anyone who ever planted a fruit tree? They would love to get the immediate benefit from the tree, but it takes time. How is your growth in Christ like a fruit tree?
- Like a seed in the ground, you should be always growing; yet the results may not be always visible. Look back over your life since you trusted Christ. What kind of fruit do you have to show?

PRAYER THOUGHTS

- Ask God to help you bring forth fruit with patience.
- Ask the Lord to help you grow every day.

SONG: *LITTLE IS MUCH WHEN GOD IS IN IT*

Day 252: (Saturday)
Be Patient Toward All Men

1 Thessalonians 5:14 Now we exhort you, brethren, warn them that are unruly, comfort the feebleminded, support the weak, be patient toward all men.

INTRODUCTORY THOUGHTS

Today's text includes the exhortation to be *"patient toward all men."* Every sincere Christian realizes and recognizes the graciousness that God displays toward His children. Regardless of the goodness of God toward us, it still remains difficult to consistently demonstrate patience toward others. However, exhibiting patience is especially important for anyone in a leadership position, especially those involved in the work of God. According to God's word, the apostle Paul exemplified patience in his dealings with other believers *(2 Corinthians 6:4; 2 Corinthians 12:12).* This should come as no surprise since one of the basic requirements for the man of God involves patience *(1 Timothy 3:3; 1 Timothy 6:11; 2 Timothy 2:24).* God's people ought to be known for their patience. In the homes, we should be patient with our spouses and children. At work, we should be patient with our coworkers, employers, and employees. In the Lord's work, we ought to be especially patient.

DEVOTIONAL THOUGHTS

- **(For children):** Do you get upset when a younger child takes your toys and plays with them? You know that they should learn to ask politely before doing this because you are older. You need to be patient toward others and help them to learn what you have already learned.
- **(For everyone):** Do you get frustrated because others might be slow to show progress? Do you think the Lord could get frustrated with you because of your pace of growth?
- Are you patient with your children or your spouse; your coworkers; and those you lead in Christian service? Were others patient with you?

PRAYER THOUGHTS

- Ask God to give you patience in your dealings with others.
- Ask the Lord to remind you of His graciousness with you.

SONG: *O TO BE LIKE THEE!*

Notes: _____

_____

_____

_____

_____

_____

_____

_____

_____

_____

_____

_____

_____

Quotes from the next volume

(VOLUME 2, WEEK 36)

Subject: Reading and Studying

The Lord gave man His word with the expectation that each believer would read it and heed what it says.

The Bible is not meant to be read merely for the sake of reading. It is to be read with a deliberate purpose! God's purposes may be missed when one indiscriminately hastens through the scriptures.

Many people who fail to understand the Bible's contents foolishly judge the Bible as a closed book except to those academically superior. The problem does not rest with God's words but with man's spiritual inabilities.

37

Patience (con't)

Occurrences: found three times in the Old Testament and forty-six times in the New Testament

First usage in the New Testament: *Matthew 18:26* (patience)

Last usage in the Old Testament: *Ecclesiastes 7:8* (patient)

Interesting fact: Patience only shows up three times in the Old Testament with Ecclesiastes extolling the virtues of the patient in spirit. The other two instances, both in the book of Psalms, refer to waiting patiently for the LORD.

Bible study tip: When studying a particular virtue, consider what Bible characters are said to possess the particular virtue. Explore the reasons why the Bible associates the virtue with those individuals. Study to find out if the virtue is likewise attributed to the Lord. These findings should help to further define and explore the particular virtue.

Sunday, Day 253—Church Day (no devotional)
Monday, Day 254—*Wait Patiently for the Lord*
Tuesday, Day 255—*The God of Patience*
Wednesday, Day 256—Church Night (no devotional)
Thursday, Day 257—*The Patience of Job*

Friday, Day 258—*Run with Patience*
Saturday, Day 259—*Patient in Suffering*

Day 253: Church Day

Psalm 40:1 I waited patiently for the LORD; and he inclined unto me, and heard my cry.

Day 254: (Monday)
Wait Patiently for the Lord

Psalm 37:7 Rest in the LORD, and wait patiently for him: fret not thyself because of him who prospereth in his way, because of the man who bringeth wicked devices to pass.

INTRODUCTORY THOUGHTS

In this Psalm, David spoke of a perceived injustice that even today tempts many believers to envy. David recognized the prosperity of the wicked and the corresponding trials of the righteous. Yet, believers are admonished to *"Rest in the LORD, and wait patiently for him."* Why would the righteous be instructed to wait patiently? Because *"yet a little while, and the wicked shall not be" (Psalm 37:10)*. The Lord in His time will work everything out. As believers, we will face trials. There are going to be times of injustice. There are going to be times of loss and mourning. However, we can wait patiently knowing that the Lord will right every wrong and settle every injustice.

DEVOTIONAL THOUGHTS

- **(For children):** The apostle Paul told the Christians at Rome to do good to those who did them wrong and not to respond with evil. Why would he say this? Because the Bible says that vengeance belongs to God *(Romans 12:14, 17, 19)*.
- **(For everyone):** What trials do you face? What causes you to fret? Are you waiting on the Lord in these areas? Are you exemplifying patience in your waiting on the Lord? Do you murmur and complain about what you perceive as the Lord's delay in responding to your needs?
- In **Deuteronomy 8:2**, the Bible reveals that God led the Israelites through the wilderness to prove them. Is it possible that the Lord might allow you to go through trials to prove your patience?

PRAYER THOUGHTS

- Ask God to help you patiently wait on Him.
- Ask the Lord to help you trust Him more in times of trial.

SONG: *BE STILL, MY SOUL*

Day 255: (Tuesday)
The God of Patience

Romans 15:4 *For whatsoever things were written aforetime were written for our learning, that we **through patience and comfort of the scriptures might have hope.***

*5 Now **the God of patience** and consolation grant you to be likeminded one toward another according to Christ Jesus:*

INTRODUCTORY THOUGHTS

Modern society dictates that everything needs to be fast and ever increasing in speed. If our food, news, communication, and technology are not delivered at lightning speeds, we will look for solutions to end the delay. We lack the patience for any obstacle impeding our instant gratification. Yet, the Bible declares that men need patience *(Hebrews 10:36)*. Where can patience be found in such a fast paced world? God! He alone understands the reality of time, patience, and longsuffering. Not only does He understand, but He wants us to have patience; so much so, that He will, at times, allow difficulties to enter our lives merely for the purpose of teaching us patience. Fortunately, the God who allows the trials also willingly grants the patience to endure any trial.

DEVOTIONAL THOUGHTS

- **(For children):** When you are hungry, it is sometimes hard to wait for supper. Regardless, we need to learn to be patient. Mom delays serving the food for our own good. If food isn't cooked properly, we could get sick. Sometimes we want things from the Lord and He makes us wait. It is always for our own good.
- **(For everyone):** Do you need patience? Do you endure trials with grace and joy? Do you need to ask God to do a work of patience in your heart? Are you willing to trust Him fully to fulfil this need?

- Have you allowed the pace of this world to fill your mind with doubts concerning the timeliness of the Lord's aid in your life? Do you believe your doubts are pleasing to the Lord?

PRAYER THOUGHTS

- Ask the Lord to give you the patience that you need in order to endure the present difficulties of life.
- Ask God to help you realize that He works in His time.

SONG: *MOMENT BY MOMENT*

Day 256: Church Night

Revelation 2:2 I know thy works, and thy labour, and thy patience, and how thou canst not bear them which are evil: and thou hast tried them which say they are apostles, and are not, and hast found them liars:

Day 257: (Thursday)
The Patience of Job

James 5:10 Take, my brethren, the prophets, who have spoken in the name of the Lord, for an example of suffering affliction, and of patience.

11 Behold, we count them happy which endure. Ye have heard of the patience of Job, and have seen the end of the Lord; that the Lord is very pitiful, and of tender mercy.

INTRODUCTORY THOUGHTS

Likely, no mere mortal endured more difficulty over a short period of time than did Job. Job suffered several awful trials with most of them coming simultaneously. Perhaps Job should not be remembered so much for the trials, but for how he handled those trials. When Job received the news that his children had perished, he said, *"Naked came I out of my mother's womb, and naked shall I return thither: the LORD gave, and the LORD hath taken away; blessed be the name of the LORD" (Job 1:21).* The verse which follows Job's statement conveys volumes, *"In all this Job sinned not, nor charged God foolishly."* Job's endurance of such trials led the Lord to point to Job as an outstanding example of patience *(James 5:11).*

DEVOTIONAL THOUGHTS

- **(For children):** God knew the apostle Paul would suffer through some hard times for Him *(Acts 9:16)* and Paul testified that he certainly did *(2 Corinthians 11:23-28)*. Through it all, Paul kept serving God. Paul was a good example to Timothy and told him to follow after patience *(1 Timothy 6:11)*. When things go wrong, are you a good example for others?
- **(For everyone):** Have you had to endure the amount of trials that Job endured? Most would honestly answer no; but even if you had, would you like to display that same level of patience through it all?
- We remember Job for the trials, but we should remember him for his patience. How will you be remembered when you leave this world? Will people remember you as a person of patience?

PRAYER THOUGHTS

- Ask the Lord to give you the patience of Job.
- Ask God to make you an example of patience.

SONG: *O GOD, OUR HELP*

Day 258: (Friday)
Run with Patience

*Hebrews 12:1 Wherefore seeing we also are compassed about with so great a cloud of witnesses, let us lay aside every weight, and the sin which doth so easily beset us, and let us **run with patience the race that is set before us,***
2 Looking unto Jesus the author and finisher of our faith; who for the joy that was set before him endured the cross, despising the shame, and is set down at the right hand of the throne of God.
3 For consider him that endured such contradiction of sinners against himself, lest ye be wearied and faint in your minds.

INTRODUCTORY THOUGHTS

The Bible likens the life of a believer to many things, one of these being a race. Our life's race is likened more to a marathon or cross-country run rather than a short-lived sprint. In these types of endurance races, the strategic runner outlasts the impatient contender. A sprint initiated at the starting line may place the runner at the head of the pack but always yields a disappointing outcome. The same holds true concerning the Christian race. Believers are to run this race patiently. The Christian must never allow present trials and difficult circumstances to disqualify him from his perspective race. In fact, the long-term goal of winning the race must be ever present in every thought and action. The Christian race is not only about how much we can accomplish in the present, but what the Lord has accomplished before our crossing of the finish line.

DEVOTIONAL THOUGHTS

- **(For children)**: Elimelech and Naomi did not have the patience to wait on God when there were food shortages in Bethlehem. They took their two sons and moved to Moab. While they were there, Elimelech and his two sons died. Their lives may have turned out differently if they had simply waited on God to take care of them in Bethlehem.
- **(For everyone)**: In what ways could patience actually help you reach the finish line first? How could patience in the race keep you from quitting when times get tough?
- How are you running your race? Are you attempting to sprint, or are you allowing the Lord to guide your direction and control your pace?

PRAYER THOUGHTS

- Ask God to help you run with patience.
- Ask God to show you that the best path and pace to run is His path and His pace.

SONG: *BY AND BY* (BLACKALL)

Day 259: (Saturday)
Patient in Suffering

1 Peter 2:19 For this is thankworthy, if a man for conscience toward God endure grief, suffering wrongfully.

*20 For what glory is it, if, when ye be buffeted for your faults, **ye shall take it patiently**? but if, when ye do well, and suffer for it, **ye take it patiently**, this is acceptable with God.*

21 For even hereunto were ye called: because Christ also suffered for us, leaving us an example, that ye should follow his steps:

22 Who did no sin, neither was guile found in his mouth:

23 Who, when he was reviled, reviled not again; when he suffered, he threatened not; but committed himself to him that judgeth righteously:

INTRODUCTORY THOUGHTS

Many fine Christians know what it means to live a life filled with suffering or pain. This suffering may come as a result of wrongdoing or in spite of righteous living. No matter the circumstance, one fact remains constant: suffering, whether merited or not, is never pleasant. The Bible instructs Christians regardless of the circumstances to greet suffering with the utmost patience. In fact, the Bible emphasizes that patience during times of suffering for well doing is *"acceptable with God"* (*1 Peter 2:20*). Enduring suffering may seem difficult and our nature certainly opposes it, but it remains part of God's calling (*1 Peter 2:21*). The Lord exhibited great patience as He suffered as our example as He that *"did no sin, neither was guile found in his mouth"* (*1 Peter 2:22*). Instead of retaliating in time of suffering, He *"committed himself to him that judgeth righteously"* (*1 Peter 2:23*). Christians should learn from Christ's example and consistently strive to entrust their well-being to the mercy of God.

DEVOTIONAL THOUGHTS

- **(For children):** Joseph was hated by his brothers who sold him into slavery. He went through many troubles but we have no record of him complaining. Many years later, he became second in command in Egypt. When his wicked brothers came to him for food, Joseph gladly forgave them and was kind to them. Joseph displayed a great example of what God wants us to be.
- **(For everyone):** Do you long to take vengeance into your own hands when others cause you to suffer wrongfully? Do you grow impatient waiting on the Lord to resolve matters that seem so unfair?
- Do you find that you are short on patience when you know that others say things about you that are wrong? Do you wait on the Lord or do you seek to clear your name no matter whom you might hurt?

PRAYER THOUGHTS

- Ask the Lord to give you patience in suffering.
- Ask the Lord to help you trust Him in times of trial and trouble.

SONG: *UNDER HIS WINGS*

Notes: _____

_____

_____

_____

_____

_____

_____

_____

_____

_____

_____

_____

_____

_____

_____

_____

Quotes from the next volume

(VOLUME 2, WEEK 37)

Subject: Reading and Studying (con't)

No other book ever written apart from the Bible can offer the spiritual blessings received from reading, hearing, and heeding it.

One can read through the scriptures on a daily basis without ever truly studying the scriptures.

Interestingly, man's flesh can sit for hours reading a novel or watching television, but studying the scripture manifests a weariness of the flesh rather quickly.

38

Peace

Occurrences: found 450 times in 420 verses

Variations: peace, peaceable, peaceably, peacemakers

First usage: *Genesis 15:15* (peace)

Last usage: *Revelation 6:4* (peace)

Defined: a quietness of the mind and calmness that can be accompanied with or without adversity

Interesting fact: *Jeremiah 6:14* and *Jeremiah 8:11* both refer to the saying *"Peace, peace when there is no peace."* In the tribulation, when people expect peace, sudden destruction will come in its place *(1 Thessalonians 5:3)*. The final use in Revelation refers to the red horse rider taking *"peace from the earth."*

Bible study tip: There are instances when the Bible uses unfamiliar words brought over from the original languages. God, in His faithfulness, will oftentimes offer a translation or definition in the context of the verse. For an example, *John 20:16* defines *Rabboni* as Master in the same text: *"Rabboni; which is to say, Master."*

Sunday, Day 260—Church Day (no devotional)
Monday, Day 261—*What Is Peace?*
Tuesday, Day 262—*The God of Peace*
Wednesday, Day 263—Church Night (no devotional)
Thursday, Day 264—*Sources of Peace*
Friday, Day 265—*No Peace to the Wicked*
Saturday, Day 266—*Publishing Peace*

Day 260: Church Day

Galatians 5:22 But **the fruit of the Spirit is** love, joy, **peace**, *longsuffering, gentleness, goodness, faith,*
23 *Meekness, temperance: against such there is no law.*

Day 261: (Monday)
What Is Peace?

Isaiah 32:17 And **the work of righteousness shall be peace**; *and the* **effect of righteousness quietness** *and assurance for ever.*
18 *And* **my people shall dwell in a peaceable habitation**, *and in sure dwellings, and in quiet resting places;*

INTRODUCTORY THOUGHTS

On the surface, one might superficially define *peace* as an absence of war, troubles, or trials. Yet, the Bible indicates a much broader concept. Two words in our passage suggest as much. The Bible says, *"the work of righteousness shall be* **peace***; and the effect of righteousness* **quietness** *and* **assurance** *for ever."* The next verse states that God's *"people shall dwell in a* **peaceable** *habitation, and in* **sure** *dwellings, and in* **quiet** *resting places."* Both verses incorporate the words *quietness* and *assurance* revealing that peace offers a quiet assurance. Fortunately, this means that peace for the child of God is not contingent upon the circumstances of life. Christians can experience peace even while enduring the worst of circumstances.

DEVOTIONAL THOUGHTS

- **(For children):** What things do you fear in life? thunderstorms? sleeping in the dark? being somewhere all by yourself? God promises to give us peace. Peace means that your heart is not troubled or afraid no matter the circumstances *(John 14:27)*.

- **(For everyone):** Why is it important to understand that peace does not simply mean an absence of troubles and trials? Should we have access to peace in the midst of our troubles and trials? When is peace needed the most?
- Do you have a quiet assurance when going through difficult times? Are you able to trust God during uncertain times? Are you confident that God will bring you through the trials of life?

PRAYER THOUGHTS

- Ask God to grant you His peace.
- Ask God help you trust Him in times of difficulty.

SONG: *FROM EVERY STORMY WIND*

Day 262: (Tuesday)
The God of Peace

Romans 15:33 Now the God of peace be with you all. Amen.

INTRODUCTORY THOUGHTS

Society has become increasingly tumultuous offering vast distractions yet supplying little peace of mind. Unfortunately, most people seeking peace do so through the wrong means. Some seek it through entertainment, some through medication, some through relationships, and others through materialism; but their desire for peace remains an ever elusive quest. God is the only source offering true and lasting peace. In fact, the word of God identifies the Lord five times as the *"God of peace" (Romans 15:33; Romans 16:20; Philippians 4:9; 1 Thessalonians 5:23; Hebrews 13:20)*. Another passage identifies Him as the *"Lord of peace" (2 Thessalonians 3:16)*. Additionally, the Lord Jesus is identified as *"The Prince of Peace" (Isaiah 9:6)*. Not only do these truths affirm that the Lord has peace to offer, but that He is the One in control of providing peace. Trying to find peace apart from God's working is comparable to salvation without a Saviour.

DEVOTIONAL THOUGHTS

- **(For children):** Children usually run to dad or mom for help. As we grow older, mom and dad may not always be near for us to go to them for help. However, God is always near. He said, *"I will never leave thee nor forsake thee" (Hebrews 13:5).* He promises to be *"a very present help in trouble" (Psalm 46:1).*
- **(For everyone):** What do you do when you find yourself in the midst of trials? Where do you run or to whom do you run for help? The answer to these questions will help you to understand what or to whom you seek for peace.
- The things of this world to which we turn for peace often provide the opposite outcomes. However, when God provides peace, He does not add to our burdens and frustration.

PRAYER THOUGHTS

- Ask God to help you understand that He is the source of peace.
- Ask God to help you to seek Him and Him only during times of trouble.

SONG: *WONDERFUL PEACE* (CORNELL)

Day 263: Church Night

*Psalm 29:11 The LORD will give strength unto his people; **the LORD will bless his people with peace.***

Day 264: (Thursday)
Sources of Peace

*Isaiah 26:3 Thou wilt **keep him in perfect peace**, whose mind is stayed on thee: because he trusteth in thee.*

INTRODUCTORY THOUGHTS

Previous studies explored the source of peace. Today's study may seem to contradict these previous studies; however, peace is always contingent upon its single source which is God. Nevertheless, peace manifests itself through multiple sources. Each of these sources fully relies upon the Lord and is given by Him as means to finding peace. Today's passage reveals that peace is contingent upon our minds staying upon

God. The last part of the verse further defines what it means to have one's mind stayed upon the Lord. It involves trusting in God, or having **faith**. The Bible stresses that those who love **God's law** will have *great* peace *(Psalm 119:165)*. Ultimately, peace entails loving and trusting what God has said. Failure to trust God's words inhibits true and lasting peace.

DEVOTIONAL THOUGHTS

- **(For children):** God made everything and has power over everything. He once said to a great storm on the sea, *"Peace, be still."* Immediately, the wind ceased and the sea was calm. He can and wants to bring you peace when you feel troubled.
- **(For everyone):** The Bible is full of promises given by God to man. Do you trust His promises? Do you believe the words of the Bible to be true and without error?
- Do you ever meditate on God's power and goodness? Do you ever think about how He never failed His people in both the Old and New Testaments? Do you realize He can do the same for you?

PRAYER THOUGHTS

- Ask God to give you faith to trust His words.
- Ask God to help you meditate on His goodness.

SONG: *CONSTANTLY ABIDING*

Day 265: (Friday)
No Peace to the Wicked

*Isaiah 57:19 I create the fruit of the lips; **Peace, peace to him that is far off, and to him that is near**, saith the LORD; and I will heal him.*

20 But the wicked are like the troubled sea, when it cannot rest, whose waters cast up mire and dirt.

*21 **There is no peace**, saith my God, to the wicked.*

INTRODUCTORY THOUGHTS

It is important to realize that the perception of peace in a person's life can be truly deceptive. Those who live for the Devil and for themselves may seem to prosper and enjoy peace. They may even testify of the peace that they seem to enjoy while those living for the Lord honestly exhibit trials and temptations associated with such a relationship. Yet, we have God's word on the matter: the wicked have no peace. This truth is so important that the Lord repeated the thought of the wicked having no peace in *Isaiah 57:21*. The wicked may enjoy times of calm in their lives, but these times are not the true and enduring peace that only comes from a relationship with the Saviour. Consider this vivid description before embarking on such a life: *"the wicked are like the troubled sea, when it cannot rest, whose waters cast up mire and dirt" (Isaiah 57:20)*. Peace comes from God!

DEVOTIONAL THOUGHTS

- **(For children)**: Briefly tell your children the story of Naboth's vineyard. Wicked king Ahab was happy when he thought he got his way. Yet, he had no peace; he was told his *"end" (1 Kings 21:19)*. Whatever God says will happen does come to pass *(1 Kings 22:34-38)*.
- **(For everyone)**: Do you ever envy the wicked for the prosperity they seem to enjoy? Asaph had this problem until he *"went into the sanctuary of God"* and understood *"their end" (Psalm 73:17)*.
- Do you have your eyes on the Lord or upon others? Peace is associated with righteousness *(Psalm 85:10; Romans 14:17)* and will only be given to those who seek the Lord and His strength.

PRAYER THOUGHTS

- Ask the Lord to help you understand the end of the wicked.
- Ask God to help you seek peace through righteousness.

SONG: *CHRIST RECEIVETH SINFUL MEN*

Day 266: (Saturday)
Publishing Peace

*Isaiah 52:7 How beautiful upon the mountains are the feet of him that bringeth good tidings, that **publisheth peace**; that bringeth good tidings of good, that publisheth salvation; that saith unto Zion, Thy God reigneth!*

INTRODUCTORY THOUGHTS

Believers understand why the world seems completely oblivious to its true need. Yes, the world needs peace but not the peace they suspect

– absence of war! Bible students recognize that trusting Jesus Christ is the means whereby individuals can quench their thirst for peace. This knowledge of the truth carries with it a grave responsibility along with a marvellous privilege. The scripture points to the beauty of the feet of those that *"bringeth good tidings, that publisheth peace; that bringeth good tidings of good, that publisheth salvation; that saith unto Zion, Thy God reigneth!"* Why are the feet mentioned as being so beautiful? The feet of the man carry him to publish peace. Similar phraseology appears in **Nahum 1:15**. Those who know God's peace are blessed with the responsibility and granted the opportunity to take that message of peace to others.

DEVOTIONAL THOUGHTS

- **(For children):** Ask dad or mom for a good gospel tract that you can give to others. When you give someone a tract with the gospel message, God says your feet are beautiful because you are telling others about Him.
- **(For everyone):** Do you know God's peace? Are you publishing that peace to a lost and dying world so cumbered with fear and distress?
- If you had the cure for cancer, would you tell cancer patients about the cure? If you had the answer to somebody's problem, would you tell him the solution? You should! Do you know the One who offers peace? Whom have you loved enough to tell?

PRAYER THOUGHTS

- Ask the Lord to burden you for the lost.
- Ask God to give you strength to publish peace.

SONG: *SEND THE LIGHT*

Notes: _____

_____

_____

_____

_____

_____

_____

Notes: _____

_____

_____

_____

_____

_____

_____

_____

_____

_____

_____

_____

_____

Quotes from the next volume

(VOLUME 2, WEEK 38)

Subject: Rebuking

Scripturally rebuking someone never involves any self-gratifying acts, but rather focuses upon helping others grow, improve, and spiritually mature.

The purpose of rebuking someone has been completely distorted in these days of emphasizing political correctness and personal self-esteem. The world now associates a scriptural rebuke with hatred, anger, and envy. In reality, a godly rebuke demonstrates a supreme act of love.

As the believer gains additional Bible knowledge, he begins to see the world in a far different light. These insights remain unavailable to those who ignore the truths of scripture.

39

Peace (con't)

Occurrences: found 334 times in the Old Testament and 116 times in the New Testament

First usage in the New Testament: *Matthew 5:9* (peacemakers)

Last usage in the Old Testament: *Judges 21:13* (peaceably)

Interesting fact: Several Bible phrases use the word *peace* to suggest that men remained silent (i.e., *"held his peace" (Genesis 24:21)*, *"hold your peace" (Exodus 14:14)*). There are times when men should hold their peace and other times when remaining silent would be sinful.

Bible study tip: The Bible contains phrases meant to teach specific Bible doctrines. Two phrases can be identical except for one word and be meant to convey two completely different truths. For instance, the *"peace **of** God"* offers a completely different connotation than being at *"peace **with** God."*

Sunday, Day 267—Church Day (no devotional)
Monday, Day 268—*Peace like a River*
Tuesday, Day 269—*False Peace*
Wednesday, Day 270—Church Night (no devotional)
Thursday, Day 271—*Seek Peace*

Friday, Day 272—*Peace with God*
Saturday, Day 273—*The Peace of God*

Day 267: Church Day

Romans 8:6 *For to be carnally minded is death; but **to be spiritually minded is life and peace.***

Day 268: (Monday)
Peace like a River

*Isaiah 48:18 O that thou hadst **hearkened to my commandments! then had thy peace been as a river**, and thy righteousness as the waves of the sea:*

INTRODUCTORY THOUGHTS

There are few sights and sounds like that of a majestically flowing river. For this reason, the Lord promised His people that they would have *"been as a river"* through simple obedience. This analogy using the river not only speaks of quality but also of quantity. Israel's obedience would bring a peace similar to the calming effect of a flowing river. This peace would also be quantitatively associated to the vast amounts of water which flow down a river. The Lord reaffirmed this truth when He said of Jerusalem, *"Behold, I will extend peace to her like a river"* **(Isaiah 66:12)**. This peace too was dependent upon the obedience of the people of God. Unfortunately, for most people, life is more like the raging waves of the sea rather than the pristine flowing waters of a river. God in His grace desires to reward the obedient with peace like a river, but disobedience has its own set of unmanageable outcomes.

DEVOTIONAL THOUGHTS

- **(For children):** Put some water in a bowl. Blow hard on it as though you were making waves. When we disobey God, our insides feel troubled like the raging waves of the sea. However, when we obey God, our insides feel calm and peaceful like the still water in the bowl when you quit blowing upon it.
- **(For everyone):** Have you ever sat down beside a gently flowing river? Did the sound of the water give you a sense of calmness? Do you enjoy that same calmness in your daily walk with the Lord?

- Would you describe your level of peace as a raging sea or a calm river? Do you feel as though your life seems more like the crashing waves rather than the peacefulness of gently running water? If you lack the peace promised of God, what do you think you can do about it?

PRAYER THOUGHTS
- Ask the Lord to grant you peace like a river.
- Ask God to show you that peace is dependent upon obedience.

SONG: *IT IS WELL WITH MY SOUL*

Day 269: (Tuesday)
False Peace

Deuteronomy 29:18 Lest there should be among you man, or woman, or family, or tribe, whose heart turneth away this day from the LORD our God, to go and serve the gods of these nations; lest there should be among you a root that beareth gall and wormwood;

19 And it come to pass, when he heareth the words of this curse, that he bless himself in his heart, saying, **I shall have peace, though I walk in the imagination of mine heart,** *to add drunkenness to thirst:*

INTRODUCTORY THOUGHTS

As previously discussed, every man desires inner peace. Yet, some individuals know peace while others live a life of unrest and instability. Those who have peace are considered wise as they strive to keep it. Unfortunately, many people who do not understand true peace convince themselves that they possess it already. According to scripture, these are the type of people who walk in the imagination of their own heart. They do things their own way rather than God's way and claim to experience peace in the process. Claiming peace without possessing it is unsafe, unwise, and certainly unscriptural. Hope in a false peace has destroyed many nations, peoples, homes, and individuals. Sadly, God's people have never been immune to this regrettable deception. In fact, the Lord declared His fury because the prophets and priests dealt falsely *(Jeremiah 6:13)*. How did they deal falsely? They proclaimed, *"Peace, peace; when there is no peace" (Jeremiah 6:14)*.

DEVOTIONAL THOUGHTS

- **(For children):** A woman in the book of Proverbs disobeyed God. Yet, she thought she was okay. She ate, wiped her mouth, and said, *"I have done no wickedness" (Proverbs 30:20)*. This was a false peace. True peace only comes from obeying God.
- **(For everyone):** Do you have genuine God-given peace? On what evidence do you base your answer? Are you walking in the ways of God or following after the imaginations of your own heart?
- Why do so many people claim peace when they have no peace? How can this be dangerous? What are some of the bad things that could happen to those who trust in a false peace?

PRAYER THOUGHTS

- Ask God to help you enjoy His peace.
- Ask God to teach you that obedience yields true peace.

SONG: *NO HOPE IN JESUS*

Day 270: Church Night

*2 Thessalonians 3:16 Now **the Lord of peace himself give you peace always by all means**. The Lord be with you all.*

Day 271: (Thursday)
Seek Peace

*Psalm 34:14 Depart from evil, and do good; **seek peace, and pursue it.***

INTRODUCTORY THOUGHTS

Though peace may seem illusive, God instructs all believers to pursue after it. True inner peace is not something that one can afford to live without. The Bible says, *"seek peace, and pursue it."* Peter reiterates this truth by saying, *"seek peace, and ensue it" (1 Peter 3:11)*. Men should seek after peace; and when found, they should allow nothing to prevent them from fully seizing upon it. The Lord said, *"therefore love the truth and peace" (Zechariah 8:19)*. Several New Testament verses repeat the importance of peace by admonishing the believer to follow after it *(Romans 14:19; 2 Timothy 2:22; Hebrews 12:14)*. God certainly wants us to seek peace *(1 Corinthians 7:15)* and makes peace attainable. Yet, He demands that we pursue after His peace His way because any other peace is really no peace at all.

Devotional Thoughts

- **(For children):** Would you like to experience thunderstorms every day? Some people feel upset and troubled all the time. *Psalm 119:165a* tells us how to have peace. When you love God's word, you will learn what it says and obediently follow after it. Then you experience peace on the inside.
- **(For everyone):** Are you seeking peace? Have you found true peace? If so, what are you doing to pursue it? Are you fighting with everything inside to keep it?
- People pursue many things in life. What are you pursuing right now? Is it popularity, wealth, or love? The most important thing you can find is true inner peace.

Prayer Thoughts

- Ask the Lord to give you strength to seek peace.
- Ask God to help you pursue peace once you have found it.

Song: *LIKE A RIVER GLORIOUS*

Day 272: (Friday)
Peace with God

> **Romans 5:1** *Therefore being justified by faith,* **we have peace with God** *through our Lord Jesus Christ:*

Introductory Thoughts

The New Testament sheds light on two types of peace: peace *with* God and the peace *of* God. Peace *with* God is *"through"* the Lord Jesus Christ *(Romans 5:1; Colossians 1:20).* According to today's passage, this *"peace with God"* is experienced only upon one's justification at the moment of salvation. Trusting Christ's payment through His death, burial, and resurrection remains the only basis for attaining this peace. Before a man trusts in Christ, he is God's enemy *(Romans 5:10)*, but after salvation, he has been gloriously reconciled to God through the work of

God's Son. No man earns this peace and no man can lose this peace to again become God's enemy because this peace is an everlasting peace.

DEVOTIONAL THOUGHTS

- **(For children):** What do toothpaste, soap, and shampoo clean? Though these products help to clean the outside of your body, your heart without Christ remains wicked because of sin. The Bible says that the blood Jesus shed on the cross *"cleanseth us from all sin."* We need to ask the Lord to clean us up by saving our souls.
- **(For everyone):** Do you remember a time in your life when you realized that you were a sinner and an enemy of God without Christ's forgiveness so you called upon Him to save you? This is known as trusting Christ as your Saviour; have you done it?
- Do you have the peace that we speak of in this devotion? Have you been reconciled to God or do you remain His enemy?

PRAYER THOUGHTS

- Ask God to show you the blessing of having *"peace with God"* through salvation.
- If you have never been saved, acknowledge to God that you are His enemy and desire to be reconciled.

SONG: *WHY DO YOU WAIT?*

Day 273: (Saturday)
The Peace of God

Philippians 4:6 *Be careful for nothing; but in every thing by prayer and supplication with thanksgiving let your requests be made known unto God.*

*7 **And the peace of God,** which passeth all understanding, shall keep your hearts and minds through Christ Jesus.*

INTRODUCTORY THOUGHTS

Salvation brings God's peace to His enemies by transforming them into His allies. However, *"the peace of God"* mentioned in today's passage involves a daily work in the believer's life. *"Peace with God"* remains an indissolvable bond, yet experiencing the daily *"peace of God"* entails an ongoing blessing that may be gained and lost. The *"peace of God"* comes through prayer and the Bible says this peace is beyond mortal comprehension. It truly comforts a believer's heart and mind through Christ Jesus. This is why the Lord admonishes believers to *"let the peace of God rule in"* their hearts *(Colossians 3:15)*. The saved will always be at peace *with* God, but each Christian must *"let"* the peace *of* God work effectually in him on a daily basis.

DEVOTIONAL THOUGHTS

- **(For children):** Once you ask the Lord to save you, you will always be His child; but that doesn't mean you will never disobey Him again. When you do disobey, pray and ask God to forgive you for this disobedience. He always forgives through prayer and His forgiveness will give you peace on the inside.
- **(For everyone):** Do life's trials seem to cause you to constantly be troubled and fretting? Do you find yourself struggling to keep your heart and mind at peace? Will you seek the Lord to renew His peace within you?
- Do you talk to the Lord on a daily basis? Do you take time to read His word? Do you faithfully attend worship services with those of like faith? Do you strive to please the Lord in all that you do? If not, you are likely void of the *"peace of God."*

PRAYER THOUGHTS

- Ask the Lord to grow His peace within you.
- Ask God to give you strength to seek Him daily for the *"peace of God."*

SONG: *SWEET PEACE*

Notes: _____

_____

_____

_____

_____

_____

Notes: _____

_____

_____

_____

_____

_____

_____

_____

_____

_____

_____

_____

_____

_____

_____

_____

_____

_____

_____

Quotes from the next volume

(VOLUME 2, WEEK 39)

Subject: Rebuking (con't)

Peter rebuked the Lord because the Lord's teaching did not align with Peter's perception and plans. Likewise, believers today "rebuke" the Lord when they respond carnally to God's working within their lives.

40

Prudence

Occurrences: found twenty-eight times in twenty-eight verses

Variations: prudence, prudent, prudently

First usage: *1 Samuel 16:18* (prudent)

Last usage: *Ephesians 1:8* (prudence)

Defined: Prudence implies more caution and reserve than wisdom in deliberating and consulting, especially as it deals with foreseeing and avoiding evil rather than simply devising and executing that which is good.

Interesting fact: The book of Proverbs refers to prudence more than any other book, thirteen times. The first use in Proverbs refers to wisdom dwelling with prudence *(Proverbs 8:12)*.

Bible study tip: Pay particular attention to the use of coordinating conjunctions (i.e., for, and, yet, but, etc.). Learn their distinct purposes and how God uses them in the scripture.

Sunday, Day 274—Church Day (no devotional)
Monday, Day 275—*The Prudent Foreseeth*
Tuesday, Day 276—*The Prudent Deal with Knowledge*
Wednesday, Day 277—Church Night (no devotional)

Thursday, Day 278—*The Prudent Looketh Well*
Friday, Day 279—*The Prudent Regardeth Reproof*
Saturday, Day 280—*Wisdom Dwells with Prudence*

Day 274: Church Day

Ephesians 1:8 Wherein he hath abounded toward us in all wisdom and prudence;
9 Having made known unto us the mystery of his will, according to his good pleasure which he hath purposed in himself:

Day 275: (Monday)

The Prudent Foreseeth

Proverbs 22:3 A prudent man foreseeth the evil, and hideth himself: but the simple pass on, and are punished.

INTRODUCTORY THOUGHTS

Prudence is commonly connected to the word *providence*. With this in mind, one can understand that prudence involves the ability to foresee the possibility of future events. Of course, this does not refer to the work of modern day "prophets" who claim to have supernatural visions from God, but is related to wisdom that originates with God. These truths are borne out in our passage where we read, *"A prudent man foreseeth the evil, and hideth himself."* The importance of this truth bears repeating in *Proverbs 27:12*. Wisdom and prudence work together *(Proverbs 8:12)* to help us to consider possible future results when making decisions. In our passage, the prudent foresees the evil and makes a decision to hide himself, while the simple fail to steer clear of the evil and are punished for it.

DEVOTIONAL THOUGHTS

- **(For children):** It is raining so you must play indoors with your friend. Would it be better to play with a ball and bat inside or quietly work some puzzles together? Why? When you consider the consequences of your actions and decide to avoid trouble by making the right choice, the Bible says you are prudent.

- **(For everyone):** Do you try to think about the outcome of your decisions before you make them or do you make decisions only to be surprised by their effects? Prudence will help in this area.
- Do you pray and read your Bible before making decisions? Do you seek godly counsel before making choices that will affect your life?

PRAYER THOUGHTS

- Ask the Lord to bless you with prudence.
- Ask the Lord to help you seek His guidance before making decisions.

SONG: *THE MORE I'M VERSED IN WISDOM'S SCHOOL*

Day 276: (Tuesday)
The Prudent Deal with Knowledge

Proverbs 13:16 Every prudent man dealeth with knowledge: but a fool layeth open his folly.

INTRODUCTORY THOUGHTS

People base decisions on different things: some make choices based on their feelings, others by chance or counsel, and some by knowledge. A prudent man does not trust his feelings for making the right choices lest he be led astray. He does not believe in chance and verifies counsel before choosing his direction. When he decides, he only trusts one foundation; and that is knowledge that comes from God. His certainty for decisions only comes from facts that he can verify. Proverbs has much to say about the association of knowledge and prudence. *"A prudent man concealeth knowledge"* **(Proverbs 12:23)**; *"the prudent are crowned with knowledge"* **(Proverbs 14:18)**; *"The heart of the prudent getteth knowledge"* **(Proverbs 18:15)**. A prudent man demands knowledge and seeks after it with his whole heart. By doing so, he avoids the terrible fate of the fools and the simple.

DEVOTIONAL THOUGHTS

- **(For children):** The prodigal son thought it would be great to leave home and have "fun." He would no longer have to obey his father's rules. However, he ended up miserable and so hungry that he would have gladly eaten the slop given to the pigs. By basing our decisions upon God's word, we can avoid the trouble that comes from making bad decisions.

- **(For everyone):** Where can we find incorruptible knowledge? Where can we look for perfect knowledge when making difficult decisions? How can we find knowledge untainted by man's shortcomings?
- Do you base your decisions upon the right foundation? Do you make these decisions based upon your feelings? Do you make choices based on chance? Do you take counsel without verifying the counsel with the Bible? If so, you likely lack prudence.

PRAYER THOUGHTS

- Ask God to give you the right foundation for your choices.
- Ask the Lord to help you seek after true knowledge.

SONG: *THE DEAR OLD BIBLE*

Day 277: Church Night

*Hosea 14:9 **Who is** wise, and he shall understand these things? **prudent**, and he shall know them? for the ways of the LORD are right, and the just shall walk in them: but the transgressors shall fall therein.*

Day 278: (Thursday)
The Prudent Looketh Well

*Proverbs 14:15 The simple believeth every word: but **the prudent man looketh well to his going.***

INTRODUCTORY THOUGHTS

Today, man has access to more information than at any time in history. Yet people generally seem to incorporate less spiritual research. Today's text contrasts two people and their modes of research. *"The simple believeth every word."* A simple man reads something and accepts it as truth without due consideration. He hears an advertisement and buys a product without additional research. He hears something taught and believes it without considering that the source may be tainted. However, a prudent man does not behave like the simple. The Bible says that he *"looketh well to his going."* He doesn't believe something merely because he considers the teacher smart. He doesn't buy a product simply because someone said he couldn't do without it. He studies, he researches, and he learns the facts before making his choices or decisions.

DEVOTIONAL THOUGHTS

- **(For children):** An older child tells you that it is okay to hit another child because he took your toy. But before you hit someone, ask yourself, *"What would the Lord want me to do?"*
- **(For everyone):** Do you consider the facts before making decisions? How many decisions have gone wrong because you failed to look well into your goings before you chose?
- What are some of the most important decisions you will make or have made in your life? Concerning those decisions made in the past, did you use prudence in deciding? How have those decisions worked out? How will you decide in the future?

PRAYER THOUGHTS

- Ask the Lord to help you incorporate prudence in your decision-making process.
- Ask God to guard you from simplicity in your decision making.

SONG: *THY WORD HAVE I HID IN MY HEART*

Day 279: (Friday)
The Prudent Regardeth Reproof

*Proverbs 15:5 A fool despiseth his father's instruction: but **he that regardeth reproof is prudent**.*

INTRODUCTORY THOUGHTS

Many people, including Christians, find criticism hard to accept, especially when the criticism seems to be unjustified. However, criticism (or reproof as the Bible refers to it) remains a useful tool in developing one's character. Today's text says, *"A fool despiseth his father's instruction."* In fact, the fool refuses to readily receive instruction, certain that he does not need to hear it. Yet, the prudent *"regardeth reproof."* A prudent man will listen to the instructions or reproofs of others knowing that the Lord uses reproofs to adjust one's shortcomings. The prudent man may or may not totally agree with the criticisms, but will listen to them knowing that God can still use these reproofs to change his heart.

DEVOTIONAL THOUGHTS

- **(For children):** When adults point out something wrong, most of the time they are really trying to be helpful. Children really need to pay attention when these things are pointed out to them. These adults are simply helping us to grow in the Lord and be more like what God wants us to be.
- **(For everyone):** The last time you received reproof, did you do so with the right attitude? Were those things said, true or false? Have you asked God to verify the truth? Have you sought His face about this particular reproof?
- Do you see reproof as a good thing or a bad thing? When do you grow most in your Christian life: in times of unwarranted praise or in times of reproof and correction?

PRAYER THOUGHTS

- Ask God to help you see the benefits of reproof.
- Ask God to bring you into contact with people who will reprove you when needed.

SONG: *NEARER, MY GOD, TO THEE*

Day 280: (Saturday)
Wisdom Dwells with Prudence

Proverbs 8:12 *I wisdom dwell with prudence,* *and find out knowledge of witty inventions.*

INTRODUCTORY THOUGHTS

Every astute Bible student knows the importance God places upon wisdom. Accordingly, the Bible says, *"Wisdom is the principal thing"* **(Proverbs 4:7)**. The verse continues, *"therefore get wisdom."* No doubt, wisdom serves as one of the most important gifts for which a believer should seek God. In fact, the Lord promises, *"If any of you lack wisdom, let him ask of God, that giveth to all men liberally, and upbraideth not; and it shall be given him"* **(James 1:5)**. More than likely, these truths are not new, but some Christians fail to recognize the association of wisdom with prudence. We ought to rejoice knowing that by seeking prudence, we are seeking wisdom; and by seeking wisdom, we are seeking prudence.

DEVOTIONAL THOUGHTS

- **(For children):** Sheep get into much trouble when they fail to follow their shepherd. Sometimes they get lost, hurt, or come face-to-face with an enemy. Sometimes they will mistakenly eat some poisonous plants. The Bible likens us to sheep. The Lord is our Shepherd. Every morning, ask the Lord to help you follow Him *(Proverbs 3:5-7)*.
- **(For everyone):** What does the Bible mean that wisdom and prudence dwell together? Why should the believer seek either prudence or wisdom?
- Are you seeking wisdom from the Lord daily? The Bible teaches us to ask God for wisdom. Are you asking Him for wisdom or for prudence?

PRAYER THOUGHTS

- Ask the Lord to help you grow in wisdom and prudence.
- Ask God to show you the importance of prudence.

SONG: *THE CONSECRATION HOUR IS NIGH*

Notes: _____

_____

_____

_____

_____

_____

_____

_____

_____

_____

_____

_____

_____

Notes: _____

_____

_____

_____

_____

_____

_____

_____

_____

_____

_____

_____

_____

_____

_____

_____

Quotes from the next volume

(VOLUME 2, WEEK 40)

Subject: Self-Examination

Though some preachers suggest that believers should never question their own salvation experience, the scripture encourages self-examination *(2 Corinthians 13:5)*.

Life is a journey. Oftentimes, people spend far too much time and strength traveling in the wrong direction.

41

Prudence (con't)

Occurrences: found twenty-three times in the Old Testament and five times in the New Testament

First usage in the New Testament: *Matthew 11:25* (prudent)

Last usage in the Old Testament: *Amos 5:13* (prudent)

Interesting fact: The scripture specifically identifies only two people as having prudence: David *(1 Samuel 16:18; 2 Chronicles 2:12)* and Christ *(Isaiah 52:13)*.

Bible study tip: Determine how you learn and retain information. Some people learn best by reading, others through sight, others by hearing, yet others with more hands-on type experience. You will benefit most by implementing within your studies various effective methods of learning. Paul refers to learning, receiving, hearing, and seeing *(Philippians 4:9)*.

Sunday, Day 281—Church Day (no devotional)
Monday, Day 282—*The Worth of a Prudent Man*
Tuesday, Day 283—*False Prudence*
Wednesday, Day 284—Church Night (no devotional)
Thursday, Day 285—*A Prudent Wife Is from the Lord*

Friday, Day 286—*My Servant Shall Deal Prudently*
Saturday, Day 287—*The Prudent Desire to Hear the Word*

Day 281: Church Day

Proverbs 12:16 *A fool's wrath is presently known: but **a prudent man covereth shame**.*

Day 282: (Monday)
The Worth of a Prudent Man

Isaiah 3:1 *For, behold, **the Lord**, the LORD of hosts, **doth take away** from Jerusalem and from Judah the stay and the staff, the whole stay of bread, and the whole stay of water,*

*2 The mighty man, and the man of war, the judge, and the prophet, and **the prudent**, and the ancient,*

3 The captain of fifty, and the honourable man, and the counseller, and the cunning artificer, and the eloquent orator.

INTRODUCTORY THOUGHTS

The context of our passage speaks of judgment against Jerusalem and Judah. In this judgment the Lord vowed to remove much of the strength of the land. He promised to remove the mighty man and the man of war, the judge and the prophet, the honourable man and the counseller. The removal of these people would certainly weaken any city, town, or nation. Yet, it is in the midst of this list that the Lord included the *prudent*. Apparently, the prudent are the strength of any people just as much as their great warriors and judges. When all things are considered, this makes perfect sense. Those who are prudent make decisions that stabilize any people and provide future stability as well.

DEVOTIONAL THOUGHTS

- **(For children):** Daniel was taken from his parents and carried captive into Babylon. Though he was surrounded by paganism, he still feared God. He refused unclean foods, prayed before giving answers to questions, and prayed though the government commanded him not to pray. God blessed him and kings came to him for guidance because he was wise.

- **(For everyone):** How important are you to those around you? Do they come to you for counsel in times when they need wisdom and guidance? Are you a trusted source for wise and prudent advice?
- In what ways could prudence help a nation in war, finances, and moral issues? How could the prudent man be considered as important as the aged person, the man of war, or the judge?

PRAYER THOUGHTS

- Ask God to make you a pillar of strength for those around you.
- Ask the Lord to help you to be a person of prudence.

SONG: *BE FIRM AND BE FAITHFUL*

Day 283: (Tuesday)
False Prudence

Isaiah 5:18 Woe unto them that draw iniquity with cords of vanity, and sin as it were with a cart rope:

19 That say, Let him make speed, and hasten his work, that we may see it: and let the counsel of the Holy One of Israel draw nigh and come, that we may know it!

20 Woe unto them that call evil good, and good evil; that put darkness for light, and light for darkness; that put bitter for sweet, and sweet for bitter!

21 Woe unto them that are wise in their own eyes, and prudent in their own sight!

22 Woe unto them that are mighty to drink wine, and men of strength to mingle strong drink:

23 Which justify the wicked for reward, and take away the righteousness of the righteous from him!

INTRODUCTORY THOUGHTS

This passage provides a list of grievous sins in the eyes of the Lord. It speaks of those who call evil good, and good evil *(Isaiah 5:20)*. It speaks of the wickedness of those who justify the wicked for reward *(Isaiah 5:23)*, and pronounces a woe upon those who mingle and drink strong drink *(Isaiah 5:22)*. By all appearances, this is a list of wicked and vile sins. Yet, it is in the midst of this list that we find a woe declared against

"them that are wise in their own eyes, and prudent in their own sight"
(Isaiah 5:21). As with everything in this world, there is a true prudence
and there is a counterfeit. The Bible warns us to make sure our prudence
is not just in our *"own sight,"* but is true in a scriptural sense.

DEVOTIONAL THOUGHTS

- **(For children):** Naaman was a famous leper. Elisha sent a messenger to tell him to wash in the Jordan River seven times to be healed. Naaman became angry and wanted to wash in a cleaner river. He thought he knew better than God, but God always knows best.
- **(For everyone):** Where is the best place to find evidence confirming that we indeed have prudence? To what authority can you cling for proof that you have genuine prudence?
- Do you think it is wise to claim prudence when you lack it? Are you willing to repent if you have been deceived? Are you willing to seek the Lord for true prudence?

PRAYER THOUGHTS

- Ask the Lord to help you see the reality of your prudence.
- Ask God to help you see the wickedness of a lack of prudence.

SONG: *HIGHER GROUND*

Day 284: Church Night

Proverbs 16:21 *The wise in heart shall be called prudent: and the
sweetness of the lips increaseth learning.*

Day 285: (Thursday)
A Prudent Wife Is from the Lord

Proverbs 19:14 *House and riches are the inheritance of fathers: and **a
prudent wife is from the LORD.***

INTRODUCTORY THOUGHTS

An inheritance can come in many forms from those who have departed this life. It may include homes, cars, furnishings, and even one's
entire life savings. These treasures can help and bless those in need.
However, no material blessings can surpass the spiritual blessings that

come directly from the Lord. Material inheritances usually come from parents or other relatives, but the Bible points to an inheritance that only comes from the Lord: a prudent wife. We may consider prudence as an irreplaceable trait for a man, but this blessing holds true for a woman also. A prudent wife is of great worth and a wonderful gift from God. The Bible confirms that a man blessed with a prudent wife and children blessed with a prudent mother should thank the Lord.

DEVOTIONAL THOUGHTS

- **(For children):** Elijah told a widow woman (who was gathering sticks to prepare the last bit of food she had) to first fix him a cake and God would bless her. Because the woman believed God, He kept filling her barrel of meal and cruse of oil. She was truly a wise mother.
- **(For everyone):** What are some of the benefits of being a prudent wife and mother? In what ways could prudence be a necessity for a lady who serves her family on a daily basis?
- In what ways could a prudent wife be a much better gift than the houses and riches of loved ones? Which one offers the most assuring and long lasting blessings?

PRAYER THOUGHTS

- Thank God for blessing your wife or mother with prudence.
- Ask God to show you the importance of prudence in your life.

SONG: *HAPPY THE HOME WHEN GOD IS THERE*

Day 286: (Friday)
My Servant Shall Deal Prudently

Isaiah 52:13 Behold, my servant shall deal prudently, he shall be exalted and extolled, and be very high.

14 As many were astonied at thee; his visage was so marred more than any man, and his form more than the sons of men:

15 So shall he sprinkle many nations; the kings shall shut their mouths at him: for that which had not been told them shall they see; and that which they had not heard shall they consider.

INTRODUCTORY THOUGHTS

Isaiah chapter 52 illustrates a well-beloved prophecy concerning the Lord Jesus Christ and His crucifixion. Verse 14 testifies to the seriousness of His crucifixion as it points out that Christ's *"visage was so marred more than any man, and his form more than the sons of men."* These truths point to His physical sufferings, but in no way detract from the spiritual sufferings Christ suffered on the cross. The fact that He took our sins upon Himself remains beyond our comprehension. This same truth applies to the physical sufferings that were more than any man could withstand. With the crucifixion as its context, Isaiah chapter 52 declares that Christ would deal with prudence. The book of Hebrews reinforces this truth as it points out that He *"for the joy that was set before him endured the cross" (Hebrews 12:2)*. The Lord's every action was performed with prudence. We, as the Lord's servants, ought to follow the example He set for us.

DEVOTIONAL THOUGHTS

- **(For children):** Jesus sacrificing Himself for our sins was no easy feat. He gave His life because He wanted to obey the Father's will and He knew that no one could otherwise go to heaven. He thought ahead to the time we would be born, and knew each of us would need a Saviour.
- **(For everyone):** How did the Lord exemplify prudence in His earthly ministry? How did He exemplify it in His crucifixion? How does He exemplify it in His daily dealings with His people?
- How should we, as servants of the Lord, strive to show prudence in our daily walk with the Lord? How can we learn to be better servants from the Son of God?

PRAYER THOUGHTS

- Ask the Lord to show you the prudence of Christ.
- Ask God to give you a desire to be a better servant for Him.

SONG: *IVORY PALACES*

Day 287: (Saturday)
The Prudent Desire to Hear the Word

Acts 13:7 Which was with the deputy of the country, Sergius Paulus, **a prudent man;** *who called for Barnabas and Saul, and* **desired to hear the word of God.**

INTRODUCTORY THOUGHTS

The apostle Paul, through the leading of the Holy Ghost, made his way through Paphos preaching God's word. While in that country, Paul faced great resistance especially from the likes of a false prophet named Bar-jesus. Yet, in the midst of this chaos, the Bible mentions a *prudent* man named Sergius Paulus, the deputy of the country. He desired to hear the message preached by God's man. Sergius Paulus wanted to hear the truth because a prudent man desires to hear it no matter the opposition and the attempts to silence the words of God. Unfortunately, there seem to be many more people like the false prophet today. They want little or nothing to do with the word of God. Yet, a prudent man, whether he agrees or disagrees with what he hears, will desire to hear the words of God. He then ponders those words as he makes his decisions concerning his daily life and eternal destination.

DEVOTIONAL THOUGHTS

- **(For children):** When Cornelius learned that Peter could tell him what God wanted him to do, Cornelius immediately sent for Peter. He gathered his family and friends to hear all the things that God commanded Peter to tell them. Are you that excited to hear God's words?
- **(For everyone):** Do you desire to hear more of God's word? Do you long to read and hear the passages that deal with your sins and shortcomings?
- What are some reasons why Bar-jesus resisted Paul's efforts to preach the word? Are you guilty of the same things? Do you ever try to quench the effect of the word of God in your life?

PRAYER THOUGHTS

- Ask the Lord to give you an unquenchable love for His word.
- Ask God to help you receive His word above all else.

SONG: *TELL ME THE STORY OF JESUS* (CROSBY)

Notes: _____

_____

_____

_____

_____

_____

_____

_____

_____

_____

_____

_____

_____

Quotes from the next volume

(VOLUME 2, WEEK 41)

Subject: Separation

Twenty-first century believers hold a common misconception about the Lord's desire for harmony, supposing that the Lord desires it at all costs.

Separation is not something accomplished through diligence, but should occur naturally after a person comes to know the Lord as Saviour.

Separation is good and it is right. However, when it becomes based more on personal conviction rather than scriptural principles, it can lead to a false sense of holiness.

42

Purity

Occurrences: found 153 times in 139 verses

Variations: pure, purely, pureness, purer, purification, purifications, purified, purifier, purifieth, purify, purifying

First usage: *Exodus 25:11* (pure)

Last usage: *Revelation 22:1* (pure)

Defined: freedom from contamination through unscriptural physical intimacy; freedom from sinister or improper views

Interesting fact: First Timothy contains the only two references to the word *purity* and refers to the youth being an example to the believers in purity *(1 Timothy 4:12)* and the younger women being entreated with all purity *(1 Timothy 5:2)*.

Bible study tip: Pay close attention to the punctuation within scripture. One misplaced comma can greatly affect a Bible doctrine. Consider the implications of removing the comma after "for ever" in *Hebrews 10:12*. Further, consider the change in meaning without the comma in *Luke 23:32: "And there were also two **other, malefactors,** led with him to be put to death."* The comma before malefactors separates Jesus from the malefactors.

Sunday, Day 288—Church Day (no devotional)
Monday, Day 289—*Purity Defined*
Tuesday, Day 290—*The Purity of God's Word*
Wednesday, Day 291—Church Night (no devotional)
Thursday, Day 292—*A Purified People*
Friday, Day 293—*The Lord Requires Purity*
Saturday, Day 294—*Purity Before the King*

Day 288: Church Day

1 Timothy 5:22 Lay hands suddenly on no man, neither be partaker of other men's sins: **keep thyself pure.**

Day 289: (Monday)
Purity Defined

Deuteronomy 32:14 Butter of kine, and milk of sheep, with fat of lambs, and rams of the breed of Bashan, and goats, with the fat of kidneys of wheat; and **thou didst drink the pure blood of the grape.**

INTRODUCTORY THOUGHTS

Reading commentaries offers varying opinions concerning the definition of purity. However, the Bible offers some exacting details which give the right definition. Today's passage speaks of the *"pure blood of the grape."* In other words, nothing was added to the juice—it was pure. There are several other substances in scripture identified as *pure*: gold *(Exodus 25:39)*, olive oil *(Exodus 27:20)*, myrrh *(Exodus 30:23)*, incense *(Exodus 37:29)*, and language *(Zephaniah 3:9)*. Each instance emphasizes that nothing exists to corrupt the nature of the original. These substances are not combined with other materials to dilute or defile them. In essence, purity demands the absence of any substance that corrupts, defiles, or taints in any way.

DEVOTIONAL THOUGHTS

- **(For children):** A fly lands in your glass of milk and drowns. Do you still want to drink the milk? No, the milk became unclean and is no longer pure. We can become unclean on the inside by sinning (being selfish, mean, lazy, etc.). God wants us all to be pure and clean.

- **(For everyone):** Some of the things mentioned in this study require a process to become pure. Only the Lord can make wicked and vile sinners pure in His sight.
- What are some things that exist in your life (anger, pride, deceit, unclean thoughts or actions, etc.) that are contrary to purity? How can you focus on purging these unholy things from your life?

PRAYER THOUGHTS

- Ask the Lord to purify you on a daily basis.
- Ask God to show you the imperfections in your life.

SONG: *HIS WAY WITH THEE*

Day 290: (Tuesday)
The Purity of God's Word

Psalm 12:6 The words of the LORD are pure words: as silver tried in a furnace of earth, purified seven times.

INTRODUCTORY THOUGHTS

God is pure in every way. It logically follows that a pure God speaks only pure words. The Bible insures that we know the truth about these matters. According to scripture, *"the commandment of the LORD is pure, enlightening the eyes" (Psalm 19:8)*. The writer later adds, *"Thy word is very pure: therefore thy servant loveth it" (Psalm 119:140)*. Both verses speak of the word of God in its entirety. In other words, the word of God (all 66 books) is without any foreign substance that would defile it in any way. The scripture also declares that the *"words of the LORD are pure words" (Psalm 12:6)*. Again, which words? The Lord insures that there is no excuse for not understanding that *"Every word of God is pure" (Proverbs 30:5)*. The Devil hates God and the things of God. He wants the world to believe that the Bible has been defiled. God claims otherwise. Who will you believe; God or the Devil?

DEVOTIONAL THOUGHTS

- **(For children):** We do not see God now, but one day we will. Until then, He wants us to read and believe the Bible just as much as if He were standing right in front of us and speaking. The Bible is the most important book you'll ever own or read.

- **(For everyone):** What does it mean to you to think that the Bible is God's pure words? Are you willing to accept God's word as being free from error and man's defilement?
- The purity of God's word should motivate believers to love it. Do you love the word of God? Do you spend time in it on a daily basis? Do you meditate on its contents throughout the day?

PRAYER THOUGHTS

- Ask the Lord to help you accept every word of God as pure.
- Ask God to give you a deeper love and appreciation for His word.

SONG: *THE BIBLE STANDS*

Day 291: Church Night

*Matthew 5:8 Blessed are the **pure in heart**: for they shall see God.*

Day 292: (Thursday)
A Purified People

*Titus 2:14 Who gave himself for us, that he might redeem us from all iniquity, and **purify unto himself** a peculiar people, zealous of good works.*

INTRODUCTORY THOUGHTS

Purity often involves a process. The twofold purification process in the believer's life commences at the moment of salvation. This process then progresses as the believer walks with the Lord. The individual's faith in the finished work of Christ washes away one's sin in Christ's blood. Christ's blood cleanses completely and purifies every believer from his sin. This cleansing and purification remains forever settled between the Lord and the believer. The born-again Christian will never and can never again be any less pure in his position with the Lord. Peter confirms the positional purity when he wrote that his audience had *"purified"* (past tense) their souls *(1 Peter 1:22)*. Our purity in position, settled by trusting Christ as Saviour *(Titus 2:14),* cannot be reversed. However, positional purity does not guarantee purity on a daily basis during our walk. The Christian's practice (his walk) must by choice remain pure.

DEVOTIONAL THOUGHTS

- **(For children):** Someone spills a drink on your toe right after you took a bath. Would you need another bath or could mom just wipe off your toe? Ask dad or mom to explain why Peter just needed his feet washed in John chapter 13.
- **(For everyone):** Have you trusted the Lord Jesus as your personal Saviour? Have you had your soul "purified" by the blood of Christ? If not, you are not pure in your position and cannot be in your walk.
- The Lord wants to purify people. Initially, He demonstrates this in His offer of salvation, but follows with a call to personal purity. Are you walking before the Lord in purity?

PRAYER THOUGHTS

- If you are saved, thank the Lord for purifying your soul.
- Ask the Lord to help you live a pure life before Him.

SONG: *ARE YOU WASHED IN THE BLOOD?*

Day 293: (Friday)
The Lord Requires Purity

*Ezra 6:20 For the priests and the Levites were **purified together, all of them were pure,** and killed the passover for all the children of the captivity, and for their brethren the priests, and for themselves.*

INTRODUCTORY THOUGHTS

From the Old Testament to the New Testament, many things change; however, some themes remain constant. One such theme involves the Lord's desire to use pure things and pure people. God commanded His people in the Old Testament to make sure the things used in the tabernacle were purified *(Leviticus 8:15)*. He also commanded that His servants be purified *(Ezra 6:20)*. In the New Testament, the apostle Paul confirmed the continuation of this theme by saying that *"pureness"* approved him as a minister of God *(2 Corinthians 6:4-6)*. God still requires those who serve to strive to live pure and holy lives. Impurities hinder the Lord's effectiveness in our lives though we may not be aware of the hindrance.

DEVOTIONAL THOUGHTS

- **(For children)**: You would not want to eat from a bowl with dirt in it. You would wash the bowl first. The Bible compares our hearts to vessels and containers. Our hearts need to be clean so God will want to use us to help others *(2 Timothy 2:20-21)*.
- **(For everyone)**: Do you desire to serve the Lord? Do you want to please Him? Do you strive to live a life that is free from the corruptions of this world so that you might better serve Him?
- How should we, as servants of the Lord, strive for purity in our daily walk with the Lord? How can this increase the Lord's effectiveness in our lives?

PRAYER THOUGHTS

- Ask the Lord to give you a desire to serve Him in purity.
- Ask God to show you the things that displease Him.

SONG: *I BRING MY SINS TO THEE*

Day 294: (Saturday)
Purity Before the King

Esther 2:1 After these things, when the wrath of king Ahasuerus was appeased, he remembered Vashti, and what she had done, and what was decreed against her.

2 Then said the king's servants that ministered unto him, Let there be fair young virgins sought for the king:

*3 And let the king appoint officers in all the provinces of his kingdom, that they may gather together all the fair young virgins unto Shushan the palace, to the house of the women, unto the custody of Hege the king's chamberlain, keeper of the women; and let their **things for purification** be given them:*

4 And let the maiden which pleaseth the king be queen instead of Vashti. And the thing pleased the king; and he did so.

INTRODUCTORY THOUGHTS

The story of Esther is a wonderful story. As she and the other ladies prepared to present themselves before king Ahasuerus, they were provided with *"things for purification."* The king considered their purity extremely important. The same principle holds true for the believers to-day. The Bible says, *"Beloved, now are we the sons of God, and it doth not yet appear what we shall be: but we know that, **when he shall appear, we shall be like him;** for we shall see him as he is. And **every man that hath this hope in him purifieth himself, even as he is pure"** (1 John 3:2-3).* Christians, soon to be presented to king Jesus, should grow increasingly concerned about their purity.

DEVOTIONAL THOUGHTS

- **(For children):** The Lord could come back at any moment to take Christians home to heaven. Would you rather be obeying or disobeying? We will give an account (a reason) to God for things we have done or not done.
- **(For everyone):** How long do you think it will be before the Lord Jesus returns for the saved? Do you have a hope that it will be soon? What does this hope do for your desire to live pure?
- What would be most important to you if you somehow knew Christ was coming tomorrow? What would you change? What would you stop doing or start doing differently?

PRAYER THOUGHTS

- Ask the Lord to remind you that His coming is nearing.
- Ask the Lord to purify you as He is pure.

SONG: *FACE TO FACE WITH CHRIST, MY SAVIOUR*

Notes:

_____

_____

_____

_____

_____

_____

_____

Notes: _____

_____

_____

_____

_____

_____

_____

_____

_____

_____

_____

_____

_____

_____

_____

_____

_____

_____

Quotes from the next volume

(VOLUME 2, WEEK 42)

Subject: Singing

Rarely does man have the opportunity to participate in heavenly activity while still on earth. Singing is one of those rare events that enables the Christian a glimpse into a heavenly behaviour.

43

Purity (con't)

Occurrences: found 115 times in the Old Testament and thirty-eight times in the New Testament

First usage in the New Testament: *Matthew 5:8* (pure)

Last usage in the Old Testament: *Malachi 3:3* (purifier, purify)

Interesting fact: The various forms of purity are found thirty-one times in the book of Exodus. This serves as confirmation of the importance of purity in the worship of God. The book of Numbers is second in mentioning purity eleven more times.

Bible study tip: Be cautious when entertaining new and unusual doctrines that you discover. Though one may find truths less known by others, it is a dangerous practice to always be looking *"to tell, or to hear some new thing" (Acts 17:21)*. If you consider something new, do not be overly anxious to express these truths before serious prayer and counsel.

Sunday, Day 295—Church Day (no devotional)
Monday, Day 296—*The Words of the Pure*
Tuesday, Day 297—*Pure in Their Own Eyes*

Wednesday, Day 298—Church Night (no devotional)
Thursday, Day 299—*All Things Are Pure*
Friday, Day 300—*An Example in Purity*
Saturday, Day 301—*Treating the Ladies with Purity*

DAY 295: CHURCH DAY

*1 Peter 1:22 Seeing ye have purified your souls in obeying the truth through the Spirit unto unfeigned love of the brethren, see that ye love one another **with a pure heart fervently:***

Day 296: (Monday)
The Words of the Pure

*Proverbs 15:26 The thoughts of the wicked are an abomination to the LORD: but **the words of the pure are pleasant words.***

INTRODUCTORY THOUGHTS

"*Out of the abundance of the heart the mouth speaketh*" (*Matthew 12:34*). As such, the words that proceed from our mouths provide helpful insights into the condition of our hearts. A man can only deceive with his words for so long; eventually, his speech exposes the reality of his heart's condition. The Bible reinforces this truth when it says, "*the words of the pure are pleasant words*" (*Proverbs 15:26*). The Bible also identifies words of praise to God as "*pleasant*" words (*Psalm 135:3; Psalm 147:1*). Impure words manifest an unpleasantness. Whereas, a pure heart utters pure words and speaks of the Lord and of His goodness.

Devotional Thoughts

- **(For children):** The Lord wants us to use pleasant words in speaking to others. Pleasant words are sweet and kind. Read *Proverbs 16:24* out loud. These types of words make others feel better inside.
- **(For everyone):** What kind of words frequently come out of your mouth? Are you surprised by the nature of your language? Do you use profane or vulgar language? Does your language sound similar to the world?
- Name some instances that qualify as pleasant words. Are those the kind of words that come from your lips? Do you praise the Lord,

quote His word, and edify the saints with your words? If not, you may be dealing with an unclean heart.

PRAYER THOUGHTS

- Ask the Lord to give you pleasant words to speak to others.
- Ask the Lord to help you realize when your words are unclean.

SONG: *MORE HOLINESS GIVE ME*

Day 297: (Tuesday)
Pure in Their Own Eyes

*Proverbs 30:12 There is a generation that are **pure in their own eyes**, and yet is not washed from their filthiness.*

INTRODUCTORY THOUGHTS

Our flesh makes us naturally prone to rebellion and uncleanness. Yet, fewer and fewer people seem willing to accept this Bible truth. Most men would rather continue in uncleanness while pretending to live pure before the Lord. According to our passage, *"There is a generation that are pure in their own eyes, and yet is not washed from their filthiness."* It is impossible to be simultaneously pure and filthy. We may understand this from a practical standpoint but refuse to accept it spiritually. True purity is never based on man's opinion but upon God's unwavering point of view. The word of God remains the only mechanism for determining truth and error. Instead of repenting and striving to align with God's viewpoint, the worldly Christian will claim purity while walking in his filthiness. Unfortunately, Christians are moving away from the truth rather than toward it.

DEVOTIONAL THOUGHTS

- **(For children):** The children of Israel knew God's laws. Yet, they thought they were doing right in asking Aaron to make them a god. God was displeased and brought judgment. We should always do what God's word says, not simply what we think or feel is right.
- **(For everyone):** Why do so many claim purity while living in the filth of this world? How should our love for God change this? Do you love God or this world?

- When we stand before the Lord, He is going to judge us based on His word. He and His word will be the absolute standard of purity. How should this change the way we live today?

PRAYER THOUGHTS

- Ask the Lord to help you seek after genuine purity.
- Ask God to help you make His word your standard of purity.

SONG: *LET THOUGHTLESS THOUSANDS CHOOSE*

Day 298: Church Night

*2 Timothy 1:3 I thank God, whom I serve from my forefathers **with pure conscience**, that without ceasing I have remembrance of thee in my prayers night and day;*

Day 299: (Thursday)
All Things Are Pure

*Titus 1:15 **Unto the pure all things are pure**: but unto them that are defiled and unbelieving is **nothing pure**; but even their mind and conscience is defiled.*

INTRODUCTORY THOUGHTS

Believers should seek to be pure in every facet of life. One might consider limiting this to the places he goes or the things he hears and sees, but purity demands a much greater focus. Believers ought to think on pure things *(Philippians 4:8)* with pure minds *(2 Peter 3:1)* and pure consciences *(1 Timothy 3:9; 2 Timothy 1:3)*. In particular, believers should have pure hearts before the Lord *(1 Timothy 1:5; 2 Timothy 2:22)*. A pure heart will lead to a pure conscience and a pure mind. A pure heart changes where a man goes, what he looks upon, and the things he allows to enter into his ears. Every Christian should strive to make sure that all things are pure.

DEVOTIONAL THOUGHTS

- **(For children):** God tells us to keep our hearts clean and think upon good things. He reveals that what we continue to think on in our hearts is where we end up *(Proverbs 23:7)*. Would it be good to think about how to play nicely with others? Why?

- **(For everyone)**: Why is it so important to have a pure mind, conscience, and heart? How can impurities in one area of our life harmfully affect the purity of other areas?
- What are some things that could harm your purity of mind? What could happen to cause you to lose the purity of your conscience? What could enter your heart to make it impure?

PRAYER THOUGHTS

- Ask the Lord to guard you from impure thoughts.
- Ask the Lord to show you the importance of inward purity.

SONG: *TAKE TIME TO BE HOLY*

Day 300: (Friday)
An Example in Purity

*1 Timothy 4:12 Let no man despise thy youth; **but be thou an example** of the believers, in word, in conversation, in charity, in spirit, in faith, **in purity**.*

INTRODUCTORY THOUGHTS

Timothy was a young man who had been nourished up on the pure words of God since childhood *(2 Timothy 3:15)*. His mother and grandmother invested the necessary time to teach him about good and bad, right and wrong. This early development helped him to understand the importance of purity *(2 Timothy 1:5)*. Because these two women brought him up in the nurture and admonition of the Lord, Timothy had been shielded from much of the wickedness and filth to which others were exposed. With this upbringing in mind, Paul called upon Timothy to be an example in purity. Paul stressed the importance of Timothy maintaining his purity so that other believers might be able to see his life and follow in his example.

DEVOTIONAL THOUGHTS

- **(For children)**: Unfortunately, some children have never read a Bible or ever been to church. If they watched and studied how you talked and behaved, would they want to come with you to church and learn of God's love?

- **(For everyone):** Do you seek to live a pure life before your friends, family, and coworkers? Is your life an example of what it means to live pure before the Lord?
- Think of some people that you would consider to be a good example of purity. What makes you think they are a good example? Should you try to incorporate these things in your own life?

PRAYER THOUGHTS

- Ask God to make you an example of purity.
- Ask the Lord to provide you with living examples of purity.

SONG: *CHRIST LIVETH IN ME*

Day 301: (Saturday)
Treating the Ladies with Purity

*1 Timothy 5:1 Rebuke not an elder, but **intreat** him as a father; and the younger men as brethren;*

*2 The **elder women** as mothers; the **younger** as sisters, **with all purity.***

INTRODUCTORY THOUGHTS

The church meetinghouse has historically been viewed as a spiritually safe haven. Unfortunately, the Devil has increasingly been able to turn this haven into a place of abuse by those with impure motives. It all began when "Christian" men allowed themselves to deal with ladies in ways that lead to impure thoughts, resulting in impure actions. In today's passage, Paul warned Timothy about these dangers and provided wisdom on how to safely deal with these relationships. He told Timothy to treat the elder women as though they were his mother. Concerning the younger ladies, Paul told Timothy to treat them as he would his sister. Christian gentlemen naturally avoid improper thoughts toward their mothers and sisters. Paul was aware that such dangers within a body of believers would exist between men and women so he cautioned Timothy and the church how to behave appropriately.

DEVOTIONAL THOUGHTS

- **(For children):** Paul wrote to Timothy about how to behave in the house of God. Most dedicated Christians have experienced the joy of extended families within the church. Christians are not just a family at home but are blessed with one at church too. Boys should always treat girls at church with respect. Ask Dad to go over a few rules with you (do not hit, hold open doors for them, etc.).
- **(For everyone):** What would be some wise steps to take to insure that you are pure in your dealings with the opposite gender? Do you consider how your words will be perceived before speaking to others?
- If you are married, speak to your spouse about ways that you can ensure purity when dealing with those of the opposite gender. Resolve to be totally committed to only your spouse.

PRAYER THOUGHTS

- Ask the Lord to protect you from impure thoughts at church.
- Ask the Lord for wisdom in dealing with the opposite gender.

SONG: *HOW DAVID, WHEN BY SIN DECEIVED*

Notes: _____

_____

_____

_____

_____

_____

_____

_____

_____

_____

_____

Notes: _____

_____

_____

_____

_____

_____

_____

_____

_____

_____

_____

_____

_____

_____

_____

_____

_____

_____

Quotes from the next volume

(VOLUME 2, WEEK 43)

Subject: Thoughts

Only a foolish man thinks he can hide anything from the Lord. This includes his thought life.

When a man trusts in his own thoughts over the words of God, that man shows a complete disregard for truth.

44

Reverence

Occurrences: found fifteen times in fourteen verses

Variations: reverence, reverenced, reverend

First usage: *Leviticus 19:30* (reverence)

Last usage: *Hebrews 12:28* (reverence)

Defined: fear mingled with respect and esteem; veneration mixed with love and affection especially toward God, His word, and His statutes

Interesting fact: God tells His children to reverence His sanctuary and all people are to reverence God *(Psalm 89:7)*. Even God's name is to be held in reverence *(Psalm 111:9)*. Hebrews refers to reverence as man's service to God along with godly fear.

Bible study tip: What you choose to believe serves as your ultimate authority. Always willingly accept the truth of scripture over your allegiance to traditional teachings, man-made doctrines or even alma maters. Rejecting scriptural light will cause the elimination of future light from your studies. Many very intelligent and learned individuals are scripturally ignorant because they refuse to receive the truth when faced with it.

Sunday, Day 302—Church Day (no devotional)
Monday, Day 303—*What Is Reverence?*
Tuesday, Day 304—*Holy and Reverend Is His Name*
Wednesday, Day 305—Church Night (no devotional)
Thursday, Day 306—*Reverence the Son*
Friday, Day 307—*Reverence for the House of God*
Saturday, Day 308—*See That She Reverence Her Husband*

Day 302: Church Day

Psalm 89:7 *God is greatly to be feared in the assembly of the saints, and **to be had in reverence** of all them that are about him.*

Day 303: (Monday)
What Is Reverence?

Hebrews 12:28 *Wherefore we receiving a kingdom which cannot be moved, let us have grace, whereby we may **serve God acceptably with reverence** and godly fear:*

INTRODUCTORY THOUGHTS

Reverence denotes giving respect and honour. The scripture demonstrates this truth when men bow before a person of high office reflecting their reverence for the office. The Bible marks this bowing down out of respect as an act of reverence *(2 Samuel 9:6; 1 Kings 1:31)*. God's word marks the refusal to bow as showing disrespect and a lack of reverence *(Esther 3:2, 5)*. Every Christian should consistently demonstrate an adequate understanding of biblical reverence. Why? There is only one way to serve God acceptably: with *"reverence and godly fear."* Today's verse teaches that reverence entails some relationship to fear, though reverence is not fear. Since men cannot serve God *"acceptably"* without reverence, living reverently toward God remains an essential element for a healthy Christian life.

DEVOTIONAL THOUGHTS

- **(For children):** God needs to be honoured as our Creator, Father, and Master. He has the right to tell us what to do. Read *Malachi 1:6* for a deeper appreciation of this truth. The best way to honour God is to do what He says in His word. When we don't obey Him, He says we despise His Name.

- **(For everyone):** How can we serve the Lord with reverence and godly fear? How does this make our service acceptable in His sight? How does reverence make our service better?
- Since reverence is connected to respect, honour, and fear, to whom should we show reverence? Do people always have to deserve reverence or should it be given based on who they are or the office they hold?

PRAYER THOUGHTS

- Ask God to help you reverence Him above all others.
- Ask the Lord to help you show reverence to those around you.

SONG: *HOW GREAT THOU ART*

Day 304: (Tuesday)
Holy and Reverend Is His Name

*Psalm 111:9 He sent redemption unto his people: he hath commanded his covenant for ever: **holy and reverend is his name.***

INTRODUCTORY THOUGHTS

The Bible employs the word *"reverend"* only once. Studying the context offers one appropriate definition and acceptable usage. Unfortunately, the vast majority of believers are unaware that the title *"reverend"* has been inappropriately usurped to apply to men. This reflects how far so-called Bible teachers and preachers have strayed from God's holy precepts. God wants Christians to show proper respect to a man of God, but the title *"reverend"* should never be used to address him. There is only one Name that is reverend and that is the Lord's. An English Baptist pastor and author, Robert Robinson, who wrote the hymn, *Come Thou Fount of Every Blessing,* abhorred the pomp assumed by many of his ministerial colleagues. He once said, *"I wonder why any man should be so silly as to call me Reverend."* Only one is worthy of all praise and honour and that is the Lord *(Psalm 99:3; Revelation 4:8)*.

DEVOTIONAL THOUGHTS

- **(For children):** You can show the Lord that you honour Him and His Name by doing what He says. Read *Luke 6:46*. God promised life and peace to His people because they feared Him and were afraid before His Name *(Malachi 2:5)*.
- **(For everyone):** What does it mean that God's name is reverend? Does reverend mean a specific title for Him or a declaration concerning His name? How can we show the appropriate reverence to God and His name?
- Is it possible that we grieve the Lord when we inappropriately use titles like *"Reverend"* or *"Father" (Matthew 23:9)* when addressing men? We should never be guilty of using one of God's titles or descriptions when addressing those who seek to serve Him.

PRAYER THOUGHTS

- Ask the Lord to help you show reverence to His Name.
- Ask God to enlighten others who have strayed from the truth.

SONG: *HOLY AND REVEREND IS THE NAME*

Day 305: Church Night

*Hebrews 12:9 Furthermore we have had **fathers** of our flesh which corrected us, and **we gave them reverence**: shall we not much rather be in subjection unto the Father of spirits, and live?*

Day 306: (Thursday)
Reverence the Son

*Luke 20:13 Then said the lord of the vineyard, What shall I do? I will send **my beloved son**: it may be they will **reverence him** when they see him.*

INTRODUCTORY THOUGHTS

Today's passage comes from a portion of one of Christ's many parables *(Luke 20:9)*. The interpretation of the parable declares that God sent prophets and priests to deliver His message to the Jewish people, but in the end He sent His own Son *(Hebrews 1:2)*. In the parable, the Lord said, *"I will send my beloved son: it may be they will reverence him when they see him" (Luke 20:13)*. The lack of reverence by the Jews did not take God by surprise. It was simply a legitimate offer to be right with God. Additionally, God intended for this parable to express an important truth: the Father expects mankind to reverence His Son. The world mocked Him, beat Him, and eventually executed Him as though He was a hardened criminal. Should we be surprised when people today fail to reverence the Son as they refuse to trust Him as Saviour?

DEVOTIONAL THOUGHTS

- **(For children):** God the Son loves us and gave His life for us. In turn, God the Father wants His Son to be honoured (respected and obeyed). Some people do not love the Son, but the Bible says one day He will be their judge and they will bow before Him *(Philippians 2:8-11)*.
- **(For everyone):** When the Lord came to this earth, a small minority showed Him reverence. Much of what He suffered was directly attributed to our personal sins.
- Do you show a daily reverence to the Son of God? Do you serve Him in reverence? Do you speak of Him with respect and awe? Do you live holy knowing that He is ever watching?

PRAYER THOUGHTS

- Ask God to show you how to truly reverence His Son.
- Ask the Lord to let your reverence for His Son change your life.

SONG: *ALL HAIL THE POWER OF JESUS' NAME*

Day 307: (Friday)
Reverence for the House of God

Leviticus 26:2 Ye shall keep my sabbaths, and reverence my sanctuary: I am the LORD.

INTRODUCTORY THOUGHTS

Many things have changed since Old Testament times. For instance, the Lord visited His people in the temple or tabernacle in the Old Testament by dwelling between the cherubims on the ark of God *(Psalm 80:1)*. This ended especially with the onset of the New Testament and the permanent indwelling of God's Spirit within believers. The Lord stressed, "*. . . that ye are the temple of God, and that the Spirit of God dwelleth in* you" *(1 Corinthians 3:16)*. For this reason, the New Testament does not place as much emphasis on reverence in the physical house of God. Regardless, the Lord is not silent concerning our behaviour in His house. We should behave ourselves both respectfully and properly *(1 Timothy 3:15)*. Of all people, Bible believers should demonstrate reverence in the house of God so that others get a sense for our awe of God and His goodness.

DEVOTIONAL THOUGHTS

- **(For children):** When someone comes to visit our family, we generally do some extra cleaning of our homes and exhibit our best behaviour. God's house is a very special place. People come to meet together with other like-minded believers who love Him and want to hear God's truths. Sometimes we have visitors. How can we take special care of God's house and how should we behave?
- **(For everyone):** What are some of the ways that we ought to behave differently in the house of God? Are there things that we may do at home or in public that we would not do at church?
- Develop some rules of behaviour for your family when they are in the house of God. Discuss why we should behave differently in the house of the Lord than at home.

PRAYER THOUGHTS

- Ask God to help you show reverence for His house.
- Ask the Lord to help you be faithful to church.

SONG: *GREAT KING OF GLORY, COME*

Day 308: (Saturday)
See That She Reverence Her Husband

Ephesians 5:33** Nevertheless let every one of you in particular so love his wife even as himself; and **the wife see that she reverence her husband.

INTRODUCTORY THOUGHTS

The Bible reflects the special relationship that should exist between a husband and his wife. The Lord wants us to recognize the importance of this relationship by likening it to the Lord's relationship with His church.

Three times the Lord commands the man to love his wife as Christ loved the church. He commanded this because He knew man's biggest problem would be faithfully and unconditionally loving his wife. The Lord was not one-sided in His commandments concerning the marriage relationship. He commanded that the woman in the marriage relationship should obey her husband. Our passage also says that she should reverence him. A woman craves the love of her husband. Likewise, the man needs respect from the woman God gave him. A godly wife will not belittle or humiliate her husband but instead show him respect as the head of their home.

DEVOTIONAL THOUGHTS

- **(For children):** Would it be fun to play the game *"follow the leader"* if everyone wanted to be the leader? No, if everyone tried to lead, the game would simply devolve into confusion and probably fighting. God set up the order of leadership within the home so our homes would be happy: dad first, mom second, and children last.
- **(For everyone):** In what ways can a wife ensure that she reverences her husband? What can a wife learn about reverence from *1 Peter 3:1-6*? What does it mean to truly reverence your husband?
- Why should a wife reverence her husband? Of all the reasons, which reason is the most important? To whom will you have to give account for any disobedience in this area?

PRAYER THOUGHTS

- Ask the Lord to make your home pleasing to Him.
- Ask the Lord help you love your wife or reverence your husband.

SONG: *HOW CLOSELY JOINED ARE MAN AND WIFE*

Notes: _____

_____

_____

_____

_____

_____

_____

Notes: _____

_____

_____

_____

_____

_____

_____

_____

_____

_____

_____

_____

_____

_____

_____

_____

_____

Quotes from the next volume

(VOLUME 2, WEEK 44)

Subject: Trusting

An individual cannot trust in vanity, riches, or lies while simultaneously trusting in the Lord.

When man trusts in nothing, he receives nothing in return.

The real needs of mankind cannot be satisfied by man, even the best of men.

45

Submission

Occurrences: found sixteen times in as many verses

Variations: submit, submitted, submitting

First usage: *Genesis 16:9* (submit)

Last usage: *1 Peter 5:5* (submit)

Defined: to yield, resign or surrender power, will, or authority; to commit to the discretion of judgment of another

Interesting fact: Husbands and wives are instructed to submit themselves to each other *(Ephesians 5:21)*; Christians are told to submit to those who rule over them *(Hebrews 13:17),* and all are to submit to God *(James 4:7)*. Additionally, the younger are to submit to the elder *(1 Peter 5:5)*. Yet, true godly submission seems to be a fading characteristic even amongst believers.

Bible study tip: Draw two circles with part of each circle overlapping the other circle. Take a pen or pencil and shade in the overlapping area. This picture is a good physical semblance of how oftentimes two Bible words have overlapping, yet different meanings. When studying a word, consider the words that share some overlapping meanings and yet how they differ in other respects.

Sunday, Day 309—Church Day (no devotional)
Monday, Day 310—*Obedience and Submission*
Tuesday, Day 311—*Submission and Humility*
Wednesday, Day 312—Church Night (no devotional)
Thursday, Day 313—*Submit Yourselves unto God*
Friday, Day 314—*Submitting unto God's Righteousness*
Saturday, Day 315—*Submitting Yourselves One to Another*

Day 309: Church Day

*Psalm 66:3 Say unto God, How terrible art thou in thy works! through the greatness of thy power shall **thine enemies submit** themselves unto thee.*

Day 310: (Monday)
Obedience and Submission

*Hebrews 13:17 **Obey them that have the rule over you, and submit yourselves**: for they watch for your souls, as they that must give account, that they may do it with joy, and not with grief: for that is unprofitable for you.*

INTRODUCTORY THOUGHTS

The passage may appear to directly equate obedience and submission together, but each word conveys a separate and distinct concept. Although today's passage includes both obedience and submission, it is important to recognize that these two words involve separate acts. Earlier studies noted a twofold definition of *obedience*: first, having an attentive ear, followed by acting upon what has been said. Dividing *submission* into two parts helps to better understand it too (*sub* + *mission*). The prefix *sub* means under (thus a submarine travels under the water), and the root word *mission* means to be sent out. Obedience, therefore, emphasizes the act of hearing and doing, while submission emphasizes the act of placing oneself under the authority of another.

DEVOTIONAL THOUGHTS

- **(For children):** While Jesus was living with Joseph and Mary, the Bible says that He *"was subject unto them" (Luke 2:51)*. Jesus was God, yet He placed Himself under the authority of His earthly parents. He is a great example of how children ought to behave.
- **(For everyone):** Submission is an act of the heart, but it also directly affects our will. If this is true, what is the root problem when we fail to submit our will to another?
- To whom does the Lord want you to submit? Why would He want you to submit to them? Does the Lord desire for you to submit to Him? If so, why do you think this is so very important to Him?

PRAYER THOUGHTS

- Ask the Lord to help you submit to His will for your life.
- Ask God to give you a surrendered heart.

SONG: *I'LL GO WHERE YOU WANT ME TO GO*

Day 311: (Tuesday)
Submission and Humility

1 Peter 5:5 *Likewise, ye younger,* **submit yourselves unto the elder.** *Yea, all of you be subject one to another, and be clothed with humility: for God resisteth the proud, and giveth grace to the humble.*

INTRODUCTORY THOUGHTS

Everyone naturally wants to be in charge and do things for their own self-fulfillment. We want to set our own schedule, plan our own activities without regarding others. Life, however, is not that simple. Everyone must willingly submit to various authorities. A lack of humility is the primary reason why we find submission so difficult. Today's passage clearly conveys this important truth. The Bible says that the younger believers are to clothe themselves with humility thus enabling them to submit themselves to the elder. Yet, pride wants to rule our hearts and squash any humble spirit. Pride wants to sit on the throne of our hearts. The Devil displayed this attitude when he was lifted up with pride and many young Christians elevated too early in life fall into this same condemnation *(1 Timothy 3:6)*. The Devil sought to make himself like the most High *(Isaiah 14:12-14)* and rob God of His rightful position. Those who want to please God must do so by submitting to Him and to others in authority. Humbling oneself before the Lord is the only means of submission.

DEVOTIONAL THOUGHTS

- **(For children):** God the Son came to earth and took upon Himself a body of flesh. He was still God and could have been in charge of everything; yet, He willingly put Himself under the authority of God the Father. Read *Philippians 2:5-8* to see how He acted.
- **(For everyone):** Do you long to be in charge? Do you want to be the boss? Do you enjoy telling others what to do? How do you feel when others tell you what to do? Be honest with yourself and the Lord if you truly sense rebellion as your first choice.
- Are you so rebellious and full of pride that others cannot lead you? Will there be others in heaven who can give a good account of your submission to authority *(Hebrews 13:17)*?

PRAYER THOUGHTS

- Ask the Lord to help you humble yourself before Him.
- Ask God to help you accept the leadership of others.

SONG: *OFT HAVE I TURNED MY EYES WITHIN*

Day 312: Church Night

1 Peter 2:13 Submit yourselves to every ordinance of man for the Lord's sake: whether it be to the king, as supreme;

Day 313: (Thursday)
Submit Yourselves unto God

James 4:7 Submit yourselves therefore to God. Resist the devil, and he will flee from you.

INTRODUCTORY THOUGHTS

God directs believers to submit to various authorities; yet, above all these authorities, we must submit ourselves unto God. This submission entails submitting our whole being (body, soul, and spirit) to God. Christ purchased us with His own blood on Calvary *(1 Corinthians 6:20)*, and we are no longer our own. This means that God has the authority to tell us what to eat, where to go, what to watch, what to listen to, what to read, where to attend church, how to worship Him, and the list continues without end. Every aspect of our lives, from our thought life to our every action, remains God's business. We should wisely submit every aspect of our lives to Him. Submitting to God enables us to resist the Devil and when we resist him, the Devil flees.

DEVOTIONAL THOUGHTS

- **(For children):** When the apostle Paul first met the Lord, he asked, "Lord, what wilt thou have me to do?" *(Acts 9:6)*. Paul's life later revealed that he asked this question often as he served the Lord. We should follow Paul's example.
- **(For everyone):** Think about various areas within your life. Does the Lord reign in each of these areas? Does He have authority in your life, or are you living according to your own will and way?
- Who dictates what you wear? Who dictates the language you use? Who dictates your prayer life and Bible study? Who dictates what you believe? If the answer is not the Lord in each area, you are not fully submitted to Him.

PRAYER THOUGHTS

- Ask God to help you submit every aspect of your life to Him.
- Ask God to show you when you are in authority instead of Him.

SONG: *IN ALL MY LORD'S APPOINTED WAYS*

Day 314: (Friday)
Submitting unto God's Righteousness

*Romans 10:1 Brethren, my heart's desire and prayer to God for **Israel** is, that they might be saved.*
2 For I bear them record that they have a zeal of God, but not according to knowledge.
*3 For they being ignorant of God's righteousness, and going about to establish their own righteousness, have **not submitted themselves unto the righteousness of God.***

INTRODUCTORY THOUGHTS

Man-made religions have always unwisely taught followers to establish their own righteousness. In the garden in Eden, Adam and Eve clothed themselves with fig leaves in an attempt to cover their nakedness caused by sin. Men built the tower of Babel hoping that this device could help them reach into heaven. The Bible describes man's righteousness as *"filthy rags" (Isaiah 64:6)*. Today's passage tells of a people who went about to establish their own righteousness by refusing to submit to God's righteousness. Man-made religions all err in the same way. They think that some work or act of obedience can somehow establish a level of righteousness that will ultimately and eventually satisfy God. Yet, the Bible points out the repeated futility of failing to submit to the righteousness of God.

DEVOTIONAL THOUGHTS

- **(For children):** God is holy, perfect, and righteous. In order to get to heaven on our own, we would need to keep each of God's laws. Have you ever lied or disobeyed your parents? No one but Jesus kept all of God's laws. Because He satisfied God's demand (sinless perfection), He sacrificed Himself on the cross to pay for our sins. Only by believing and trusting in Him can we get to heaven.
- **(For everyone):** Upon what are you depending to get you to heaven? Upon what are you depending to gain favour with the Lord? If you are counting on your works, you will be eternally disappointed.
- What use are filthy rags? What does this tell you about the greatness of your righteousness? The only way to please God is to submit to His righteousness.

PRAYER THOUGHTS

- Ask God to show you when you are trusting in your own righteousness.
- Ask the Lord to help you accept His righteousness.

SONG: *THE SOLID ROCK*

Day 315: (Saturday)
Submitting Yourselves One to Another

Ephesians 5:21 Submitting yourselves one to another in the fear of God.

INTRODUCTORY THOUGHTS

One important aspect of submission to the Lord involves submitting to one another. Grasping this important truth would solve many of the problems in the world, home, and church. The Bible tells us that the younger are supposed to submit to the elder *(1 Peter 5:5)*. Husbands and wives are to submit to each other *(Ephesians 5:21-22; Colossians 3:18)*. Christians are to submit to those who labour in the work of the Lord *(1 Corinthians 16:16)*, and those who rule over them *(Hebrews 13:17)*. Instead of fighting for authoritative positions, we should first seek opportunities to submit ourselves to others for the glory of God. A pride-filled heart remains the biggest stumblingblock in the way of full submission.

DEVOTIONAL THOUGHTS

- **(For children):** Why should we submit to our parents, our pastor, our Sunday School teacher? *Ephesians 5:21* says to do it *"in the fear of God."* We are to submit because God wants us to submit. He is on our side. Our home and our church will be happier when we submit to the will of God.
- **(For everyone):** To whom does God want you to submit? How could your obedience in this area bring glory to God? Why do you think people struggle so much submitting to authority?
- What happens when two people who are working together both want to be in charge? What would happen if the same two people were willing to submit to one another?

PRAYER THOUGHTS

- Ask the Lord to give you a heart of humility.
- Ask God to help you to submit to others.

SONG: *OUR BEST*

Notes: _____

_____

_____

_____

_____

_____

_____

_____

_____

_____

_____

_____

_____

_____

_____

_____

_____

Quotes from the next volume

(VOLUME 2, WEEK 45)

Subject: Trusting (con't)

Trusting in worldly safety, uncertain riches, vanity, other people, or even self always yields disappointment and defeat.

46

Temperance

Occurrences: found seven times in six verses, all in the New Testament

Variations: temperance, temperate; Note: though not included here, you could also include the words *temper, tempered, untempered.*

First usage: *Acts 24:25* (temperance)

Last usage: *2 Peter 1:6* (temperance—twice)

Defined: habitual moderation in regard to the various aspects of life

Interesting fact: Temperance is the last of the nine-fold fruit of the spirit mentioned in *Galatians 5:22-23*.

Bible study tip: Be careful not to structure some new doctrine based upon one or two verses or single passages. Every cult can be traced to those who claimed to be different from everyone else by purporting to be the single purveyors of truth. They claim their unique doctrines make them sole possessors of the truth. The more evidence existing from scripture concerning any particular doctrinal claim, the better founded the teachings, though never a guarantee of accuracy in itself.

Sunday, Day 316—Church Day (no devotional)
Monday, Day 317—*What Is Temperance?*
Tuesday, 318—*Temperate in All Things*
Wednesday, Day 319—Church Night (no devotional)
Thursday, Day 320—*The Fruit of the Spirit*
Friday, Day 321—*Temperance in Ministry*
Saturday, Day 322—*Add Temperance to Knowledge*

DAY 316: CHURCH DAY

Titus 2:1 *But speak thou the things which become sound doctrine:* 2 ***That the aged men be*** *sober, grave,* **temperate,** *sound in faith, in charity, in patience.*

Day 317: (Monday)
What Is Temperance?

Acts 24:24 *And after certain days, when Felix came with his wife Drusilla, which was a Jewess, he sent for Paul, and heard him concerning the faith in Christ.* 25 ***And as he reasoned of*** *righteousness,* **temperance,** *and judgment to come, Felix trembled, and answered, Go thy way for this time; when I have a convenient season, I will call for thee.*

INTRODUCTORY THOUGHTS

Searching a modern dictionary for the words *temperance* or *temperate* likely yields a definition limiting temperance to self-control or abstinence from alcohol. However, the scripture infers a much broader and deeper definition. Studying the root word *temper* offers a better biblical definition of the word than today's typical dictionary definition. *Temper* is an action word that means to mix something. Although the Bible contains only a few uses of the words *temperate* and *temperance*, these words mean to be balanced or to have a proper mix. Paul's message, as he reasoned with Felix, included a message of temperance. Improper balance is one of greatest problems plaguing modern Christianity. It can best be seen in the tendency to lean either toward absolute truth without love or love without seeking the balance of presenting the whole counsel of God.

DEVOTIONAL THOUGHTS

- **(For children):** Our bodies work best with a proper balance of eating, sleeping, working, and playing. To be the best we can for the Lord, we must read the Bible, pray, go to church, and do what the Lord would have us to do.
- **(For everyone):** The Bible says, *"a false balance is not good" (**Proverbs 20:23**).* This is speaking of a balance that measures weights, but the practical application of this truth holds true within the Christian life and walk. A false balance is never good.
- Why is it so important for believers to grasp a proper balance? What problems can exist when we lose sight of temperance in our daily walk with the Lord and with others?

PRAYER THOUGHTS

- Ask the Lord to show you the importance of temperance.
- Ask God to help you reason with others concerning temperance.

SONG: *WHOLLY THINE* (HAWKS)

Day 318: (Tuesday)
Temperate in All Things

1 Corinthians 9:24 Know ye not that they which run in a race run all, but one receiveth the prize? So run, that ye may obtain.

25 **And every man that striveth for the mastery is temperate in all things.** *Now they do it to obtain a corruptible crown; but we an incorruptible.*

INTRODUCTORY THOUGHTS

Athletes understand the importance of being temperate in their training. They incorporate a variety of exercises to strengthen each body part thus maximizing their potential. Limiting training to one aspect causes the athlete to lose his edge. It is important to realize that exercise is only one part of the training regimen. For instance, no serious athlete ignores the importance of a balanced diet rich in nutrients. Dedicated athletes strive for a corruptible crown by implementing temperance in all things. Believers seeking a spiritually incorruptible crown should learn from the athletes who incorporate temperance. An athlete missing out at the finish line results in sadness. The Christian's failure to incorporate balance will cause him to lose rewards at the judgment seat of Christ. This is the greater loss.

DEVOTIONAL THOUGHTS

- **(For children):** Discuss *Proverbs 25:16, Proverbs 20:13a,* and *Mark 6:31.* God wants us to have a proper balance. Some children who love to sing have trouble listening to the message. Children need to learn to do both. God chose preaching to make known His word and to save people.
- **(For everyone):** What are some ways to implement temperance within your Christian life? What troubles might exist if you fail to be temperate in your service to the Lord?
- Do you balance Bible reading and prayer? Do you balance compassion with your zeal? Do you exemplify temperance in the way you treat others?

PRAYER THOUGHTS

- Ask the Lord to help you balance your walk with Him.
- Ask God to show you the importance of each part of your walk.

SONG: *BY AND BY (BLACKALL)*

Day 319: Church Night

Proverbs 11:1 A false balance is abomination to the LORD: but a just weight is his delight.

Day 320: (Thursday)
The Fruit of the Spirit

Galatians 5:22 But the fruit of the Spirit is love, joy, peace, longsuffering, gentleness, goodness, faith,
*23 Meekness, **temperance**: against such there is no law.*

INTRODUCTORY THOUGHTS

Fruit thrives within the right environment with the proper living conditions. The same holds true concerning God's virtues in the life of a Christian. It is God's indwelling Spirit that provides the fertile environment necessary for every believer to cultivate these virtues. They include love, joy, peace, and faith. Only as Christians submit to the leading of the Holy Ghost can we fully access these virtues. Though mentioned last in the list from Galatians, *temperance* is another of the important virtues making up the fruit of the Spirit. Though frequently neglected, temperance is no less important than the other virtues naturally growing in the life of a fertile believer. A disregard for the proper mix in the Christian life causes imbalance. Believers who fail to cultivate stability and peace by not yielding control to God's indwelling Spirit never realize their God-given potential.

DEVOTIONAL THOUGHTS

- **(For children):** A tree needs a proper amount of sunshine, rain, and good soil to produce fruit. The fruit of the Spirit mentioned above comes as a child of God reads his Bible, prays, and lives obediently according to what God says.
- **(For everyone):** Does your life reflect balance? Would the Lord describe your life as stable, consistent, and balanced? Or are you tossed to and fro by the troubles and cares of this world?
- Do you recognize the fruit of the Spirit naturally growing in your life? If not, what is hindering your spiritual growth? Are you reading your Bible? Are you spending time in prayer with the Lord?

PRAYER THOUGHTS

- Ask the Lord to help you yield more completely to Him.
- Ask God to help His fruit grow and mature in your life.

SONG: *WHEN GENTLE SPRING RENEWS THE EARTH*

Day 321: (Friday)
Temperance in Ministry

Titus 1:7 For a bishop must be blameless, as the steward of God; not selfwilled, not soon angry, not given to wine, no striker, not given to filthy lucre;
8 But a lover of hospitality, a lover of good men, sober, just, holy, **temperate***;*
9 Holding fast the faithful word as he hath been taught, that he may be able by sound doctrine both to exhort and to convince the gainsayers.

INTRODUCTORY THOUGHTS

Today's passage presents a list of qualifications for a man who desires to be a pastor holding the office of a bishop. Though this list specifically deals with a ministry office, it could serve as a list of admonitions for anyone desiring to serve the Lord. Bible teachers and preachers often focus on a few of the most publicized qualifications while neglecting some of the others. For instance, very rarely is much attention focused on the necessity of temperance in the life of the man of God. Temperance plays an important part in the life of God's servant. Failure of those in leadership to be balanced will lead to a whole church full of people lacking temperance. This same truth holds for anyone who leads or serves in any ministry of a church.

DEVOTIONAL THOUGHTS

- **(For children):** Paul wrote two letters to Timothy giving him instruction on how to faithfully serve the Lord. Among other things, Paul told Timothy to study, to pray, and to pay attention to reading. He also emphasized the importance of doctrine (the teachings of the Bible), and exhortation (urging people strongly and encouraging them to do the right thing).
- **(For everyone):** What ways would temperance be useful to someone in a teaching and preaching position in the church?
- Temperance is contagious. Are you encouraging others to lead balanced lives or a slack life?

PRAYER THOUGHTS

- Ask God to help you minister to others with temperance.
- Ask God to show you the value of temperance in your walk.

SONG: *GOOD GOD IN WHAT VAIN AGE WE LIVE*

Day 322: (Saturday)
Add Temperance to Knowledge

2 Peter 1:5 And beside this, giving all diligence, add to your faith virtue; and to virtue knowledge;

6 **And to knowledge temperance**; *and to temperance patience; and to patience godliness;*
7 *And to godliness brotherly kindness; and to brotherly kindness charity.*
8 *For if these things be in you, and abound, they make you that ye shall neither be barren nor unfruitful in the knowledge of our Lord Jesus Christ.*

INTRODUCTORY THOUGHTS

The scripture contains many admonitions to seek for knowledge. Today's passage says that knowledge is something that should be added to the foundation of faith. Yet, knowledge brings with it a set of temptations. Knowledge increases sorrow *(Ecclesiastes 1:18)*, has potential to pervert *(Isaiah 47:10)*, and when not handled properly, *"knowledge puffeth up" (1 Corinthians 8:1)*. With this understanding, it should come as no surprise that the Lord would instruct us to add *temperance* to our knowledge. Knowledge without temperance leads to many pitfalls in an individual, church, or ministry. Our knowledge must be balanced by temperance.

DEVOTIONAL THOUGHTS

- **(For children):** What things are easy for you to learn and do well? Do you think this knowledge makes you better than others? Study and discuss *1 Corinthians 4:7*. Why not commit to use your God-given abilities to help others?
- **(For everyone):** Pride is one of the greatest pitfalls of knowledge. Do you find your pride and humility frequently getting out of balance because of the things that you know?
- What are some reasons why you think the Lord said that we should add temperance to our knowledge? How can temperance be beneficial with knowledge?

PRAYER THOUGHTS

- Ask the Lord to help you add temperance to your knowledge.
- Ask God to help you maintain balance during times of temptation.

SONG: *ALMIGHTY MAKER OF MY FRAME*

Notes: _____

_____

_____

_____

_____

_____

_____

_____

_____

_____

_____

_____

_____

Quotes from the next volume

(VOLUME 2, WEEK 46)

Subject: Unity

Unity only comes from and through the Lord Jesus Christ, but once it comes, the saints of God must endeavour to keep that unity.

Only saints who exercise "lowliness and meekness, with long-suffering" will experience unity.

When believers are united, they are like multiple cords woven together. When someone sows discord, he attempts to undo or "discord" the threefold cord.

47

Tenderhearted

Occurrences: found twice in the Bible

Variations: tenderhearted; (Note: although the details are not considered here, it would also be helpful to study the word *tender.)*

First usage: *2 Chronicles 13:7*

Last usage: *Ephesians 4:32*

Defined: having great sensibility; susceptible to impressions or influence

Interesting fact: Christians are told to be kind to each other and *tenderhearted* resulting in the forgiveness of others because Christ has forgiven each of us *(Ephesians 4:32)*. We are to forgive as we are forgiven, unconditionally.

Bible study tip: The Bible student cannot fully understand any event or teaching until having considered each of the varied accounts. The most common scenario involves an event found in more than one gospel. However, there are many other instances where an event may be mentioned in more than one passage and book of the Bible.

Sunday, Day 323—Church Day (no devotional)
Monday, Day 324—*What Is a Tender Heart?*
Tuesday, Day 325—*Humility Yields a Tender Heart*
Wednesday, Day 326—Church Night (no devotional)
Thursday, Day 327—*A Hard Heart Will Not Hearken*
Friday, Day 328—*A Heart as Firm as a Stone*
Saturday, Day 329—*A Hard Heart Leads to Mischief*

Day 323: Church Day

*Ephesians 4:32 And be ye kind one to another, **tenderhearted**, forgiving one another, even as God for Christ's sake hath forgiven you.*

Day 324: (Monday)
What Is a Tender Heart?

*Deuteronomy 28:54 So that the man that is **tender** among you, and **very delicate**, his eye shall be evil toward his brother, and toward the wife of his bosom, and toward the remnant of his children which he shall leave:*

INTRODUCTORY THOUGHTS

Sometimes the most effective means of defining a Bible word involves researching those words commonly associated with the word in question. *Delicate* is such a word. On four occasions, the Bible associates the word *delicate* with variations of the word *tender* (**Deuteronomy 28:54, 56; Isaiah 47:1**). This association provides the Bible student with the sense that a delicate person is easily broken spiritually. Additional Bible study demonstrates that a tender heart remains pliable and prone to brokenness before the Lord. Conversely, the Bible points to a hardened heart as remaining obstinate. The word *obstinate* conveys an inflexibleness or stubbornness. As believers, we should aspire to be tenderhearted before the Lord with a heart easily moved to accomplish His will.

DEVOTIONAL THOUGHTS

- **(For children):** Ezra is a great example of someone with a tender heart toward the things of God. The Bible says he prepared his heart (got it settled that he would do things God's way and not his own)

(Ezra 7:10). He, therefore, searched God's word and greatly desired to do what it said.

- **(For everyone):** Is your heart easily moved by reading God's word? Does the Lord prick your heart when His word is preached? Do you find that the Lord frequently compels you to be faithful?
- What kind of things might assist a believer in developing a tender heart? What other things might lead to a hardened heart? Which things are a consistent diet in your life?

PRAYER THOUGHTS

- Ask the Lord to use these studies to tenderize your heart.
- Ask God to show you the things in your life that could harden your heart.

SONG: *ALMIGHTY GOD, THY WORD IS CAST*

Day 325: (Tuesday)
Humility Yields a Tender Heart

*2 Kings 22:19 Because **thine heart was tender, and** thou hast **humbled** thyself before the LORD, when thou heardest what I spake against this place, and against the inhabitants thereof, that they should become a desolation and a curse, and hast rent thy clothes, and wept before me; I also have heard thee, saith the LORD.*

INTRODUCTORY THOUGHTS

Pride shows itself as an unyielding adversary of a tender heart. A prideful heart remains hard and obstinate toward the things of the Lord. According to scripture, such a heart is stubborn and self-willed. However, those who choose to humble themselves actually tenderize their heart so that God can work according to His purpose and will. The humbled heart does not focus on whether the outcome looks good, nor does it focus upon who receives credit for a certain act. Today's passage reveals Josiah accepting the coming judgment, repenting by rending his clothes, and weeping before the Lord. The Lord heard his servant's plea. Yet, Josiah's tender heart kept him from complaining or arguing with the Lord concerning God's looming judgment.

DEVOTIONAL THOUGHTS

- **(For children):** A friend speaks ugly to you for no reason and you respond harshly. Then God reminds you to *"Keep thy tongue from evil" (Psalm 34:13).* You tell your friend you are sorry. When you submit to what God tells you to do, you display a tender heart.
- **(For everyone):** Do you gripe and complain about the things taking place in your life? How do you handle bad news? Do you submit yourself to the Lord's will and cry out to Him for help?
- When is the last time you sincerely wept before the Lord? When is the last time you were moved of the Lord to prayer because of something you read in His word?

PRAYER THOUGHTS

- Ask God to help you humble yourself before Him.
- Ask the Lord to help you submit to His will for your life.

SONG: *I SURRENDER ALL*

Day 326: Church Night

Psalm 95:8 Harden not your heart, *as in the provocation, and as in the day of temptation in the wilderness:*

Day 327: (Thursday)
A Hard Heart Will Not Hearken

Exodus 7:13 And he hardened Pharaoh's heart, *that he hearkened not unto them; as the LORD had said.*

INTRODUCTORY THOUGHTS

The Bible seems to point to Pharaoh most often as an example of someone with a heart hardened through sin and the deceitfulness of power and fame. Pharaoh's hardened heart led him from one rebellious act to the next. He constantly fought against the Lord and the Lord's man. Even after all of the miracles in Egypt and the abundance of judgments, he chose to pursue the children of Israel as they departed from Egypt. Pharaoh's hardened heart led him to pursue them to the Red Sea. Out of all the troublesome effects of a hard heart, the most troubling aspect is that it refuses to hearken to the words of the Lord. On at least five occasions, the Lord makes this connection *(Exodus 7:13, 22; Exodus 8:15, 19; Exodus 9:12)*. A hard heart closes the ears to the truth and sets the individual up for greater judgment.

DEVOTIONAL THOUGHTS

- **(For children):** King Zedekiah would not listen to God's word and hardened his heart from turning unto the Lord *(2 Chronicles 36:11-13)*. If he would have listened, Jerusalem would not have been burned, and his sons would not have been slain.
- **(For everyone):** Is your heart pliable to the word of God? Do you allow your Bible reading to change your thoughts and actions? Do you repent when you find yourself contrary to the word of God?
- Are others able to show you truth from the word of God? Does pride harden your heart when others seek to rebuke you in love from the Bible?

PRAYER THOUGHTS

- Ask God to give you ears to hear what He would say to you.
- Ask the Lord to give you a special love for His word.

SONG: *I SET MYSELF AGAINST THE LORD*

Day 328: (Friday)
A Heart as Firm as a Stone

*Job 41:24 His heart is as firm as a stone; yea, **as hard as a piece of the nether millstone.***

INTRODUCTORY THOUGHTS

The Bible admonishes believers to be *stedfast* and *unmoveable (1 Corinthians 15:58)*. We are to be *grounded* and *settled (Colossians 1:23)* in the faith—much like a tree planted by the rivers of waters *(Psalm 1:3)*. Yet, today's passage points to the dangers of a hardened heart set in rebellion. It is likened to a stone and a millstone. We should remain stedfast in our commitment to serve the Lord, yet our hearts should remain tender and pliable to Him and His will. A stony heart hinders the seed of God's word from taking root *(Matthew 13:5-6)*. This hardness hinders the possibility of spiritual fruit from taking root and maturing. A soft heart and a stedfast walk exhibit the godly balance that God desires for each of us.

Devotional Thoughts

- **(For children):** There are many different kinds of stones. Some are more easily broken than others. The Bible tells us that God's people made their hearts like an adamant stone, an extremely hard or unbreakable one. They refused to hear God's law and the messages of His prophets. They only hurt themselves and for this reason God sent them into captivity *(Zechariah 7:12-14).*
- **(For everyone):** Is your heart hard? Are you cold and indifferent toward the workings of God in your heart? Have you repented of your sins and asked the Lord to work in your heart?
- What are some of the effects you would expect to see from someone who has a hardened heart? Are those traits present in your life? Are you willing to seek the Lord's help in softening your heart?

Prayer Thoughts

- Ask the Lord to show you the true condition of your heart.
- Ask God to help you repent at the first indication of a hardening heart.

Song: *COME, O THOU ALL VICTORIOUS LORD*

Day 329: (Saturday)
A Hard Heart Leads to Mischief

*Proverbs 28:14 Happy is the man that feareth alway: but **he that hardeneth his heart shall fall into mischief.***

Introductory Thoughts

A tender heart quickly and readily yields when offered correction; however, as a heart becomes hardened, the times of yielding become fewer and farther apart. During the hardening process, the individual finds the true nature of the heart more difficult to grasp. As the heart further hardens, the individual finds himself involved in further defiance. The mischief may start as seemingly insignificant, but a hardening heart will ultimately lead to greater depths of wickedness, some seemingly unimaginable only a short time ago. Some of the worst sins committed in the Bible by God's people were committed by those who shortly before had displayed a tender heart. Yet, they allowed their hearts to be hardened by the deceitfulness of sin.

DEVOTIONAL THOUGHTS

- **(For children):** King Saul did not abide by what God wanted him to do as told to him by Samuel. He simply offered excuses when asked about his wrongdoings and blatant disobedience. His hard heart eventually led him to attempt to kill David who had done him no harm *(1 Samuel 23:9)*.
- **(For everyone):** How far away from the Lord do you have to wander before the Lord deals with your heart? Do you find it easier to ignore His dealings the more you refuse to repent?
- Why do we long to get involved in mischief? Why do we struggle so much to do right? Is it because we have allowed our hearts to become hardened by sin?

PRAYER THOUGHTS

- Ask the Lord to help you repent when He corrects you.
- Ask the Lord to protect you from the mischief that a deceitful heart desires.

SONG: *COME, THOU FOUNT*

Notes: _____

_____

_____

_____

_____

_____

_____

_____

_____

_____

_____

_____

Notes: _____

_____

_____

_____

_____

_____

_____

_____

_____

_____

_____

_____

_____

Quotes from the next volume

(VOLUME 2, WEEK 47)

Subject: Vanity

Regardless of worldly accomplishments and accolades, a life void of God remains meaningless.

The Bible says that vanity is meaningless and empty, yet men love vanity.

When men follow after vanity, they themselves become vain.

In order for an individual to be saved he must repent. One aspect of repentance involves ceasing to trust vanity and turning one's faith toward the living and true God.

48

Tenderhearted (con't)

Occurrences: the word *tender* is found thirty-nine times in the Bible and the word *tenderness* occurs only once

Interesting fact: A man's strength in one area of his life may prove to be a weakness in another. For instance, Rehoboam's tenderheartedness made him vulnerable to those who were void of character *(2 Chronicles 13:7)*.

Bible study tip: Christians today have access to the completed canon of scripture. Old Testament saints did not understand all that we understand today. Progressive illumination teaches that not all truths were known or understood equally throughout Bible history. Be careful not to project New Testament understanding upon Old Testament saints. In other words, not every doctrine or truth can be applied forward nor should they all be applied retroactively though prophesied. The prophecy usually came without the illumination of its complete application.

Sunday, Day 330—Church Day (no devotional)
Monday, Day 331—*The Hard Heart Does Not Believe*
Tuesday, Day 332—*A Law for Hard Hearts*
Wednesday, Day 333—Church Night (no devotional)
Thursday, Day 334—*A Hard Heart Will Not Hearken*

Friday, Day 335—*Hard Hearts Grieve the Lord*
Saturday, Day 336—*A Tender Heart for Others*

Day 330: Church Day

*John 12:40 He hath blinded their eyes, and **hardened their heart;** that they should not see with their eyes, nor understand with their heart, and be converted, and I should heal them.*

Day 331: (Monday)
The Hard Heart Does Not Believe

*Mark 16:14 Afterward he appeared unto the eleven as they sat at meat, and upbraided them with their unbelief and **hardness of heart,** because they believed not them which had seen him after he was risen.*

INTRODUCTORY THOUGHTS

Today's passage explores the scene as the Lord met with His eleven apostles for the first time following His resurrection. The word *afterward* pinpoints the timing of the passage as having occurred after He had appeared to others. For instance, the Lord had already appeared to Mary Magdalene. She told the disciples the great news of Christ's resurrection, but the Bible says that they did not believe her. Shortly thereafter, the Lord appeared directly to the apostles and scolded them for their *"unbelief and hardness of heart."* A heart that is tender serves as fertile ground for faith. However, a hardened heart does not allow the seed of faith to grow. *Mark 6:52* confirms this principle as it points out that *"they considered not the miracle of the loaves: for **their heart was hardened.**"* Hardness of heart prevented faith in the disciples during that time and will do the same now in any believer who fails to remain tenderhearted.

DEVOTIONAL THOUGHTS

- **(For children):** When the people were told to possess the promised land after seeing God's power and miracles, they chose to send in spies to search out the land for themselves. Twelve men entered the land, but only two of them believed God. The other ten men gave a bad report. These disobedient men all died in a plague shortly after and never lived in the promised land.

- **(For everyone):** Do you find it difficult to consistently trust the Lord? Is it easier for you to doubt than to believe the promises of God? If so, it is likely that your heart has become hardened.
- The disciples saw multiple miracles from the Lord, but continually struggled with faith. Faith is not a matter of sight, but a matter of the heart. A hardened heart sprouts forth doubt and despair.

PRAYER THOUGHTS

- Ask the Lord to strengthen your faith.
- Ask the Lord to help you see the role of the heart in faith.

SONG: *TENDERHEARTED*

Day 332: (Tuesday)
A Law for Hard Hearts

Matthew 19:3 The Pharisees also came unto him, tempting him, and saying unto him, Is it lawful for a man to put away his wife for every cause?

4 And he answered and said unto them, Have ye not read, that he which made them at the beginning made them male and female,

5 And said, For this cause shall a man leave father and mother, and shall cleave to his wife: and they twain shall be one flesh?

6 Wherefore they are no more twain, but one flesh. What therefore God hath joined together, let not man put asunder.

7 They say unto him, Why did Moses then command to give a writing of divorcement, and to put her away?

*8 He saith unto them, Moses **because of the hardness of your hearts** suffered you to put away your wives: but from the beginning it was not so.*

INTRODUCTORY THOUGHTS

The Pharisees repeatedly sought to trap the Lord by attempting to draw Him into controversial discussions. Today's passage demonstrates much more than a simple response to entangling questioning. Interestingly, we learn from the Lord's response that God's law made allowances for man based upon God's understanding of man's nature. In other words, the Lord Jesus indicated that God gave some of the law simply because of the hardness of man's heart! Unfortunately, these laws are used today by men to justify decisions contrary to God's will thus further validating the hard-hearted nature of man. In either case, God's ways are never thwarted. God's laws allow even man's wickedness to bring about God's justice and His laws further expose the inherent shortcomings of man. God graciously gave some of His laws to make allowances for man's weaknesses caused by sin.

DEVOTIONAL THOUGHTS

- **(For children)**: Read *Matthew 18:23-33*. The wicked servant had the right to have the man who owed him money thrown into prison. The king was angry when he heard that the wicked servant wanted justice rather than expressing mercy and grace. Being entitled to do something does not always mean God is pleased with what you do.
- **(For everyone)**: Do you abuse certain Bible verses as justification for your actions when you know that these actions displease God? Do you allow God's concern for justice to become the grounds for which you violate God's will for your life and the lives of others?
- Are you satisfied when you find a justification for doing something that God allows but doesn't will for you to do? The Bible says that allowances were created because of man's hard-heartedness.

PRAYER THOUGHTS

- Ask the Lord to give you a tender heart toward His will.
- Ask God to keep you from the sin of justifying your sin.

SONG: *FULLY TRUSTING*

Day 333: Church Night

*Isaiah 48:4 Because I knew that **thou art obstinate**, and thy neck is an iron sinew, and thy brow brass;*

Day 334: (Thursday)
A Hard Heart Calls for Wrath

Romans 2:1 Therefore thou art inexcusable, O man, whosoever thou art that judgest: for wherein thou judgest another, thou condemnest thyself; for thou that judgest doest the same things.

2 But we are sure that the judgment of God is according to truth against them which commit such things.

3 And thinkest thou this, O man, that judgest them which do such things, and doest the same, that thou shalt escape the judgment of God?

4 Or despisest thou the riches of his goodness and forbearance and longsuffering; not knowing that the goodness of God leadeth thee to repentance?

*5 But after thy **hardness and impenitent heart** treasurest up unto thyself wrath against the day of wrath and revelation of the righteous judgment of God;*

INTRODUCTORY THOUGHTS

No sensible person would ever ask to be on the receiving end of the wrath of God. The thought is completely illogical! Yet, this scenario takes place every day in the lives of those who live with hardened hearts toward the things of God. The Bible affirms that a humble spirit begs God's attention and brings His corresponding blessings *(Isaiah 66:2)*. Contrariwise, a hard heart also garners God's attention but for judgment rather than blessing. Today's passage points out that the hard heart treasures up wrath against itself. This wrath rarely takes place immediately, but it will come in the *"day of wrath."* It is important to recall that hardness of heart brought the plagues upon Egypt and it brought blindness to the Jews in Jesus' day. Ultimately, it will bring eternal damnation in the lake of fire to all those who fail to accept God's payment for sin.

DEVOTIONAL THOUGHTS

- **(For children):** God gave Nebuchadnezzar a year to change his ways. He refused so God brought judgment upon him *(Daniel 5:20-21)*. Belshazzar too hardened his heart even though he knew what had happened to Nebuchadnezzar. It comes as no surprise when we read of God's judgment upon him also *(Daniel 5:22-30)*.
- **(For everyone):** Do you want to be on the receiving end of God's judgment or His blessings? Do you want to treasure up the wrath of God or experience the goodness of God? Your only hope is to humble yourself before the Almighty.
- Do you want God's attention? How do you hope to get His attention? There is a right and a wrong way. Do you seek His attention and bless-

ing through a contrite spirit? Or do you seek his attention and rebuke through a heart hardened by sin?

PRAYER THOUGHTS

- Ask God to give you a broken and contrite spirit.
- Ask the Lord to keep you from His wrath.

SONG: *JUST AS I AM*

Day 335: (Friday)
Hard Hearts Grieve the Lord

Mark 3:1 *And he entered again into the synagogue; and there was a man there which had a withered hand.*

2 And they watched him, whether he would heal him on the sabbath day; that they might accuse him.

3 And he saith unto the man which had the withered hand, Stand forth.

4 And he saith unto them, Is it lawful to do good on the sabbath days, or to do evil? to save life, or to kill? But they held their peace.

*5 And when he had looked round about on them with anger, being grieved for **the hardness of their hearts**, he saith unto the man, Stretch forth thine hand. And he stretched it out: and his hand was restored whole as the other.*

INTRODUCTORY THOUGHTS

Today's passage tells the story of Jesus entering the synagogue. He immediately noticed a man with a withered hand. This man's physical infirmity moved Christ to compassion. Unfortunately, the religious leaders were simply calloused toward the man's predicament. The Pharisees watched Jesus closely, not because they were pleased with His gracious act, but because they sought opportunity to accuse the Lord for breaking their man-made rules. As the Lord observed the crowd, the Pharisees' hardened hearts grieved the Lord to the point of anger. Of course, the Lord knew their thoughts and first sought to reason with them. He did the very thing which the Pharisees hoped He would. The hearts of the religious leaders that should have been tender and welcoming to God's miracles were instead full of pride and completely calloused. Christ's acts of compassion served to further harden their deceitful hearts rather than softening them.

DEVOTIONAL THOUGHTS

- **(For children):** God's Spirit comes to live inside of those who accept Christ as Saviour. *Ephesians 4:30* tells us not to grieve the Holy Spirit of God. We grieve the Spirit when we do things that the Lord does not want us to do.
- **(For everyone):** Do you find joy when God's Spirit works through you to do His will? Do you rejoice when God does something wonderful in the lives of those around you, or are you constantly finding fault in others?
- Look up the definition of the word *"grieve."* Why do hardened hearts grieve the Lord? Why was He so angry when the Pharisees sought to accuse Him?

PRAYER THOUGHTS

- Ask the Lord to help you rejoice in His work.
- Ask God to keep you from the sin of a hardened heart.

SONG: *MY FAITH LOOKS UP TO THEE*

Day 336: (Saturday)
A Tender Heart for Others

*Ephesians 4:32 And be ye **kind** one to another, **tenderhearted**, **forgiving** one another, even as God for Christ's sake hath forgiven you.*

INTRODUCTORY THOUGHTS

God's children are supposed to be easily recognizable through their love one for another *(John 13:35)*. Today's passage teaches Christians to be both kind and forgiving. In the midst of these two exemplary qualities, the Lord desires His children to show forth a tender heart. This means that our hearts ought to be easily moved when other believers are experiencing either joy or distress in their lives *(Romans 12:15)*. Unfortunately, instead of exemplifying a tender heart, far too many believers are becoming more like the world by displaying a divisive spirit and by devouring one another *(Galatians 5:15)*. Believers who are hard-hearted toward others are generally hard-hearted toward the Lord as well *(1 John 3:17)*.

DEVOTIONAL THOUGHTS

- **(For children):** Would you want another child to feel happy for you if you got something new? Do you feel happy for others when they do? If you're sick, do you want people to pray for you? Do you do the same for them? *Luke 6:31* says that we should.
- **(For everyone):** Are you easily moved to pray for others? Are you moved to tears at the sorrows of your brothers and sisters in Christ? Do you rejoice when others rejoice?
- Do you bite and devour other believers? Do you grow jealous when God blesses your brother or sister in Christ? Do you pray for God's blessings upon them?

PRAYER THOUGHTS

- Ask the Lord to give you the right love for others.
- Ask God to stir you for the needs of others.

SONG: *HE WAS NOT WILLING*

Notes: _____

_____

_____

_____

_____

_____

Quotes from the next volume

(VOLUME 2, WEEK 48)

Subject: Vengeance

Sometimes the most difficult and significant tasks involve the simplest truths. For instance, every Christian should quickly learn that vengeance belongs unto the Lord.

When a believer takes vengeance into his own hands, he robs the Lord of His right and responsibility to exact vengeance at the right time and in the right manner.

49

Thanksgiving

Occurrences: found 141 times in 136 verses

Variations: thank, thanked, thankful, thankfulness, thanking, thanks, thanksgiving, thanksgivings, thankworthy, unthankful

First usage: *Leviticus 7:12* (thanksgiving—twice)

Last usage: *Revelation 11:17* (thanks)

Defined: rendering thanks or expressing gratitude for good received

Interesting fact: *1 Timothy 4:3-4* reveals why we pray before a meal and explains that there are no foods forbidden during this age. It also shows that thanks should be given to God for providing the food. The apostle Paul uses *thank* eleven times in his epistles, each time thanking God for His goodness.

Bible study tip: Sometimes the search for a scriptural definition can be as simple as reversing the order of a compound word. For instance, the word *careful* quite simply means to be *full of care*. Other compound words often follow the same pattern and supply the same result.

Sunday, Day 337—Church Day (no devotional)
Monday, Day 338—*It Is Good to Give Thanks*
Tuesday, Day 339—*Giving Thanks Magnifies the Lord*
Wednesday, Day 340—Church Night (no devotional)
Thursday, Day 341—*The Audience of Our Thanksgiving*
Friday, Day 342—*A Time for Thanksgiving*
Saturday, Day 343—*Let the Redeemed of the Lord Say So*

Day 337: Church Day

Psalm 100:4 *Enter into his gates **with thanksgiving**, and into his courts with praise: **be thankful unto him**, and bless his name.*

Day 338: (Monday)
It Is Good to Give Thanks

Psalm 92:1 ***It is a good thing to give thanks*** *unto the LORD, and to sing praises unto thy name, O most High:*

INTRODUCTORY THOUGHTS

"What is the will of God for my life?" serves as one of the most oft asked questions by Christians. Unfortunately, far too many Christians complicate their search and fail in their desperate attempts to find God's will for their lives. They invest considerable time and energy looking for a field of service. All the while, they fail to notice the plain truth revealed in the scriptures concerning God's will. The truth is likely very simple. The Bible declares it good to give thanks unto the Lord and failure to do what is good is sin *(James 4:17)*. It stands to reason, therefore, that giving God thanks serves as one of the most basic ways for man to obey the will of God. *"In every thing give thanks: for **this is the will of God** in Christ Jesus **concerning you"** (1 Thessalonians 5:18)*. Conclusion: Giving God thanks serves as the simplest way to fulfil God's will in a Christian's life.

DEVOTIONAL THOUGHTS

- **(For children):** Learn this poem: *"Jesus healed ten lepers* (hold up all ten fingers); *they were very glad* (put a big smile on your face); *but nine did not say, 'Thank you'* (shake your head and hold up nine fingers); *and that made Jesus sad* (frown)." Now read *Luke 17:12-18.*

- **(For everyone):** What does God want you to do for Him? Are you called to serve in missions, or to preach, or teach, or to serve in some other field of service? Have you been faithful in doing the things you already know to do?
- Since it is right to offer heartfelt thanks to the Lord, then it is sin when we fail to do so. Have you ever felt it necessary to repent of the sin of unthankfulness? Do you ever ask the Lord to forgive and to cleanse you?

PRAYER THOUGHTS

- Ask the Lord to forgive you for not thanking Him.
- Ask the Lord to give you a heart of thankfulness.

SONG: *IT IS GOOD TO SING THY PRAISES*

Day 339: (Tuesday)
Giving Thanks Magnifies the Lord

*Psalm 69:30 I will praise the name of God with a song, and will magnify him **with thanksgiving.***

INTRODUCTORY THOUGHTS

Thankfulness strengthens and builds one's faith in the Lord. Christians need more outward and vocal expression of their thankfulness for God's provisions and blessings. Giving of thanks simply exalts the Lord. According to scripture, man can *"magnify him* [God] *with thanksgiving."* Something magnified is made easier to see. Therefore, when men give thanks to the Lord, they make God more visible to a world overcome by sin. For what do you have to be thankful? Try giving God thanks for answered prayers, deliverance from trials, or simply His daily provisions. This thankfulness would help the world to see Him better. Ungrateful Christians have helped to convince the world that it does not need to give God credit for creation (and redemption among other things). Long before these perversions of truth, Christians ceased to give thanks.

DEVOTIONAL THOUGHTS

- **(For children):** Do you bow your head and reverently close your eyes at home when thanks is offered to God for the food He provides? You can be a witness for God by doing the same thing in a restaurant. As our example, Jesus thanked His Father openly when He fed the 5,000 *(John 6:11).*

- **(For everyone):** Do you have family members, neighbours, friends, or coworkers who do not know the Lord? Do you give thanks to God in their presence?
- Do you thank the Lord for His blessings on your life? Do you thank Him for answered prayers or for deliverance from trials, temptations, or troubles?

PRAYER THOUGHTS

- Ask the Lord to help you magnify Him in your giving of thanks.
- Ask God to help you to be more thankful.

SONG: *BREAK FORTH, O JOYFUL HEART*

Day 340: Church Night

1 Chronicles 16:8 Give thanks unto the LORD, call upon his name, make known his deeds among the people.

Day 341: (Thursday)
The Audience of Our Thanksgiving

Psalm 35:18 I will give thee thanks in the great congregation: I will praise thee among much people.

INTRODUCTORY THOUGHTS

Churches and believers have been intimidated by the world and lukewarm Christianity. Many believers have allowed the world to convince them that Christianity should not be openly practiced except in the confines of the home or within a place of worship. Religion (to include Christianity) has been classified as a private matter. Far too many churches have curtailed efforts of going to the lost to present the gospel to them. Believers have even become increasingly intimidated in mentioning the name of Jesus in publick for fear of ridicule or offending others. The Bible points out that failing to give God thanks in the sight of others thwarts the will of God. According to scripture, we should give God thanks and praise Him *"among much people."* Before limiting this to giving of thanks within church meetings, the Bible specifically says that we should *"give thanks unto thee, O LORD, among the heathen"* **(Psalm 18:49)**.

DEVOTIONAL THOUGHTS

- **(For children):** Read **Psalm 126:1-3**. After being held captive for seventy years, the children of Israel openly told unbelievers who did not love God that it was God who brought them back into their land. How can we learn from their example?
- **(For everyone):** Are you embarrassed in the presence of others to vocally give thanks to the Lord? Do you offer excuses for your unwillingness to obey the clear commands found in God's word?
- Are you more concerned about pleasing the Lord even if others might not agree with what you are doing? Are you prepared to stand at the judgment seat of Christ and give an answer for your unwillingness to thank Him?

PRAYER THOUGHTS

- Ask God for boldness to publickly thank Him.
- Ask the Lord to constantly remind you of the coming judgment.

SONG: *O FOR A THOUSAND TONGUES TO SING*

Day 342: (Friday)
A Time for Thanksgiving

Daniel 6:10 *Now when Daniel knew that the writing was signed, he went into his house; and his windows being open in his chamber toward Jerusalem, he kneeled upon his knees three times a day, and prayed, and **gave thanks** before his God, as he did aforetime.*

INTRODUCTORY THOUGHTS

Christians seem to be getting ever busier and yet living spiritually less productive lives. It is dangerous to neglect taking the time to give God thanks. A cursory prayer at mealtime will not suffice to show God your gratitude. The Bible has many instances where men set aside specific times for the giving of thanks to God. For instance, the Bible refers to giving of thanks in the morning and again in the evening **(1 Chronicles 23:30)**. Have you ever resolved to give God thanks first thing in the morning and again before retiring for the day? How would our walk with the Lord be different if we aspired to focus on thankfulness first thing in the morning and again the last thing in the evening? Another passage speaks of a man rising at midnight to give God thanks *(Psalm 119:62)*. The Bible then talks of Daniel who took the time to give God thanks three times a day *(Daniel 6:10)*. Christians should make time for thanksgiving on a daily basis!

DEVOTIONAL THOUGHTS

- **(For children)**: Count the rooms in your house. Name a few things found in each room for which you are thankful. Thank the Lord for these blessings. Can you do the same thing with your family members by giving thanks to God for them? Be sure to also thank them for how they have blessed your life.
- **(For everyone)**: Do you spend time daily thanking the Lord for His goodness toward you? If not, is it because He fails you or because you do not appreciate Him like you should?
- Do you thank others when they do nice things for you? Why do we find it easier to take time to thank others, yet difficult to make time to thank the Lord?

PRAYER THOUGHTS

- Ask God to help you get in the habit of thanking Him.
- Ask the Lord to show you reasons for which you should be thankful.

SONG: *COUNT YOUR BLESSINGS*

Day 343: (Saturday)
Let the Redeemed of the Lord Say So

Psalm 107:1 O give thanks unto the LORD, *for he is good: for his mercy endureth for ever.*
2 Let the redeemed of the LORD say so, whom he hath redeemed from the hand of the enemy;

INTRODUCTORY THOUGHTS

Many believers are familiar with the phrase, *"Let the redeemed of the Lord say so,"* but far too few consider its immediate context in scripture. As the Lord's children, we are to *"say so,"* but what are we to be saying? Believers are to offer thanks to the Lord and continually speak of His goodness and mercy. Oftentimes, the Bible admonishes God's people to give thanks unto God for His mercy, especially those who have been redeemed from the hand of the enemy *(Psalm 107:2)*. We also need to give thanks to God because of His redeeming mercy *(Psalm 136:1, 2, 3, 26)*. One who is redeemed can best say so by giving God thanks. Let others know you are not ashamed to belong to God and that you are truly grateful for His working in your life.

DEVOTIONAL THOUGHTS

- **(For children):** God gave us His best gift ever because it lasts forever. He gave us His Son. Jesus died on the cross so that we could have the free gift of salvation. Have you ever said, *"Thank you,"* for this wonderful gift *(2 Corinthians 9:15)*?
- **(For everyone):** How often do you spend time giving thanks to the Lord? Do you let others know how good God has been to you, or do you find yourself ashamed of Him?
- For what could you give God thanks? Has He redeemed you from the hand of the enemy? Has He provided for your needs? Has He blessed you by answering prayers? Has He worked in your life?

PRAYER THOUGHTS

- Ask the Lord to help you verbally give thanks to Him.
- Thank the Lord for His goodness and mercy.

SONG: *REJOICE, THE LORD IS KING*

Notes: _____

_____

_____

_____

_____

_____

_____

_____

Notes: _____

_____

_____

_____

_____

_____

_____

_____

_____

_____

_____

_____

_____

_____

_____

Quotes from the next volume

(VOLUME 2, WEEK 49)

Subject: Warfare

The fact that the Bible describes the Christian life as the good *"fight of faith" (1 Timothy 6:12)* reveals that the believer's warfare is spiritual and never fleshly.

Dedicated soldiers are a dying breed, especially amongst Christians. This is why so many people quit when the going gets tough or obstacles surface. The average Christian believes that God's will involves no hurdles.

50

Thanksgiving (con't)

Occurrences: found sixty-eight times in the Old Testament and seventy-three times in the New Testament

First usage in the New Testament: *Matthew 11:25* (thank)

Last usage in the Old Testament: *Jonah 2:9* (thanksgiving)

Interesting fact: The first mention of thanksgiving points to an Old Testament sacrifice of thanksgiving to God *(Leviticus 7:12)*. The New Testament reveals that we *"are built up a spiritual house . . . to offer up spiritual sacrifices, acceptable to God by Jesus Christ"* *(1 Peter 2:5)*. According to Hebrews, by Jesus Christ, we *"offer **the sacrifice of praise** to God continually, that is, the fruit of our lips giving thanks to his name"* *(Hebrews 13:15)*.

Bible study tip: The first and last usage of a word can introduce helpful insights into a particular word's Bible meaning. That is why each introduction to the week's devotionals mentions the first time a word is used in scripture. Recognizing this observable fact is called the law of first mention. However, like all study tools, overzealous application can cause error by applying the first usage definition to each and every other occurrence.

Sunday, Day 344—Church Day (no devotional)
Monday, Day 345—*Giving Thanks for Others*
Tuesday, Day 346—*A Stepping Stone Away from God*
Wednesday, Day 347—Church Night (no devotional)
Thursday, Day 348—*But Rather, Giving of Thanks*
Friday, Day 349—*Giving Thanks for All Things*
Saturday, Day 350—*Prayer and Thanksgiving*

Day 344: Church Day

Psalm 107:21 Oh that men would praise the LORD for his goodness, and for his wonderful works to the children of men!
*22 And let them **sacrifice the sacrifices of thanksgiving**, and declare his works with rejoicing.*

Day 345: (Monday)
Giving Thanks for Others

Romans 1:8 First, I thank my God through Jesus Christ for you all, that your faith is spoken of throughout the whole world.

INTRODUCTORY THOUGHTS

Are you thankful for the people God has placed in your life? Most Christians could spend hours expressing their thankfulness for the godly influences. Oftentimes, however, we neglect to recognize the true blessings of these people. Once again, the apostle Paul provides an excellent example for each of us to emulate. Reading his epistles reveals an honour roll of thankfulness. He expressly thanked God for the believers at Rome *(Romans 1:8)*, Ephesus *(Ephesians 1:16)*, Philippi *(Philippians 1:3)*, Colosse *(Colossians 1:3)*, and Thessalonica *(1 Thessalonians 1:2)*. Paul realized the blessings of his associations with these believers and publickly thanked God for them. We too should be thankful for the godly influences God allows to cross our paths and influence our lives. Yet, the Bible goes a step further by indicating that Paul gave thanks *"for all men" (1 Timothy 2:1)*.

DEVOTIONAL THOUGHTS

- **(For children):** God says give thanks for all men. It should be easy to give thanks for policemen, firemen, doctors, teachers, but what about those who are mean to you? Do you spend time giving thanks for family who love you and friends who care about you?
- **(For everyone):** When is the last time you thanked God for placing special people in your life? Have you thanked Him for your family, your friends, or your brothers and sisters in Christ?
- Have you thanked the Lord for the people in your life who seem to cause you trouble? Perhaps God uses these people to help you remain humble or stay on track. If so, you ought to thank God for them too.

PRAYER THOUGHTS

- Ask the Lord to help you be thankful for the people in your life.
- Take time to thank God for the people you know.

SONG: *BLEST BE THE TIE THAT BINDS*

Day 346: (Tuesday)
A Stepping Stone Away from God

Romans 1:20 *For the invisible things of him from the creation of the world are clearly seen, being understood by the things that are made, even his eternal power and Godhead; so that they are without excuse:* 21 *Because that, when they knew God, they glorified him not as God,* **neither were thankful***; but became vain in their imaginations, and their foolish heart was darkened.*

INTRODUCTORY THOUGHTS

The first chapter of Romans concludes with a list of horrendous sins. These sins reveal people who were completely void of the relationship God intended for His creation. Most believers could never imagine the possibility of being guilty of the sins of sodomy **(Romans 1:26-27)**, murder **(Romans 1:29)**, and hating the Lord **(Romans 1:30)**. Yet, egregious sins begin through a rather simple process. The list in Romans reveals that the downward spiral begins when men fail to glorify God and refuse to give Him thanks **(Romans 1:21)**. Sadly, many of God's people are laying the groundwork for a downward spiral into further degradation.

Becoming a child of God empowers the Christian but does not eliminate his freedom to choose his path, right or wrong. Unfortunately, traveling the wrong path can lead a Christian into the depths of inexpressible depravity.

DEVOTIONAL THOUGHTS

- **(For children):** The Israelites were *not* thankful for how God had blessed them *(Ezekiel 16:17-19)*. Instead, they took God's blessings and focused their attention upon idols that had no power to help them *(Psalm 115:4-7)*. Unthankfulness eventually causes even those with scriptural knowledge to turn away from God.
- **(For everyone):** Do you faithfully give God thanks for the things within your life? Do you take time to give Him credit for the blessings as well as the trials that draw you close to Him?
- How do you think someone ends up committing the sins mentioned at the end of Romans chapter 1? Is it possible that failing to repent of unthankfulness could lead you into such wickedness?

PRAYER THOUGHTS

- Ask the Lord to identify any unthankfulness within your heart and life.
- Ask the Lord to protect you from the sins of Romans chapter 1.

SONG: *I AM RESOLVED*

Day 347: Church Night

*Colossians 3:17 And whatsoever ye do in word or deed, do all in the name of the Lord Jesus, **giving thanks** to God and the Father by him.*

Day 348: (Thursday)
But Rather, Giving of Thanks

Ephesians 5:1 Be ye therefore followers of God, as dear children; 2 And walk in love, as Christ also hath loved us, and hath given himself for us an offering and a sacrifice to God for a sweetsmelling savour. 3 But fornication, and all uncleanness, or covetousness, let it not be once named among you, as becometh saints;

4 Neither filthiness, nor foolish talking, nor jesting, which are not convenient: **but rather giving of thanks.**

INTRODUCTORY THOUGHTS

God's children are to faithfully follow God. We are to obey His will for our lives and follow the example of His Son. Today's passage provides some insight into the details of this calling. We see that believers are to walk in love *(Ephesians 5:2)* and avoid sins like fornication and covetousness *(Ephesians 5:3)*. Additionally, believers are to have no part in foolish and inconvenient talking or jesting *(Ephesians 5:4)*. These things are unprofitable and unbecoming to the child of God. Instead, the Lord would rather His people put forth their strength in giving Him thanks *(Ephesians 5:4)*. God does not need His creation to thank Him but knows that a thankful people are the only ones who can truly live spiritual lives. Those who feel like they lack opportunity to give God thanks should cease from the sinful practices that monopolize their time and strength. Focus on God and a thankful spirit will blossom and mature.

DEVOTIONAL THOUGHTS

- **(For children):** Sometimes when we enter into God's house, we talk about everything but Him. *Psalm 100:4* tells us that we should be praising and thanking Him and not focusing on the things of this world.
- **(For everyone):** How do you expend your strength when you are around others? Do you get caught up in foolish talking and inconvenient jesting? Are you embarrassed at the thought of publickly giving God thanks?
- God prefers giving of thanks over foolish talking. Upon which do you tend to focus? Why do we choose to do and say things displeasing to the Lord when He has made clear how He expects us to behave?

PRAYER THOUGHTS

- Ask God to help you thank Him more with each passing day.
- Ask the Lord to help you recognize the content of your conversations.

SONG: *PRAISE THE SAVIOUR, YE WHO KNOW HIM*

Day 349: (Friday)
Giving Thanks for All Things

Ephesians 5:20 Giving thanks always for all things unto God and the Father in the name of our Lord Jesus Christ;

INTRODUCTORY THOUGHTS

Men generally find time to thank God for things which they deem to be good or strictly positive. Yet, the Bible admonishes us to be thankful *"for all things."* This means that we should thank God for blessings and trials; for health and sickness; for gain and loss; for peace and troubles. This may seem strange but becomes much more feasible when we understand the truth of **Romans 8:28**. God takes all things, good and bad, and makes them work together for our good. As such, we ought to be willing to give God thanks *"for all things"* knowing that He will, in turn, use them for our benefit. Failure to grasp this truth is a failure to trust God's goodness and wisdom. God can and will use even the negative things in your life to help you grow and develop as His child.

DEVOTIONAL THOUGHTS

- **(For children):** It is no fun being sick. But when it happens, you can still find things for which to be thankful. You can thank God for the doctor who prescribes the medicine, for mom who gives special care and attention, and for brothers and sisters who pray for you.
- **(For everyone):** What trials are you facing today? What burdens are you bearing? What are the things troubling your soul? Have you thanked God for those things?
- Murmuring and thanksgiving are at opposite ends of the spectrum. We cannot do both simultaneously. Are you murmuring or trying to be truly thankful for even the trials, heartaches, and troubles?

PRAYER THOUGHTS

- Ask God to forgive you for complaining about your trials.
- Ask God to help you to be thankful *"for all things."*

SONG: *THANKS TO GOD*

Day 350: (Saturday)
Prayer and Thanksgiving

Philippians 4:6 *Be careful for nothing; but in every thing by prayer and supplication* **with thanksgiving** *let your requests be made known unto God.*

INTRODUCTORY THOUGHTS

Our heartfelt giving of thanks should always coincide with our prayers to God. Today's passage from Philippians confirms this truth, as do a host of other passages *(Daniel 6:10; Ephesians 1:16; Colossians 1:3; Colossians 4:2; 1 Thessalonians 1:2; 1 Timothy 2:1)*. However, an unthankful spirit always affects one's prayer life eventually developing into a vicious repetitive cycle. A lack of prayer instills a lack of thankfulness. Those who fail to be thankful, fail to cultivate a consistent prayer life. Fortunately, this lack of thankfulness exposes our true problem which is a heart lacking humility. As our heart fills with pride, we fail to realize the goodness of God and our need to continually seek His face with this spirit of thankfulness. The solution involves conditioning ourselves to have a prayer life consisting of a genuine time of thanksgiving. True thankfulness should eliminate many of the prayers consisting of nothing but self-serving desires.

DEVOTIONAL THOUGHTS

- **(For children):** The Bible tells us to keep on praying *(1 Thessalonians 5:17)* and to be thankful *(Colossians 3:15)*. How would mom and dad feel if you didn't talk to them or thank them for what they do for you? How do you think God feels when we do not talk to Him and say, *"Thank you, Father"*?
- **(For everyone):** How is your prayer life? How faithful are you in giving thanks to God? Do you give thanks to God during your time of prayer, or do you just make your requests known to Him?
- Is giving thanks important to you? Is your prayer time selfish in that it only acts as a means by which you seek to get things from God? Why not begin your time of prayer thanking the Lord for His goodness to you?

PRAYER THOUGHTS

- Take time to thank the Lord for His faithfulness to you.
- Ask the Lord to help you be more thankful during times of prayer.

SONG: *I LOVE TO STEAL AWHILE AWAY*

Notes: _____

_____

_____

_____

_____

_____

_____

_____

_____

_____

_____

_____

_____

Quotes from the next volume

(VOLUME 2, WEEK 50)

Subject: Watching

While preaching sounds the trumpet of alarm in the ears of men, prayer sounds the alarm in the ears of God.

God's enemies always search for the weak spot where the hedge has been cut down or ignored. This is why there is no angle in the believer's life that can be safely ignored.

51

Thanksgiving (con't)

Occurrences: found thirty-two times in thirty verses in the Book of Psalms

First usage in Psalms: *Psalm 6:5* (thanks)

Last usage in Psalms: *Psalm 147:7* (thanksgiving)

Interesting fact: The first verse of Psalms 105, 106, and 107 each contain the phrase, *"O give thanks unto the LORD."* This phrase appears seven times in scripture *(1 Chronicles 16:34; Psalm 105:1; Psalm 106:1; Psalm 107:1; Psalm 118:1, 29; Psalm 136:1)* with six instances being followed by a statement of God's goodness and His enduring mercy.

Bible study tip: When studying the psalms, do not discount the value of the subtitles. These subtitles often provide context to the psalm and at times even help define words or phrases. Additionally, other subtitles help to provide insight into events described in other parts of scripture.

Sunday, Day 351—Church Day (no devotional)
Monday, Day 352—*In Every Thing Give Thanks*
Tuesday, Day 353—*Giving Thanks for God's Provisions*
Wednesday, Day 354—Church Night (no devotional)
Thursday, Day 355—*A Sin for the Last Days*

Friday, Day 356—*A Sacrifice of Praise*
Saturday, Day 357—*Giving Thanks Will Continue*

Day 351: Church Day

Psalm 50:14 *Offer unto God thanksgiving;* and pay thy vows unto the most High:

Day 352: (Monday)
In Every Thing Give Thanks

***1 Thessalonians 5:18 In every thing give thanks:** for this is the will of God in Christ Jesus concerning you.*

Introductory Thoughts

Men should willingly give thanks *"for all things" (Ephesians 5:20),* but today's passage teaches a somewhat different truth: men should give thanks *"in every thing."* The subtle differences between these two truths turn out to be quite profound. They express two different facets of the Christian's call to give thanks: give thanks to God *for* all things, but our thanks should take place *in the midst* of all things, good and bad. This means that we should not simply give God thanks once a certain trial of life has ended, but the thankfulness should take place while these trials are ongoing. Very few believers seem to recognize the importance of giving thanks for trials, but even fewer seem willing to give that thanks during the heat of the trial. Why is this so important? God says that the giving of this thanks, even in the midst of trials, is God's will for our lives.

Devotional Thoughts

- **(For children):** Think about it: if you thank God when you are sick, won't it be much easier to thank Him when you are well. Thank God when others are mean to you and it will be easier to keep that spirit of thankfulness when you are having fun together with others. Remember to give thanks to God every day.
- **(For everyone):** Do you give thanks to God for your trials? When do you give thanks for them? Is it after the trial is ended or while you are in the midst of the trial?

- What are you going through right now? Have you thanked God for allowing it? Are you willing to give God thanks *"in every thing"*? Does it concern you that this is God's will for your life?

PRAYER THOUGHTS

- Thank God for the trials that you are facing.
- Ask God to give you a heart that overflows with thanksgiving.

SONG: *IF ON A QUIET SEA*

Day 353: (Tuesday)
Giving Thanks for God's Provisions

1 Timothy 4:4 For every creature of God is good, and nothing to be refused, if it be received **with thanksgiving:**

INTRODUCTORY THOUGHTS

Preachers oftentimes wish for simpler days when people seemed more attuned to the things of God. Unfortunately, many believers have lost sight of how much we need God for our daily provisions. Far too many people today believe that their jobs provide their needs or that their efforts at their jobs have provided for their needs. Yet, the truth remains, God is the great provider. When people gathered food from their fields, they had a better understanding of how dependent they were upon God's hand of blessing. They thanked Him for providing the rain and the sunshine to make their crops to grow. They saw God's hand directly involved in the feeding of their families. We too ought to take time to give God thanks for the basic necessities and never neglect them simply because we have an easier life. Today's passage speaks specifically of food, but we ought to thank God for clothing and shelter as well.

DEVOTIONAL THOUGHTS

- **(For children):** Do you have food to eat? Do you have clothes to wear? Do you have a place to live? Do you have a bed in which you sleep? Thank God for these simple things because He loves you and things could be so very different.
- **(For everyone):** Are you truly thankful to God for His provisions? Do you whisper a quick repetitious prayer before eating a meal, or do you sincerely take time to thank God for His provisions and blessings?

- Do you complain about the food that you eat, the clothes that you wear, and the house in which you live; or are you grateful for what the Lord has provided for you?

PRAYER THOUGHTS
- Ask the Lord to help you recognize His hand in your provisions.
- Thank the Lord for all the things with which He has blessed you.

SONG: *GREAT IS THY FAITHFULNESS!*

Day 354: Church Night

Colossians 1:12 Giving thanks unto the Father, which hath made us meet to be partakers of the inheritance of the saints in light:
13 Who hath delivered us from the power of darkness, and hath translated us into the kingdom of his dear Son:
14 In whom we have redemption through his blood, even the forgiveness of sins:
15 Who is the image of the invisible God, the firstborn of every creature:
16 For by him were all things created, that are in heaven, and that are in earth, visible and invisible, whether they be thrones, or dominions, or principalities, or powers: all things were created by him, and for him:
17 And he is before all things, and by him all things consist.

Day 355: (Thursday)
A Sin for the Last Days

*2 Timothy 3:1 This know also, that in the last days **perilous times** shall come.*
*2 For men shall be lovers of their own selves, covetous, boasters, proud, blasphemers, disobedient to parents, **unthankful**, unholy,*
3 Without natural affection, trucebreakers, false accusers, incontinent, fierce, despisers of those that are good,
4 Traitors, heady, highminded, lovers of pleasures more than lovers of God;
*5 Having a form of godliness, but denying the power thereof: **from such turn away.***

INTRODUCTORY THOUGHTS

The Bible describes the last days of the church age as perilous times overwhelmed by excess of sin. However, dedicated Christians living within God's will desire righteousness to reign. No matter, sins such as pride, blasphemy, despising the good, and loving pleasures more than God prevail during the last days. Believers are admonished not to get caught up in them and forewarned to turn away from these activities. These areas are all recognized as problems increasingly prevalent in to-day's societies, but sometimes "we miss the forest for the trees." We recognize these obvious sins as severe and sore displeasing to the Lord; but in their midst, the Lord also mentions *unthankfulness*. This is another of the identifying marks of the end times. People have grown increasingly unthankful. Unfortunately, these earmarks are not limited to the world but have also infiltrated the church.

DEVOTIONAL THOUGHTS

- **(For children)**: *Psalm 68:19* says that God *"daily loadeth us with benefits."* Have mom and dad help you to recognize these things and then thank God for them. Many people become unthankful because they fail to admit that it is God who gives us good gifts *(James 1:17)*.
- **(For everyone)**: Are you proud when you recognize that you are not like the world when it comes to blasphemy and pride? Do you then find yourself excusing the sin of unthankfulness?
- Christians often think it important to *"turn away"* from those who are blasphemous, but what about those who are simply not thankful toward God? Should we surround ourselves with those who refuse to be thankful toward God?

PRAYER THOUGHTS

- Ask God to deliver you from the sin of unthankfulness.
- Ask the Lord to more clearly show you how He feels about unthankfulness.

SONG: *INGRATITUDE'S A SIN*

Day 356: (Friday)
A Sacrifice of Praise

*Hebrews 13:15 By him therefore let us offer the sacrifice of praise to God continually, that is, **the fruit of our lips giving thanks to his name**.*

INTRODUCTORY THOUGHTS

Far too many believers live with a skewed perspective concerning God's expectations. They desperately desire to do some *"great thing"* for the Lord. They ponder on thoughts of what would cause God to take notice of them and gain His favour. Would selling everything and going to the mission field help? Do they need to quit their job and go into full-time Christian service? Do they need to travel in order to spread the gospel far and wide? No doubt this serves as the Lord's will for some, but one's intent needs to be God-focused and not self-centered. Regardless of one's calling, God has given Christians a great way to give Him a well-pleasing sacrifice. Today's passage mentions the fruit of our lips as a means of giving thanks to God and calls it a sacrifice of praise. Maybe the Lord does have *"great things"* in store for your life, but offering Him a sacrifice of praise serves as the best place to begin.

DEVOTIONAL THOUGHTS

- **(For children):** Read *Psalm 126:3*. Name some great things God has done for you. Would you like to do something for Him that He considers great? You can do so by just saying, *"Thank you"* (*Psalm 107:21-22*). That pleases Him.
- **(For everyone):** Do you wish to give the Lord something special? Do you want to do something that would be pleasing to Him? Are you willing to offer Him thanks as a precious sacrifice?
- Why are we so ready to focus on the *"great things,"* yet seem so hesitant to do the things that God asks? This may be our nature *(2 Kings 5:13)*, but it greatly displeases the Lord.

PRAYER THOUGHTS

- Ask God to help you thank Him for who He is and what He does.
- Give God a sacrifice of praise by thanking Him.

SONG: *O WORSHIP THE KING*

Day 357: (Saturday)
Giving Thanks Will Continue

Revelation 7:12 Saying, Amen: Blessing, and glory, and wisdom, and **thanksgiving**, *and honour, and power, and might, be unto our God for ever and ever. Amen.*

INTRODUCTORY THOUGHTS

Far too much of the Christian's focus has little to no impact beyond the here and now. When Christians leave this world to meet the Lord, there are some things that will carry through to eternity *(1 Timothy 6:19)*. One involves the *thanksgiving* we present to our Creator. In fact, death will heighten our desire and ability to offer thanks to God. Departed believers, along with angels and other spirit beings are already giving thanks to God in heaven. Our thanksgiving like theirs already will become more frequent and increasingly pure when we finally see our Saviour face-to-face. One day, we too will join that throng to thank the One who gave His everything for us. Why wait to face any regret of not having obeyed the Lord while on earth? Give God thanks now!

DEVOTIONAL THOUGHTS

- **(For children):** Read *Psalm 145:1-2*. Blessing and praising God include thanking Him. King David said he did that daily and that he would do it forever. Can you picture this king in heaven right now thanking God?
- **(For everyone):** How much time do you spend on spiritually perishable matters? How much time do you spend on things God calls vanity? What more could the Lord have done to encourage you to give Him thanks?
- Are you excited about the prospect of spending an eternity in heaven? Do you ever find yourself longing to be with the Lord? Why not begin doing some of the things that will continue forever? You can. Give Him thanks!

PRAYER THOUGHTS

- Thank God for eternal life.
- Ask God to help you begin thanking Him today.

SONG: *NOW THANK WE ALL OUR GOD*

Notes: _____

_____

_____

_____

_____

_____

_____

_____

_____

_____

_____

_____

_____

Quotes from the next volume

(VOLUME 2, WEEK 51)

Subject: Witnessing

In order to offer an adequate witness of the Lord's saving grace, an individual must first have experienced the new birth combined with the witness of God's indwelling Spirit *(1 John 5:10).*

Modern Christianity focuses on self, while biblical Christianity focuses on the Saviour and others.

Everyone needs the opportunity to hear the gospel, despite their background or current living conditions. The whole world needs to hear that Christ has risen!

52

Zeal

Occurrences: found twenty-six times in the Bible

Variations: zeal, zealous, zealously

First usage: *Numbers 25:11* (zealous)

Last usage: *Revelation 3:19* (zealous)

Defined: passionate ardor in the pursuit of something; eagerness of desire to accomplish or obtain some object

Interesting fact: Zeal is a good thing directed toward the right object *(Titus 2:14)*, but the Bible provides many examples of those who have zeal while lacking knowledge *(Romans 10:2, 1 Corinthians 14:12, Galatians 1:14; Galatians 4:17)*.

Bible study tip: Using a concordance or Bible study software to discover words and phrases oftentimes communicates the best helps in finding good cross-references. Search words and phrases throughout scripture comparing each of your findings. The discovered associations could fill in additional details to a parallel account. Or the discovery may display the New Testament fulfillment of an Old Testament passage. Or the multiple uses could give new insights to truths that you did not before know. For instance, the study of *justice* and *judgment* reveals many amazing insights.

Sunday, Day 358—Church Day (no devotional)
Monday, Day 359—*Zealous of Good Works*
Tuesday, Day 360—*Zeal Without Knowledge*
Wednesday, Day 361—Church Night (no devotional)
Thursday, Day 362—*Zeal: It's Life or Death*
Friday, Day 363—*Godly Sorrow Yields Zeal*
Saturday, Day 364—*Zealously Affected*

Day 358: Church Day

Psalm 119:139 My zeal hath consumed me, *because mine enemies have forgotten thy words.*

Day 359: (Monday)
Zealous of Good Works

Titus 2:14 *Who gave himself for us, that he might redeem us from all iniquity, and purify unto himself a peculiar people,* **zealous of good works.**

INTRODUCTORY THOUGHTS

Zeal involves a fervent desire to accomplish some particular feat. The Bible tells us that Christ died on the cross to redeem a people who would then become zealous of good works. Every Christian should strive to be zealous in his service to the Lord. Many believers during periods of great persecution zealously gave their lives for the gospel's sake. *Acts 15:26* tells of men who *"hazarded their lives for the name of our Lord Jesus Christ."* These people recognized that they were no longer their own but God's. They had been redeemed by the precious blood of the Lord Jesus Christ and willingly sealed that testimony with their own blood. The more the enemies of God persecuted them, the more freely the gospel spread.

DEVOTIONAL THOUGHTS

- **(For children):** Read *Ecclesiastes 9:10* and *Romans 12:11*. Now, consider some of the acts of David's mighty men. They were eager and had a burning desire to serve the Lord. They did not quit but finished their jobs. They lived and served God zealously.

- **(For everyone):** How zealous are you in your service for the Lord? Do you find ways to witness to others? Do you strongly desire opportunities to serve the Lord?
- What would it take to keep you from serving the Lord? If circumstances easily thwart your efforts towards the work of the Lord, then it is likely that you are not zealous of good works.

PRAYER THOUGHTS

- Ask the Lord to give you more zeal.
- Ask the Lord to remind you of His zeal toward saving you.

SONG: *MORE HOLINESS GIVE ME*

Day 360: (Tuesday)
Zeal Without Knowledge

Romans 10:1 Brethren, my heart's desire and prayer to God for Israel is, that they might be saved.

*2 For I bear them record that they have **a zeal of God, but not according to knowledge.***

INTRODUCTORY THOUGHTS

Believers should be zealous of good works, but their zeal must not spring from a position of ignorance. The Bible points to the Jews as a zealous people, but their zeal was not according to knowledge. Nobody worked harder trying to reach a righteous state than did the Jews. However, they failed to realize that true righteousness comes as an unmerited gift from God. Yet, the Jews were *"ignorant of God's righteousness,"* and went *"about to establish their own righteousness" (Romans 10:3)*. Paul repeatedly testified concerning the futility of trying to earn God's favour through one's own efforts *(Acts 22:3; Philippians 3:6)*. Before Paul came to know Christ, he thought he should fight against Christ's followers and zealously persecute the church of God. He even placed many of the new believers into prison and caused their deaths. Yet, he declared that all this was done in ignorance *(1 Timothy 1:13)*. He, like the Jews, had a tremendous zeal, but that zeal was not according to knowledge.

DEVOTIONAL THOUGHTS

- **(For children):** *2 Timothy 2:15* teaches some very important truths concerning God's word. Many people eagerly serve God but will miss heaven because they believe that their works will somehow merit them a place in heaven. They have failed to realize that salvation remains God's free gift to lost people solely based on what the Lord has already done.
- **(For everyone):** Are you zealous for the Lord? Is your zeal based upon knowledge of the truth of God's word? Zeal without knowledge leads to ignorance which functions as a seed of false doctrine.
- No groups are as zealous as the cults at propagating their message, yet they exhibit zeal without knowledge. How much more zealous should we be who know and love the truth?

PRAYER THOUGHTS

- Ask the Lord to give you zeal founded upon sound knowledge.
- Ask God to help you serve Him with the right fervency.

SONG: *WHO IS ON THE LORD'S SIDE?*

Day 361: Church Night

*Revelation 3:19 As many as I love, I rebuke and chasten: **be zealous therefore,** and repent.*

Day 362: (Thursday)
Zeal: It's Life or Death

Numbers 25:10 And the LORD spake unto Moses, saying,

*11 Phinehas, the son of Eleazar, the son of Aaron the priest, hath turned my wrath away from the children of Israel, while **he was zealous for my sake** among them, that I consumed not the children of Israel in my jealousy.*

12 Wherefore say, Behold, I give unto him my covenant of peace:

*13 And he shall have it, and his seed after him, even the covenant of an everlasting priesthood; because **he was zealous for his God,** and made an atonement for the children of Israel.*

INTRODUCTORY THOUGHTS

Today's passage refers to the zeal of one man. Zeal can serve to save a nation or it can cause the shedding forth of innocent blood. The book of Numbers tells of a time when Israel allowed sin into their camp and began experiencing God's wrath. Fortunately, one man took it upon himself to save the nation of Israel from God's impending judgment. He spared a great number of lives because he was zealous to take action. It should be noted that his zeal was for the Lord's sake *(Numbers 25:11)*. Unfortunately, the Bible reveals others like king Saul whose zeal brought about a far different outcome. His zeal ended the lives of innocent people. According to *2 Samuel 21:2*, Saul, in his zeal to the people, slew the Gibeonites bringing a famine upon God's people in the days of David. The famine only ended when seven men of Saul's house lost their lives.

DEVOTIONAL THOUGHTS

- **(For children):** Nehemiah had zeal to serve God and encouraged others to likewise serve the Lord. This one man led God's people to rebuild the wall of Jerusalem, even when faced with vicious threatening from their enemies. Read about the conditions in which they worked in *Nehemiah 4:21-23*.
- **(For everyone):** Are you zealous for the Lord or just zealously active in temporal matters? What could go wrong if your zeal is simply for people or things? What good outcomes could take place if your zeal is in line with God's will and for God's purposes?
- Does your zeal encourage people to turn toward the Lord or turn away from Him? Are you a magnet for the godly or do you attract the ungodly through your zeal? Is your zeal for the Lord contagious?

PRAYER THOUGHTS

- Ask God to use your zeal to righteously affect others.
- Ask the Lord to protect you from harmful zeal.

SONG: *TO THE WORK*

Day 363: (Friday)
Godly Sorrow Yields Zeal

*2 Corinthians 7:11 For behold this selfsame thing, that **ye sorrowed after a godly sort**, what carefulness **it wrought** in you, yea, what clearing of yourselves, yea, what indignation, yea, what fear, yea, what vehement desire, yea, what **zeal**, yea, what revenge! In all things ye have approved yourselves to be clear in this matter.*

INTRODUCTORY THOUGHTS

People often consider *sorrow* as something that breeds discouragement or even depression. However, there exists another type of sorrow called *godly* sorrow. It serves to positively influence the lives of those devoted to Christ. In fact, godly sorrow works to develop other godly traits such as carefulness, righteous indignation, fear of God, vehement desire, and zeal in the life of the believer. When we experience sorrow of a godly sort from having failed the Lord, it helps us to learn to serve Him with renewed fervency and zeal. This truth is further validated by the biblical principle that those who are forgiven much by the Lord will love Him more *(Luke 7:41-47)*. Those who consistently reflect upon where God brought them will experience the right type of sorrow. Further scriptural study reveals that the most zealous Christians are those who were deeply influenced by godly sorrow.

DEVOTIONAL THOUGHTS

- **(For children):** Can you imagine how the apostle Peter must have felt after he denied he knew the Lord three times? The Bible says that he wept bitterly over his sin and shame. Yet, he ultimately became a great servant for the Lord who was exceedingly blessed by being chosen of God to write two epistles in the New Testament.
- **(For everyone):** Have you ever sensed severe remorse after failing the Lord? Does that sorrow make you to want to serve Him with a greater fervency and zeal or cause you to lose faith?
- Many people can testify that before salvation they gave many years zealously to the Devil's ways. Have you determined to serve the Lord as zealously as you once served the works of the flesh?

PRAYER THOUGHTS

- Ask God to give you zeal in His service.
- Ask the Lord to work sorrow in your heart over your failures.

SONG: *IN EVIL LONG I TOOK DELIGHT*

Day 364: (Saturday)
Zealously Affected

Galatians 4:17 They zealously affect you, but not well; yea, they would exclude you, that ye might affect them.

18 But it is good to be zealously affected always in a good thing, and not only when I am present with you.

INTRODUCTORY THOUGHTS

A zealous person is contagious, both positively and negatively. The apostle Paul cautioned that the early believers had been zealously affected, but not in a good way. Those who opposed the gospel were adamant, yet they unwisely waged war against the truth. Night and day, they zealously fought in order to hinder the ministry of the believers. Ultimately, their zeal affected the people of God. These believers who started strong were hindered by the enemies' efforts to the point that it affected their race for the Lord *(Galatians 5:7)*. Modern day enemies of the gospel are aware of this potential pitfall for the believers. They often display more zeal than those who knowingly possess the truth. Yet, today's passage also teaches that *"it is good to be zealously affected always in a good thing."* Zeal breeds zeal. Zeal in righteousness will yield righteous results.

DEVOTIONAL THOUGHTS

- **(For children):** When the woman at the well met Jesus, she excitedly told others about him *(John 4:28-29)*. These people gathered to hear Jesus and many gloriously believed on Him *(John 4:30, 39)*. We too should have the same excitement in telling others about Jesus.
- **(For everyone):** Your zeal affects others so how is your zeal affecting them? Are you affecting others with a righteous zeal or in some ungodly and worldly fashion?
- Have you ever been excited about something you purchased? Did your excitement persuade you to tell others about this particular product?

Did those whom you told also become excited about the product? How does this relate to how zealous you should be concerning the Lord and what He has done for you?

PRAYER THOUGHTS

- Ask God to give you zeal to tell others about Him.
- Ask the Lord to help you affect others positively.

SONG: *MY FAITH LOOKS UP TO THEE*

Notes: _____

_____

_____

_____

_____

_____

_____

_____

_____

Quotes from the next volume

(VOLUME 2, WEEK 52)

Subject: Witnessing (con't)

If a believer lives a life to the glory of God, there will come a time when the world wants to know "a reason of the hope" that lies within him.

Every unsaved person will have windows of opportunities when he becomes most receptive to the gospel of Christ.

There exists no adequate excuse for a believer not to give the gospel to others.

Scripture Index